WORDS FOR
MY COMRADES

WORDS FOR MY COMRADES

A POLITICAL HISTORY OF

TUPAC SHAKUR

DEAN VAN NGUYEN

WHITE
RABBIT

First published in the United States in 2025 by Doubleday,
a division of Penguin Random House LLC
First published in Great Britain in 2025 by White Rabbit,
an imprint of The Orion Publishing Group Ltd
Carmelite House, 50 Victoria Embankment
London EC4Y 0DZ

An Hachette UK Company

The authorised representative in the EEA is Hachette Ireland, 8 Castlecourt Centre,
Dublin 15, D15 XTP3, Ireland (email: info@hbgi.ie)

1 3 5 7 9 10 8 6 4 2

A CIP catalogue record for this book is
available from the British Library.

ISBN (Hardback) 978 1 3996 1543 3
ISBN (Export Trade Paperback) 978 1 3996 1544 0
ISBN (Ebook) 978 1 3996 1546 4
ISBN (Audio) 978 1 3996 1547 1

Printed and bound in Great Britain by Clays Ltd, Elcograf S.p.A.

MIX
Paper | Supporting
responsible forestry
FSC
www.fsc.org   FSC® C104740

www.whiterabbitbooks.co.uk
www.orionbooks.co.uk

To Amy

The Shakurs have been guided by struggle, prepared or not, whenever . . . . forever. We've exposed our existence, naked from fear, to those who would hear the positive.

—Mutulu Shakur

CONTENTS

PART III. Hands Up: Afterlife, Legacy, and a Future Not Set

WORDS FOR MY COMRADES

Tupac Amaru Shakur, 1994

PROLOGUE

THE TEXT ON his original birth certificate read: Lesane Parish Crooks. It was a name with no history, assembled from various sources, and bestowed on the son of Afeni Shakur to prevent the boy from being targeted by enemies of a Black Panther Party mother just weeks after she was acquitted of conspiracy to bomb a series of public buildings around New York City. This covert identity proved to be nothing more than a placeholder. When she felt it was safe to do so, Afeni amended the document to ensure history would recognize the chosen child by his true form, Tupac Amaru Shakur.

It was a name selected to honor Túpac Amaru II, descendant of the last Incan ruler and Indigenous cacique. Amaru II was executed in 1781 after leading a large Andean rebellion against Spanish rule; he died a martyr and symbol of anti-colonial resistance. For Tupac Shakur, it proved to be a chilling prophecy that came to be. But, as Afeni explained, "I wanted him to have the name of revolutionary, Indigenous people in the world. I wanted him to know he was part of a world culture and not just from a neighborhood."

Afeni's hopes became reality. Through music, her son became embedded in America's urban centers, spanning from New York, the city of his birth, to Baltimore, where he came of age, to various points of California, where he reached artistic maturity. But since his early death, Tupac has transcended his status as merely a maker of socially conscious music to become a figurehead of righteous resistance, of socialist activism, of revolution, all over the world. He is America's last great revolutionary figure—and his influence and iconography resonate across the continents.

When Tupac was fatally wounded on Las Vegas Boulevard in 1996, a link to a generation of radical Black political activism was irreparably severed. Tupac wasn't just the child of Black Panthers—a "Panther cub," as the membership dubbed their kids—he represented the continuum of the organization's ethos. Though the Panthers had dissolved a decade and a half before his death, its soul lived on within the rapper's five-foot-nine-inch muscle-and-bone frame.

Tupac cut into America's heart of darkness with surgical precision. He had the eloquence to illustrate oppression, the charisma to make people listen, and the musical chops to filter it all through the tight margins of a rap song. An astute observer and expressive stylist, 2Pac's lyrics could be imbued with complex narratives, humanizing the downtrodden with tender understanding and righteous indignation. (Throughout this book, "Tupac" will refer to the person and "2Pac" to the recording artist.) But he could also be manic and hostile—on record and in real life.

These qualities are not mutually exclusive. In fact, it's the plurality of Tupac that has made him such a symbol of rebellion: the orator and the outlaw; the activist and the extremist. His discography bears this out, running from socially conscious hip-hop (particularly his earlier work) to uncompromising gangster rap (most prominent toward the end of his life). His achievements are even more remarkable when you consider that he died at the young age of twenty-five. As legendary music producer Quincy Jones said, "If we had lost Oprah Winfrey at 25, we would have lost a relatively unknown, local market TV anchor-woman. If we had lost Malcolm X at 25, we would have lost a hustler named Detroit Red."

It's tempting to believe that Tupac's destiny was coded when he was still in the womb. After Afeni's bail was revoked during her trial on the conspiracy charges brought against her and a group of compatriots known as the Panther 21, she spent some of her pregnancy in prison and had to battle authorities to receive a daily egg and glass of milk to help safeguard her unborn child's health. Through the horrible rattle and clank of cells and chains, and the howls of agitated prisoners, Tupac was soothed by the whispered psalms of a mother who, if convicted, was facing decades in these conditions.

Tupac's family tree has radicals sprouting from every branch. Afeni's first husband was Lumumba Shakur, leader of the Panthers in Harlem and another member of the Panther 21. Tupac's step-father, Mutulu Shakur, was a community activist who ran medical facilities that maintained that heroin addiction could be treated with acupuncture and political education; in 1982, he was placed on the FBI's Ten Most Wanted Fugitives list after masterminding the robbery of an armored car that ended in three deaths (Tupac would not become properly acquainted with his biological father, Billy Garland, until adulthood). Tupac's godparents were said to be high-ranking Black Panther Elmer "Geronimo" Pratt and Assata Shakur, a leading figure in the 1970s Black Liberation Army, who escaped to political asylum in Cuba after being convicted of murder in 1977. None of the elder Shakurs were related by blood, but rather took the name from an Islamic god. "In my family every Black male with the last name of Shakur that ever passed the age of fifteen has either been killed or put in jail," Tupac said. "There are no Shakurs, Black male Shakurs, out right now, free, breathing, without bullet holes in them or cuffs on his hands. None."

It was a powerful dynasty and a heavy mantle to bear, but Tupac embraced his Black nationalist ancestry. "It was like their words with my voice," he said. "I just continued where they left off. I tried to add spark to it, I tried to be the new breed, the new generation. I tried to make them proud of me." The rebelliousness that Tupac exuded aligned with the militancy of the Panthers, who deemed passive resistance as a blunt weapon in the fight against institutional racism.

But Tupac did not want to be a replica of his Panther forebears. He'd grown up in the wasteland of a revolution that had not come to pass and bore witness to his mother's struggles with addiction with no help forthcoming from her former comrades. Walking his own path, he increasingly began to see rap as a weapon to strike at empire. A man of righteous fury, 2Pac used music to voice social injustices endured by Black Americans as racial tensions were hitting another bleak apex in the mid-1990s. His words encapsulated the struggle of his people, but the message was made accessible to the worldwide disenfranchised. He spoke words of wisdom, of freedom, of truth and life and love. Of course he did. But he could also show the fullness of his wrath, on record and in front of a camera, inspiring rebellion with one swaggering swivel of his middle finger.

His early music resembled a societal manifesto, full of messages about Black liberation, women's liberation, social unity—music for "the masses, the lower classes, ones you left out." Later, 2Pac's version of gangster rap had a heavy focus on blood-in-your-mouth realism: undiluted anger, unflinching depictions of violence, and a sense of otherworldliness that felt like a consequence of the accumulating incidents of violence he experienced. The sweep of his body of work made him a spokesperson not just for his own generation, but for subsequent generations, domestic and abroad, who endure similar fights against hardship, poverty, and tyranny. Even today, 2Pac's songs and words are being continually revisited, applied to new situations, and adopted by groups who identify in him something of themselves. And though he was perhaps too much of a contradiction—as much an antagonist as he was an activist—and too driven by from-the-gut emotion to have presented finely tuned political ideas, it has made his image even more malleable; in death, he remains a figure to be interpreted and reinterpreted, a lodestar for disciples the world over when hope is depleted.

The hero often becomes an icon in death. Following his murder in 1996, Tupac became a symbol of radical politics and revolutionary thought. His image has come to exist in the same sphere as Che Guevara, similarly destined to be worshipped on the walls of young people's bedrooms, college dorms, and any space radicals assemble forevermore, instantly recognizable even to people who can identify few of his songs other than maybe "California Love" and "Changes." All over the world you'll find murals of Tupac, but his image resonates most prominently in zones of conflict and uprising. Following the Siege of Sarajevo, the words "2Pac for Life" could be observed scrawled on bullet-scarred walls. The Bosnian War was not alien to Tupac himself. As he told MTV in 1994, "What makes me saying 'I don't give a fuck' different from Patrick Henry saying 'Give me liberty or give me death'? What makes my

freedom any different than Bosnians or whoever [America] wants
to fight for this year?"

During the civil war in Sierra Leone—which began in 1991, the
year 2Pac put out his first album, and ended in 2002, six years after
his death—the Revolutionary United Front used Tupac T-shirts as
uniforms, and the guerrillas referred to themselves as the "Tupac
Army." Palestinian rappers cite him as an inspiration as they seek to
infuse their message of liberation with Tupac's teachings. As Tamer
Nafar, a member of the group DAM who emerged from the harsh
area of Lod, near Tel Aviv, has said, "When I heard Tupac sing 'It's a
white man's world,' I decided to take hip-hop seriously." The world
has embraced Tupac as an icon of anti-establishment defiance, a
cipher of self-determination who could speak truth to power with
charisma and courage. The persistent rumors that Tupac is not dead
and in fact living in either Africa or South America almost have
a veil of plausibility, partially because he seems to have so many
admirers among underground activist groups across the planet.

It's natural that Tupac should have become associated with
rebellion given his Panther roots. The party is probably best
known for presenting a militant image of Black pride and Black
power: guns, leather jackets, hard-hitting public protest. Too often
excluded from the narrative is that the Black Panthers was an intellectual movement rooted in Marxist-Leninist theory. Tupac's ideas
somewhat diverged as he was driven less by overarching ideas about
how society should be restructured and more by his own sense of
realpolitik. Railing against the establishment, he had a particular
hatred for American imperialism, once suggesting in an interview
that it was the bloodiest form of gang violence. Tupac was sickened
by the wealth structures of U.S. society, too. One of the threads
of his musical output is his disgust at this imbalance. He instinc-
tively knew the inequality created by capitalism was immoral and,
as he once fired out in an interview, that there was "no way Michael
Jackson should have, or whoever Jackson, should have a million-
thousand-druple-billion dollars and then there's people starving."

Words for My Comrades borrows its title from a lyric from 2Pac's
song "Blasphemy," from his 1996 album *The Don Killuminati: The
7 Day Theory*. The use of the traditional form of address between

communists, leftists, and the proletariat signals that his worldview, though altered to meet the demands of the 1990s, was forged in the radical left-wing activism of the Panthers and others.

Tupac's mantra of "Thug Life" was balanced by the Notorious B.I.G.'s more boastful "ashy to classy." "Thug Life," an acronym for "The Hate U Give Little Infants Fucks Everybody"—the idea that the racism and oppression end up folding back on society like a wave of the sea, carried forward by the wind one moment and driven back the next—encapsulated Tupac's social justice spirit. "Ashy to classy" represented Biggie's commitment to the all-American "come up" from poverty to prosperity. Biggie, 2Pac's historic rival and musical equal, was murdered in 1997, age twenty-four. In his absence, "ashy to classy" was taken to extremes by two of his former associates, Jay-Z and Sean "Puffy" Combs, who pitched themselves as guardians of Biggie's legacy while becoming extremely rich models of rap capitalism. We'll never know how Tupac and Biggie would have viewed such acquisitiveness.

Growing up in Dublin, Ireland, I saw Tupac as omnipresent in the schoolyard. In the late 1990s, kids with distinct musical taste tended to fit into two camps: there were the rockers, who wore thick black hoodies, often bearing the face of their deity, Kurt Cobain. And there were those who gravitated toward gangster rap, then reaching the peak of its global influence. To the latter, 2Pac CDs were a currency of cool; "Thug Life" was a slogan scrawled on many notebooks and bookbags. When some Irish kids were old enough, they got Tupac tattoos inked on their skin.

The first 2Pac song I remember being enthralled with was "Do for Love," a posthumous single that sees him chart a rocky romantic relationship. I was twelve years old, browsing for CD singles in chain record store HMV, when the creeping, funky bass line grabbed me. Then there was 2Pac's voice, so often parodied but always so powerful. I stayed in the store until the end of the song and bought it immediately. Included on the disc was "Brenda's Got a Baby," 2Pac's famous single-verse saga of a preteen girl molested by her cousin, impregnated, forced to turn to sex work, and slain on the streets. It was a heavy song for me, not yet a teenager. But a dose of realism from beyond my gray, narrow, all-boys Catholic school upbringing was no bad thing, and nobody could paint these portraits as vividly as 2Pac. Perhaps this is why his albums were passed around the schoolyard like precious contraband.

It should come as no surprise that Tupac appeals to the children of Ireland, a nation that after four hundred years of British colonial rule embraced the ideals of resistance, rebellion, and revolution. Unlike Public Enemy, whose songs had more specificity, or N.W.A., whose portraits of dissent felt undetachable from the South Central Los Angeles streets that inspired them, Irish people could transplant meaning onto Tupac. He was an icon of righteous defiance, cut from the same cloth, we surmised, as Irish freedom fighters. I believe he grew more popular in Ireland after he died because that's what Irish heroes did: James Connolly, Patrick Pearse, Thomas MacDonagh, Roger Casement, Michael Collins—they all died for their cause. "I will live by the gun and die by the gun" is a quote often attributed to Tupac. To Irish revolutionaries, it could have been a rallying cry.

In 2008, popular comedy rap duo the Rubberbandits recorded a song called "Up Da Ra," which playfully examined the lasting popularity of this slogan of support for the Irish Republican Army (IRA). The song includes the line "And to all the patriots who have died before in the Irish wars? / I know you're up in heaven smoking a joint with Tupac and Bob Marley." I spoke to Blindboy Boatclub, the group's core creative turned author and podcaster, about the lyrics. It was, he said, partially influenced by seeing drawings on bus stops of Tupac with a speech bubble saying *"Tiocfaidh ár lá,"* an Irish-language slogan of defiance that translates to "Our day will come." He also remembered a mural in Ballynanty, Limerick, that portrayed Tupac alongside a group of rugby players with horses in the background. It was, Blindboy asserted, "beautiful."

"The lads would have been booting around in Honda Civics in '97, '98, they were playing the Wolfe Tones, Bob Marley, and 2Pac," Blindboy said. "The Wolfe Tones and 2Pac, you played them alongside each other and whatever it was, it represented the same thing. I don't know if people were thinking about it but there was a similarity. I always compare certain Irish rebel songs to gangster rap."

Ireland's affinity for Tupac is just the latest in a mutual sense of kinship shared by Irish people and Black American activists that can be traced across centuries. In 1845, Frederick Douglass fled to Ireland to escape slave catchers after the publication of his book *Narrative of the Life of Frederick Douglass, an American Slave*. He encountered Daniel O'Connell, an Irishman fighting for Catholic emancipation in Ireland. At the time, Catholics were a majority in Ireland, but subject to harsh rule by the Protestant minority and the British Empire. O'Connell was opposed to all forms of oppression and was one of the few political leaders who spoke out against American slavery. Douglass drew comfort and inspiration from O'Connell: "I have heard many speakers within the last four years—speakers of the first order; but I confess, I have never heard one, by whom I was more completely captivated than by Mr. O'Connell."

After the Irish War of Independence, a guerrilla struggle fought from 1919 to 1921 by revolutionary paramilitary organization the IRA against British rule, there was the establishment of the Irish Republic, which resulted in partition of the island. Six of Ireland's thirty-two counties located in the north of Ireland remained under British rule. Irish Catholics in the north suddenly found themselves on the opposite side of a border from their countrymen and kin. Living among a Protestant majority who saw themselves as British, the Catholics were denied basic rights such as votes, housing, and jobs. By the 1960s, they were taking their cues from the civil rights movement in the United States by organizing protests, but these were ruthlessly suppressed. A need for protection revived Irish paramilitary operations, with some identifying as the successors of the old IRA. "Everyone was very radicalized at that stage," said Tim Brannigan, a west Belfast Black Irish Catholic who went to prison in the 1990s on IRA weapons charges. "But, of course, what the IRA did was rather than see the potential for a mass movement, they saw the potential for clandestine guerrilla struggle."

The kinship between the Black American struggle and the Catholic struggle was sharply felt in Derry, a city in Northern Ireland. In August 1969, a march was organized to protest discrimination, but participants faced counterdemonstrations and a police force, the Royal Ulster Constabulary (RUC), its officers deploying water cannons and batons. Residents of the Bogside neighborhood responded by rioting. In what became known as the Battle of the Bogside, Catholic resisters declared the area autonomous territory. They erected barricades to prevent the police entering. Radio Free Derry played rebel songs as a call to locals to resist. A famous mural reading "YOU ARE NOW ENTERING FREE DERRY" was painted on a corner house signifying a police-free zone. It's still there today, an enduring symbol of the resistance.

Lasting intermittently for three years, Free Derry showed the power of a community united against oppressive forces. Yet Derry would be deeply wounded by some of the most brutal sectarian violence in what would become known as the Troubles. In 1972, there was Bloody Sunday, a peaceful protest that was attacked by the British Army and resulted in the murder of fourteen civilians, a case which is still unresolved.

Imprisoned for a short period for her role in the Battle of the Bogside was Bernadette Devlin. A working-class revolutionary socialist, Devlin was elected as an MP to the British Parliament aged only twenty-one. In 1969, she toured the United States to raise funds for political prisoners in Ireland. Such was her celebrity that she even made an appearance on *The Tonight Show Starring Johnny Carson*. As the tour stretched on, Devlin spoke increasingly about the Black American struggle, criticizing Irish Americans for failing to show unity despite the obvious parallels occurring back in their motherland. They may have been opening their wallets for her cause, but to Devlin, these Irish Americans were complicit in a similarly oppressive policing system that brought tyranny to marginalized communities. After being awarded the freedom key to New York by the city's mayor, John Lindsay, she delivered it to the local Black Panthers via her comrade, Eamonn McCann, with a message: "To all these people, to whom this city and this country belong, I return what is rightfully, theirs, this symbol of the freedom of New York."

Devlin befriended Angela Davis after visiting the imprisoned Panther in 1971. Years later, Davis joined the campaign to free Devlin's daughter, Róisín McAliskey, jailed on IRA bombing charges. Addressing a protest in San Francisco, Davis declared, "Róisín must be freed and Northern Ireland released from the shackles of British imperialism!"

(In his book *How the Irish Became White*, author Noel Ignatiev explains how the new Irish immigrants in America achieved acceptance among an initially hostile population by proving that they could be more brutal in their oppression of Black Americans. This was the start of a chasm between Irish people and Irish Americans that exists today. While in general, Irish Americans look fondly at the island many see as their ancestral home, the descendants of the Irish who stayed look at them with less affection.)

The IRA and the Black Panther Party were founded to fight back against oppressive states. Both established networks of community services to provide what the state failed to offer. Both faced suppression through counterintelligence. And both sought a radical left-wing reorganization of society. The two groups, not failing to spot the parallels, used their own newspapers to report on and support each other's cause.

It was instinctual for Irish freedom fighters to express solidarity with other political prisoners given their long history of imprisonment at the hands of the British state. Throughout the twentieth century, Irish prisoners used hunger strikes to protest British authority, many condemning themselves to the horrible fate of death by starvation. Playwright and politician Terence MacSwiney died after a seventy-four-day hunger strike in 1920; his demise was known to have had a profound impact on Marcus Garvey, the Jamaican Black nationalist leader. Garvey even sent telegrams to both British prime minister David Lloyd George, urging him to compromise so MacSwiney's life could be spared, and to MacSwiney's priest, asking him to "convey to McSwiney [*sic*] sympathy of 400,000,000 Negroes."

Garvey's admiration for the Irish response to colonial rule had been total. The year before MacSwiney's death, he declared, "The time has come for the Negro race to offer up its martyrs upon the altar of liberty even as the Irish has given a long list, from Robert Emmet to Roger Casement."

As the Troubles in Ireland continued throughout the 1980s and into the '90s, and the Provisional IRA's bombing campaign, undertaken with the goal of ending British rule in the six counties, claimed more and more innocent lives, they struggled for support at home and abroad, dubbed terrorists rather than freedom fighters. Still, after peace on the island was achieved through the Good Friday Agreement in 1998, a younger generation, with no war to fight, but who still shout "Up the Ra," have found alternative ways to keep the spirit of resistance as part of their identity. Expressing kinship with Tupac is the contemporary version of the same mutual understanding between Irish and Black American struggle.

Around the one hundredth anniversary of the 1916 Easter Rising, a key event in the Irish struggle for independence, a Facebook page was set up with the purpose of ensuring Tupac received credit for his contributions to the cause. The group's admins photoshopped Tupac into old photos, alongside Connolly, Pearse, and other heroes of the armed rebellion who'd almost all been executed for the part they played. It was for laughs, yes, but through meme culture, the group was ambiently solidifying the bond. It made a weird kind of sense: Tupac Shakur was in the original IRA. The joke wouldn't have worked with any other rapper—maybe, even, no other American.

Words for My Comrades is the story of how Tupac Shakur came to exemplify radicalism and revolution not just in the United States and Ireland, but among any people caught up in revolutionary struggle or seeking socialist solutions to capitalist problems. By charting his story, we understand how the spirit of insurgency can and does manifest because it must. Yet as Tupac's standing grows, there's a risk that his image becomes as flat as the two-dimensional posters fans hang on their walls—that a public appetite for a particular imagining of Tupac is fed, and, like the Panthers, his meaning is reduced to its lowest form. It's crucial that this is resisted.

In 2004, artist Jordan Fripp created *Martyrs*, an art piece featuring the stencil outlines of the faces of Martin Luther King Jr., Malcolm X, and Tupac with green, yellow, and red coloring on them, respectively. The colors reflected Fripp's interpretation of each man's philosophical ideologies: King—assigned green, the color of money—believed social injustices were rooted in economics. Malcolm—yellow, the color of envy—believed the Black community needed to attain power to achieve upliftment. While Tupac, red, believed in the oppressed using force to overcome subjugation. "I really started to see a connection and was asking myself, 'What if?'" explained Fripp. "When anyone dies prematurely, that's a question that you have to ask yourself, especially someone who is as prominent and adored as Tupac. And so, I posed the question to myself when I created this piece: What would have come if he had lived to his full potential?"

Martyrs was created just a few years after comedian Chris Rock poked fun at the idea of Tupac and Biggie as Black American icons comparable to Martin and Malcolm. ("I don't think you'll see their pictures hanging up . . . in your grandmamma's living room. 'That's Abraham, Martin, and Pac.'") Yet as time goes on, it's clear that to many people Tupac does exist in their righteous realm.

I needed to discover how this happened. How did this rap artist become the greatest icon that the culture produced? How did a young man who sought to define what it was to live and die in L.A., "the only place for me," become a symbol to those fighting the system in my home country and so many others across the planet? How did a man who made music to dance to find himself elevated to a status that's commonly held by civil rights leaders and guerrilla warfare commanders?

Part of the answer lies in Tupac's Panther heritage. The most lasting radicals to emerge from a time of turmoil, the Panthers helped shape Tupac's worldview and gave his actions and message a sense of historic continuity—to tell *this* story of Tupac is to chart a half century of radical politics and revolutionaries, including his mother, Afeni Shakur, and their suppression. But his portrait was forged in the 1990s, a new era of dissent, winter of the American century. This was a mythology decades in the making, and I knew the answers I sought required threading many disparate strands of political and cultural history.

Words for My Comrades is that attempt.

PART I

THE MEANING OF AFENI:
PANTHERS, FEDS, AND RESISTANCE ON THE STREETS OF BABYLON

A group of Lumbee Indians stand next to a makeshift cross abandoned by the Ku Klux Klan following a confrontation between both groups in Maxton, North Carolina, in 1958. The clash became known as the Battle of Hayes Pond.

1

OF JIM CROW SOIL

O NE OF THE MOST touching moments in hip-hop history took place under a huge, dangling effigy of the Empire State Building, with the Fresh Prince holding court. On September 9, 1999, Afeni Shakur and Voletta Wallace, mothers of fallen phenoms Tupac and the Notorious B.I.G., stood on either side of Will Smith on the Metropolitan Opera House stage in New York City to present the MTV Video Music Award for Best Rap Video. Mira Sorvino and Freddie Prinze Jr. would later hand out the Best Male Video prize to Smith himself for "Miami." Ricky Martin took home the most awards. This was America in the late 1990s.

Smith had been the first rapper to triumph in the Best Rap Video category ten years earlier with DJ Jazzy Jeff and the Fresh Prince's "Parents Just Don't Understand." A decade on, he welcomed Shakur and Wallace to the stage with a line that, with a touch of corniness, referenced that win: "I'd like to introduce to you two parents who do seem to understand."

Entering the arena from opposite corners to the weepy sounds of "A Song for Mama" by Boyz II Men, the mothers embraced like old friends in front of the speaker's stand at center stage. Shakur—wearing a gray jacket, pants, and prominent chain, not dissimilar to a look her son once sported, her hair cut short and styled with orange dye—spoke first: "In keeping with both our sons' memories and contributions to the arts, we stand united as mothers preserving their legacies." Wallace, behind sunglasses and with the tall Smith still looming behind, added, "The fact that we are even standing here shows what the power of faith, friends, family, loved ones, and fans can do to bring us all closer."

From there, Shakur expressed her hope that Tupac and Biggie would continue to inspire children to achieve their goals; Wallace pointed to the power of music to make the world a better place. These were vague statements, likely pruned to avoid any controversy. The real message was in the image of the two grieving mothers united, the anger and hate that drove their sons from friends to enemies banished for good.

The idea of having Shakur and Wallace co-present an award had been concocted by MTV and pitched to them—Michele M. Dix, senior creative director of the VMAs, later referred to Afeni and Voletta as "the legacy moms." It's tempting to consider the extreme MTV-ness of the situation and wonder if it exuded the dignity the moment required. But many of the stars in the room, including Sean "Puffy" Combs and Snoop Dogg, had also been present during the infamous 1995 Source Awards, when words exchanged on the podium ratcheted up tensions during the East Coast–West Coast feud to stiflingly high levels. Tupac and the Notorious B.I.G. had become entangled in conflict, setting them on paths that led to their deaths. They were gone, unable to reconcile, yet here were their mothers, together, and maybe their words—their solidarity— could ensure other parents did not suffer the same fate. The public coming together of Shakur and Wallace symbolized a moment of healing for hip-hop.

You'd be forgiven for not remembering this part, but it was Jay-Z who won the award for the video to his single "Can I Get A . . . ," featuring Amil and Ja Rule, from the movie *Rush Hour*. The clip sees Jay in an extravagant club, rapping over a bubbling electro-bop beat, in front of an all-woman dance troupe dressed in matching black outfits, one of the movie's supporting actors, Chris Penn, behind the bar mixing cocktails. It was the kind of song and video that epitomized the changing nature of mainstream rap in the wake of 2Pac and Biggie's deaths: flashy but not dangerous, glamorous but not violent. This is sometimes called the "bling-bling era," when large jewels and shiny suits became a symbol of opulence, and music videos became extremely expensive to reflect the value of exuding wealth. Awarding "Can I Get A . . ." seemed to affirm that rap was mutating to survive the loss of its two greatest talents.

For Afeni, the appearance at one of the American music industry's premium banquets solidified her role as custodian of Tupac's legacy and public figure in her own right. By 1999, the child of Jim Crow soil turned revolutionary was now a music mogul, deep into her work with her own record label, Amaru Entertainment, as well as the various foundations and programs she's founded in her son's name. Her reputation as hip-hop's First Mother had begun when Tupac was alive, due, in part, to his success, but also because of the notion that Afeni's Black Panther background had infused her son with his rebellious spirit and the socially conscious streak in his music. And, of course, there's 2Pac's song "Dear Mama," the archetypical ode to one's mother in a genre where moms are endlessly venerated. Yet even before becoming a parent, Afeni Shakur lived a life worthy of immortalization.

Returning to New York for the MTV Video Music Awards in the last gasps of the twentieth century brought Afeni to the city that forged much of her political ideology, where she became a nationwide story as one of the Panther 21, and where she gave birth to two children, Tupac and Sekyiwa. But her saga begins in Lumberton, North Carolina, where on January 10, 1947, Afeni was born Alice Faye Williams to parents Walter Williams Jr. and Rosa Belle Williams (née McLellan), their second and final child after eldest daughter Gloria Jean. The couple lived in Norfolk, Virginia, at the time, and Alice's birth some 250 miles away was the result of Rosa Belle journeying to visit her sickly mother. It was a difficult delivery. Rosa Belle brushed up against death when the midwife declined to remove the afterbirth. And so from nativity, Alice's world was marred by trauma.

Rosa Belle's family had strong roots in Lumberton, where the women in her lineage had gone from slaves to sharecroppers to domestic and factory workers. North Carolina had been a Confederacy state, albeit initially a reluctant one. While seven states seceded upon Abraham Lincoln's election to the presidency in 1860, North Carolina initially opted to remain within the Union. But when Lincoln responded to Confederate soldiers attacking Fort Sumter in Charleston, South Carolina, by seeking 75,000 volunteers to crush the rebellion, North Carolina opted to become one of the eleven states of the Confederacy rather than fight its neighbors. Almost 125,000 North Carolinians served in the Confederate army during the American Civil War—more than 80 percent of the white male population between the ages of fifteen and forty-nine when the conflict began, and more than any other Confederate state.

The Confederacy fell and slavery was abolished, but into the Reconstruction era, the Black residents of North Carolina immediately felt the cruelty of continued segregation. In the late 1800s, Rosa Belle's grandmother Millie Ann married a white man named Powell. For the perceived transgression of wedding a Black woman, Powell's family disowned him—but not before attaching him to the back of a wagon and dragging him around town as punishment. But Millie Ann had unshakable faith. She would walk the dirt roads of Lumberton singing gospel songs and reciting Bible verses to the neighbors who would listen, the Holy Scripture seemingly running counter to the hellish reality of her people since they were kidnapped and hauled across the Atlantic—and that of her husband just by association. Millie Ann was one of the many Black landowners of the era to have their little corner of America stolen away. The way Afeni told it, her great-grandmother was forced to offer her house up for bail when her sons got busted. The structure was later burned down.

By this point, Jim Crow laws had begun infecting the South and would hold firm until Alice's birth. With a childhood spent moving between Lumberton and Norfolk, the world Alice was born into was one where Black Americans had suffered a century of brutality, oppression, and disenfranchisement. They were second-class citizens, denied access to the best jobs and schools, and regularly subjected to violent tyranny, such as the torture and killing of fourteen-year-old Emmett Till in Mississippi in 1955, when Alice was eight years old. She had memories from as early as age five of white North Carolina locals spitting racist insults in her direction from their passing cars. For Alice, this was the desperate normality. She expected little from America and little is what she got.

"There wasn't anything different about it," she said of her childhood, "it was fucked up like everybody else's is, all the rest of my comrades and all the rest of my friends, their lives and my life are not really that different."

Desperate conditions can give rise to resistance. In 1958, Lumberton became the scene of a conflict between the local indigenous population and the robed and hooded racists of the Ku Klux Klan.

The Lumbee Indians are recognized as the largest tribe east of the Mississippi River, but in 1950s Lumberton, tribe members and the local Black community were united in the oppression they faced. "There was a lot of camaraderie there insofar as what they were facing," said John Lowery. Born years after the clash, he was inaugurated as the seventh Lumbee tribal chairman in 2022. "In Lumberton, at the downtown theater, which is called the Carolina Civic Center now, the Indians and the Blacks sat up top on the balcony, and the Indians had one side of the balcony and Blacks had the other side of the balcony. So once again, you were hand in hand facing discrimination."

Klan activity had intensified after 1954's *Brown v. Board of Education of Topeka, Kansas,* the landmark decision outlawing school segregation. The group's leader in North and South Carolina was James W. "Catfish" Cole, a Second World War veteran and self-styled holy man on a mission from God to lead the white fight against civil rights. Cole targeted the Lumbees, denying their Indigenous identity by accusing them of being a "mongrel" race, partly white and partly Black. Led by the preacher, the Klan entered Robeson County to stage its favored tactic of intimidation: cross burnings. One crucifix was lit up to confront a Lumbee family who moved into a "white neighborhood"; another to threaten a Native American woman who was dating a white man.

Cole's next play was to stage a Klan rally at Hayes Pond, near Maxton, on January 18, 1958, to "put Indians in their place." Word spread quickly around the county. Lumbee leaders Sanford Locklear, Simeon Oxendine, and Neil Lowry mobilized their people.

As darkness descended, fifty or so Klansmen began assembling in the bitterly cold field, playing religious music over a loudspeaker. They bore a banner emblazoned with "KKK," illuminated with a single light bulb attached to a long pole. But the Klansmen soon found themselves surrounded by nearly six hundred Lumbee men and fifty Lumbee women armed with guns and knives. Locklear and his brother-in-law Lowry approached Cole.

"We come to talk to these people," the Klan leader insisted.

"Well, you're ain't gon' talk to these people tonight," replied Locklear.

Lowry grew tired of talk. He shot out the lone light bulb brightening the scene. The sound of Lumbee gunfire filled the air, panicking Cole and his followers, who fled into nearby swamps. History remembers the confrontation by a suitably dramatic name: the Battle of Hayes Pond. The triumphant Lumbees celebrated their victory by holding up a claimed spoil of war: the abandoned KKK banner. The next day, Oxendine and fellow Lumbee Charlie Warriax, smiling proudly, wrapped themselves in it for a *Life* magazine photo shoot. The published picture sees them smiling goofily, transposing the emblem of racism and hate to mock its creators.

In the aftermath, the soundly beaten Cole called the Lumbees "lawless mongrels" and blamed local police for not coming to his aid. There would not be a second battle. With public sentiment firmly on the side of the Lumbees, Cole was convicted for inciting a riot and given a two-year prison sentence. He died in 1967 from injuries sustained in a car accident.

Alice was among the local Black population who rejoiced when they heard what went down in Maxton. Years later, she would regale an impressionable Tupac with tales of the conflict. "There was no real bloodshed, there was no death, thankfully," said Chairman John Lowery over six decades later. "But, at the same time, we got them in the soul. And probably killed a lot of their internal desire to want to come back and to push that type of ideology on our people."

While North Carolina's Indigenous population was resisting white supremacists, the state was seeing early stirrings of a new form of radical Black militarism. The year 1958 was also the year of the very sad "Kissing Case." In Monroe, two Black boys, aged seven and nine, had played a childhood kissing game in which a white girl had pecked them both on the cheek. For this transgression, the boys were arrested for molestation, jailed, beaten, and sent to reform school. Their defense was led by Robert F. Williams, a Black native of Monroe who had returned home after traveling to Detroit as part of the Great Migration, and president of the local NAACP chapter. In this role, Williams had formed the Black Armed Guard, arguing that armed self-reliance was necessary to defend against the Klan. "If the 14th Amendment to the United States Constitution cannot be enforced in this social jungle called Dixie at this time, then Negroes must defend themselves, even if it is necessary to resort to violence," he said in a 1959 press conference.

The Kissing Case received international attention—in Rotterdam, the Netherlands, a Catholic boys club organized a writing campaign that led to twelve thousand letters being sent to the U.S. embassy with instructions they be forwarded to First Lady Mamie Eisenhower. The pressure was enough for North Carolina officials to release the two boys, and Williams used the boost in his profile to argue openly for armed Black self-defense. "We must be willing to kill, if necessary," he said, a potential challenge to the anti-violence position of Dr. Martin Luther King Jr. The statement earned Williams a suspension from the NAACP, but his form of radical Black militarism would only proliferate over the next two decades.

Life inside the home of Alice Williams had its own troubles. Her father, a trucker, was ill-tempered and violent toward Rosa Belle. With her husband an unreliable provider, Rosa Belle kept a record of the amount of money he'd hand her every Friday—the sum inevitably being light, depending on how much he'd squandered on booze and other frivolities. For the most part, Rosa Belle took the beatings, and Alice considered her mother weak because of it. But on one occasion, with Alice and Gloria Jean looking on, Rosa Belle fought back, dousing Walter in burning hot grease straight from the skillet.

Trauma had been passed down from the previous generation. Walter's father, Walter Sr., was a diminutive preacher—about five foot two inches by Afeni's estimates—who married Lena, a woman as tall as six feet. Afeni's cousin, the musician J. Kimo Williams, would later contend that "the tragedy of our family tree stems from our paternal grandfather, Walter Williams Sr." One of the stories J. Kimo heard about his wanton grandfather is that when Walter Sr. spoke from the pulpit, he could look out at his wife in one pew and mistress in another.

The Williams family were relatively well off, working as share-croppers on a large farm in North Carolina. But Lena died when Walter, one of "like fifteen children," was just eleven years old, leaving him with a cold and domineering father. Walter Sr. had hoped Walter Jr. would follow in his footsteps and become a preacher. His son's refusal outraged him. Walter Jr.'s rebellion was complete when he ran away from home. "That was my dad's first heartbreak," said Afeni. "That was the first notch in his spirit."

Afeni's own dominating memory of her grandfather was his refusal to give her a watermelon from his garden unless the little girl coughed up some cash. When she did, Alice found the fruit had not yet ripened. Walter Sr. pocketed the money, she said, in full knowledge of the swindle he'd pulled on his own flesh and blood.

Rosa Belle eventually couldn't take any more of Walter Jr. She called her brother to come and help her migrate north to the developing Black principality of the South Bronx. Once there, she secured a low-paid job in a factory making lampshades and summoned her two children.

Alice was eleven years old when she was transplanted to New York City. While Gloria Jean found the rhythm of the city invigorating, Alice didn't make for a natural New Yorker. The smell of the city upset her. She couldn't run out of the house at midnight to play hide-and-seek anymore. And when she looked toward the sky at night, she found the stars were missing, lost in the impurity of the city air.

Compounding her misery was the family's living situation. On a salary of about forty dollars a week, Rosa Belle could only afford a single room within another woman's apartment for her, Gloria Jean, and Alice to cram into. And there was the food. So she wouldn't overstep her means, the local butcher would only allow Rosa Belle to buy certain things on credit, typically kosher bologna and hamburger meat—not exactly Alice's idea of a comfort meal.

This was not the glamorous utopia the southern girl had been conditioned to expect. "Every time somebody came down [south] from New York, they looked so good," she later explained. "But the reason for that, I found out later because I did it myself, was that when you go down South you bring your whole wardrobe, and you make people think that it's only a small part of it. You borrow a car, a flashy, snazzy car, and you go down there and you pretend. But because of that and because of ignorance, up the road was always what was happening. Everything in the world was better up the road. Food was better, everything was better. White people didn't call you a bunch of motherfuckers up the road. It was like heaven, it was the land of milk and honey up the road. And when I got up the road I was disgusted."

Going from an all-Black school in the South to a majority-white school caused issues too, and Alice discovered a taste for responding to conflict with her fists. When one kid said she looked like something from outer space, she beat him up. When the teacher attempted to break up the fight, Alice tried to kick her ass too. Back in class there was an inquiry into the incident. Another boy told the teacher about the outer space jibe, drawing laughter from the rest of the kids. Of course, Alice went for every single last one of them. "Because I was just ferocious. I wasn't bad, I was just ferocious because I didn't know any better," she later said. "I was trying to protect myself and I felt like I just didn't belong there, you know. And I was very scared. I was really scared of all those white people all around me. I wasn't used to that."

Alice later attended Benjamin Franklin Junior High School in the Bronx, where her grades qualified her for honors. Taking an interest in journalism, she wrote for the school newspaper, *The Franklin Flash*, and in the ninth grade won a journalism award, receiving a letter of congratulations from Mayor Robert F. Wagner. Yet money was too tight to allow Alice to maintain her interest. Rosa Bell would recall in 1970 that her daughter "seemed to be yearning, to express a lot of talent that never got out."

High school provided little stability in Alice's life. She was initially drawn to Hunter College High School, but it refused to grant her an entrance test based on IQ scores. Alice's English teacher suggested she take the tests for Bronx High School of Science and for the High School of Performing Arts, typically referred to as PA and the future setting of the teen musical *Fame*. She passed the qualifying exams to get into both. The idea of rubbing shoulders with rich white kids every day put Alice off the Bronx High School of Science, so in 1962, like Coco Hernandez would in *Fame* eighteen years later, she walked through the doors of PA in Midtown Manhattan. Alice soon discovered that the kids were rich there too. Some would pull up for class in limos. Meanwhile, with no cafeteria at PA, Alice couldn't even afford lunch, let alone all the items needed for dance classes.

Still, Alice struck up a young romance with an actor named Glynn Turman, already noted for playing Travis Younger in the original Broadway production of the play *A Raisin in the Sun*, alongside Sidney Poitier and Ruby Dee. (Later, he would be best known for playing Mayor Clarence Royce in HBO's *The Wire*.) Glynn lived in Greenwich Village and ran in circles with famous actors, a world unfamiliar to Alice. But the relationship ended when, Afeni would later claim, Glynn slapped her during an argument.

"I bet you won't slap me again," Alice hissed back, to which, she'd later say, Glynn responded by striking her in the face again, this time with more force, scrambling her senses.

Hell-bent on revenge, Alice stormed PA the next day armed with every knife she owned plus a zip gun, which she stashed in her locker with the full intent to kill Glynn. If she had, it's fair to say that both hip-hop and HBO history would look very different today.

Miserable with life at the school, Alice found herself getting drunk off Thunderbird wine just to get through the day. She failed all but one subject and crashed out of PA after one term.

"I couldn't relate to that," Afeni later said of the school. "It was my first time out of the community. I couldn't afford the materials we were supposed to have. Most of the other girls had come from private schools. I couldn't relate to them, so I started hanging out."

For Alice, "hanging out" meant, like many troubled kids before and after her, finding solace in a gang. She started running with the Disciples, a Bronx street clique. Alice even earned the role of president of its female wing, the Disciple Debs. A lot of their crimes were small-time—taking the antennas off parked cars and whipping bystanders, foolishness of that nature. But things could get intense. Because of its location on the border of two different gang territories, a pool in Crotona Park would turn red from fights between the Disciples and local Puerto Ricans. Knives would be drawn as the two rival factions fought furiously.

"We were killing each other. I mean every week there was a body in Crotona Pool," said Afeni. "Every week. It wasn't funny . . . and at the same time that I was going to Performing Arts and my mother was bragging about me for that, I was running around shooting and cutting people."

For a time, there was some relief in Alice's life through a boyfriend named Ray, who, at thirty-three, was significantly older than she was. The pair would sit out on a fire escape listening to Jimi Hendrix and Sly and the Family Stone, drop LSD, and fantasize about being contract killers, like a Blaxploitation generation Bonnie and Clyde.

Then there was her dear friend Sandra, who had dated Glynn previously. Though they were the same age, Sandra came across as a little more grown-up than Alice. They would hang out in a Harlem bar, dressed to the nines, sipping Hennessy or Bacardi 151, entertaining the attention of men who could afford to keep their drinks topped up, and playing Nina Simone's beautiful "Four Women" on the jukebox, a song that charts a genealogy of Black women from slavery to the 1960s through four characters.

One night, a man Sandra knew happened to come into the bar. His name was Omar, though Alice took to calling him Cheyenne and he took to calling her All I See, a mangled pronunciation of Alice. She thought he was pretty slick. After leaving the bar, the pair moved on to the Bronx's after-hours spots, getting high well into the night. A little over a week later, they were living together. With cash on the hip, Omar would treat Alice to all sorts of gifts—clothes and jewelry, but also reefer and cocaine, which they'd do casually as they spoke for hours on end.

"Black is the best color on the planet Earth," Omar would say.

This man was not just any smooth talker. He had been a member of the Nation of Islam under Elijah Muhammad but broke his five-year association with the organization in 1964, to defect with Malcolm X. Omar told Alice of the first few weeks after the bitter split, when many of Malcolm's followers had to hole up in basements with guns, not quite sure what the reprisals would be. But he also opened her mind to Malcolm and the Nation's own form of Black nationalism. With everything she'd grown up around, the message hit home.

"This dude was the first person who started teaching me about any kind of politics," Afeni said. "The politics he was talking were apolitical, but it was the beginning of my having any knowledge at all of the teachings of Elijah Muhammad. Well that shit just blew my mind."

The genesis of the Nation of Islam is shrouded in mystery and myth, the kind of ethereal enigma you could build a new religious sect on. It begins with W. D. Fard, a man—or, as his followers claim, the physical manifestation of God—of about fifty aliases, whose existence on this planet has no recorded beginning or end.

His mission is said to have begun in 1930. As a door-to-door salesman of silks, Fard began preaching Black exceptionalism, regaling those who welcomed him into their home with tales of Africa, where his fine wares originated from. Fard soon graduated to basement sermons. His stories were somewhat fantastical, involving an underhanded Black scientist, Yakub, who, through eugenics, had created the white race some 6,600 years earlier, thus orchestrating the destruction of global Black rule. But easy to get to grips with was Fard's message that Black people were righteous and white people were the instrument of the devil—proclamations that squared with his captivated audience's experiences and history.

But then something strange happened—Fard vanished into the ether. In 1934, he requested that his student, whom he had named Elijah Muhammad, drive him to the airport. Through tears, Elijah begged his teacher not to leave him. Fard answered with a list of books for the protégé to read and the order that Elijah fulfill the work on his own. And then he was gone, never to be seen in material form again.

For twenty years, Elijah Muhammad spread Fard's word, building the Nation into a vocal, socially conservative, immaculately dressed sect of Black Muslim separatists, but one with never more than a few hundred members or accepted by mainstream Islam. It was with Malcolm in the spotlight that the group began to wield serious influence.

Most tellings of the Malcolm X story begin when he was still prenatal. It was in Omaha, Nebraska, 1925, when out of the winter night rode a group of robed Klansmen on horseback, torches and rifles in hand, surrounding the home of Earl Little, his pregnant wife Louise, and their three small children. They'd come with a warning for Earl: cease preaching the word of Marcus Garvey to the local Black residents. But with her husband away in Milwaukee, it was left to Louise to resist the threat at her door. Windows were smashed and guns were caressed; mercifully, no harm came to the family. The rebellious Earl, however, had set himself down a path from which he could not veer. Six years later, he was killed in what authorities called a streetcar accident. Malcolm would forever maintain that his father was murdered by the KKK.

After eighth grade, Malcolm moved to his half sister's house in Boston and, at seventeen, he absconded to Harlem, where he survived as a hustler, pimp, and petty criminal. Back in Boston, the versatile crook found a new racket: burglarizing the homes of well-off whites, which led to a prison sentence for larceny and breaking and entering.

It was in jail that Malcolm became enlightened. He ravenously consumed books recommended by older inmates. But it was his brother Reginald who first pointed him toward the Nation of Islam. This mix of knowledge and Islamic belief freed his mind from what he came to see as the trapping of his previous existence. He discarded the name Little and took the marker X, symbolizing that his identity had been lost when his ancestors were kidnapped in Africa and sold into slavery. Upon his release, Malcolm became Elijah Muhammad's protégé and, in 1954, less than two years out of prison, he was selected to lead Temple Number 7 (later Mosque Number 7) in Harlem.

An electrifying public speaker, Malcolm drew in followers like Omar with his blistering expressions of Black identity, morality, and independence from white America. Crucially, he differentiated himself from the mainstream civil rights movement by challenging the message of integration and nonviolence preached by Martin Luther King Jr. Malcolm called on his followers to defend themselves "by any means necessary"—the image of him peering out the window of his home in Queens, New York, with an M1 carbine in hand is one of the most lasting depictions of Black militantism. Because of his previous life as a street hustler and close association with Harlem, Malcolm held a standing throughout America's growing ghettos that eclipsed that of King. With Malcolm as its up-front spokesman, the Nation claimed a membership of five hundred thousand, but many more with no desire to convert to Islam also heeded his words.

By 1963, Malcolm's star had risen far beyond the Nation itself, which perturbed Elijah Muhammad, who, as a messenger of God, coveted the notoriety for himself. Malcolm, meanwhile, became disillusioned when he discovered that Muhammad lived a less-than-pious life: the seer had fathered children by six of his personal secretaries. Tensions between both men came to a head when Malcolm declared publicly that John F. Kennedy's assassination in November 1963 was an example of "chickens coming home to roost"—the consequences of a violent society reaching the very top of government. It repulsed an American public in mourning. In response, Muhammad forbade Malcolm from speaking publicly for ninety days. There would be no reconciliation between both men, and Malcolm's exodus from the Nation became permanent.

The final year of Malcolm's life was one of conversion, pilgrimage, and discovery. Just weeks after leaving the Nation in March 1964, he founded Muslim Mosque, Inc. A journey to Mecca that same year led him to embrace Sunni Islam, adopt the Muslim name el-Hajj Malik el-Shabazz, and renounce the separatist beliefs of his former teacher. In 1965, Malcolm founded the Organization of Afro-American Unity (OAAU) as a secular vehicle to unify Black Americans with the people of Africa and the developing world. But he could not run from the anger and hostility of his former associates in the Nation who considered him a traitor and heathen. On February 21, 1965, Malcolm was shot dead while speaking at the Audubon Ballroom in Washington Heights, New York. Three members of the Nation of Islam were arrested. During the trial, one of the defendants, Talmadge Hayer (birth name Thomas Hagan; later known as Mujahid Abdul Halim), confessed to the killing, but insisted the other two accused—Norman 3X Butler (Muhammad Aziz) and Thomas 15X Johnson (Khalil Islam)—were not involved. Nonetheless, all three men were convicted of the murder. Scholars continued to have doubts about the conviction and, in 2021, Aziz and Islam were finally exonerated.

Though Malcolm was gone, his critiques of America, made during his time inside and outside of the Nation of Islam, provided the underlying principles of the burgeoning Black Power and Black Consciousness movements. Under the leadership of Louis Farrakhan, the Nation would have a new day of influence in the 1990s, right when Tupac Shakur was at the height of his fame. But in the wake of Malcolm's murder, it retracted. Heartbroken former Malcolmites scattered to spread shards of his doctrine to fresh ears—with followers like Omar passing the word to people like Alice, albeit in conditions that Malcolm would surely not have approved of.

"I wasn't doing anything else except snorting dope and talking about how great Malcolm was and this drag about the misunderstanding he and Elijah had," Afeni later said. "I was very naive."

Sandra's narcotic of choice was also heroin, which she'd snort after copping some from her white boyfriend, Henry. She was still using when she became pregnant. The situation was a shock to Sandra—in fact, she didn't realize she was carrying a child until five months into the pregnancy. How could this have happened, Sandra wondered, after she'd had what she thought was a total hysterectomy? "They just removed one tube and didn't tell her that they had only removed one tube," Afeni later claimed angrily.

One morning, at about five a.m., Sandra rose to use the bathroom but collapsed on the way. She died of a brain hemorrhage. At the hospital, doctors operated and rescued the baby from her body, but the child died soon after. "They wouldn't put the baby in an incubator or something," Afeni later said. "You know, like the nurses told us that they just killed the baby. They just let the child die."

The terrible news had yet to reach Alice when, later that night, she received a call from her mother summoning her. Once she arrived at the house, Rosa Belle and Gloria Jean, with tears in their eyes, told her of Sandra's death. Alice couldn't believe it. Dazed, she staggered back outside and began walking the New York streets. Alice kept on walking. For a full twenty-four hours she wandered the city, processing the tragedy. "I was really fucked up. It was the first time in my life I'd ever felt somebody's death, you know, because she was all I had."

Sandra's death motivated Alice to turn away from drugs and seek a more stable path in her life. She took a postal job, becoming one of the first women mail carriers in New York. But she did not stay in the role long because, as she put it, "that kind of work is geared to making you a machine."

Mourning her loss, lacking a formal education, and unable to hold down regular work, Alice was at risk of drifting into another period of instability. But things changed in early 1968, when the wandering soul walked down 125th Street and got to Seventh Avenue. At first, she saw the same old scene; somebody was perched on top of a box to draw attention. This was unremarkable; speakers had always chosen this corner to preach to the community, even heavyweights like Marcus Garvey and Malcolm X. But Alice was struck by the crowd: it wasn't just the usual dashiki-wearing nationalists looking on. This gathering included mothers and children, teachers and domestics, hoods and hustlers.

On the wooden platform was a diminutive man dressed in all black, a small group of men resembling foot soldiers flanking him on both sides. He spoke of Black pride, igniting within Alice a feeling of self-love, a feeling of purpose, that she had never experienced before. He was the co-founder of the Black Panther Party for Self-Defense. He was Bobby Seale.

Bobby Seale, chairman of the Black Panther Party for Self-Defense, leads a close-order drill during funeral services for member "Little" Bobby Hutton, a seventeen-year-old Panther killed in a shoot-out with police in Oakland, California, in 1968.

2

SELF-DEFENSE

Fury Filled Bobby Seale's eyes, tightened a knot in his guts, and pressed his actions toward the ill-advised. It was February 21, 1965, and Seale's hero Malcolm X was dead, assassinated in Washington Heights, New York, in the gruesome final act of a campaign of threats and intimidation waged on the good minister by his former acolytes in the Nation of Islam. In faraway Oakland, an ashen-faced comrade delivered the news through a rolled-down car window as Seale sat in the passenger's seat of another friend's car. Immediately, he was hit with feelings of loss and loneliness, feelings that quickly mutated into a frenzy. With the car in motion, the enraged Seale spotted a parked motorcycle cop. Without warning, he clambered out of the window of the moving vehicle. "You racist white motherfucking cop!" Seale bellowed. "We going to kill you! You-all *killed* Malcolm!" It was a potentially lethal thing to do, but Seale felt ready to die that day.

Behind the wheel was Kenny Freeman—who would take the name Mamadou Lumumba in the late 1960s—chauffeuring Seale and a couple of fellow Black nationalists. They were friends a more radical Seale would later dismiss as "cultural nationalists," or, to be more descriptive, "punk motherfuckers who sit in a fucking armchair and try to articulate the revolution while black people are dying in the streets." Freeman took the incandescent Seale home in the hope of calming him down. But his rage couldn't be contained. Instead, Seale picked up six bricks from his garden, breaking each in half to give him twelve projectiles in all. Now crudely armed, he began throwing the bricks at any passing car he'd see with a white person inside.

"Whatever I do from now on," Seale declared, "it's this racist society's fault."

After causing more trouble in a local burger joint, Seale returned home. Once more the anger rose up inside him, manifesting as a balled fist, which he forced right through a glass porch window.

"Fuck it," Seale told Freeman in the kitchen, nursing his injured hand. "I'll make my own self into a motherfucking Malcolm X, and if they want to kill me, they'll have to kill me."

The assassins may have been Black, but there was no doubt in Seale's mind: Malcolm's death was a consequence of the destructive, racist oppression of a white world. The cops, the FBI, the president—all shared the blame. None were free of sin.

Grief, rage—useless without direction. Like his idol, Seale would come to eschew pacifist civil rights activism and instead advocate that Black Americans be ready to use violence if necessary. Because there's no such thing as semi-Malcolms, and you don't overthrow oppressive regimes by simply hurling dried clay. The way Seale and his comrades would come to see it, you need guns, black leather, and the psyche of a nocturnal jungle cat.

Bobby Seale's road to revolutionary politics had unlikely pit stops in music and the military. He was born in Liberty, Texas, in 1936 to George and Thelma Seale (née Traylor). The couple would regularly separate and reconcile, moving the family through various cities in Texas, but unable to outrun poverty. When they upended to California, George struggled to find work. Being a carpenter of such skill that he once built a home from the ground up didn't mean much when the unions routinely excluded African Americans. George finally did get his union card, and Bobby would later proudly claim that his father was one of only three Black men in the state at the time to attain membership.

Formal education didn't interest Bobby much, but he showed awareness in social justice after learning in school about the crimes inflicted on Native Americans by European colonizers. He dropped out at sixteen and sought meaning in life by joining the air force, though he also had notions of becoming a professional jazz drummer. Those musical ambitions ended up infringing on his military career in the strangest way when a colonel, who happened to have a relationship with debt collectors pursuing Seale for missed payments on a drum kit, started sweating him to pay up. An argument broke out between the two, leading to Seale being court-martialed and discharged. He left as an expert sheet mechanic in aircraft production and repair, but the bad conduct charge on his record meant he struggled to hold down a permanent job. Deciding to give education another shot, Seale enrolled at Merritt College in Oakland with hopes of becoming an engineer. But his life skewed toward a drastically different path when, at a protest at Merritt against President John F. Kennedy's 1962 naval blockade of Cuba, he came across a kid with a penchant for Marx and Malcolm.

It's tempting to venerate the first time Bobby Seale and Huey P. Newton made each other's acquaintance. It's like considering the first unions of Castro and Guevara, Lenin and Trotsky, Lennon and McCartney—chance encounters that alter the planet in inextricable ways, inviting "what if" scenarios if one had simply not been in that place at that time. Stop the meeting from occurring and the Jenga blocks of history collapse.

In truth, the two Merritt College students' interests were so aligned that they were always going to collide. On this day, Newton, then a member of the Afro-American Association, had just finished preaching to a crowd when Seale decided to test him on civil rights laws, the NAACP, and whether he thought either was doing Black people any good. Newton immediately tore them apart, calling the NAACP a waste of money and the laws pointless, as they were not being enforced. Impressed, Seale looked for Newton in the school library a couple of days later and asked where the next Afro-American Association meeting was being held. Newton gave him the address and the title of the book they'd be discussing— *Black Bourgeoisie* by E. Franklin Frazier. Seale was twenty-five at the time, Newton just nineteen.

He's the single most lasting icon to come from the Panthers; the man closest to igniting the cult of personality that revolutionary heroes cultivate, perhaps even require. Huey, the use of his surname optional, like Martin, Malcolm, Che, and Tupac. From birth, it was Huey Percy Newton, a child of Monroe, Louisiana, the youngest of a brood of seven—four boys and three girls. His father, a share-cropper and Baptist minister, once came dangerously close to being lynched for talking back to his white bosses. Such incidents likely motivated the family to abandon the south for Oakland when Huey was only one year old. Word was that the wartime industrial boom meant job opportunities were plentiful. Still, the Newton family struggled financially and frequently relocated throughout Huey's early life.

Though he graduated from high school, he did so without having acquired literacy, later teaching himself to read with Plato's *Republic* as his textbook. "I read it through about five times until I could actually understand it," Newton later claimed. This thirst for further education brought Newton to Merritt, but his life was regularly blighted with troubles with the law, starting in his teen years and continuing through to college, including busts for vandalism and burglary.

The sum of Newton's Merritt education might have been just six months of classes when the pair connected, but Seale was impressed with his intellect, his revolutionary politics, and his acceptance that violence is often necessary to change society. This was a duo that went together like rifle wood and leather berets. Seale had an affable demeanor—in fact, he spent his early years in activism moonlighting as a stand-up comic. But Newton had a steely magnetism. His features appeared forged in iron. The image of him sitting in a wicker chair—a rifle in one hand, a spear in the other—is one of the defining images of Black American militarism. And though Newton was not a physically imposing man, with a voice that sounded bookish and cerebral when compared to some of the booming orators considered his contemporaries, a taste for street fighting had toughened him, a toughness that he projected through his eyes.

Seale and Newton did not actually spend the period after their initial meeting in close collaboration. In fact, for about a year they didn't see each other at all. In 1964, Newton served six months in prison for felony assault with a deadly weapon after stabbing a man at a party with a steak knife. Newton later claimed the move was in reaction to what he perceived as a threat, and would have been recognized as such had the jury been made up of his own peers. But with Newton back on the streets, it wasn't long before the magnetic pull of the Bay Area's leftist activity brought Seale back to him. Both worked with local community organizations like the North Oakland Neighborhood Anti-Poverty Center. Alongside activists such as Kenny Freeman, Seale invested time in the Revolutionary Action Movement (RAM), a Marxist-Leninist Black nationalist group, but grew frustrated by its soft underbelly. When he burst into one of the group's houses after dusk and found that the ruckus had caused members to hide under their beds, Seale knew it was time to split.

Their revolutionary principles and experience of on-the-ground activism left Seale and Newton eager for a new kind of Black politics, one that embraced inner-city youth as a revolutionary proletariat, a movement that would further Malcolm X's message of "freedom by any means necessary" to new levels. All they needed was a final push.

The pyre was lit in broad daylight. Tuesday, September 27, 1966, was a sweltering day in San Francisco. Under the sun, three Black teenagers were joyriding in a stolen 1958 Buick through the hilly terrain of impoverished Hunters Point until the car stalled on Griffith Street near Oakdale Avenue. A police cruiser approached, though the Buick had not yet been reported as stolen.

Noticing the cop car, the boys—Darrell Mobley, Clifton Bacon, and Matthew "Peanut" Johnson, all aged between fourteen and sixteen—decided to make a run for it. Clambering out of the vehicle, Bacon and Johnson darted into an open field, while Mobley sought refuge behind a parked car. All three were unarmed.

Alvin Johnson, a white patrol officer with twenty-three years on the force, gave chase in his cruiser, tracking sixteen-year-old Matthew Johnson as he ran uphill toward Navy Road and around a building. The suspect in his sights, the patrolman jumped out of his car and yelled, "Stop! Hold it, or I'm going to shoot!" As the boy ran down a hill near a housing project, Alvin Johnson fired four shots, one of which penetrated Matthew Johnson's heart. The cop would claim that the initial three shots were intended to be warnings, but one witness said that all the shots were aimed directly at Matthew Johnson. He died within minutes.

The response from locals was chaos and rage. Residents demanded a meeting with Mayor John Shelley to voice their discontent. Shelley obliged, but by the time he arrived at the scene, the anger had swelled and dialogue was impossible. Pelted with bricks and even a firebomb, the mayor was forced to retreat.

The killing of Matthew Johnson ignited three days of civil unrest that would become known as the Hunters Point Uprising. In response, California governor Edmund G. Brown called a state of emergency and dispatched two thousand National Guard troops with tanks. Police coordinated with local volunteer group the Peace Patrol to keep residents off the streets. But even the Peace Patrol found it difficult to ally with cops who fired over the heads of protesters and into a community center protecting two hundred children from the violence. Forty-two Black protesters were injured in all, ten with gunshot wounds.

Two weeks later—and eighteen months since the killing of Malcolm X—Seale and Newton initiated their vision. Joined by a cadre of local comrades they'd come to trust—Elbert "Big Man" Howard, Sherman Forte, Reggie Forte, and "Little" Bobby Hutton—the righteous duo announced the formation of a new political party on October 15, 1966: the Black Panther Party for Self-Defense. Their roles were set by chance: that Seale became chairman and Newton the minister of defense came down to the literal tossing of a coin.

Their early activity centered on Newton's belief in the explosive, rebellious anger of the ghetto as a social force. The Panthers downplayed its campus origin story in favor of a spiritual connection to the streets and the youths, hustlers, and disenfranchised denizens who roamed them. This was the Panthers' base. Inspired by Robert F. Williams's book *Negroes with Guns*, Newton reasoned that if the people could stand up to the police, he could organize them into a political power. It was not illegal to carry guns in California if they were not concealed, so the nascent group was free to arm itself. The first weaponry the Panthers acquired came from a Japanese American radical and gun collector who was talked into donating an M1 rifle and 9-millimeter pistol to the cause. There was a little issue for the legally astute Newton: he was on probation for the stabbing conviction. Therefore, he wasn't permitted to carry a handgun, and so the rifle became his hardware of choice. The Panthers' early activities involved Huey, armed with his musket and a lawbook, shadowing cops as they performed their duties and loudly reciting the relevant portions of the penal code. In scenes that were stiflingly tense, Newton's mind stayed impossibly clear and his demeanor stoic and cool. It was a daring enough action to garner him a righteous reputation across the Black neighborhoods of the Bay Area.

Funds for the nascent Panthers were raised by purchasing copies of *Quotations from Chairman Mao Tse-tung*, commonly called Mao's Little Red Book, at a local bookstore for thirty cents and flipping them on college campuses for a dollar—money that was duly invested in shotguns.

The Panthers' motto has been quoted so often in the decades since that it's lost some of its impact, yet it's always worth repeating: "All Power to the People." A rallying cry that challenged the rich ruling-class domination of society.

Inspired by Malcolm X's critiques of America, the Panthers developed an intellectual framework that went beyond policing the police (or the "racist, Gestapo pigs," to use a preferred Panther term, retaliatory language against the bigoted epithets cops used against Black people on a daily basis). Seale described the group as "a righteous revolutionary front against this racist decadent, capitalistic system." Neither he nor Newton was in accord with the Nation of Islam's vehement theology of racial separatism that characterized white people as metaphysically evil. And while the NOI would accept a capitalism that served Black interests, the Panthers' outlook leaned on Marxist theory: capitalism was at the root of Black oppression, its abolition was a precondition of social justice and could be achieved by the awakening of the lumpenproletariat. The Panthers drew distinction between racist and nonracist whites, and, crucially, between the exploited Black masses and Black capitalists, whom they saw as propping up the crooked system. In this regard, they were in synchronicity with James Farmer, co-founder of the Congress of Racial Equality (CORE), who argued that Black entrepreneurial capitalists supported Jim Crow laws because they created a consumer market outside of the interest or influence of white businessmen.

Toward the end of his life, Malcolm had often reflected on an incident from his NOI days. It occurred in a Muslim restaurant in Harlem, when the minister was approached by a blond coed student who had journeyed to New York to pledge her loyalty after seeing him speak at her New England college. What could a white ally like her do for the movement? she inquired. "Nothing," Malcolm retorted. The young woman burst into tears and ran out of the building. It was an interaction Malcolm would come to regret. In contrast, when Newton was asked during a radio interview what white people could do to support his party, he suggested they should form their own organizations in solidarity. His urgings were enough to inspire a group of antiracist hippies in Ann Arbor, Michigan, to establish the White Panther Party. "We thought the Black Panther Party was the vanguard of the revolution in America," cofounder John Sinclair told me. "We thought they were head and shoulders above everybody else, and we regarded them as the leaders of our movement."

There was also no tangible religious element to the Panthers, a departure from the Muslim faith of Malcolm X. Newton, who had been raised by devout Christian parents, had attended Nation of Islam mosques to see if their particular word of God would impact him. Instead, he adopted what he called "revolutionary humanism." "I have had enough of religion and could not bring myself to adopt another one," he wrote. "I needed a more concrete understanding of social conditions. References to God or Allah did not satisfy my stubborn thirst for answers."

The brilliant apex of Seale and Newton's political ideology was the Panthers' Ten-Point Program. Drafted upon the party's foundation and first published on May 15, 1967, in the second issue of its weekly newspaper, *The Black Panther*—and included in all 537 issues thereafter—it was presented under a title that reflected that change was long overdue: "What We Want Now!" Structured like the Constitution, the Ten-Point Program was a list of demands that the Panthers deemed crucial if they were to achieve the true emancipation of Black people. Some are easily recognizable as left-ist concepts, such as the universal right to housing. But others were more controversial. There was Point 7: "We Want an Immediate End to Police Brutality and the Murder of Black People." It was enough to make Clayborne Carson, acolyte of Martin Luther King Jr. and attendee at the 1963 March on Washington, reflect on the plan as "a human rights document."

Of course, politicians, even supposedly freedom-loving conservatives, were not going to stand having armed Black men patrolling the streets. Six months after the foundation of the Panthers, Seale and Newton heard about a bill being presented by Oakland Republican Don Mulford that would prohibit the open carry of loaded firearms in public spaces. Their response would be swift and dramatic. On May 2, 1967, about two dozen Panthers led by Seale marched on the California Capitol in Sacramento to demonstrate their opposition. Newton, considerably more quick-tempered than Seale, sat out the eighty-mile journey. As fate would have it, when they arrived, Ronald Reagan, then at the beginning of his eight-year stint as governor, was on the Capitol lawn, hosting a gathering of eighth-graders. As the armed group came into view, decked out in their fearsome black leather jackets and berets, Reagan was hustled inside. Nobody stopped Seale and his unit as they made their way inside the building, roaming the halls with purpose, in search of the state assembly chamber and the legislators within.

The action was bold, punchy, and elevated the Panthers into a whole new tier of infamy.

On the opposite side of America, Alice Faye Williams was in a transitional period of her life. Personal traumas had left scars; attempts to find new meaning in gainful employment had flatlined. Through it all, she discovered a passion for West African Yoruba culture. Alice would often spend Saturdays attending *bembes*, ceremonial gatherings that centered on African drumming. It inspired a new name and vision of herself—Afeni, an appellation with beautiful dual meaning: "dear one" and "lover of people."

Then, in early 1968, nearly two years after the formation of the Panthers, with no oracular warning or obvious sense of grandeur, there he was in front of her, Bobby Seale. From his small platform on Harlem's 125th Street—its selection an intended homage to his hero, Malcolm X—Seale's words electrified Afeni.

Among the seven or so Panthers flanking Seale that day were Emory Douglas, Joudon Ford, and Aaron Dixon, the latter a Seattle recruit who'd been asked to accompany the party co-founder on his mission to establish new chapters. "We had our leather jackets on, we had our berets, so we were dressed differently from everybody else who was walking by," Dixon described to me. "So people were interested in 'Who's this new organization? Who's this new militant organization? And who was this guy, Bobby Seale?' And Bobby Seale was a fiery speaker. When you heard him speak, you were ready to join the movement."

In the Black Panthers, Afeni saw pride and purpose. But she couldn't join the party right then and there—she had to wait for the organization to officially set up in her city. "Somebody told me they were coming [to New York]; you know, I knew they just *had* to come, they just couldn't stay on the coast, I just couldn't relate to that," she later said. "Nothing that strong could stay in one area. I just knew from the beginning that it would branch out into something beautiful—it had to. I just knew there were n*****s all over the place that felt like I did."

Needless to say, this relied on the Panthers not unraveling. The hyperfocus of police significantly stress-tested the burgeoning group's foundations. Eventually, the harassment led to bloodshed.

In the small hours of October 28, 1967, patrolman John Frey was working a lonely shift monitoring Oakland's west side. Keeping his mind occupied were two lists of license plate numbers he was to look out for. One contained information on stolen cars. The other was an inventory of vehicles owned by members of the Black Panther Party for Self-Defense. Frey was twenty-three years old, a father of one, and, as would be claimed by numerous Black witnesses later in court, a bully and racist.

The squad car idled on darkened, dilapidated Seventh Street at 4:51 a.m. when headlights illuminated the rearview mirror. Behind the beams of light was a tan Volkswagen carrying two men. After checking with dispatch that it was, as he suspected, a "known Panther vehicle," Frey (pronounced "Fry") pulled the car over at the corner of Seventh and Willow Street. In minutes, it was confirmed that the car was registered to LaVerne Williams, the girlfriend of the group's minister of defense, Huey P. Newton. Listening in on the radio communication was nearby patrolman Herbert Heanes, who soon rolled up to the intersection and found the two stationary vehicles.

Waiting in the Volkswagen were Newton and second Panther Gene McKinney. As he approached the driver's window, Frey instantly recognized the man in front of him. "Well, well, well, what do we have? The great, great Huey P. Newton," the cop uttered mockingly. Frey asked for Newton's driver's license and inquired as to the ownership of the Volkswagen. Newton complied, stating that the car belonged to Williams. Frey then ordered Newton out of the Volkswagen.

What happened next was scrutinized in detail in a trial that began in July 1968. During deliberations, the jury felt confident they could put together the chain of events: Newton emerged from the car with no gun, but with his usual lawbook. According to Newton's testimony, Frey said, "You can take that book and stick it up your ass, n****r," before the officer, over six feet tall and more than two hundred pounds, hit him with a left hook to the face. The two men brawled awkwardly; a round went off. "I was dazed and went down to one knee," testified Newton. "I saw him draw his service revolver and felt something like boiling hot soup spilled on my stomach. There were shots all around and the world was spinning. I don't know what happened."

Startled, the second cop, Heanes, fired into the darkness, hitting Frey in the shoulder and causing him to lose the gun. Newton, the jury determined, then seized the loose weapon and emptied it into Frey's back. Somehow, in the darkness and gun smoke, Heanes was also hit three times.

As the two shot cops lay on the street, Frey dying and Heanes wounded, the injured Newton and McKinney fled on foot, desperately clambering into the passing car of a man Newton would later be accused of kidnapping. The Panther leader eventually made it to Kaiser Hospital, where he was simultaneously arrested and treated for his wounds. A photograph was snapped showing him weakened yet handcuffed to a medical bed.

The nature of the events seemingly settled, the jury then had to determine whether Newton had committed a crime. A split emerged as to whether his actions constituted an unlawful killing or self-defense. They landed somewhere in between—voluntary manslaughter. Huey Newton was found guilty in September 1968.

Right from the initial arrest, the Free Huey campaign became the Panthers' priority. Chief of Staff David Hilliard and Newton's brother Melvin began spreading the word in the most guerrilla fashion: by borrowing a psychedelically painted double-decker bus from one of the local white political communes and driving it through the streets blaring, "Free Huey! Free Huey! Can a Black man get a fair trial in America—even if he was defending his life against a white policeman?"

From these beginnings, the campaign intensified. Free Huey provided the Panthers with a fulcrum to attract more support and build broader coalitions among the left. Thousands attended rallies; the courthouse grounds during his appearances would be awash with protesters.

Though the ultimate aim of the Free Huey campaign was burned into its name, it also had a second, more modest ambition: to save Newton from the death penalty.

Despite focusing attention on the West Coast on its Free Huey campaign, the Panthers spent much of 1968 expanding outward from California and into several other major American cities. As Afeni had hoped, an office was established in New York, right in historic Harlem. That August, she was pushed once more toward these new radicals when a friend recommended she see another key member at a rally in Mount Morris Park. This was Eldridge Cleaver.

Tall, handsome, broad-shouldered, and imposing, with fierce masculine energy and a cool eloquence, Cleaver initially represented something of the intellectual wing of the Black Panther Party. His book, *Soul on Ice*, had been released the previous spring. An elegantly written collection of essays penned in Folsom Prison and first published through *Ramparts* magazine, it was hailed as a definitive tome on Black rage and, despite its brutal depictions of his crimes as a serial rapist, earned Cleaver reverence among white liberal circles—*The New York Times* even named it one of its ten best books of the year.

Fresh out of jail, Cleaver was assigned to cover a Malcolm X memorial for *Ramparts* on the second anniversary of the minister's death. It was the Panthers, decked out in their typical black leather and grasping high-powered weaponry, who acted as security for Malcolm's widow, Betty Shabazz. When twenty armed Panthers arrived at San Francisco International Airport to meet Shabazz, startled security were anxious to seize the weapons. Newton refused, correctly pointing out that they were breaking no laws. Shabazz and her escorts soon left for the *Ramparts* office, where Cleaver and his colleagues were waiting, but the shaken security guards called the cops. Police soon arrived at *Ramparts*, eager to engage the group. Cleaver was struck by Newton, who stared down nosy cops and countered their racist taunts by calling them pigs. Weapons were stroked and tensions ran high. But the cops eventually backed off and the memorial took place with no more drama. Energized by what he witnessed, Cleaver joined the Panthers in February 1967 and soon became the party's minister of information and editor of its newspaper, *The Black Panther*, a crucial instrument in spreading the party's revolutionary doctrine, broadcasting its activities to communities nationwide, and raising funds through sales.

Some people, though, are born to chaos.

On April 4, 1968, Martin Luther King Jr. was assassinated in Memphis. The irony was not lost on the Panthers—the paradigm of nonviolent resistance had been violently slain. It emboldened these children of Malcolm in their belief that force was a necessary implement in liberation. In a private phone call with Hilliard, Cleaver declared, "Nonviolence has died with King."

Tensions in America ran stiflingly high in the wake of King's death. Oakland mostly avoided the whirlwind of fire and rioting that hit many American cities. Peace, though, was not absolute.

Two days after the murder, Cleaver was involved in a shoot-out between Panthers and police that left founding member "Little"

Bobby Hutton, still only seventeen years old, dead. Immediately, the Panthers maintained that the tragedy was, once more, the result of police harassment: Cleaver and Hutton were among a group of innocent members riding in a car when they were confronted by Oakland police. Years later, however, Cleaver admitted the cabal "went after the cops that night," while Hilliard, also present, claimed they were part of a caravan of Panther vehicles deployed with the intention of ambushing police. Clueless cops approached the group after spotting Cleaver urinating down a side street. Guns were drawn; two officers were wounded. In the melee, Hutton and Cleaver fled to a nearby apartment building. For ninety minutes the cornered pair shot it out with police. Finally, with Cleaver wounded, Hutton opted to give himself up. Cleaver later claimed that Hutton had stripped down to his underwear and had his hands raised in the air to prove that he was unarmed when cops shot him more than twelve times. Police reports claimed that Hutton, dressed in a trench coat, was attempting to escape. An early death made a martyr of "Little" Bobby, whom Seale called the first member of the Black Panthers. His funeral was attended by approximately fifteen hundred mourners. Marlon Brando gave the eulogy and, afterward, addressed an even bigger crowd at a local park.

The shoot-out didn't immediately derail Cleaver's rise. In August, he accepted the nomination of the fringe Peace and Freedom Party to run for president, beating the challenge of comedian Dick Gregory. "I'm not going to let the people down that gave me this nomination. I'm going to get the job done," Cleaver told delegates, despite being legally too young to be president. He also began teaching an experimental course on racism at the University of California, Berkeley. It incensed Reagan, who, foreshadowing future right-wing pushbacks against the telling of Black history such as the *New York Times*'s 1619 Project on the legacy of slavery, proclaimed, "If Eldridge Cleaver is allowed to teach our children, they may come home one night and slit our throats."

No amount of liberal idolatry, however, would save Cleaver from the grasp of the California Department of Justice. Staring at a return to prison for a parole violation, he vowed to his wife, Kathleen Cleaver, a fierce and dedicated Panther in her own right, that he would never return to jail. Eldridge jumped bail in November 1968, first fleeing to Montreal and then Cuba. He toured the country and mused on writing a follow-up to *Soul on Ice*. But Fidel Castro grew tired of his troublesome guest and soon stuffed him on a plane to Algeria, a nation that had broken off diplomatic relations with the United States the previous year due to its support of Israel during the Six-Day War. Algeria was not long independent from France and since fighting a bloody war of liberation had shown allegiance to various revolutionary movements, including the Vietcong. Viewing the Black Panthers as the closest thing America had to a socialist uprising, Algerian president Houari Boumédiène allowed Cleaver to establish what was dubbed the International Section of the Black Panther Party. Its home became a pleasant three-story white villa in the gated El Biar neighborhood, near a square named after John F. Kennedy. The digs were a gift from its former residents, the official delegation of the Vietcong, after they moved into larger quarters. Hung on the wall was the image of a Black Panther with the caption "In the Revolution One Wins or One Dies."

For a time, Cleaver did good work, drumming up support for the Panthers as he visited various Asian cities in what he called a "tour of solidarity" to "cement political alliances." But the Algiers office became an important outpost for fellow Panthers who, like Cleaver, needed a sanctuary outside of America. The onetime rising star of the literary world became one of the most vocal champions of violent rebellion.

Months earlier, at Mount Morris Park, Afeni felt Cleaver's speech reverberate through her, much like the feeling that Seale had previously ignited. "When I heard him it was the same thing— it was like, that was the dope, man," she said. But Afeni was also struck by the sense of comradeship among the Panthers and their supporters that day.

"I mean, on top of listening to all of this, I would still be confronted with these dudes that were walking around there taking care of the crowd, and they were brothers—they were concerned about the people that were in the audience. They were concerned about something happening to them. I couldn't understand all this danger—I couldn't imagine all that much danger, I couldn't see it, but they were concerned about it, and they were serious about what they were doing. And there were just so many people that said so many things that made so much sense, you know. They told you about love. It was just something different, it wasn't like that same old thing that I'd heard and dismissed. It was different, because they were talking about fighting at the same time that they were talking about things that were relevant to me right now. I just had to relate to it."

Joining the Panthers turned out to be an easy endeavor. Cleaver encouraged those attending his speech to go to a political education class the next day, chaired by the deputy minister of defense in New York, Joudon Ford. In the middle of the meeting, Ford suddenly asked, "How many people in here are Panthers or plan to become Panthers?"

Afeni's hand shot in the air. And that was it, initiation over. "All of a sudden I was a Panther."

The final shots of the 1960s was the perfect time for rediscovery. Flower power was in the ether. John Lennon and Yoko Ono's shaggy dream that peace would be given a chance didn't feel outside the realms of possibility. Acid shaped liberation; sex was plentiful and transgressive. The polychromatic visions of Jimi Hendrix, Brian Wilson, and Jim Morrison appeared to expand the potential of human endeavor. But for many, peace and love were insufficient tools in the fight against oppression.

The rattle and hum of student protest could be heard all over the world. In 1968 alone, resistance ignited across campuses in Germany, Brazil, Mexico, Finland, and France. In the Land of the Noble Free, the war in Vietnam offered a fulcrum to build a youth movement centered on left-wing radicalism. "The New Left" was a broad umbrella of activists who sought to make political gains in civil rights, social order, and the war. A survey of college students showed that in the late 1960s, "350,000 considered themselves as revolutionaries." Of course, revolution means many different things to different people—not all would advocate for armed insurrection. But to some, like Eldridge Cleaver, it meant exactly that. To these hardened hearts and minds, what America needed was akin to Russia's Bolsheviks or Cuba's 26th of July Movement. The political stability of the United States needed to be shattered, no doubt about it. The goal was to overthrow the government. Cleaver had even hoped to establish camps in Cuba to train soldiers to fight a guerrilla war across the plains of America.

As the Black Panthers gained a foothold in New York, the city was being pockmarked by bombs as revolutionaries attempted to assert themselves. There was Sam Melville, connected to eight New York bombings throughout 1969 (no loss of life) before being arrested. During sentencing, he gave the judge a clenched-fist salute, a symbol of solidary adopted by, among others, the Panthers and reinforced as a Black Power salute when thrown in the air by American sprinters Tommie Smith and John Carlos during a medal ceremony at the 1968 Olympics.

There was the Weathermen, which sprouted out of the Students for a Democratic Society (SDS) after becoming disillusioned with its peaceful tactics. The group's intent was simple: to overthrow an imperial and racist government, to slay the beast from within. "The very first question people in this country must ask in considering the question of revolution," the group declared, "is where they stand in relation to the United States as an oppressor nation, and where they stand in relation to the masses of people throughout the world whom US imperialism is oppressing."

The Weathermen had hoped to announce itself in October 1969 with what it dubbed "Days of Rage," a series of protests in Chicago to coincide with the trial of the Chicago Eight, a group of political activists—Bobby Seale among them—who were arrested for their roles in the inflamed anti-war protests that took place during the August 1968 Democratic National Convention. To "bring the war home" was the mantra. Turnout, however, was low, as most of the group's ex-SDS comrades weren't willing to drop their placards and engage in urban guerrilla warfare. In the end, Days of Rage largely consisted of mild demonstrations and petty vandalism. It was condemned by Fred Hampton, rising leader of the Panthers' Chicago branch. "We believe that the Weathermen's action is anachronistic, opportunistic, individualistic," said Hampton. "It's chauvinistic, it's Custeristic. And that's the bad part about it. It's Custeristic in that its leaders take their people into situations where the people can be massacred and they call it a revolution. It's nothing but child's play. It's folly. We think these people may be sincere, but they're misguided."

Maybe it was more contained than its organizers had plotted, but this small uprising left a legacy. As the *Chicago Tribune* wrote in the 1990s, "The Days of Rage symbolized a marked fissure in American society, the end of the carefree '60s, when rich, white college kids clashed with police, their parents, the government in protest against the Vietnam War, racial intolerance and just about everything else that had served as the status quo."

The Weathermen's leadership and hardcore followers disappeared into the underground to conduct a bombing campaign that targeted government buildings, police stations, and financial institutions; its only casualties were three members of the group who were killed in an accidental Greenwich Village townhouse explosion. But if what the Weathermen wanted above all else was revolution, the second most important thing to them might have been the admiration of the Black Panthers. "In our hearts," said member Cathy Wilkerson, "I think what all of us wanted to be were Black Panthers."

"One of the things we felt very strongly was that we weren't merely allies of the Panthers, we wanted to be comrades," Weathermen co-founder Bill Ayers told me over the phone as he drove to his annual talk to high-school kids in Columbus, Ohio. "And that means that we didn't think of ourselves as providing support, we thought of ourselves as members of the same struggle, trying to accomplish the same things. We felt like comrades. This is something that often gets lost, but it was the heart of our politics: We were in solidarity with the Black movement, not in service to it. We were in solidarity with it, we were in solidarity with the international anti-imperialist movement."

Even the acid-crazed hippies of the White Panther Party became convinced to skip peace and love and move straight to the nitroglycerin. In September 1968, dynamite exploded outside the Central Intelligence Agency (CIA) office in Ann Arbor, leaving the space a twisted wreck of glass and steel. So loud was the explosion that it woke the local police chief at his home more than two miles away. After a yearlong investigation, three members of the group—Lawrence "Pun" Plamondon, John Sinclair, and John Waterhouse Forrest—were indicted by a federal grand jury. By this point, Sinclair was already in prison after being hit with a ten-year sentence for being in possession of a couple of joints. The severity of the sentence made him a cause célèbre among many celebrities. John Lennon even recorded a song about him, appropriately titled "John Sinclair." "They gave him ten for two," sang Lennon. "What else can the bastards do?" Plamondon went on the lam to escape arrest for the CIA office explosion and even made the FBI's Ten Most Wanted list before finally being captured.

The bombing case was eventually tossed out due to an illegal wiretap and Sinclair was freed on the marijuana charges. Until the end, his supporters insisted the bombing charges were drummed up. But speaking to me months before his death in April 2024, Sinclair admitted, "Our people did the bombing. So there's no . . . that was the reason they charged us, because we did it. I didn't happen to be part of the bombing group, but I knew about it. And I've just confessed publicly since Pun Plamondon died. I said, 'Now I can tell you that he blew up the CIA' [laughs]. Because you can't arrest him now because he's dead, you motherfuckers."

Though militarism was embedded in the Black Panthers' image, it remained largely theoretical, and Cleaver's ambition to develop the organization into a more militaristic force would eventually cause the group to rupture. In the late 1960s, the Panthers moved beyond Newton's police surveillance to focus on community action. Operating out of its New York offices, initiatives included a youth section called the Black Panther Athletic Club and a health clinic in the Bronx that provided medical and dental services to the community at a reduced fee. Panther-operated health-care clinics were established in thirteen cities in all, dispensing basic medical care, housing assistance, and legal aid. In Winston-Salem, North Carolina, the Panthers even ran an ambulance service. The New York Panthers had guns, of course, but unlike their Oakland predecessors', they were mostly kept in closets or drawers, removed only for weekly weapons safety training and military drills, which trained young members in defending the office.

Core to being a rank-and-file Panther was attending political education classes. The curriculum was revolutionary principles and the evils of capitalism; the writings of Chairman Mao were among the assigned texts. Often complementing the radical literature was the classic movie *The Battle of Algiers*. In New Haven, Panthers would show up at housing projects, hang a white bedsheet in front of a projector, and screen one of their "liberated" copies of the film that depicts Algerian rebels of the 1950s and '60s and their campaign against the French colonialists.

The Battle of Algiers depicts the true story of Ali La Pointe, who is transformed from a petty criminal to a hardened and effective guerrilla fighter. In one crucial section of the film, the National Liberation Front (FLN) calls an eight-day general strike to defy the French during a United Nations debate on Algeria. It bothers La Pointe, who'd rather focus on winning independence through the blood and babel of armed struggle.

"It's hard to start a revolution," Ben M'Hidi, a senior FLN leader, tells La Pointe in the film. "Even harder to continue it. And hardest of all to win it. But, it's only afterwards, when we have won, that the true difficulties begin. In short, Ali, there's still much to do."

Afeni quickly became a section leader and communications secretary. West Coast Panther Bill Jennings remembered a "strong Black sister. Don't take no shit. She was just to be respected. You know how you meet some sisters who have that strong aura about themselves without saying anything? She's one of them kind of people." Afeni ran a breakfast program, one of the Panthers' nationwide flagship initiatives that provided a free meal to children before school. The first breakfast program was inaugurated by Seale in early 1969 after a party member observed that schoolchildren passing his home often looked hungry. Churches and other public halls were used as makeshift lunchrooms. Donations from the public were accepted; local businesses provided food and equipment. Additionally, the Panthers established free clothing programs, free busing to prison programs that helped people visit their jailed loved ones—wherever there was a need in the community, the Panthers sought to fill it. One of Afeni's passions was leading rent strikes against the kind of hoggish New York landlords who'd show up expediently to evict a tenant who'd fallen behind on their rent but leave them waiting months on end to fix a broken staircase.

From morning to midnight, the Panthers served breakfast to hungry kids, hawked newspapers on city streets, and studied the curriculum required of every true revolutionary. When the day was finally done, many weary bodies retreated to what were called "Panther pads": shared, low-rent communal accommodation within the same communities they were servicing. In New York, the buildings were often crumbling due to neglectful landlords. Dinner for the whole house could be served from a single pot. Mattresses would be strewn across various rooms, with Panthers huddled together for warmth so they could sleep through the cold nights. Then the next morning they'd rise, put their black leather uniforms back on, and do it all over again.

The breakfast program helped net the group support beyond revolutionary circles, but the Panther hierarchy viewed these initiatives as a temporary relief for the Black masses—a short-term fix until their revolt was complete. Newton wrote, "We recognized that in order to bring the people to the level of consciousness where they would seize the time, it would be necessary to serve their interests in survival by developing programs which would help them to meet their daily needs . . . These programs satisfy the deep needs of the community but they are not solutions to our problems. That is why we call them survival programs, meaning survival pending revolution."

Speaking decades later, Aaron Dixon reached for Newton's turn of phrase—the "pending revolution." "Because the people weren't ready for revolution, and so we decided to create programs that would serve the people and help the people because kids were going to school hungry. And we said, 'How can kids go to school hungry and learn when they haven't had anything to eat? So let's provide them some food, let's make sure they have breakfast before they go' . . . That was our way of organizing the people—by providing them with services."

Afeni believed strongly in the Panthers' principles and plan. In the spectrum of the party's membership, it's fair to place her on the more moderate wing, drawn more to community uplift than military struggle. "Those programs would have helped my mother with her two girls tremendously," she later said. "And those programs would have helped my mother in a way that would have saved her dignity. I joined because the Panthers answered the needs of the people in my community."

Yet it was during this period that Afeni entered the orbit of two men of a more hardened revolutionary mindset, two men who'd become important figures in her life. It was in the Harlem office that Afeni met Sekou Odinga, a former neighborhood gang member who followed Malcolm X's example out of criminality and into his Organization of Afro-American Unity, a religiously secular group formed after the split with the Nation of Islam. Having become disenchanted by the group after Malcolm's death, Odinga instead put his efforts into the Panthers by becoming a founding member of the New York chapter, as well as the Black Panther International Section.

And it was roughly the same time that Afeni first laid eyes on another Panther leader: Lumumba Abdul Shakur. Spotting him at a rally for the Panthers—dressed in a black naval three-quarter-length coat decorated with red, black, and green bars, the colors of the Pan-African flag—Afeni was immediately drawn to the man who was clearly running things. Soon the two became lovers. Lumumba fed the furnace of revolution that burned deep in Afeni's soul.

Odinga and Lumumba went way back. Both were the children of southerners who had migrated to the South Jamaica section of Queens, a historically white neighborhood that during the 1950s, as part of the Great Migration, saw an influx of Black families from the Deep South. They met at Edgar D. Shimer Junior High in the assistant principal's office, inevitable given both had a reputation for causing trouble. Odinga—then named Nathaniel Burns, known in the streets as Beany—was a member of the gang the Sinners and in 1961, aged sixteen, he was arrested for mugging and sent to the state prison in Comstock, New York. There, he found Lumumba, and the pair renewed their friendship within the concrete and steel surroundings.

Lumumba was born Anthony Coston, and before coming of age he too was running with gangs. In the late 1950s, when he was still a minor, Anthony got in trouble with the police for an altercation on a Queens bus. As Afeni told it years later, a white man punched him in the face for daring to sit next to him. Anthony was hauled in front of a judge, who told him he shouldn't have retaliated before handing down a five-year sentence. But as Malcolm X once said, "The penitentiary has been the university for many a Black man," and like the man who would become his hero, Lumumba became enlightened in prison.

Little did Anthony know that his father was way ahead of him. In the summer of 1962, the elder Coston came to see his son in prison. During their conversation, Anthony was trying to find the words to express his appreciation of Malcolm when his father unexpectedly asked what he thought of him.

"Malcolm X is a very beautiful brother and all the brothers in prison love Brother Malcolm X," Anthony replied. He told his father he had become a Black nationalist and Muslim, even if he couldn't quite adapt to praying. "I never before saw anything that affected my father like what I just said," he later wrote. "His facial expression became one of complete satisfaction."

Anthony's dad became known as Saladin Shakur. In Arabic, Shakur means "thankful to God"; as a surname, it would adorn a veritable family tree of Black revolutionaries. Shortly after, Anthony took the name Lumumba Shakur, and his older brother, James, who would also become a senior Panther, became Zayd Shakur. Saladin would take up a role as spiritual guide for his sons and many other Black Panthers. It was the Shakurs who introduced Nathaniel Burns to Malcolm's teachings.

Burns was freed in December 1963. "I went in search of Malcolm and saw him preaching on a street corner," he'd later remember. "He was mesmerizing." After a brief drift toward weed, gambling, and bouncing around different jobs, an epiphany came at the 1964 World's Fair in Queens when a group of Black women asked if he'd mind modeling some dashikis. Burns was so entranced, he not only took to wearing the garments, he also learned to sew them to sell to friends. The following year, he shed his birth name and, inspired by Guinean revolutionary socialist leader Sékou Touré, was remade as Sekou Odinga. When Lumumba emerged from prison, the pair reconnected. But their hopes of joining Malcolm X's movement were brutally dashed when the minister was assassinated. And so the Panthers became their vehicle for change.

Lumumba became a section leader in Harlem, with Odinga taking on the same role in the Bronx. The pair reflected the popular Afrocentric customs of East Coast members of the party that caused tension with the West Coast hierarchy. The Oakland leadership initially banned the wearing of dashikis and the taking of African names, sending none other than Cleaver to enforce the rule. But after a protracted negotiation, the New Yorkers were allowed to keep the customs on condition that they wore black leather at official party functions.

Suddenly, Afeni was in the company of positive male role models. There was Odinga and Lumumba and Lumumba's family. In the Shakurs, she recognized what she felt in her heart was the true role of fathers and husbands. Afeni may have been iron willed, tough to the core, but, let down by the men in her life since childhood, she had been searching for a male protector, and here, finally, he was. In turn, Lumumba loved Afeni's spirit and candor. He was tender, too; Lumumba introduced Afeni to, of all things, bean pie. They'd pick up the pastry at a store on 126th and Lenox and eat the whole thing in a single sitting. The ritual would make Afeni brim with happiness.

The couple married in the bedroom of Malcolm X's sister Ella Little-Collins at the 139th Street headquarters of Malcolm's OAAU organization in what may have been something of an ad hoc Muslim ceremony. With his brothers as witnesses, Lumumba declared three times, "This is my wife, this is my wife, this is my wife," and the union was sealed. "Once I read the Koran later, I could see what a perversion the whole ceremony was," Afeni later said. Moreover, Lumumba already had a wife and children. In November 1966, he had married a woman named Sayeeda, and three months later, she gave birth to twins. Sayeeda wasn't exactly thrilled by the revelation that her marriage was now polygynous, but Afeni moved in and lived with the family anyway. "No, she didn't like it at first," said Afeni, "but once she realized I was no threat to her, she calmed down after a while."

Afeni was now a Shakur, fierce and powerful. She wasn't interested in playing house like Sayeeda; the Panthers and the revolution were her concern. "I didn't care because I don't think I ever cared about being an only woman. I never would give that much of my time to any one man anyway. It was a very welcome thing to me."

The Black Panther Party was founded and led by men, but women made up a huge proportion of the rank-and-file membership. As a woman in the party, Afeni was in a struggle within a struggle: to be viewed by male counterparts as comrades-in-arms in the impending revolution. It was Panther philosophy that revolutionaries had no gender, a radical and progressive step from Malcolm's relatively patriarchal views on women. Yet day to day, Panther women undeniably experienced sexism. Within the Panther pads, they were often expected to perform a disproportionate percentage of the household chores. In the era of free love, and under the supposed rules of living in a socialist commune, some were told that their duties should include sex.

"You had a revolutionary duty to have sex with somebody because they need sex and that kind of garbage," Kit Kim Holder told me. Just twelve years old when he became a Panther, Holder nonetheless flittered between staying with his parents and hanging out at the Panther pads, where he witnessed pressure applied to women to have sex with the men. "That did happen. I was there, I seen it happen, and people denied that it happened."

Studying theory was one thing, but as Panther Safiya Bukhari saw it, male Panthers alone couldn't always easily disentangle themselves from the mindset instilled in them by a sexist society. "It is extremely important that we remember that even though the Black Panther Party had a built in process to deal with male chauvinism within its ranks, the members of the Party were products of the society in which they lived," she wrote. "We struggled against these tendencies whenever possible, but they were reinforced by the society in which we lived."

As one of the highest-ranking members of the Panthers on the East Coast, Afeni inspired many young women to join the party. Being part of a power couple also brought additional respect and influence. "Didn't nobody fuck with me because I was someone in the party," she said. "They'd have to answer to Lumumba." And still, she continued to rise at five a.m. to prepare meals for the free breakfast program, handled various administrative duties, and took part in political education classes.

When fifteen-year-old Jamal Joseph (né Eddie Joseph) entered the Brooklyn office for the first time with two friends, he worried that the stoic militants might shoot them just for having the audacity. Instead, the high-schoolers walked right into one of the Panthers' classes. Afeni was there, spitting her raw truths about bourgeois Black people who barely cared about the cause and just wanted to look good in the Panthers' trademark fashion. "The struggle," she said, "is about love, sacrifice, and being willing to die for the people." Jamal left with copies of Cleaver's *Soul on Ice*, Mao's Little Red Book, *The Wretched of the Earth* by Frantz Fanon, and a sense of purpose that would see him have one of the longest and most colorful revolutionary existences of his generation.

As a Black Panther, Afeni Shakur's life had structure and purpose. Yet she was still a hardened lawbreaker from her time in the Disciples. Afeni insisted on having parity with the Panther men when it came to firearms and didn't balk at being part of one of the group's "missions." In her case, that meant leading the robbery of a tollbooth. The only account of this has come from Afeni herself, who was scant on detail and did not specify why she'd been sent on the assignment, but the sanctioning of armed robbery was among the Panthers' sources of funding and volunteers came from within.

Armed with a pistol, Afeni emerged from a vehicle being driven by one of her comrades and approached the tollbooth attendant.

"Give me your money," she yelled.

"No!" the worker replied defiantly as he slammed the glass barrier shut.

Spurned, Afeni squeezed the trigger and unloaded a single round at the glass. But the bullet ricocheted, leaving her with powder burns on her neck. The would-be stickup girl barely managed to clamber into the moving getaway car.

"That's why I know God is good because I was stupid beyond belief," she later said.

The line between survival and disaster is often thin, and divine intervention can't be relied upon to keep a person on the right side. Afeni fell under the watch of a different kind of power. Being a Panther placed her under the gaze of J. Edgar Hoover's FBI, and she would become a target as the bureau moved to maim the group, with no illicit tactic off the table.

Portrait of Afeni Shakur, 1970

3

THE SWEEPING OF THE BARS

WHAT THEY KNEW for sure is that the FBI couldn't be trusted with its secrets. That was the kernel notion, the impulse that drove a well-drilled cadre of activists to make a daring raid on a small satellite office in the bureau's vast empire. They did so certain of the FBI's propensity for corruption. But even these radicalized campaigners did not foresee the scale of insidiousness their operation would bring to light.

Skeletons were discovered in the low-key backdrop of Media, a borough outside of Philadelphia, Pennsylvania, where the population has never breached 6,500. It's a postcard picture of American suburban town idealism where residents take great pride in their harmonious way of life—its nickname doubles as a motto: "Everyone's Hometown." But if you visit the scene of the crime, you'll find a plaque recognizing that it was a felonious act of breaking and entering that proved to be the most significant event ever to occur within Media's borders.

It took place on the night of March 8, 1971, a date selected by the burglars because the attention of the town, like every corner of America, would be drawn to Madison Square Garden and Joe Frazier's heavyweight title defense against former champion Muhammad Ali. A son of Elijah Muhammad's Nation of Islam, Ali had been stripped of his crown by boxing authorities after he refused to submit to the draft for the Vietnam War. It made Ali a hero and symbol of the anti-war movement, but the personal and professional cost to him was enormous. Though he managed to avoid jail, Ali was fined

$10,000 and banned from the sport for what would have been three of his peak years. In contrast, Frazier supported U.S. involvement in the war and was comfortable enough in the presence of Richard Nixon to ask if the president could pull a few strings to get Ali's ban lifted so the two pugilists could finally get it on. "Sure, I'd like that," replied the eternally charmless Nixon. Both Frazier and Ali had claims on being the true heavyweight champion, were undefeated, and possessed intense personal animosity toward each other. Their rivalry besotted the American public; Frazier versus Ali was sold as the "Fight of the Century."

As Frazier brawled his way to a points victory—capped with a thunderous left hook to Ali's jaw in the final round that put the former champion flat on his back—the burglars were at work. Led by physics professor and anti-war activist William C. Davidon, the group called itself the Citizens' Commission to Investigate the FBI, a name that appeared to hold official status when, in fact, it was a clandestine collection of dissident protesters. The commission's goal that night was to find documents that proved the bureau was illegally spying on and harassing anti-war protesters.

There was Keith Forsyth, a twenty-year-old college dropout who had moved from Ohio to Philadelphia to connect with the city's peace movement. Once recruited by Davidon, Forsyth busied himself by joining a locksmith association so he could purchase and study books from the Locksmith Library. For weeks Forsyth practiced picking a lock just like the one on the door to the FBI office, which was located on the second floor of a drab multiuse building that included residential apartments, right across the street from the Delaware County Courthouse. In the corner of the attic hideout that served as the burglars' research and development center, Forsyth picked that lock, practicing over and over like a protégé violinist, using self-made tools that could not be traced, until he felt supremely confident that he could access the bureau's sanctum in thirty seconds or less.

The attic was part of the home of John and Bonnie Raines, married with three children. It was twenty-nine-year-old Bonnie who, prior to the break-in, cased the FBI office by impersonating a scruffy coed there to interview an agent for a school paper about job opportunities for women in the FBI, manipulating her all-American good looks into an intel-gathering weapon. It was a dangerous move to turn up at the scene of the yet-to-occur crime; sure enough, the mystery woman with the long black hair tucked under a stocking hat was soon identified as a suspect in the case. But the scouting mission provided a crucial piece of information—the presence of a second door, blocked from the inside by a filing cabinet.

When Forsyth showed up alone to pick the lock on the primary door, he noticed something that had either recently been changed or gone unnoticed in the group's reconnaissance: a second, more sophisticated lock. Forsyth was stunned—this was a lock he could not pick. Foiled, he left the building to find a pay phone and inform the team, who were waiting at a nearby motel, of the major hitch. Some of the group considered aborting the operation. There was, however, that second door to consider. As an entry point, it had initially been dismissed. But if Forsyth could move the file cabinet without making too much noise, it could provide entry. So having composed himself back in the motel, Forsyth returned to the office, picked the second door's lock, and snapped off the deadbolt. He lay on the floor and, using his leg muscles and part of a jack he happened to have in his car, slowly pushed the file cabinet enough to open the door—a daring move, as a resident of the building could have walked by at any time. But Forsyth's luck held. Minutes later, four of his colleagues swooped in and filled multiple suitcases with FBI files.

From this small office, American history was altered. Because what the Citizens' Commission to Investigate the FBI found led to the uncovering of the culture of surreptitiousness, racism, and lawlessness overseen by the bureau's untouchable director, J. Edgar Hoover. Over the course of his near half century leading the FBI, Hoover had become a legend in his own time. He was viewed by the public and government institutions alike as the righteous figurehead of an agency with the reputation of being clean-cut, virtuous, and incorruptible. After Media, nothing would be that innocent again.

For months following the raid, the activists leaked the information to select members of the government and press. The first news reports described the FBI's surveillance of students, Black activists, and peace groups. One document encouraged the interrogation of individuals identified with the New Left to "enhance the paranoia endemic in these circles and will further serve to get the point across there is an F.B.I. agent behind every mailbox."

The initial news reports lacked crucial context. Within the pages of the files was a strange and mysterious acronym: COINTELPRO. Without an overt explanation among the documents, neither the burglars nor the public at first grasped what the word meant. It took the dogged reporting of Carl Stern for all to be revealed. The journalist took the ultimate action of suing the Department of Justice and FBI in federal court for access to COINTELPRO documents under the Freedom of Information Act (FOIA). His efforts revealed it to be a nationwide program of illegal surveillance and harassment. For fifteen years, the FBI coordinated a program of infiltration, distortion, and subversion against those it deemed a threat—or, more accurately, those Hoover deemed a threat—to the government and society. COINTELPRO (or Counterintelligence Program, to give it its full, forbidden name) manifested in the 1950s as a symptom of the Red Scare as the bureau concocted an aggressive campaign against communism at home. By the late 1960s, its target was anti-war activists, the Black liberation movement, and Black people in general.

The public may have assumed that its FBI was mostly concerned with organized crime, foreign espionage, and the corruption of power. In fact, Hoover, with his commitment to keeping America a white Christian republic, devoted significant resources to monitoring Black student organizers. Among the documents stolen by the Citizens' Commission to Investigate the FBI was a memo from Hoover to bureau offices ordering agents to "expose, disrupt, misdirect, discredit, or otherwise neutralize" Black nationalist organizations. Another revealed that *every* Black student at Swarthmore College was under surveillance. Hoover ordered that COINTELPRO's existence be kept secret and that every office report directly to him.

With its efforts to create a revolutionary socialist movement in the Black community, and that movement to take the form of a struggle against capitalism, the Black Panther Party represented a significant threat to Hoover's ideals. Informed that capitalism was at the core of their oppression, young Black people were joining a group that not just advocated for free meals for those living in poverty, it executed the plan via initiatives such as its breakfast programs. The group was both articulating and putting into practice an alternative to good old American capitalism, which Hoover was not going to stand for. As Beverly Gage wrote in her book *G-Man: J. Edgar Hoover and the Making of the American Century*, "If Hoover had been asked at almost any point in his career to conjure up his most terrifying vision of domestic insurrection, he might have described the Black Panthers."

COINTELPRO could be sinister, cruel, and violent. But some stories of the FBI's actions during its era are almost comical, like schemes concocted by high-schoolers, not the agency that brought you such fabled lawmen as John Dillinger's pursuer Melvin Purvis and Mafia infiltrator Joseph D. Pistone. The Nation of Islam experienced its insidious nature when the FBI dreamed up a simple plan to derail the organization. In April 1968, it anonymously mailed 273 members of Temple Number 9 in New York a twenty-page booklet detailing the mosque's finances. With crude illustrations, it depicted NOI leaders living the high life while their followers struggled in poverty. Recipients were likely bemused by the whole thing, and the NOI weathered the incident.

Hoover's ire extended to white allies. In 1970, he approved a plan to target the actress Jean Seberg for the sin of donating money to the Black Panthers. The scheme involved feeding gossip pages a rumor that the father of her unborn baby was not her husband, the French author and diplomat Romain Gary, but a Panther. Soon after reading the story, the upset Seberg went into premature labor. Her daughter was delivered by emergency cesarean section and died three days later. Gary later claimed that Seberg attempted suicide every year thereafter on the anniversary of the child's death. In 1979, two weeks after the anniversary of her daughter's passing, Seberg died of an overdose of barbiturates. Her body was found in Paris, wrapped in a blanket and lying in the back seat of her car, next to a suicide note.

No rules applied; no tactic was off the table. Cops' willingness to sidestep best practices to achieve violent ends was laid bare in Chicago, when Fred Hampton, the dynamic spokesman for the city's Black Panthers, was shot and killed in his bed during a predawn raid of his apartment. The operation was carried out by a tactical unit of the Cook County State's Attorney's Office, but the FBI had been lurking in the shadows. Hampton did not live to discover that the bureau had invaded his inner circle. William O'Neal was in charge of his security and possessed keys to Panther headquarters and safe houses. At the same time, he was serving as an informant for the FBI.

In mid-November 1969, O'Neal sat down with his handler, FBI Special Agent Roy Mitchell, at the Golden Torch restaurant in downtown Chicago. Tragedy formulated when O'Neal offered up a detailed floor plan of Hampton's West Side apartment, including information on where Chairman Fred slept. Mitchell took the diagram to Assistant State's Attorney Richard Jalovec, who authorized an arms raid on the Hampton residence for the early hours of December 4, 1969.

Ahead of time, O'Neal slipped Hampton a large dose of secobarbital in a glass of Kool-Aid. It sent Hampton into a deep and blissful slumber in his bed; at about four a.m., a heavily armed fourteen-man police team burst into his home. The apartment became a killing cage. Though Hampton never stirred, he was shot three times, once in the chest and twice in the head, at point-blank range, his heavily pregnant girlfriend, Akua Njeri (then known as Deborah Johnson), nearby. Killed by a single bullet to the heart was Mark Clark, head of the Panthers in Peoria, Illinois. Several others were wounded. No Panther had fired a shot, with the exception of Clark, who firearms experts determined squeezed off a single round during death convulsions as he was falling to the floor. In contrast, the police had fired at least ninety-eight rounds into the apartment. As the Hampton family lawyer Jeffrey Haas described it to me, "It was not a shoot-out, it was a shoot in." Despite this, the survivors were charged with aggressive assault and the attempted murder of members of the unit. Bond was set at $100,000 apiece.

Among themselves, the triumphant G-men had no interest

in downplaying their role in Hampton's demise. A week after his death, FBI agent Robert Piper sent a memo to headquarters noting that Hampton was killed in the raid and that this was due, in large part, to the "tremendous value" of O'Neal's work as an informant. Piper then suggested a three-hundred-dollar cash bonus for O'Neal was in order. The request was quickly approved.

In 1977, M. Wesley Swearingen, an FBI agent with a quarter century of service, became a whistleblower. Among the catalog of offenses he revealed to investigators, Swearingen divulged that an FBI supervisor in Chicago told him the bureau had "deliberately set up" the situation in which Hampton was killed.

After his cover was blown, O'Neal entered the federal Witness Protection Program. "Do I feel like I betrayed someone? Absolutely not. I had no allegiance to the Panthers," he told a TV reporter in 1989. Nine months later, O'Neal was struck by a car as he made a late-night run across Chicago's Eisenhower Expressway in an apparent suicide. His infamy was sealed in 2021 with the release of Shaka King's movie *Judas and the Black Messiah*, a telling of the story of O'Neal and Hampton, with O'Neal forevermore branded with the name from the Gospels most closely associated with betrayal.

These are just some of the stories that must have rattled around Hoover's mind as he contemplated the devastating consequences if COINTELPRO were to be publicly exposed. Almost daily he wrote memos pressing agents to solve the Media burglary. This continued for almost fourteen months, from the day he first heard about the raid until the eve of his death, on May 2, 1972. Hoover was laid to rest as an American hero. Death spared him witnessing the full uncovering of COINTELPRO and other secret operations. After Stern's reporting, there was the Church Committee's long investigation into abuses. The Socialist Workers Party instigated a thirteen-year lawsuit that revealed how the FBI spent decades harassing the party and its members in ways that, according to the federal judge, had "no legal authority or justification." Hoover's maniacal obsessions were laid bare, significantly recoloring his legacy.

And the burglars? They got away with it. Despite an extensive investigation, no member of the Citizens' Commission to Investigate the FBI was caught. Agreeing to never reunite, they moved on to new acts of resistance, enjoyed the company of family, turned middle-aged, and then elderly, as people tend to do, keeping their secret safe as the years slipped by. It wasn't until 2014 that former *Washington Post* reporter Betty Medsger, who broke the initial stories contained within the stolen documents, revealed the identities of Davidon, Forsyth, Bonnie and John Raines, and most of their compatriots in her book *The Burglary: The Discovery of J. Edgar Hoover's Secret FBI*.

Serious police raids occur under the cover of darkness, when cops have the safety blanket of knowing their prey are likely at their most vulnerable. Fred Hampton's surviving comrades discovered this to be true in the most brutal fashion. In the arrest of Afeni and Lumumba Shakur, daybreak was again judged to be overly delayed.

It was five a.m. on April 2, 1969, half an hour before sunrise, when five NYPD officers stormed the couple's home at 112 West 117th Street. The circumstances of the Shakurs' capture were unscrupulous. One cop lit a rag while the officers collectively shouted "Fire!" to draw Afeni and Lumumba to them. Guns were pressed against her stomach and his forehead; vicious threats were issued. "Police! If you move, I'll blow your fuckin' brains open!"

It was a single capture in a wider web. That morning, more than 150 NYPD officers executed a mass arrest of the city's Black Panthers. Each squadron included at least one Black officer, as the NYPD believed that their voices would be more likely to secure safe entry to the Panthers' dwellings. The tactic appears to have been entirely self-serving. Once inside the home of Cetewayo (often referred to in the media by his original name, Michael Tabor), white detective Joseph Coffey held a gun to the suspect's head and declared, "If you move, I'll blow your brains out." Cetewayo testified that the cop added, "I got you, you Black bastard. You Panthers say you like to shoot policemen—well, let's see you try now."

More courteous was the arrest of Robert Collier at 336 East Eighth Street. Later in court, a detective would say Collier behaved "like a gentleman." Good manners didn't stop the cops' hauling off to jail the two homeless Puerto Rican boys whom Collier had let crash in his apartment the night before. More problematic for a Panther who already had a conviction for conspiring to bomb the Statue of Liberty was that the arresting officers also found a shopping bag of brass pipe.

By eleven a.m., before most of the captured had appeared before a judge, Manhattan district attorney Frank Hogan was in front of a gathering of journalists, announcing the indictment: twenty-one Black Panthers were being charged with 186 counts of attempted arson, attempted murder, and conspiracy to bomb police stations, schools, department stores, and the New York Botanical Garden. Hogan identified Macy's, Alexander's, Bloomingdale's, Abercrombie & Fitch, and Korvette as targets and "tomorrow" as the planned date of execution. In doing so, he depicted law enforcement's interception as a heroic last-minute play that saved lives and protected livelihoods.

In all, police made ten arrests that morning. As well as Afeni, Lumumba, Cetewayo, and Collier, they picked up Dharuba (Richard Moore), Ali Bey Hassan (John Casson), Abayama Katara (Alex McKeiver), Jamal Joseph, Baba Odinga (Walter Johnson), and Joan Bird. That afternoon, Lonnie Epps arrived at a police station with his father to turn himself in. Curtis Powell was preparing to surrender peacefully when he returned to his apartment with two white filmmaker friends. As they stepped through the door, police in bulletproof vests with rifles rose from behind the furniture. Sundiata Acoli (Clark Squire) was also arrested later in the day. There was no need to go looking for Richard Harris and Kuwasi Balagoon (Donald Weems), who were sitting in a Newark jail for robbery. No roughhouse tactics were necessary to take Lee Berry, as police arrested the Vietnam War veteran in his hospital bed while he was receiving treatment for epilepsy. Shaba Om (Lee Roper) and Kwando Kinshasa (William King) managed to slip out of the city and evade capture until being arrested in Columbus, Ohio, in November, making it eighteen arrests in total.

Justice Charles Marks—who'd come to court at 12:30 a.m. that morning to receive the indictment, such was its perceived time sensitivity—set an inflated $100,000 bond for each apprehended Panther. The defendants, still not having talked to their lawyers, were separated and sent to various different jails, where they could grieve for freedom in Dickensian squalor. Afeni's destination was the Women's House of Detention at 10 Greenwich Avenue, an art deco coffin in its final months of use after allegations of prisoner mistreatment, known to those forced to loiter in its locked-down interiors as the House of D.

Determined to avoid the NYPD's dragnet that April 2 morning, however, was Afeni and Lumumba's close comrade Sekou Odinga. Asleep in an upper-floor apartment near Brooklyn's Prospect Park, he was awoken by the sound of cops creeping up the stairs. Pressing his ear to the door, Odinga quickly realized a raid was going down. He could hear footsteps on the roof; police were all around, like cockroaches. Quickly dressing himself, Odinga grabbed the rifle at his bedside and yelled, "Who's there?"

"The police! Open the door."

"Gimme a minute. I'm putting my clothes on."

Stepping to the front door, Odinga clicked a round into the gun's chamber. The action was audible to the cops, who quickly moved to cover.

With just seconds to escape, Odinga ran into the bathroom and cracked open the tiny window. Below was a four-story drop. Abandoning his rifle, he squeezed through the narrow gap and sought freedom via a concrete drainpipe that ran down toward the street. Shimmying down the wall, he heard a voice shout out, "There he is! There he is!"

Odinga leapt from the wall, falling almost thirty feet and landing on the roof of a garage, his knee smashing into his chin on landing. Disoriented, he jumped into a tree, then to the pavement below. Limping away in pain, Odinga sought sanctuary by trying the doors of random brownstones until he found an unlocked basement. Inside, he hid behind an oil tank. And there he stayed as the police cordoned off the block and began their search. Hours passed, but unbelievably, Odinga remained undetected. He waited until the sun went down, hailed a taxi, and made off. By 1970, Odinga had reached the Panthers' Algeria outpost, via a stop-off in Cuba, to the warm embrace of Eldridge Cleaver, alongside Larry Mack and Mshina (Thomas Berry), the final two names on the indictment.

A twenty-second soul, Fred Richardson, was added after the trial began.

The investigation into the New York Panthers was led by the Bureau of Special Services (BOSS), a localized department within the NYPD that tracked political and activist groups that it ostensibly believed to be a threat to the city. To what extent the indictment of the Panther 21 was a direct result of activities that fell under the umbrella of COINTELPRO is unclear. Writing in 1974, law scholar Peter Zimroth reported that the Feds were completely blindsided by the indictment. However, there is good reason to believe that, as with the killing of Hampton in Chicago, the FBI was quietly guiding the NYPD in its attempts to disrupt and neutralize Panthers. The relationship certainly appeared cozy on August 29, 1968, when FBI special agent Henry Naehle reported on his meeting with a member of an NYPD special unit investigating the Panthers. Naehle acknowledged that the FBI's New York Field Office "has been working closely . . . in exchanging information of mutual interest and to our mutual advantage."

Before her arrest, Afeni had sensed an unsettling presence in the form of Yedwa Sudan. Like Afeni, he had joined the Black Panthers soon after its establishment in New York. But as she forged strong connections with many of her new comrades, there was something suspicious about Sudan's energy. Hot-tempered with lunatic vibrancy, he seemed an over-the-top parody of what a Black militant should be. Jamal Joseph had once observed Sudan pull a .38 pistol from under a couch cushion and fire a round at a television set to shut Richard Nixon up. None of it impressed Afeni. The suspicion tugged at her heels. She told anybody who would listen that she thought Sudan was a cop, a charge he strenuously denied. How could he be police, he argued. Had they not heard about all the burglaries he committed? Or the time he pointed a gun at his own landlord? Not even Lumumba would heed his wife's suspicions. She was "an emotional sister," he told Sudan.

Afeni's instincts were correct—"Yedwa Sudan" was the creation of undercover BOSS officer Ralph White, deployed to infiltrate and destroy the Panthers from within. Though the deception had never convinced Afeni, White's façade was enough to elicit a significant amount of trust. "Man, he couldn't be a cop," Lumumba later told one of his attorneys. "You should have seen the shit he did."

White was not alone. Six NYPD officers in total successfully passed themselves off as New York Panthers. Their testimony proved crucial in securing the Panther 21 indictments.

In a tumultuous era, the prospect of oblivion—whether imprisonment or slaughter—cast a shadow over all American dissenters, disruptors, and revolutionaries. As authorities continued their hydraulic press on chapters all over the country, the remaining Panthers struggled to hold their lines. No recruit should have been blind to the inherent risk of being a Panther—the group had formed in the spirit of the murdered Malcolm X and gained infamy through its open embrace of guns. But mass indictments? Assassination? These were tremendous risks, and so many wandered from the movement, unwilling to trade their freedom or their lives for the increasingly desperate struggle. In a hostile atmosphere, others tried to stay united and focused.

"It wasn't something that we thought about all the time, because we had to worry about running the programs, and we already had decided that we were going to defend ourselves and protect ourselves," said Seattle Panther Aaron Dixon when asked about what the threat of being jailed or killed does to the psyche. "So they raided our offices, there were shoot-outs. I had two assassination attempts on my life. The first one was in July of 'sixty-eight, in Seattle, and I just barely escaped. In 1971, I had another assassination attempt. That became part of what we did—burying our dead and making sure that their memories lived on. But there were a lot of people who had joined. And when all those attacks happened, there were a lot of people who left. They weren't ready for that. There were people who were scared for their lives. And they left, they just decided that they weren't ready for that type of a commitment. But there were a lot of people who were ready to die."

The Panthers' screening process was not exactly robust—if you were Black and wanted to be a Panther, you were a Panther. This allowed the organization to grow quickly, but it also allowed relative moderates not as entrenched in the cause as Dixon to join, and for wolves like William O'Neal and Ralph White to come through the door.

The remaining New York Panthers mustered their energy and resources to help the imprisoned comrades. With many key members lost to the case, senior West Coast figures such as Field Marshal Donald L. Cox were deployed to help fill the leadership void. But the party's offices would invariably be empty when the Panther 21 were in court, as members attended large rallies that took place outside the courthouse. Police presence at these shows of support was always heavy. Photographed at one rally was a particularly interested observer: Afeni's mother, Rosa Belle, a toothpick in her mouth and stern expression etched across her careworn features.

Harassment was the daily reality. Steve Long, a fresh recruit who joined the party after attending a Panther 21 protest, was in a group pad in Harlem when there was a late knock at the door. Long went to greet the caller only to discover it was the police. The cops had no official business, just a message: "We're coming for you." Long defiantly slammed the door in their faces.

Help came from some unlikely highbrows. On January 14, 1970, legendary music composer Leonard Bernstein hosted a ritzy Manhattan fundraiser. The event inspired a *New York* magazine cover story by Tom Wolfe, who dismissed the idea of rich New Yorkers supporting Black militants as "radical chic." The ridicule stepped on the hose of potential funding for the Panthers' legal defense. "Tom Wolfe's article really made people who thought they might want to support us just disappear," Jamal Joseph told me.

Others were determined to show more forceful comradeship. On the night of February 21, 1970, the New York cell of the Weathermen, by now out of mainstream society and operating underground, arrived at the Inwood home of Justice John Murtagh, the judge overseeing the Panther 21 trial. As Murtagh, his wife, and three children slept, the group scrawled "Free the Panther 21" and "The Vietcong Have Won" on the sidewalk. A neighbor reported the activity. When the police arrived, they found the Weathermen had placed three shopping bags containing Molotov cocktails beside the front door, on a window ledge, and beneath a car in the garage. All three went off at 4:30 a.m., blowing out two of the home's windows and searing the paint off the car.

By the end of the year, the organization was pivoting toward a new strategy. Its shift in priorities was laid out in the communiqué "New Morning, Changing Weather." Deeply affected by the townhouse explosion that had resulted in the deaths of three members, the Weather Underground, as it was called after ditching "the Weathermen" for a gender-neutral name, apologized for its "tendency to consider only bombings or picking up the gun as revolutionary, with the glorification of the heavier the better" and adopted a more hippie-like position. "The hearts of our people are in a good place . . . They've moved to the country and found new ways to bring up free, wild children. People have purified themselves with organic food, fought for sexual liberation, grown long hair. People have reached out to each other and learned that grass and organic consciousness-expanding drugs are weapons of the revolution." It was signed by just one member: the woman Hoover had dubbed "La Pasionaria of the lunatic left," Bernardine Dohrn.

This sharp turn in direction was a culmination of internal anxieties that often tormented leftist groups at the time. The question was constantly humming in the background: Were the Weather Underground's goals more reachable through anarchic underground actions, or through more mainstream-palatable politics? "We couldn't resolve the question of how much or what type of action to do, and we began to split," said Bill Ayers, co-founder of the group that had itself split from the SDS.

Ayers described three factions within the Weather Underground fighting for its soul. For one group, "the more chaos and destruction the better." Another clique wanted to operate in a way that was more deliberate, and that didn't jeopardize the broader left movement. Then there was a group trying to straddle both sides. "That all got clarified when the townhouse happened," said Ayers. "The group that won the argument after the townhouse was the group that said we have to do this as part of the movement, not separate to the movement. We're not terrorists, we may think of ourselves as urban guerrillas, but we're not letting the military lead, and that was a huge argument. So 'New Morning' came out of that argument. The argument was the military should not lead, the military should follow the politics."

In response to "New Morning, Changing Weather," members of the Panther 21 issued an open letter criticizing the Weather Underground's rejection of revolutionary violence—quoting Che Guevara to underline their point—and lack of action on raising money for their cause. This put the Weather Underground, so eager for the approval of the Panthers, in a tricky position. The selected response was silence.

"We're twenty years old, we're trying to figure out how to move in this context," said Ayers. "We're experimenting, we're making mistakes, we're listening to people. So when we wrote 'New Morning' and the Panthers were critical of it, we took their criticism as a comradely criticism."

Feelings of disappointment with comrades were a minor annoyance. The more serious concern for the Panther 21 was the legal team New York was assembling against them. The prosecution was led by Joseph A. Phillips, a formidable figure not just in stature—six feet four inches tall with a crown of curly brown hair—but reputation. Phillips had spent a year with a small Brooklyn law firm before grabbing the opportunity to work in the office of Manhattan district attorney Frank S. Hogan. He was initially assigned to the appeals bureau and won a high-profile Supreme Court case involving the racketeer mob man Joseph Lanza, who charged that an illegal wiretap had been installed in his prison cell. From 1964, Phillips was assigned to the rackets bureau of Hogan's office, working on heavy cases dealing with organized crime and corrupt public officials.

In the other corner was the perfectly disheveled figure of William Kunstler, a seasoned civil rights lawyer as likely to throw a fist in the air as his radical clients. Though he had an activist spirit, Kunstler was not immune to the thrill of the spotlight. In 1970, a *New York Times* profile dubbed him perhaps the country's best-known lawyer. Kunstler departed the New York Panther 21 case to focus on the Chicago Eight, a trial he deduced would have a higher profile. Attorneys involved suspected that both trials were scheduled concurrently to split two defense teams that shared many of the same resources.

Stepping in to lead the Panther 21 defense in Kunstler's absence was twenty-six-year-old Gerald Lefcourt, leading a ticket that consisted of his sister-in-law Carol Lefcourt, Charles McKinney, William Crain, Robert Bloom, and Sanford Katz.

Gerald Lefcourt's affinity for the Panthers was innate. With Carol Lefcourt and Crain, he had co-founded the Law Commune, an institute guided by the principles of mutual aid that often took on young radicals as clients and considered law a weapon in the fight for social change. Lefcourt's relationship with the New York Panthers began in the summer of 1968, when he received a call from Huey Newton's lawyer Charles Garry inquiring as to whether he would defend three party members accused of assaulting police and fire services workers. After arriving at the courthouse, the young attorney looked on as three bruised, banged-up, bandaged Panthers were marched into their arraignment as the cops and firefighters chuckled to themselves. "It was obvious that they had beaten these three Panthers to a pulp, yet the Panthers were accused of assaulting them," Lefcourt told me.

Panther cases continued to pile up on Lefcourt's desk through late 1968 and into the new year. For a young lawyer, it was an intense crash course on radical law, positioning him as a kind of lone Spartan against the might of the state's marching Persian infantry. No call, though, could have grabbed Lefcourt's attention like the one he received about the night of January 17, 1969—three months before the Panther 21 busts—when a small explosion shattered two windows of the Forty-Fourth Precinct station in the Bronx. Minutes after the blast, two patrolmen on motorcycles happened upon a parked car watching on from the opposite side of the Harlem River. Standing at the trunk was Sekou Odinga, who was quickly joined outside the vehicle by Kuwasi Balagoon. The officers stepped off their bikes and approached the two men to ask what was the problem. Suddenly, pistols were drawn. Shots were exchanged between cops and revolutionaries from six feet apart; miraculously, nobody was hit. Both suspects quickly fled the scene, and when the smoke cleared, only one person, still in the car, was left to face the music: Joan Bird. Lefcourt represented her at the arraignment. The case was eventually folded into the Panther 21 indictment.

The only other woman in the Panther 21 could appear to be the totemic opposite personality of Afeni. Short, slender, with big eyes that conveyed her youth, Bird was a diminutive presence, nothing like her jailed comrades such as Dharuba, who took regular openings to hurl calls of "fascist" and "racist" at their judge and prosecution. "Joan is a very sensitive girl," Afeni once said. "She's the most unselfish person I know."

The daughter of hardworking Jamaican immigrants, Joan Victoria Bird had a relatively stable upbringing. Right up to her arrest she lived in her parents' five-room apartment on Eighth Avenue, near 152nd Street, and, as a Catholic, attended various parochial schools. In January 1968, Bird enrolled in Bronx Community College with hopes of becoming a nurse but flunked out. Various non-degree courses yielded the same outcome. By the summer of 1968, Bird was a Panther. "I read their Ten-Point Program," she said, "and understood completely what brothers like Malcolm, Huey, Eldridge, and Che were talking about—liberation by any means necessary for all oppressed people of the world."

As well as studying politics, as was the requirement of all Panthers, Bird helped raise funds by putting on fashion shows, and she organized Christmas parties for neighborhood kids. Depending on what lens you're inclined to view the Panthers through, Bird is either an example of authorities sparing no one in the party from their systematic attack on the Panthers, or the Panthers' ability to radicalize the unlikeliest person.

What was the fashion-conscious Catholic doing there on a cold night of cop shop blasts and exchanged gunfire? The prosecution, working from information from undercover officers, believed the January 17 explosion to be the brainchild of Lumumba. His goal, the prosecution claimed, was to bomb the Forty-Fourth Precinct station and deploy snipers across the river to pick off officers as they escaped the explosion. Odinga and Balagoon were selected as the gunmen because of their tendency to brag about their cop shooting exploits, while Bird served as their driver. Police did retrieve an unfired rifle and four bullets from the trunk of the car, though believers of their story must accept Odinga's faith that he could efficiently use such a small arsenal from four hundred yards with no scope.

The prosecution claimed that prior to the January 17 incidents, undercover cops had been shown Lumumba's dynamite and were so concerned that they and other BOSS officers secretly traded it out for a dummy concoction of molded clay and oatmeal. The explosion at the Forty-Fourth Precinct had been caused by a blasting cap and nothing more. If the police hadn't made that swap and the real dynamite had detonated, the prosecution said, the devastation would have been much worse.

That same evening, there was an explosion at a Queens Board of Education office building, blowing a hole out of the side of the building. Nobody was hurt. It was speculated that the more destructive nature of the blast was caused by a real stick of dynamite being added to the fakes. Additionally, it was claimed that a whole bundle of the phony dynamite was found two days later at a third location, the Twenty-Fourth Precinct station.

Bird was charged with helping two assailants attempt to kill policemen. In court, the defense sought to suppress a confession that allegedly was obtained from Bird, who insisted she was beaten by the police after her arrival at the Wadsworth Avenue station house. During pretrial hearings, Bird's mother testified that Bird's face was bruised the day after her arrest. The Panthers even claimed the torture had included her being dangled by the ankles from a third-story window. The police, however, maintained that her face was bruised because she ducked down in the car during the shoot-out. Balagoon would later plead guilty to assault in the first degree for the shooting after his trial was severed from the rest of the Panther 21.

Right from the outset, the Panther 21's defense team faced all manner of obstacles. The commissioner of the New York Department of Correction ordered that the imprisoned Panthers be kept apart at all times. For the men, this meant being held across seven different jails. In the first five months of their incarceration, their lawyers were only allowed to meet with them as a group for a total of three hours. It wasn't until November that Justice Murtagh ordered the Department of Correction to allow lawyers to meet them as a group for one hour per week. Such setbacks would have done little for the prisoners' hope that they'd be exonerated. The FBI, officially under the jurisdiction of the U.S. Department of Justice, was waging a war on Black Panthers, and now its imprisoned members needed to believe that the courts would give them a fair opportunity to prove their innocence. As the hammer of injustice loomed, morale among the defendants was often low. In one meeting, Dharuba confided to Gerald Lefcourt, "You haven't got a chance. We already got a ticket on this railroad. They gonna give us forever. The court will never free us. Only the people will free us."

Lumumba attempted to assert agency over his wife by selecting Carol Lefcourt as Afeni's primary defense counsel, a decision she immediately objected to. "Carol Lefcourt had a tiny, squeaky voice," Afeni later said. "And I thought hell no, she can't represent me! Not sounding like that. The judge wouldn't be able to hear her *objection*, not with that voice. There was no meat to her voice, no resonance, no assurance . . . Hey, I'm facing the same three hundred and fifty years everyone else is facing, and I am not going out like that. With this here, Carol Lefcourt, speaking for me? Shit."

None of the defense lawyers would be deemed fit to represent her. With her freedom on the line, the twenty-two-year-old high-school dropout made the extraordinary decision, the incomprehensible decision, to represent herself in court. It was a move that could be interpreted as smacking of arrogance, or desperation, or acceptance of a doomed fate. Maybe it was all those things at once. Yet Afeni had been inspired by Fidel Castro's prowess in court when defending his armed attack on the Moncada Barracks—the text of his speech became the book and manifesto *History Will Absolve Me*. Like Castro, Afeni wanted to portray herself as a freedom fighter.

According to Gerald Lefcourt, the decision was not Afeni's alone. It was the lawyers, in discussion with their clients, who came up with the idea to have a couple of them make their own defense. "Because they were so scary to the world," said Lefcourt, "we were trying to come up with a way to humanize them as people and decided that one or two of them should represent themselves, so that the jury could hear directly from them and not see them all as the same and not fear them." As well as Afeni, Cetewayo was selected for his expressiveness, his presence, and a baritone voice reminiscent of Paul Robeson's.

The way Jamal Joseph remembered it, though, was Afeni insisting she represent herself and the lawyers developing a strategy from that, rather than the other way around: "It wasn't so much that it was a mutual decision, it was Afeni's decision," he asserted. "There was a discussion and I think Charles McKinney, who was the older Black trial lawyer in the case, was the first to say that this could be a good strategy. And then people talked and everybody kind of said, yes, this is a great idea . . . So, when we say it was a collective decision, no, it was Afeni's decision. And other people kind of agreed that, yes, this could be good. She was Afeni Shakur in that moment."

As a risk, it was beyond huge. Afeni's wasn't the only freedom on the line. The jury would inevitably draw conclusions on the whole group from her presentation. Lumumba protested—his wife wasn't qualified, she could get too emotional, she could "fuck it up." But Afeni could tell herself that her instinct had been right about Detective White. If she harbored any lingering frustrations about the men in the party not taking her suspicions seriously, there was one thing she could now be sure of: her fate was in her own hands.

"When I get convicted, is anybody else here gonna do my time?" she asked her lawyers rhetorically.

"No, that's your sentence to serve."

"Well, this is my decision."

Meanwhile, bail money was being scrounged. An influx of $61,070 was provided by five Presbyterian and Episcopalian churches across New York and four ministers. Dr. Robert P. Johnson, the Black general presbyter of the Presbytery of New York City, appealed to churchmen in the metropolitan area to help raise money for the Panthers, arguing that to hold them in jail for ten months before their trial amounted to preventive detention. With enough money, the Panthers opted to free Afeni, likely seeing her oratory and organization skills as a weapon on the outside. On January 30, Afeni left the Women's House of Detention in Greenwich Village to the applause of friends, lawyers, and the ministers. Back in court three days later, she flashed a smile at prosecutor Joseph Phillips as she entered this time via the audience.

Pretrial procedures in *The People of the State of New York v. Lumumba Abdul Shakur et al.*, as it was placed on record, began on February 2. By the time it reached court, only thirteen Panthers on the indictment were facing trial. Once more, Lumumba tried to persuade his wife to backtrack on the decision to act as her own defense in court. But as Marcus Garvey said, "If you haven't confidence in self, you are twice defeated in the race of life." Afeni held firm on her decision. The trial would begin that September. It would last eight months, becoming the longest and most expensive in New York State history.

Six months after Afeni was released on bail, in July 1970, Joan Bird was finally uncaged. Without a conviction she had spent fifteen months and four days in the Women's House of Detention. Once more, it had cost the Panthers and its supporters $100,000 for this liberation. As Bird made her way into an oval holding room between the prison and outside world, it was an old prison mate who spotted her. "She's coming, she's coming," yelled Afeni, with her firsthand experience of walking through the iron gate and into that room. In an instant, Bird's tiny frame was seized by her parents, Afeni, and Jamal Joseph. There was crying, shouting, and hugging. In no time she was whisked onto the street outside, where some 150 people had gathered. Chants of "Power to the people" rang out. Yellow flowers were pushed into Bird's hands; another supporter handed her daisies. With the cheering still going on, Bird crossed the street, turned, and looked back toward the upper floors of the jail. Bird then raised a clenched fist, and cried out, "Power." From the House of D came an audible roar in response.

As the Panther 21 awaited their day in court, the rest of the party was in chaos and disorder. Since the productive days of their Oakland genesis, co-founder Bobby Seale had been drowning in legal trouble. In August 1968, he was indicted for taking part in demonstrations at the Democratic National Convention, becoming one of a group that became known as the Chicago Eight. Seale's connection to the rest of the group, who were all white, was tenuous, but his fiery speech advocating armed defense against racist police attacks was deemed enough to charge him with a violation of the 1968 Anti-Riot Act.

On September 24, 1969, thirteen months after the riots, the trial of the Chicago Eight began in the opulent oak-paneled twenty-third-floor courtroom of Judge Julius Hoffman—all the finery American justice can buy. Seale's counsel of choice, Charles Garry, was in the hospital for gallbladder surgery, and the incredulous defendant insisted upon the right either to represent himself or to have the trial halted until his lawyer was healthy. The request was denied. Regardless, Seale, a ball of fury, ignored the judge's attempt to keep him quiet. "I have a constitutional right to speak," he insisted, "and if you try to suppress my constitutional right to speak out in behalf of my constitutional rights, then I can only see you as a bigot, a racist, and a fascist, and I have said before and clearly indicated on the record." On October 29, the judge ordered that Seale be bound and gagged—literally. Though no photographs could be taken in the courtroom, the artist's sketch of Seale tied to the chair with a gag in his mouth captured the establishment's brutal feelings toward Black revolutionaries. "This is no longer a court of order," asserted defense lawyer William Kunstler. "Your Honor, this is a medieval torture chamber." Finally, on November 5, Hoffman severed Seale from the case. The Chicago Eight became the Chicago Seven. Seale avoided being convicted on the original charge, but was thrown in jail anyway, sentenced to four years for contempt.

The pursuit of Seale didn't end with him being jailed. He was tried in 1970 as part of the New Haven Black Panther trials. The previous year, nineteen-year-old party member Alex Rackley was tortured and killed by three fellow Panthers who suspected Rackley of being an FBI informant—a signal of the paranoia gripping the party. They were convicted swiftly, but Seale, who was visiting New Haven at the time of Rackley's murder, was also implicated. In total, authorities indicted nine people. After hearing the evidence, the jury became deadlocked. Many expected the judge to call for a retrial. Instead, he dismissed the charges against Seale.

As Seale festered, Huey P. Newton was finding freedom. After two years in jail and three trials for the same crime, his reprieve came in May 1970, when an appeals court found that the judge in Newton's first trial failed to inform the jury of the defendant's claims that he was unconscious at the time Officer John Frey was fatally shot. On August 5, Newton walked out of Oakland's Alameda County Courthouse to await a retrial. After the intensity of the Free Huey campaign—three years of rallies and protests all over America—his release was a scene of joy and jubilee. Crowds swelled as he emerged through the building's double metal doors. Through tears, his disciples chanted, "Huey! Huey!" Bustling through his adoring crowd, the returned Supreme Commander climbed up on a waiting Volkswagen and pulled his shirt off, perhaps cognizant that an important moment required an iconic image. Newton's body was lean and muscular, as prison exercise tends to do to a physique. The Black liberation movement had its savior back, the man to restore its potency.

One thousand dreams materialized behind prison bars suddenly seemed possible. But Newton found that the Panthers' ecosystem had been altered beyond recognition. When he was arrested in the autumn of 1967, he knew every single member of the Black Panther Party. By the time of his release in the summer of 1970, the organization had mushroomed. Many of the supporters who had driven the Free Huey campaign and knew the man only from passed-down fables had expected their messiah to be reinstalled at the top of the Panthers and bring strength, clarity, and purpose to it.

Newton's physical transformation was minimal compared to changes to his mind and spirit. Malcolm X and Eldridge Cleaver may have bettered themselves inside, but for Newton, prison had been no place to flourish. He exited more muscular but also more unhinged, unsuitable to head an organization of the infamy and scope that the Black Panthers had become. And with Seale in jail and Cleaver in exile, there were few members with sufficient cachet to share the load or rein him in. Newton's supporters had worked tirelessly to free Huey, but could Huey free them?

To Reggie Schell, the leader of the Philadelphia branch, the changes in Newton were immediately apparent: "I was out in California that summer when Huey P. Newton got out of jail, and I watched it when people from the community came up and talked with him, congratulated him for coming home and told him how much they missed him and supported him. And I saw that he couldn't talk to them. His conversation was gone, he was a million miles away from them . . . You know, everyone was talking about turning the Party around. Internally there were certain things happening that left a lot of people across the country dissatisfied."

Grim thoughts pervaded a once brilliant mind, now dimmed by drugs and alcohol. "I have never seen anybody snort that much cocaine and drink that much Johnnie Walker Red in my life," recalled Denise Oliver-Velez, a member of both the Panthers and radical left-wing Puerto Rican community group the Young Lords, who observed Newton's coke-and-scotch-fueled megalomania during a visit he made to New York. Even impulses of petty jealousy raged within him. Accompanying Newton on his trip was Connie Matthews, an educated, Jamaican-born member of the party who served as its international coordinator. Matthews had fallen in love with the bailed Panther 21 member Cetewayo and the two married, angering His Excellency.

"Huey had a fucking fit," said Oliver-Velez. "He was not happy about it." Cetewayo was worried that his wife was in the clutches of a maniac, so he connived to stay as close to his wife as possible. Knowing that Newton sought to meet Young Lords members at the Midtown hotel he was holed up in, Cetewayo asked if he could tag along.

The meeting was less than productive. "Huey was stark raving mad. He was nuttier than a fruitcake. It was bizarre," remembered Oliver-Velez. As Cetewayo spent time with Matthews, Newton declared to Oliver-Velez that he was going to expel every single East Coast Panther and instead make the Young Lords a branch of the party, a notion that would have bemused the stand-alone group. "Honestly, this dude was whacked. He was stoned out of his skull the whole time, talking mania."

Even more dangerous to the stability of the Panthers was Newton's changing ideology. After prison, he grew more convinced that the organization's community programs were its most valuable weapon, and that armed struggle in a sprawling nation like the United States would be doomed to fail. Musing on new political theory, Newton came to believe that American imperialism had rendered individual nations powerless, and therefore, nationalism could not exist. Only individual communities, united, could prevail against the American oppressor. He called this theory "revolutionary intercommunalism."

These shifts put Newton in conflict with committed militants like Eldridge Cleaver, whom Panthers called "the Rage" for his commitment to guerrilla warfare. Rank-and-file members were further confused when Newton expelled the highly respected Geronimo Pratt from the party as he awaited trial for the killing of Caroline Olsen, a twenty-seven-year-old white elementary school teacher, on a Santa Monica tennis court. Newton ordered members not to corroborate Pratt's alibi that he was at a meeting in Oakland with the Panther Central Committee at the time the murder took place. Pratt was ultimately convicted. The jury was dismissed never knowing that a key witness was an informant for the FBI.

Newton's strained mental state made him vulnerable to J. Edgar Hoover's witchcraft. Operating in the shadows, the FBI sought to drive a wedge between Newton and Cleaver, and what it recognized as two clear factions within the Black Panther Party that would be vulnerable to division. These efforts were happening as early as March 1970, while Newton was still in jail. In Algeria, Cleaver received a curious letter, unsigned, claiming that the California Panthers were seeking to undercut his influence. The target took the bait: Cleaver expelled three party members due to the mystery correspondence. More letters followed. A directive produced on counterfeit Panther stationery, and attributed to the party's chief of staff and Newton loyalist, David Hilliard, labeled Cleaver "a murderer and a punk" and warned that anyone aiding him would be "dealt with no matter where they may be located." Newton too received letters after his release. One claimed that the New York Panthers were seeking to assassinate him.

There was another blow to morale when Newton expelled the

still-imprisoned members of the Panther 21 for their response to the Weather Underground's communiqué. Newton was further enraged when the bailed Dharuba and Cetewayo took the massive decision to abandon their trial and flee the country, eventually surfacing in Algiers. The February 13, 1971, edition of the *Black Panther* newspaper splashed the faces of Dharuba, Cetewayo, and Connie Matthews across its cover with the words "Enemies of the People." In an editorial, the Central Committee denounced their "counter-revolutionary actions," calling them "jackanapes" who "jeopardized the chances of the other brothers getting bail and they propped up the dying case . . . against the New York 21."

Enlisted to assist Cetewayo and Matthews in leaving America was Oliver-Velez, who organized the necessary fake IDs and other documentation. Also on the journey was Jamal Joseph, one of the Panther 21 defendants separated from the case because he was too young to be tried as an adult, but nonetheless minded to go underground in solidarity with his comrades.

Together, the group boarded a train to Montreal, Canada, where Matthews had connections in the French-speaking liberation movement. But to move without suspicion, they concocted what they thought was a cunning plan: to disguise themselves as a Latino salsa band. The costumes were extravagant, featuring everything from polka-dot puff-sleeve shirts to fake mustaches.

A potential snag in the scheme developed. When these sham musicians reached the border, a group of Canadian Mounties boarded the train. So slapdash was his look that a nervous Joseph needed to adjust his fake mustache as the lawmen made their way down the car. The tension was overwhelming. If identified, the runaways would have to decide to be taken quietly or to not be taken quietly. *Damn, we're gonna have to throw down on this train*, thought Oliver-Velez. But the Mounties walked right past the group and instead grabbed a long-haired white hippie who was trying to beat the draft. "It was really comical," recalled Oliver-Velez. "I mean, it would be a perfect scene in a movie."

The group made it safely to Montreal, where Joseph had a change of heart about leaving his homeland. "It was something in me that said you've got to return and fight," he remembered. "And that's what I did."

Meanwhile, with tensions at an all-time high, Cleaver agreed to appear on Jim Dunbar's *A.M. San Francisco* show via telephone. As Newton sat in a Bay Area studio, Cleaver, no stranger to jumping bail himself, demanded the Panther 21 be reinstated in the party. He denounced Newton loyalist David Hilliard as incompetent and reactionary. A furious Newton immediately sought retribution. His mind may have been an increasingly blunted instrument, and his ability to command full loyalty of the party like he did in his legend-making early heyday was fast eroding. But Huey Newton still clung to an absolute authority that Eldridge Cleaver did not have. And so Newton initiated a follow-up phone call, and unleashed his fury in one great surge. In a furious tirade, he berated the "punk" Cleaver for fleeing America. The exile was told in no uncertain terms that the entire Algeria operation had been expelled.

"I think you lost your ability to reason, brother," replied the bemused Cleaver.

In the gilded halls of American power, far from the bloodied brick-and-mortar boulevards of the Panthers' base, or the ancient Casbah of Algiers, Hoover was smiling.

The quickest and most efficient telling of the Black Liberation Army (BLA) story begins with members of the Cleaver faction rising from the split. Eldridge's vision had always been guerrilla units striking terror in the heart of America's empire, and it was his loyal followers, primarily East Coast Panthers, who put it into action as he sat in the relatively comfortable surroundings of Algiers. But the murky history of this clandestine group is not so neat.

For certain, Cleaver's long-standing notion that the Panthers required a paramilitary wing was a heavy influence on the form the BLA eventually took. COINTELPRO had yet to be publicly revealed, but the lived experiences of its illicit tactics meant the metallic taste for revenge permanently swirled in the mouths of BLA recruits. Secret factions had been in development long before the split. Though reports are sketchy, there may have been groups in Los Angeles, Texas, Louisiana, Mississippi, and Alabama establishing weapons caches and training as early as late 1968 or early 1969. Other crucial precursors included the armed Louisiana group the Deacons for Defense and Justice, the writings of Robert F. Williams, and, going further back in time, Nat Turner's slave rebellion.

Further complicating the history is the lack of formal leadership, inconsistent communication, and murky timeline on when these scattered militants began using the name Black Liberation Army. As Assata Shakur (or Joanne Chesimard, as authorities continued to call her), a gutsy, hardheaded Panther who became the soul of the BLA, wrote in her autobiography, "The Black Liberation Army was not a centralized, organized group with a common leadership and chain of command. Instead, there were various organizations and collectives working out of different cities, and in some of the larger cities there were often several groups working independently of each other."

The FBI's infiltration and, for all intents and purposes, criminalization of the Black Panthers crippled the party and pushed the Black liberation movement toward more extreme actions. There had long been an ideological chasm within the Panthers between those who felt community programs should be the priority and those who saw them as peripheral to the ultimate goal of revolution. The question of military struggle as a plausible and legitimate strategy to combat racist oppression was always in the ether. And with comrades being locked up and murdered by the state, compressing the Panthers into submission, many more became convinced of an underground existence. The BLA believed that clandestine operations were a legitimate strategy until such a time when an aboveground movement became viable. Cast in Marxist-Leninist philosophies and the anti-colonial theories of Frantz Fanon that advanced armed struggle as a necessity in liberation, the BLA saw revolutionary violence against the state as a necessary response to what their members deemed an imperialist nation fixed on exclusivity and racism.

The BLA's approach was comparable to that of the Weather Underground. But while the only casualties in the Weather Underground's campaign were accidental deaths of its own members, the BLA would methodically and deliberately bring blood to the streets.

It's a paradox that the Newton-Cleaver split opened the door for the BLA, but the weakening of the Panthers hurt its case for legitimacy. A militaristic underground arm protecting the interests of an aboveground political organization with the single move toward national liberation could have been potent—after all, people in the underground require support from aboveground comrades. Writing in prison years later, ex-BLA member Jalil Muntaqim called the group's formation "premature" in its "capacity to wage a sustained protracted national liberation war."

And so with little joined-up thinking, a nebulous leadership structure, inadequate logistics, and a lack of communication between cadres, the BLA found unity in one simplified motivation: killing police. The armed wing of the state was, it reasoned, complicit in their oppression and so a legitimate target.

Striking hard and without warning, the BLA is believed to be responsible for the killings of more than ten police officers around the country. The most notorious attack occurred in Colonial Park, Harlem, a domain of low-income housing developments marked by the cops of the Thirty-Second Precinct at the time as an area of high risk.

At ten p.m. on the night of May 21, 1971, two NYPD officers, Waverly Jones and Joseph Piagentini, responded to a call about a woman injured in a knife fight. They parked their cruiser on West 155th Street, near the Macombs Dam Bridge, walked the four blocks to West 159th Street, down a set of stairs, and entered the building on foot. Finding the alleged victim uncooperative, Jones, a thirty-three-year-old Black man, and Piagentini, twenty-eight and white, made the return journey to the car.

Jones probably never heard the sonic crack of bullets that rang out that night. The first gunman crept up and fired three shots from about six inches behind him, striking the officer in the back of the head and spine, killing him instantly. Piagentini was simultaneously shot to the ground by a second hitman. Though badly wounded, the father of two daughters was cognizant enough to plead for his life. It didn't help. One of the ambushers seized Piagentini's own weapon from his holster and coldly fired one final shot at the help-less officer. In this massacre, he was hit a total of thirteen times, leaving twenty-two entry and exit wounds in his body. When a passer-by came upon the scene, Piagentini's mangled body was still moving. He died on his way to the hospital. At the scene of the murders, blood stained the sidewalk, a fence, and a lawn. As the policemen were wheeled into Harlem Hospital, many of the nurses watching began to cry. "Oh my God, it can't be," one said, sobbing.

It wasn't just the brutality that made the Colonial Park killings the BLA's most notorious action, it was the communiqué put out in its aftermath. On the evening of the shooting, two packages were delivered, one to the offices of *The New York Times* and another to Harlem radio station WLIB. Each carried a license plate num-ber that police had connected to a previous shooting to prove their authenticity. When a *Times* guard asked the mysterious courier what was in the package, the man turned and ran from the building.

"Armed goons of this racist government," the note declared, "will again meet the guns of oppressed third world peoples as long as they occupy our community and murder our brothers and sisters in the name of American law and order."

There could be no illusions—authorities now knew they were dealing with connected, politically motivated cop killings. Within days, President Richard Nixon met with J. Edgar Hoover and Attor-ney General John Mitchell in the Oval Office. Anguishing about whether the violent Black uprising he feared was here, the presi-dent told Hoover in no uncertain terms to eliminate this threat.

Scan Afeni's life and it can feel like the subject she wanted to talk about the least was Tupac's biological father, Billy Garland. But maybe that's because there was so little to say. Barely present in his son's life, Garland has always been an indistinct figure in the Tupac story. Like Afeni, he was a Panther—a rank-and-file member of the New Jersey chapter who would use his van to distribute copies of the newspaper. They first encountered each other in a friend's Manhattan loft in the fall of 1970 and a short affair began. It was Garland who often drove Afeni to court. Years later, she brushed off any sense that the pair had shared a meaningful connection. "I wanted to have sex, you know," she told *People* magazine in 1997.

Around the same time, Afeni began seeing a man named Kenneth Saunders, known on the streets as Legs, a onetime minor associate of Harlem drug lord Nicky Barnes. Years later, Tupac would tell journalist Tabitha Soren that he once believed Legs to be his biological father, signaling that, for a time, there was confusion surrounding his paternity. Any hopes Afeni had for the relationship were dashed when Legs was returned to prison on a parole violation.

When not concentrating on her case, Afeni was visible in the community. In August, she made a visit to Harlem Hospital and those receiving treatment for drug addiction. "Here she is," announced the public relations director of Harlem Drug Fighters, a drug-free detoxification and rehabilitation inpatient program, as he introduced Afeni to some patients as they played cards, "the first Black woman ever held in $100,000 bail in New York City."

"They are fixing to give us seventy-five years," she told the room. "But I am a revolutionary and I know that if I go, there will be someone to come after me."

Such moments of levity were a welcome distraction, answering the call of community service a reminder of a more carefree existence. Impossible to ignore, though, would have been thoughts of oblivion, and the trial that separated Afeni from it.

The trial began in September 1970 with the tense haggle of a jury selection that dragged on as the Panthers and their team scrapped relentlessly for a fair panel of their peers—a tenet of the Ten-Point Program. The drawn-out process eventually caused Justice Murtagh to rage, "At a time when the court's calendar is congested, six weeks have been expended to accomplish what could properly have been achieved in a matter of hours."

During one session, Assistant District Attorney Phillips protested that the defense was deliberately trying to discourage prospective jurors they didn't like with lengthy and abusive questioning. The argument ignited after Afeni interrogated a potential Black juror about his lack of activity in community affairs in Harlem.

"Are you a numbers writer?" Afeni asked.

An incensed Phillips jumped to his feet. "That was despicable!"

Decades later, Jamal Joseph reflected on the process. "We actually impaneled the most diverse jury that Manhattan had seen at that time. It seems crazy because you think of how diverse Manhattan is and what jury pools look like, but it wasn't the case. It was usually twelve white men and they were lynch mobs, not juries."

During opening arguments, Afeni, addressing the jurors as "sisters and brothers," sprinkled a little flowery eloquence into her speech. "The district attorney and his agents used a dash of truth and a cup of lies to concoct one of the most imaginative Hollywood scripts in the history of America," she said, wearing a fashionable black-and-white horizontally striped sweater, flared skirt, leather boots that went up to her calves, and a white-and-aqua silk headscarf. Afeni denied that the defendants advocated violence, declaring that "violence is nonproductive," and explained, "Acts of violent aggression are grounds for expulsion from our party."

She added, "We have a fanatical yearning for freedom, for an end to exploitation."

In the memoir *Evolution of a Revolutionary*, an older Afeni reflected on the trial. "I was young. I was arrogant. And I was brilliant in court. I wouldn't have been able to be brilliant if I thought I was going to get out of jail. It was because I thought this was the *last* time I could speak. The last time before they locked me up forever."

Just as Afeni was finding her rhythm in court, there was a devastating development. Dharuba and Cetewayo's decision to jump bail dismayed the defense lawyers, who feared it could be interpreted as an admission of guilt. But it also had major knock-on consequences for two of their abandoned comrades: Afeni and Joan Bird had their bail revoked and were once again condemned to the crumbling New York Women's House of Detention, conditions that threatened the precious life of Afeni's unborn child. A broken boiler offered no hot water. The prison's odd take on culinary science meant that dinner was cooked the previous evening and left to sit overnight. And neither Afeni nor Bird trusted the prison doctors enough to allow themselves to be examined.

"The conditions are not just abominable, as they were before; they are inhuman," Afeni told Justice Murtagh.

Afeni's pregnancy had caused unease among the defense team, who feared what it might do to the temperament of Lumumba, who had never posted bail. "I divorce thee," he repeated three times in the courtroom after she told him the news. Few words would be uttered between them for the remainder of the trial. But Afeni's focus remained on improving her conditions so the baby could grow strong. "There she stood between Lumumba Shakur and Joseph Phillips," wrote journalist Murray Kempton about her desperate pleas to Justice Murtagh, "and spoke as though she was bearing a Prince."

On March 20, 1971, Afeni wrote a letter from within prison walls to recipients that included "the unborn baby (babies) within my womb." Her participation in the book *Look for Me in the Whirlwind: The Collective Autobiography of the New York 21* hinged on its inclusion. "I've learned a lot in two years about being a woman and it's for that reason that I want to talk to you. Joan and I, and all the brothers in jail, are caught up in this funny situation where everyone seems to be attacking everyone else and we're sort of in the middle looking dumb. I've seen a lot of people I knew and loved die in the past year or so and it's really been a struggle to remain unbitter . . .

"I do not regret any of it—for it taught me to be something that some people will never learn—for the first time in my life I feel like a woman, beaten, battered and scarred maybe, but isn't that what wisdom is truly made of[?] Help me to continue to learn—only this time with a bit more grace for I am a poor example for anyone to follow because I have deviated from the revolutionary principles which I know to be correct. I wish you love."

That sense of violence was something Afeni couldn't escape. The Newton-Cleaver split had ignited bloodshed between both factions akin to a war between two rival mobsters for control of a crime family. It was reminiscent of the violence that broke out between the Nation of Islam and Malcolm X and his supporters after their split. The Panthers had been cast in the spirit of the minister and had led them to the same brutality. Shortly before

Afeni wrote her letter, Robert Webb, a Cleaver loyalist, tried to stop a group of Panthers selling the newspaper in Harlem. Three of the men drew guns and fired at Webb, killing him. On April 17, 1971, Sam Napier, the circulation manager of the Black Panther newspaper, Newton acolyte, and close friend of Afeni's, was tied to a chair and shot to death in a Panthers office in Corona, Queens. Five New York Panthers stood trial for the murder and one, Mark Holder, was convicted. At a second trial in 1973, the other four pleaded guilty to the reduced charge of attempted manslaughter in the second degree. They included two of Afeni's Panther 21 comrades: Jamal Joseph and the out-on-bail Dharuba.

Abandoned by her fellow defendants for the comforts of Algiers, divorced from her husband, and sitting in a crumbling prison, Afeni must have felt her support network shrinking. But within the walls of the House of D, she found fellowship and love. Older inmates showed the twenty-four-year-old expectant mother how to apply Vaseline to her growing belly to reduce stretch marks. They washed her court clothes, using a trick with toothpaste so they were appropriately starched for her court appearances. And they gave her a shoulder to cry on when feelings of loneliness overwhelmed her.

"I had support from women during all that," Afeni reflected. "Women have to find strength from other women, because this is what get us through."

All the while, she safeguarded her unborn child. "This is my prince," she would say, patting her pregnant belly. "He is going to save the Black nation."

Particularly drawn to Afeni was Carol Crooks, a Brooklynite packed off to the House of D at just eighteen years old after a drug bust. "I had come from court, and she was talking to a group of girls in the back of the hallway," Crooks recalled. "She was telling us whatever we asked about . . . She explained to us what [the Panthers] were fighting for . . . She had a smile, she was very, very soft in her manner, and everybody did everything for her."

Despite her youth, Crooks was a hardened presence within the tough environment. "Crooksie had a rep in the joint and nobody messed with me because I was with Crooksie," remembered Denise

Oliver-Velez, who found herself briefly imprisoned alongside both women.

Bonds fused firmly in the House of D, and Crooks and Afeni grew ever closer as their incarcerations stretched on.

Assistant District Attorney Phillips's strategy included giving the jury a blow-by-blow account of the defendants' purported actions from November 1968 to the day of their arrest. It was a catalog of bomb-building-kit purchases, reconnaissance missions, and rhetoric about offing pigs. Afeni, it was claimed, had cooked up a plan: should a Panther be arrested, their comrades would kidnap a cop and hold them for ransom equivalent to the cost of bail. Eugene Roberts, present undercover, claimed he suggested to Afeni that there was a flaw in her scheme: the captive, once released, would be able to identify their kidnappers.

"You misunderstand me," he alleged Afeni said. "After we get the Panther released, we ice the pig."

Gerald Lefcourt's approach involved exposing the clandestine nature of authorities' activities against the Panthers. This wasn't normal investigative procedure, he argued. This was secret police. "The Bureau of Special Services was an outfit that was designed to destroy things like the Panthers," he later said. "And a lot of our arguments were about that—about the secret police and what they were trying to accomplish."

Then, there was a gift from the prophets of Media, Pennsylvania. The revelations of FBI malpractice contained in documents snatched in the office burglary seemed to confirm everything the defense were arguing. "We doubled down on the strategy about the secret police and their attempts to destroy this political movement," said Lefcourt.

The state summoned sixty-five witnesses and the defense called an additional ten—none of whom were the defendants. These inflated numbers couldn't obscure that the prosecution's case was propped up by the reports of the undercover agents. Crucial to the defense was the deconstruction and delegitimization of those who had invaded the Panthers' circle.

Among four undercover cops to take the stand was Roberts, whose résumé in the covert arts was formidable. Having previously infiltrated the security detail of Malcolm X, Roberts had been close by when the minister was killed at the Audubon Ballroom in 1965. He even exchanged fire with one of the assassins—a bullet fired at him from point-blank range ripped through his jacket but remarkably missed his flesh—and tried in vain to resuscitate the stricken Malcolm. Also in the auditorium was Roberts's wife, who was haunted by the killing for decades. Following Malcolm's demise, Roberts was promoted to detective by the NYPD, and moved on to the Black Panther Party.

That experience showed in Roberts's testimony. Under questioning, he recalled many meetings and various conversations in a calm, maybe even dull, manner. Attempts were made by the defense to shake him: "Isn't it a fact that you helped murder Malcolm X?" asked Gerald Lefcourt pointedly. But even with his cool temperament and smooth delivery, Roberts struggled to put forward a compelling case that New York was at risk from a violent terrorist campaign. Grilled by Katz, he revealed that no exact date, targets, or type of explosive to be used in the alleged bombing plot had been communicated to him.

McKinney just put it to him straight: "You really didn't think anything was going to happen, did you?"

"I personally believed something was going to be done," Roberts said on the stand, "but I didn't know when."

Roberts's tedious testimony raised the importance to the prosecution of Ralph White—the man the Panthers knew as Yedwa Sudan, whom only Afeni had identified as a double agent. Nobody would listen to her concerns about White, and because of that, she was carrying a child in the terrible conditions of the House of D. And here White was again, ready to make the case that the defendants were violent terrorists on the cusp of unleashing a wave of murder and mayhem on the citizens of New York.

White described an August 1968 trip to Baltimore with Lumumba to obtain guns. During a night speed-smoking reefer and necking bourbon, the pair took a leisurely walk in the park during which, White claimed, Lumumba suggested they use the shotgun he'd bought to "shoot a pig," but an ideal opportunity never arose. This epitomized a crucial weakness in the prosecution's case. As alarming as the obtaining of arms is to most people, as upsetting as rhetoric about cop-killing is to their sensibilities, White never witnessed any violent crimes as they occurred. Did Afeni suggest kidnapping an officer and holding them for ransom if one of her comrades was arrested? Maybe she did, maybe she didn't. But Panthers *were getting arrested* and the number of officers snatched in retaliation never went above zero.

Even so, conspiracy to commit a crime, even if that crime is stopped, is still against the law. Yet on the eve of the roundup of the Panther 21, Roberts again traveled to Baltimore, this time with Cetewayo, Kinshasa, and Dharuba. Never, Roberts reported, did the conversation turn to the complicated, multi-venue bombing plot that was supposedly due to occur within days—a poor indication that any such plans had substance to them.

Clearly, though, the strongest element of the prosecution's case was the January explosions—the night Joan Bird had been arrested. This was not talk, this was real crimes. In court, White described witnessing Lumumba hiding dynamite behind a refrigerator at the Elsmere Tenants Council where they both worked. He told of hearing Lumumba and Mshina whisper about a "building off the Major Deegan Expressway," theorized, in retrospect, to refer to the Forty-Fourth Precinct, one of the locations where a phony bomb had ignited. "His testimony put dynamite in Lumumba Shakur's hands," recalled Lefcourt. "If he's believed, we're dead."

The defense attacked White's character. Here was a lawman who seemed to enjoy being a Panther a little too much. He drank, he smoked weed—he even supplied other Panthers with the drug. He slept with Panther women. And he was deceptive with his NYPD bosses, falsifying expense reports to his own financial benefit. Still, White's cohesive testimony worried the defense. "You want to know the truth?" responded one Panther lawyer when asked how the detective did. "Pretty fucking well. Pretty damn well. We've tried everything . . . His imagination seems to be helping him. His story-telling ability seems to be helping him instead of fucking him up."

Eventually, it was Afeni's turn to interrogate White. Maybe it was months of pent-up anger toward him, or frustration at how others had allowed him to infiltrate the circle. Maybe it was a tactic to personalize her story in front of the jury. But in the courtroom, wearing a smock that tightly hugged her pregnant belly, Afeni's first question was personal.

"Why, Yedwa, have you done this to us?"

And so the coursing began. With steely resolve, Afeni tried to pin White down on specifics of how she, a visible community worker, could also be judged a violent terrorist.

After some inane babbling, White admitted, "As far as your involvement, I thought you were more military than political."

"What involvement?" inquired Afeni.

"I can't remember everything you said or everything you had done or even all your actions; but . . . I was only basing my own opinion on what I saw about you or about anyone else."

"I understand that," Afeni replied. "But you said there were things you saw me doing, I just want to hear one thing."

"I remember when—excuse me—I remember a meeting at the Panther office, you were real charged up about—you went into a thing about icing the pigs, along with that military thing, and very emotional. I remember that, plus other things I can't remember offhand. I am only saying what I based my opinions on, what I had seen. What I had seen and heard and I had forgotten most of them."

White limped on. With her prey clearly floundering, Afeni kept her queries short and to the point.

"Did you ever see me at Lincoln Hospital working?"

"Yes, I have," admitted White.

"Did you ever see me at the schools working?"

"Yes, I have."

"Ever see me in the street working?"

"Yes, I have."

"Are these some of the things that led you to think I was military minded?"

"No, it was not."

"You don't remember the other things," declared Afeni.

"At the time I remembered them then. I remember—you reminded me of the good things you were doing. If you reminded me of some of the things you said, I could answer that."

"Yes, I guess so."

Afeni's questioning highlighted her record as a servant to the Black community. This was beyond reproach; not even White could deny it. But her résumé as an urban guerrilla? It was based on dubious rhetoric.

There was still the critical task of closing statements, the brightest stage and final act in the plea for freedom, where nothing less than a symphonic performance could result in a lifetime of regret. Afeni spoke second to last among the defense counsel. Standing before the jury, she allowed herself to be vulnerable.

"I don't know what I'm supposed to say. I don't know how I'm supposed to justify the charges that Mr. Phillips has brought before the court against me. But I do know that none of these charges has been proven and I'm not talking about proven beyond a reasonable doubt. I'm saying that none of the charges have been proven, period. That nothing has been proven in this courtroom, that I or any of the defendants did any of these things that Mr. Phillips insists we did do.

"So, why are we here? Why are any of us here?

"I don't know. But I would appreciate it if you end this nightmare, because I'm tired of it and I can't justify it in my mind. There's no logical reason for us to have gone through the last two years as we have, to be threatened with imprisonment because somebody somewhere is watching and waiting to justify being a spy. So do what you have to do. But please don't forget what you saw and heard in this courtroom . . . Let history record you as a jury that would not kneel to the outrageous bidding of the state. Show us that we were not wrong in assuming that you would judge us fairly."

Lefcourt remembered the scene: "Standing there in front of the jury, obviously on the verge of giving birth and arguing that 'Enough is enough. I'm tired. Let me have my baby. Let me go home.' Powerful."

In contrast, Phillips used his closing statement to revisit the evidence in fine detail, from beginning to end. The routine likely stuck in the craw of the jury, who, by that point, had already invested a huge amount of time and energy into the trial—two commodities they would need little of once inside the deliberation room.

Around four p.m. on May 12, 1971, Justice Murtagh was informed that the jury had rendered a verdict—the longest trial in New York history and it had only taken them about two hours and forty minutes to reach a decision.

The jurors arrived at 4:35 p.m., and were first asked to give their verdict on the man whose name had been burned into the title of the indictment.

"How do you find the defendant Lumumba Shakur on the charges of conspiracy to murder in the first degree?"

Juror James Ingram Fox answered in his mild West Indian accent: "Not guilty." Eleven more times Fox was prompted and eleven more times he responded: "Not guilty." As each of the defendants was systematically considered, Fox eventually gave 156 utterances of "not guilty." The verdict had been unanimous. Even the fled Cetewayo and Dharuba were found not guilty, despite the prosecution's arguments that their absence indicated guilt. The exonerated Panthers could treat themselves to a deathly sweet, perhaps previously unmentionable, sight: Phillips, who so vilified their characters over the long months, looked downcast, washed out. Spectators yelled "Right on" and "Power to the people." Afeni burst into tears, Lumumba shouted, and the defendants came together to cry, yell, and celebrate with one another. Curtis Powell, who never made bail, finally walked out the front door of the courtroom a free man with both arms held high with clenched fists.

"We went around the table saying how we felt," explained juror James Butters after the trial, "and it was boom-boom-boom all the way around."

The speedy resolution reflected that the jury had seen massive problems in the prosecution's case. They were incredulous that so many Panthers had been indicted on these charges; most they deemed linked to crimes in only extremely tenuous ways. Butters considered the arrests nothing less than a "mop up operation" against the Black Panthers. "To say Afeni Shakur is guilty of that shit when [Phillips] did not even tie her to any of it. You're making a fool out of me, man," he raged.

Many also saw the judge as biased against the defendants. The extortionate bails didn't sit right with them, and though they were told it shouldn't affect their judgment, one admitted he couldn't help it. They watched in consternation as Murtagh responded "request denied" to Afeni's motion for a fair trial.

For the Panther 21 and the broader network of American radicals protesting their government from the left, this was a great victory—a victory that deserves celebration to this day. The defendants had avoided life imprisonment and could look forward to a future not fixed. But for the authorities determined to crush the Black liberation movement, the jury's verdict was not a substantial defeat. For more than two years, the Panthers had funneled huge resources into the case. Its membership had decreased; key personnel had fled the city or been forced to spend the time since their arrest in prison on huge bonds. In New York, the party was essentially finished. Without the old cause to return to, a few Panther 21 veterans would find their way into the Black Liberation Army. When some of their actions came to light, the district attorney and his team may well have allowed themselves to feel vindicated.

Afeni Shakur had survived a tremendous ordeal, her health and dignity intact. She wouldn't receive such attention again until the release of 2Pac's "Dear Mama." It's a song that, in 2Pac's attempts to honor the many, somewhat depersonalizes his own mother's extraordinary story. There's no mention of Panthers or bombing conspiracies on "Dear Mama"; the only jail cell is the one 2Pac describes himself being held in. Yet it's dedicated to a woman who had endured what only a tiny percentage of people will ever know, and had risen to a level fewer still could ever be capable of. Crucial to understanding the Tupac story is understanding the story of a mother before she was a mother, the person who raised him in the spirit of resistance.

"Where'd you find out how to talk like that, child?" juror Benjamin Giles, a Black retired longshoreman, asked Afeni after the verdict.

"Fear, Mr. Giles," she replied. "Plain fear."

The trial over, Afeni found sanctuary in an apartment on West Fourth Street. The owner was Ann Dubole, a wealthy white woman who allowed radicals to live in the property, sometimes for months at a time. Joining Afeni in the apartment was Joan Bird and Joan's girlfriend Bern (short for Bernadette), another former resident of the House of D. Already living there was Giles Kotcher, a white man from Louisville, Kentucky, and member of the Gay Liberation Front, a group formed after the Stonewall riots. If Afeni had access to the right window in the House of D on August 2, 1969, she'd have seen the Gay Liberation Front outside protesting its conditions, the first of several weekly rallies.

Kotcher had been involved in civil rights activism down south. Fate now brought him into the circle of the Panthers, a group he greatly admired. When the FBI inevitably came by to hassle Afeni and Bird, the women would send Kotcher to the door in the hope he would quickly dismiss the agents.

Before long, it was time for Afeni to go to New York Flower–Fifth Avenue Hospital. Despite the hardships of her pregnant months, there were no major complications. On June 16, 1971, she gave birth to a baby boy with bright eyes and a strong heartbeat. But still in a state of heightened awareness after the trial, Afeni sought to deter the government from marking the child as a Panther baby and thus flagging him as a threat to society. So she gave him the name Lesane Parish Crooks. Inspiration came from various sources. Lesane was the surname of her sister Gloria Jean's children. Parish, it was claimed by friend and working-class lesbian activist Charlotte Marchant, was the name of a soap star Afeni liked. And Crooks came from Carol Crooks. "That's what was on the paper," said Afeni of the child's legal name. "But Tupac was always his name. Tupac Amaru Shakur. He was always in my mind a soldier in exile from the beginning. That's how I saw it."

Afeni brought the precious package back to the apartment on West Fourth Street. Her roommate Kotcher immediately bonded with the baby, cuddling him as a new dad might when the infant adjusting to the world needed soothing. The Tupac story would partially be defined by the lack of reliability among the men in his life and an eternal search for a father figure. You could say the first to fill the role was this gay, white, southern man who'd somehow found himself in a Panthers crash pad. This is me "romanticizing it," Kotcher protested when we spoke. But I can't deny that I do like the notion.

Afeni spoke fondly of Crooks over the course of her life without ever fully revealing that their connection was romantic. But the depth of their relationship was revealed when Crooks talked to author Hugh Ryan for his 2022 book *The Women's House of Detention: A Queer History of a Forgotten Prison*. It was around the time of the acquittal that Crooks said they became romantically involved. Afeni even directed hospital nurses to hand her newborn baby to Crooks when they first brought him back into the room after she gave birth.

For Huey Newton, Black liberation and gay liberation were not to be uncoupled. Writing in August 1970, he reflected on the conditioning that caused his own neurosis about masculinity, as though part of an attempt to deprogram a life spent in a society pushing men toward homophobia.

"We should be willing to discuss the insecurities that many people have about homosexuality. When I say 'insecurities,' I mean the fear that they are some kind of threat to our manhood. I can understand this fear. Because of the long conditioning process that builds insecurity in the American male, homosexuality might produce certain hang-ups in us. I have hang-ups myself about male homosexuality. But on the other hand, I have no hang-up about female homosexuality. And that is a phenomenon in itself. I think it is probably because male homosexuality is a threat to me and female homosexuality is not."

Newton may have been inspired by French writer Jean Genet, who traveled to the United States to support both the Panther 21 and New Haven trials. In 1958, Genet had written *Les Nègres*, translated in 1960 to *The Blacks: A Clown Show*, an absurdist piece in which the killing of a white woman is reenacted in a play within a play by Black actors for the amusement of a white establishment audience, themselves played by Black actors in makeup. It opened in New York in 1961 and ran for two years, giving future icons James Earl Jones and Maya Angelou an early platform. Genet was also one of the most provocative writers on homosexuality in the world. Refused a visa to enter the United States because of a lengthy conviction record and association with the revolutionary left in France, he entered the country by traveling to Canada, where Lumumba's brother Zayd Shakur helped slip him over the border. Though the FBI opted not to intervene, it nonetheless tracked Genet's movements.

Acting as Genet's translator was a young lesbian in the Black Panther Party named Angela Davis. She observed that not only did Genet make no attempt to hide his homosexuality, he deliberately provoked debate, on one occasion by wearing drag. Davis watched on as Genet argued with the Panthers about their homophobia and use of slurs such as "faggot." She believed it was these arguments that led Newton to support gay liberation. Newton's move pivoted him further away from the social conservatism of his hero Malcolm X's former organization, the Nation of Islam.

The message from the top of the Panthers might have been that Black and gay liberation were one and the same struggle, but Afeni sometimes found it difficult to get the male Panthers to accept she was in a same-sex relationship with Crooks. "Afeni did not get support from the powers that be over her choices," said their friend Denise Oliver-Velez. "I remember the attitude from a number of the brothers who were not happy about any woman being a lesbian because you're supposed to pay attention to them, not a woman.

"It didn't become a big deal until brothers in the party were demanding that Afeni tell them who is the father of her [child]. And Afeni's answer was Crooksie," added Oliver-Velez. "That went over like a lead brick, okay? I mean, she literally said that Crooks was the father of her child. And the Panther Party at that time, and I'm gonna be very honest with you, in the Young Lords, we were far more progressive on women's issues and on LGBTQ issues, because the Young Lords Party had not only the Women's Caucus, which struggled against male chauvinism and machismo, but we also, out of the Women's Caucus, had a Gay and Lesbian Caucus."

. . .

As Afeni settled into her hard-fought freedom, comrades now enlisted in the Black Liberation Army battled on. For these hardened guerrillas, bank robberies became a favorite source of funding. From 1971 to 1973, the BLA was held responsible for a series of sniper attacks and thefts in New York, New Jersey, St. Louis, and Detroit. The fighting was getting increasingly ad hoc and desperate. Instead of packing up and heading for the nearest sympathetic country they could find, these soldiers seemed hell-bent on prison or martyrdom.

On May 2, 1973, at about 12:45 a.m., Assata Shakur, Zayd Shakur, and Panther 21 member Sundiata Acoli were in a beat-up white Pontiac LeMans on the New Jersey Turnpike in East Brunswick when they were stopped by state trooper James Harper, twenty-nine years old. Police later said they were heading to Washington. It was not a suspicion that the car was carrying hardened violent revolutionaries that piqued Harper's attention, but a faulty taillight. Noticing the cop, Acoli, the driver, pulled over to the side of the highway. Following standard procedure, Harper called for backup. A second trooper, thirty-five-year-old Werner Foerster, rolled up moments later.

Harper approached the car and asked to see a driver's license and registration. Noticing a discrepancy in the paperwork, he asked Acoli to step out. Choosing compliance, Acoli clambered out of the LeMans and walked to the rear of his vehicle, where Foerster began to question him. Peering inside the vehicle, Harper noticed that the woman was fidgeting and the man's eyes seemed glassy. Suddenly, Foerster shouted out, "Jim, look what I found." Harper looked back and saw his fellow officer holding up an ammunition clip from an automatic pistol. Quickly, he ordered Assata and Zayd not to move. No hope of that. Assata reached beneath her right leg, drew a gun, and blasted Harper in the shoulder. Though wounded, Harper managed to draw his gun and return fire. Blood filled the back seat as both Assata and Zayd were hit. In the chaos, Acoli managed to seize Foerster's gun. The BLA soldier aimed the pistol at the trooper's head and squeezed the trigger, killing him.

Bleeding and vulnerable, Harper darted; Acoli clambered back into the LeMans and pulled away. A description of the vehicle hit the police airwaves, and in just minutes, another trooper, Robert Palentchar, found it parked five miles south, on the side of the turnpike. As he arrived on the scene, Palentchar saw a man standing fifty yards or so from the car. It was Acoli. Palentchar ordered him to freeze. Instead, Acoli charged for the wooded area near the road. The trooper emptied his clip in the suspect's direction but missed every shot. Then came quite the sight. It was Assata, blood streaming from her wounds, walking toward Palentchar from fifty feet away with arms raised in surrender. Zayd's body was found nearby in a gully along the road shoulder where he had succumbed to the gunshot injuries. Assata was taken to the hospital. Acoli was found the next day, hiding in nearby woods.

The following years became a series of court cases for Assata relating to her BLA activities. She beat case after case through a combination of dismissals and acquittals. Even the New Jersey Turnpike incident required three trials. The first saw a change of venue, the second was declared a mistrial due to her pregnancy. Then, in 1977, almost four years after the incident, an all-white jury found Assata guilty on eight charges, including first-degree murder, and sentenced her to life imprisonment. Speaking in a low voice, she said, "I am ashamed that I have even taken part in this trial," and denounced the jury as "racist."

"You have convicted a woman who had her hands in the air," she said.

Judge Theodore Appleby of Superior Court ordered the court attendants to "remove the prisoner." Assata, in a final moment of defiance, replied, "The prisoner will walk away on her own feet."

Zayd Shakur was laid to rest in Long Island. Inside the chapel, his bullet-scarred body lay wrapped in white. Alongside the coffin were flags representing the causes he stood for: Pan-Africanism, Black liberation, Puerto Rican independence, and the Black Panther Party. Before the services began, Saladin Shakur, Lumumba and Zayd's much-respected father, told mourners that his fallen son "was a struggler, he was a revolutionary—he died for a good cause."

. . .

A great distance away, the man who was once the loudest voice in calling for violent Black nationalist resistance mused over a very special pair of pants. At a small social gathering in the Latin Quarter of Paris, Eldridge Cleaver spoke proudly, and at length, about a design he envisioned as a direct attack on the unisex fashion that offended his masculine sensibilities. But simple words were not enough—a demonstration was in order. After dinner, Cleaver disappeared into an adjoining room, where he thumbed the material of his own creation, pulling the denim garment over his lower limbs, one leg after the other. Cleaver's jeans bucked the mainstream convention of concealing a man's penis and instead carried the cargo in an external sheath of cloth. Present to bear witness was a small group of Harvard undergraduates and American expat novelist Jack Caball, who commented, "I've seen writers invent plenty of ways of keeping from writing, but these pants are a disaster for Cleaver."

Needless to say, Cleaver could not sustain his position in the movement after his expulsion from the Black Panther Party. In 1972, he left Algeria and headed to Paris, where he drank copious amounts of red wine and dreamed of his lewd trousers appearing on the covers of *Vogue* and *Harper's Bazaar*. It proved a short-term distraction. Cleaver grew despondent with his new life; his children's adoption of the French language and culture over that of their American heritage perturbed him. He retreated to an apartment in Cannes, where suicidal thoughts circled his mind.

Then, one night, Cleaver gazed out at the night sky and, without warning, witnessed images of his communist heroes—Karl Marx, Lenin, Mao Tse-tung—parade across the face of the moon. One by one, each image fell away, until one set of features refused to disappear: the face of Jesus Christ. At once, Cleaver knew. His problems had never been political or economic at all, but spiritual. With new clarity of thought, he ran back into the apartment and immediately reached for the Bible. Cleaver embraced Christianity and became persuaded to return to the United States.

The airplane touched down at Kennedy Airport on the afternoon of November 18, 1975. Mixing with the hundred-odd newsmen were clean-cut FBI agents, waiting for the fugitive. The towering

Cleaver, wearing a black raincoat, stooped to clear the plane's door before descending the passenger stairs, to his first steps on home soil in seven years, and into the arms of the waiting G-men and their handcuffs. After he was moved through customs to the airport's federal building to be fingerprinted and photographed, the media were permitted to ask some questions.

"It's ridiculous to ask me questions in these circumstances," Cleaver asserted. "I came back because I wanted to."

If he had so little to say, maybe it was because his thoughts were already in print. An article penned by Cleaver appeared in *The New York Times* that same day. "Lots of people believe I left because I preferred to go live in a Communist country, and that now, several years and many Communist countries later, I find the grass not greener on the Communist side of the fence," he wrote. "So now, here I stand, locked outside the gates of the paradise I once scorned, begging to be let back in."

Cleaver offered words of conciliation to the nation in which he once saw little but evil, calling the American political system "the freest and most democratic in the world," before attempting to call time on his era of radical dissent, and making the case for the endpoint he felt it had reached: "Each generation subjects the world it inherits to severe criticism. I think that my generation has been more critical than most, and for good reason. At the same time, at the end of the critical process, we should arrive at some conclusions. We should have discovered which values are worth conserving. It is the beginning of another fight, the fight to defend those values from the blind excesses of our fellows who are still caught up in the critical process. It is my hope to make positive contribution in this regard."

After ending his exodus, Cleaver served eight months in prison, spent five years on probation, and performed two thousand hours of community service for his role in the 1968 shoot-out that left "Little" Bobby Hutton dead. His greatest hits back in the United States included a sequel to his first book titled *Soul on Fire* and an attempt to create a new religion, Chrislam, an amalgamation of Christianity and Islam. Cleaver's pivot from Black Panther socialism was completed in the early 1980s when he joined the Republican Party and endorsed Ronald Reagan in his 1984 presidential reelection campaign. He put himself forward as a potential GOP candidate in various elections too, but his campaigns struggled to gain support. By the late 1990s, Cleaver was employed by the University of La Verne, California, as a diversity consultant, spoke passionately about the need for environmental protection, and advocated for a woman president. He died on May 1, 1998, in Pomona, California, of undisclosed causes.

In the spring of 1997, Cleaver agreed to an interview with Henry Louis Gates Jr. Among the topics discussed was Tupac Shakur, murdered a year earlier. Tupac was the child of a woman once electrified by the words of a young Cleaver. Or, as Cleaver described him to Gates, the symbolic "child of Huey Newton and Malcolm."

"Huey P. Newton was a gun toting gangster, but that's not all he was. I'm saying he went through that experience as a criminal, but the thing about Tupac was his spirit and his rebellion against oppression. This comes from the way that he was raised and the values that were transmitted to him."

PART II

TO WHICH NATION DO YOU BELONG?:
A REVOLUTIONARY LIFE

"The beautiful Bronx," 1973

4

THIS SHOULD MOVE YA

L INCOLN HOSPITAL, Mott Haven, the Bronx. Like many medical centers that serve America's sprawling metropolises, this striking redbrick building is a sad temple in hip-hop history. On August 27, 1987, DJ Scott La Rock, producer and co-founder of Boogie Down Productions, died on an operating table after being shot while riding in a Jeep through the Highbridge Gardens project. The loss of La Rock has been called hip-hop's first tragedy.

Having opened its doors in 1975, the hospital was a relatively new building that replaced the old Lincoln Hospital, a pitiful, bloodstained, cockroach-infested construction known throughout the South Bronx as "the Butcher Shop." It was in this old iteration of the institution that, in 1970, a group of radicals from both the Black Panther Party and the Young Lords founded Lincoln Detox. In an old nurses' residence on the sixth floor, under posters of Angela Davis, Malcolm X, and Chairman Mao, "the People's Program" offered holistic drug rehabilitation that included acupuncture, community service, and Marxist education classes, so participants could learn about their addiction through a communist lens. Dope was framed as chemical warfare that placated minority communities, revolutionary communism taught as the cure. Lincoln Detox's director of political education was Mutulu Shakur, a committed revolutionary who would keep company with Afeni Shakur during the period and become stepfather to her young son, Tupac.

About two and a half miles north of the new Lincoln Hospital you will find the cradle of hip-hop. Rarely is it possible to pinpoint the genesis of a culture to an address and moment, but on August 11, 1973, at 1520 Sedgwick Avenue in the Morris Heights neighborhood, DJ Kool Herc unveiled his two turntables and mixer at a back-to-school party in the building's rec center. His new technique used a couple of copies of the same record to extend the instrumental break as friend Coke La Rock (no relation to Scott) jumped on the mic to work up the crowd. And with that, hip-hop was born. From these humble origins would grow a global behemoth, one of America's two biggest cultural achievements, alongside jazz.

Hip-hop created billionaires but was born in poverty. It was a youth movement that began with zero mainstream interest and few commercial concerns. Nascent emcees loved to rap about two things above all else: partying and how good they were at rapping. But a lot of them sounded off about the struggle too, penning lyrics that wouldn't have looked out of place in the *Black Panther* newspaper once hawked by the party's rank-and-file members. From the earliest recordings, rap and radical politics intertwined. The music became a soapbox for the marginalized and oppressed to deliver dispatches from the urban decay they lived in. To tell the story of Tupac Shakur, hip-hop's greatest radical, we must consider the radical origins of hip-hop.

It had to happen in the beautiful Bronx, a fiefdom of socialist thought, Marxist organization, and anti-establishment resistance since long before the Panthers or Young Lords showed up. When the Bolsheviks seized power in Russia in the October Revolution of 1917, New York's Red faction toasted the news. They were not an insignificant pocket of the city's population—Riga-born socialist leader Morris Hillquit ran for mayor that same year and won more than a fifth of the votes cast. The Communist Party USA was established in the city soon after, its membership mostly made up of poor Jewish immigrants who'd come off boats through Ellis Island. As late as 1931, four-fifths of the communists living in the city were foreign-born.

For these leftist dreamers, the Bronx was a particularly blessed domain. Consider the United Workers Cooperatives between

Allerton and Arnow Avenues, on the east side of the Bronx, known to its residents as the Coops. In the mid-1920s, thousands of immigrant Jewish garment workers pooled their resources to build two cooperatively owned and run five-story complexes comprising 750 apartments. The Coops was a self-contained world of utopian ideals of a fair and equitable society. There were no evictions or rent hikes. Children enjoyed gardens and play areas, while a kindergarten provided hot meals. Adults attended communist meetings and engaged in Marxist-Leninist discussion. Righteous slogans echoed throughout the buildings: "Wages up! Hours down!" "Make New York a union town," "Black and white unite and fight," and "Free the Scottsboro Boys," a reference to the wrongful conviction of nine Black teenagers on charges of rape in Alabama who after years of legal wrangling would eventually all be pardoned. Residents of the Coops believed they were sitting in a relative paradise and watching capitalism's end days, with communism ready to fill the void. As Vivian Gornick wrote in her 1977 oral history *The Romance of American Communism*, "There are a few thousand people wandering around America today who became Communists because they were raised in the Co-Operative Houses on Allerton Avenue in the Bronx."

With the cold wind of the Depression blowing through America in the early 1930s, the Soviet Union began to be viewed as a more intriguing proposition. Americans soon wondered if communism could be a desirable alternative to the cruel irrationality of a capitalist system and the hunger, misery, and unemployment inflicted by its failings. Before McCarthyism made such an achievement practically impossible, a New York communist, Benjamin Davis Jr., represented Harlem on the New York City Council from 1943 to 1949, succeeding prominent civil rights leader Adam Clayton Powell Jr. But as the Red Scare took hold, Davis's politics earned him a conviction for violating the Smith Act, a law that criminalized any action that was seen as advocating an overthrow of the government, and he spent five years in prison.

Membership of Communist Party USA eventually dwindled. Nikita Khrushchev's "secret speech" in 1956 revealed more about the crimes of Joseph Stalin than had been previously known, and it shattered many members' confidence in a socialist future. Still, uptown and the Bronx remained a hive of leftist action. The members of the Nation of Islam were no socialists, but Malcolm X respected the anti-racism activism of the Communist Party. After splitting with the NOI, his sermons often veered anti-capitalist as he saw capitalism and racism as bedfellows. "You can't operate a capitalistic system unless you are vulturistic; you have to have someone else's blood to suck to be a capitalist," acknowledged the minister. The Black Panthers' New York outposts were full of grieving Malcolmites who funneled his teachings into their overtly Marxist curriculum.

The Panthers operated in a very different Bronx than the ones the Coops' founders knew. The 1950s saw the middle-class residents begin to flood out of the borough, drawn to the burgeoning utopianism of the American suburb. The Bronx went from two-thirds white in 1950 to two-thirds Black and Hispanic in 1960—a process known as "white flight." New York never fell to Jim Crow laws, yet there was an undeniable air of segregation. "Black kids didn't play on white blocks; white teens didn't walk through the projects," wrote Panther 21 member Jamal Joseph, who grew up in Edenwald Houses, a project built in the 1950s in the Eastchester and Laconia neighborhoods that were once predominantly Irish and Italian working class. "Maybe we weren't being fire-hosed, clubbed, and bitten by German shepherds like the Negroes in the South we saw on TV, but white storekeepers would kick us out, white teenagers would jump us, and white cops would beat the shit out of us for being in the wrong place at the wrong time."

Devastated by the loss of hundreds of thousands of manufacturing jobs over the previous decades, blighted by heroin, and with insufficient public services, the South Bronx was fertile soil for grassroots left-wing activism. Some of it took on particularly assertive forms. In the early morning of July 14, 1970, members of the Young Lords entered Lincoln Hospital. With baseball bats and nunchakus, the activists gained control of the hospital within ten minutes. Cleo Silvers, a young Black member of the group, ordered administrators to leave the building. A Puerto Rican flag flew from the roof and signs hung from its windows read "Welcome to the people's hospital" and "*Bienvenidos al hospital del pueblo.*"

The protest didn't occur in a vacuum. For years, New York's Black and brown neighborhoods had access to health-care facilities of a disproportionately poor standard compared to those serving white New Yorkers. To draw on just one statistic, in 1952, the tuberculosis mortality rate in the Central Harlem Health District was nearly fifteen times the rate for nearby, mostly white, Flushing, Queens. To the Young Lords, the situation was intolerable, and so its primary concern was drawing attention to detrimental health conditions in their poverty-stricken neighborhoods. The group allied with the Health Revolutionary Unity Movement (HRUM), an organization of hospital workers who felt the established union was corrupt. A precursor to the hospital insurrection took place a month earlier, when the Young Lords seized a mobile chest X-ray unit used to seek out cases of tuberculosis and drove it from 116th Street and Lexington Avenue to a site in East Harlem.

But the takeover of Lincoln Hospital was a level up. The early-morning storming was the beginning of what became a twelve-hour-long occupation in protest of the hospital's poor care conditions. With the disruption of potentially lifesaving work going on in the hospital, the execution had to be smooth and precise. "It took us a couple of months to complete the full planning of it," Silvers explained.

In a press conference, the Young Lords listed seven demands, including funds for a new hospital building, increased minimum wage for all workers, and a day care center for patients and staff. The city would give no public guarantee that it would meet their requests. Feeling they'd made their point, and wary of the police lining up outside the building, the protesters crafted an escape plan. They donned hospital clothing and exited the building alongside other workers. Only two members, Pablo Yoruba Guzman and Louis Alvarez Perez, were arrested for possession of dangerous weapons—charges that were later dismissed.

That November, the Young Lords returned, with permission, to the halls of their great protest, to establish Lincoln Detox. With one in five people in Mott Haven battling addiction at the time, lines would start forming at the clinic at seven a.m., two hours before it opened. A lack of financial support meant that for the first eight months of the endeavor, everyone worked for free. Lincoln Detox eventually received city funding, and by 1971 it was detoxing six hundred people every ten days. Some participated in the clinic's political education program, where lessons involved reading and discussing former Panther 21 member Michael "Cetewayo" Tabor's pamphlet *Capitalism Plus Dope Equals Genocide* and Mao's Little Red Book.

As a staff member, Jennifer Dohrn—an associate of the Weather Underground through her sister, Bernardine, as well as the partner of Young Lords co-founder and key Lincoln Detox figure Mickey Melendez, with whom she had three children—would see patients rendered homeless by their addiction arrive at Lincoln Detox desperate and without hope. Once in its care, the clinic would try to explain to addicts why this horror was happening to them. Structure would be introduced into patients' lives by allowing them to help out with a breakfast program, school program, or tuberculosis testing van.

"To watch people coming off of heroin and suddenly having this moment of feeling that their life was not controlled by it and they could contribute in a very different way to being part of rebuilding their community was a very hopeful time," said Dohrn. "There was so much going on that you could suddenly define yourself in a different way as contributing as opposed to feeling useless and a burden."

It was during the lifespan of Lincoln Detox that a new culture swept the borough, fusing the youths from diverse backgrounds into a rainbow coalition of baggy tracksuits and fresh sneakers. Together, African Americans, Afro Caribbeans, and Latino youth fostered hip-hop. For Silvers, both an ex-Panther and Young Lord, this union of Black and Puerto Rican communities for revolutionary struggle in the late 1960s and early '70s was a crucial precursor to the grassroots creative expression that would take place in the same streets.

"It happened because of the struggle to unite African Americans and Puerto Ricans in the South Bronx," she said. "That form of music, that genre of music, arose out of that relationship and that relationship started when the Black Panther Party and the Young Lords came together and started working together in the South Bronx. There was a definite rift between the two groups of people who were fighting over a tiny amount of jobs and anti-poverty funding that was coming in. And there was unity between the Black Panther Party and the Young Lords and the struggle to bring the community together to unite, which was the basis for the further development of hip-hop. Yes, that's how it started. Black Panther Party and Young Lords again, we did a lot of work in the South Bronx and Harlem, and all around New York City."

Jamal Joseph saw hip-hop as a descendant of the Black spoken word artists who directly preceded it. "Those poets were revolutionaries," he said. "That's what they talked about. If you looked at the Last Poets, Sonia Sanchez, and Amiri Baraka, they had beats behind them. They were always people laying down African rhythms on the conga drums. Sonia Sanchez started performing with jazz ensembles and combining what she did as a poet and just using her voice and her phrasing as an instrument. So, when hip-hop came about, I saw it as kind of the next level, and that instead of the live beats, people were sampling records and cutting and scratching. But if you looked at what people were talking about, they weren't talking about money, power, and fame. They were talking about police brutality and violence and poverty and how you overcame that. And Tupac came and really infused revolutionary consciousness in that. He started using the words revolution and liberation and struggle."

There is a photograph of Tupac Shakur that provides compelling evidence that he was a child of hip-hop. It's sometimes credited as being snapped in New York in 1987, the year Tupac turned sixteen, and the streets were being filled with the sounds of Eric B. & Rakim's *Paid in Full*. In the image, Tupac, wearing an open red-pattern shirt and matching shorts or pants, sits on the hood of a sports car. In his hands is a boom box, one of those large, portable music players of the day so entrenched in urban America that they became known as "ghetto blasters." LL Cool J had codified the boom box's place in hip-hop with his 1985 debut album *Radio*—its single "I Can't Live Without My Radio," with the kind of beat that would test the most resilient speaker, became the defining anthem of the hardware. And in 1989, the character Radio Raheem in Spike Lee's Brooklyn saga *Do the Right Thing* wired it into the minds of broader America.

Tupac may have left the city and moved to Baltimore three years earlier, but looking at the photo, it's clear that growing up in New York during the inception of hip-hop fostered a love and understanding of the culture. He was likely aware of not just the sound, but the implications of extremely young people of color shaking up the culture in a way that seemed antithetical to what was happening in Andy Warhol's Factory, where the art world intertwined with celebrity. Hip-hop was raw in comparison. Soon a child of Park Slope named Jean-Michel Basquiat would go from tagging buildings with a spray paint can to bringing hip-hop's anti-establishment energy to the Lower East Side art scene.

How could hip-hop not have that sense of urgency, of combustible unpredictability, when it was forged in fire? Facing plummeting property values, landlords in the 1970s discovered a way of maximizing their bottom lines: burning the buildings to the ground for the insurance money. The South Bronx regularly became a hellish vision of ember and smoke. Apartment buildings would be emptied out, stripped for pipes and wires, and torched. Arsonists working for landlords would warn tenants of impending fires so they would not be asleep at home when the terrible deed took place, but some wouldn't take the risk of not being notified and slept with their clothes on. As the 1977 World Series took place in Yankee Stadium, television coverage cut to a nearby building ablaze. Legendary ball game caller Howard Cosell is often quoted as saying, "Ladies and gentlemen, the Bronx is burning," though those words never actually escaped his lips. By the end of the arson wave, 80 percent of the housing stock was lost.

In this backdrop, hip-hop proliferated into four elements:

MCing, DJing, B-boying (or breakdancing), graffiti art, plus a fifth element, the binding force: knowledge. It gave kids a sense of purpose that stopped them from getting into trouble—well, if they could avoid being caught bombing subway cars with spray paint—and, in the process, formed the early promise of an artistic movement. This post-Panther generation could still look out their bedroom windows and see a New York City that bore little resemblance to the glittering metropolis hawked to the rest of the world on postcards and in Hollywood movies and Sinatra tunes. The streets didn't talk much about Panthers or Young Lords anymore, but revolutionary actions are never truly forgotten, and those who walked the same boulevards absorbed the activism of the area's history. In poverty, almost anything can become protest, and hip-hop was a response to social and economic injustice by showcasing innovation, joy, and the resilience of youth despite a lack of resources. Soon enough, the lyrics of rap music would become protest too.

One kid who used hip-hop to pull himself out of gang life was a former Black Spades "warlord" from the South Bronx who, inspired by DJ Kool Herc, began hosting his own hip-hop parties. His government name is unclear—Kevin Donovan and Lance Taylor are just two monikers that have been reported. Whatever the truth of his birth certificate, the streets came to know him as Afrika Bambaataa. As a DJ, Bambaataa would quickly shuffle among an eclectic mix of songs—say, from the Rolling Stones to Hugo Montenegro to old TV theme tunes—broadening hip-hop's sonic potential. Inspired by the Black Panthers, Nation of Islam, the civil rights movement, and the movie *Zulu*, Bambaataa formed the Universal Zulu Nation, an organization and movement that promoted peace, unity, love, and having fun. While motivated to eliminate gang activity from parties, Bambaataa and the Universal Zulu Nation developed a framework for hip-hop, delineating the concept of the five elements, promoting Afrocentrism, and bringing a sense of celebration to the Bronx. (In May 2016, Bambaataa stepped down from his leadership role in the Universal Zulu Nation amid accusations that he sexually assaulted several young boys. No charges have ever been brought against Bambaataa, who has denied all allegations, though he remains persona non grata in the hip-hop nation. When the culture celebrated its fiftieth anniversary in 2023, he was absent from all events and omitted from much of the commentary.)

By 1979, rap songs were being pressed onto wax for public consumption. With its heavy use of Chic sample, hippity-skippity rapping, and focus on its lyricists' propensity for partying, hip-hop's good-time origins were reflected in the Sugarhill Gang's "Rapper's Delight." Afrika Bambaataa entered the arena with "Zulu Nation Throw Down (Cosmic Force)" in 1980 and found chart success with the fizzing electronica of "Planet Rock" two years later. These early hits had a broad public appeal, downplaying the impoverished lived reality of hip-hop's pioneers. But left-wing social and political messages were also finding their way into the music.

"How We Gonna Make the Black Nation Rise?," a 1980 song by Brother D with Collective Effort, has been referred to as the first political hip-hop tune. It was released on Clappers Records, a company masterminded by founder Lister Hewan-Lowe to have a communist disposition. "I got revved up and excited about the possibilities of forming a record company that had a Maoist approach instead of a capitalist approach," recalled Hewan-Lowe, "and I was obsessed with the fact that the shareholders should be the people who made the music."

Plotting a revolutionary hip-hop record, he put out the word that he needed some on-mic talent. Enter Brother D, or math teacher Daryl Aamaa Nubyahn as he was known by day, and Collective Effort, an anonymous group of male and female backing vocalists. Over a sample of Cheryl Lynn's disco classic "Got to Be Real," Brother D, promising to "bring the truth right on down to Earth," uses rudimentary rhyme patterns typical of old-school hiphop to warn the Black community of the perils it faced. In some of the song's most striking bars, Brother D alters a lyric of "Rapper's Delight" to point to the fate of Native Americans as a history that could be repeated on African Americans, and, in a rebuttal to hiphop songs that simply urge people to have fun, warns them not to get distracted: "While you're partying on, on, on, on and on / The ovens may be hot by the break of dawn."

Though "How We Gonna Make the Black Nation Rise?" didn't make many waves, Brother D didn't abandon his principles.

Seven years later he put out "Clappers Power," a song with an anti-colonialism message and cover that featured the image of a seventeen-year-old Mao.

Any notion that rap records with social commentary could not be hits was soon dispelled. In 1982, Grandmaster Flash and the Furious Five released "The Message." Flash, a pioneering DJ, actually had little to do with the track—it was conceived, written, produced, and largely performed by Ed "Duke Bootee" Fletcher, with Skip McDonald on guitar, Jiggs Chase as co-writer and co-producer, and, famously, ostentatious Furious Five rapper Melle Mel as co-writer and vocalist. Mel was one of the kids drawn to hip-hop as escapism from the Burning Bronx. "We were in a place where we just needed an outlet, where we just needed something to make a day normal," he later said. Now, Mel was forcing everyone to take a look.

Unlike "How We Gonna Make the Black Nation Rise?," which mostly deals in huge ideas, "The Message" brings listeners down to street level, where they can get glimpses of intolerable poverty: "It's like a jungle sometimes / It makes me wonder how I keep from going under," decries Duke Bootee. From there, Bootee and Mel build this desperate world: cockroaches, drug addicts, repo men. Mel's final, crescendo verse was actually first heard on the back end of the twelve-minute "Superappin'" from 1979. Returning to the piece, the rapper once more describes a child born in the ghetto "livin' second rate" whose admiration for the neighborhood criminals convinces him to become one of them. Handed an eight-year sentence for his crimes, the young man hangs himself in his cell. To punctuate these themes further, the song ends with the sound of Furious Five group members being arrested for no obvious reason.

"The Message" went gold within eleven days, was named *NME*'s song of the year, "the most powerful pop record of 1982" by *The New York Times*, and the floodgates of rap records with a social justice bent opened. Few, though, developed the notion of rap music as a social platform like KRS-One, an early participant in hip-hop culture who became convinced of music as a podium for political messaging. In 1984, KRS-One became one of the rappers in Scott La Rock & the Celebrity Three, which later filtered into Boogie Down Productions. Their first album, *Criminal Minded*, became best known for "The Bridge Is Over" and "South Bronx," legendary diss tracks that took issue with rivals MC Shan, Marley Marl, the Juice Crew, and anyone else from Queens and the Queensbridge projects claiming that their turf was hip-hop's true home. But prior to that, there had been the single "Advance," which discussed nuclear war prevention. KRS-One would take to calling himself the Teacher.

By the late 1980s, Public Enemy were expanding how far political rap could go. The Long Island group were unashamedly drawn to their revolutionary elders; the sonic barrages under rapper Chuck D's booming oratory captured a kind of righteous anger, made digestible by hypeman Flavor Flav's court jester buoyancy. Their albums were loud, aggressive, and full of Black Power edicts. "Most of my heroes don't appear on no stamp" became one of Public Enemy's slogans and rallying cries, a reminder of how much reckoning America had to do with Black history. Though followers of Louis Farrakhan's Nation of Islam—the video for "Shut 'Em Down" redesigned the dollar bill to bear the face of Malcolm X—Public Enemy aesthetically leaned toward the Panthers, eschewing the NOI's buttoned-up dress sense for a more militaristic style. "Public Enemy has been dubbed 'The Black Panthers of Rap' for rekindling the spirit of the '60s black power movement in a young audience," wrote *The Washington Post* in 1988.

By now, hip-hop had long escaped its New York homeland and spread across America. Rap music entered what became known as its golden age, when the sophistication of its writing and production accelerated away from its more rudimentary origins. Some of the greatest music America has ever produced came from this period. Some of the same philosophies remained, though, as did New York as a hive of revolutionary action, even as the Clinton era gave birth to a more sterile Gotham. There was the presence of Marxist philosophers such as Marshall Berman. In 1995, Fidel Castro accepted an invitation to speak in the Bronx after Mayor Rudy Giuliani opted not to invite the Cuban communist leader to a dinner to mark the United Nations' fiftieth anniversary celebration.

The name and image of Malcolm X remained interwoven into rap: on the cover of their 1992 album *Daily Operation*, Gang Starr posed with a framed portrait of Malcolm hanging on the wall. When Spike Lee's biopic *Malcolm X* was released that same year to acclaim, it codified Malcolm's image in the hip-hop nation.

As the culture gained ground in the mainstream, many were already upset by what they saw as a debasement of hip-hop's founding ethos. None more so than KRS-One. In 1988, during the aftermath of Scott La Rock's death, Boogie Down Productions released their record *By All Means Necessary*. This cover showed KRS peeking out of a window in homage to an iconic picture of Malcolm from the 1960s, an Uzi in the place of the minister's rifle. KRS used the album as his own pulpit. This sermon encouraged safe sex ("Jimmy"), told a tale of cops shaking down a local dealer ("Illegal Business"), and reasserted the Universal Zulu Nation's message of keeping brutality out of hip-hop ("Stop the Violence"). But on "My Philosophy," pointedly positioned as track one, KRS took aim at artists dumbing down and taking the almighty dollar. "And it lacks creativity and intelligence / But they don't care 'cause their company's sellin it," before urging rappers to bring back the core principles that once energized his fallen partner: "Let us get back to what we call hip-hop / And what it meant to DJ Scott La Rock."

KRS's fears proved prescient. As hip-hop began to generate serious money, some of its most powerful drivers were executives whose idea of quality and success were measured in profitability. And the only useful element of hip-hop to a capitalist culture was rapping, which became severed from the other core tenets. As the 1990s lurched on, rap music began conveying less of the righteous personality of its origins. A lot of classic records were made, that can never be denied. But adrift uptown and in the Bronx, the originators could only watch on as others got rich, their original purpose blurred by the passage of time, as forgotten by its new disciples as the forefathers themselves.

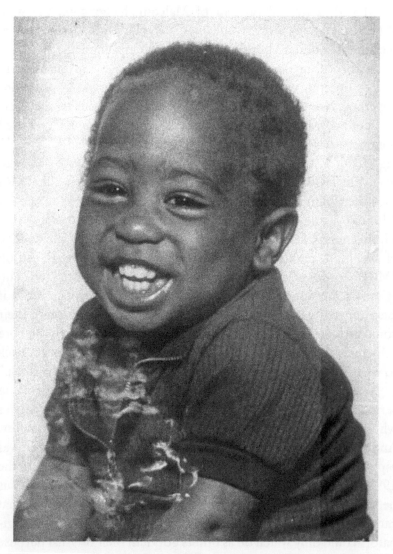

"Raised in this whirlwind": Tupac, 1972

5

REMEMBER THIS HOUSE

UPAC SHAKUR, New Yorker. Putting the two together feels strange, like asking your body to accept the transfusion of an incorrect blood type. But the boy became aware of the world to the sound of twelve-foot-high stainless steel chariots, bombed out with graffiti tags, rumbling along at fifty-five miles per hour through the city's arteries, a blur of kaleidoscopic color. Tupac will never be synonymous with the city of his birth—that's a reality he sealed when he declared war on its favorite hip-hop son, the Notorious B.I.G. But that doesn't change the fact that the molding of his mind began in New York. Perhaps he was a subject of Gotham more than any other place on the planet.

Maybe it's more accurate to say that Tupac was defined by a *lack* of roots. Even within New York, his living arrangements were in constant flux. It's difficult, therefore, to say Tupac was from any particular neighborhood or borough. On the song "My Block," he lists some of the addresses where he felt an attachment: 112th Street and Seventh Avenue, 183rd and Walt, 122nd and Morningside. By junior high, it's estimated that he had moved home twenty times in this anarchic metropolis. In their worst moments, the family was forced to seek temporary lodgings in homeless shelters.

It had at first promised to be a stable, nurturing childhood in the city. After her acquittal, Afeni Shakur courted the admiration of the liberal glitterati, which afforded her some appealing opportunities. She was invited to speak at Harvard and Yale. Afeni even found some unlikely social acquaintances: the jurors from her trial.

On December 10, 1971, a champagne party was held at Gerald Lefcourt's former law commune office at 640 Broadway. Guests included thirteen defendants and twelve jurors. Among them was Panther 21 member Robert Collier, who warmly embraced juror Jim Butters. Small talk filled the air. Collier was thrilled to discover that Butters worked with recovering drug addicts at Phoenix House, a nonprofit rehabilitation organization.

"Far out!" yelled Collier, who was excited to tell Butters of his attempts to set up a new community school.

Things got a little awkward when juror Hiram Irizarry called Kwando Kinshasa by his former name, Mr. King. Irizarry's wife, Emma, had warned her husband something like this might happen. She'd reluctantly been talked into coming to the party by Hiram, as he was eager for her to meet the Panthers. But Emma's apprehensions melted away when she seized an adorable six-month-old baby and began bouncing him on her knee. As Emma entertained the child, she traded baby talk with his mother, Afeni Shakur.

The shindig was such a success, it was even repeated the following May to celebrate the first anniversary of the Panther 21's acquittal.

In another social meetup, Afeni had lunch at the Riverside Drive home of J. Ingram Fox, a fifty-seven-year-old Guyana-born musician and foreman of the jury. After a meal of chili, green salad, and ginger, Afeni's baby slept on the sofa as Fox played sections of his three-act opera *Dan Fodio* on the grand piano, an unproduced work based on Nigerian folklore that had taken him twenty years to write. In appreciation, Afeni handed him a photograph of her infant with an inscription on the back: "To Mr. Fox, who gave me life so that I can be an attribute to humanity. Love, Parish."

It's fair to say that the child captivated anyone he encountered. He'd giggle and squeal for his occasional Panther babysitter, Cleo Silvers, full of happiness and glow. One afternoon, Afeni brought him along to lunch with Joan Bird and Edwin Kennebeck, another Panther 21 juror and an editor at Viking Press interested in publishing some of her children's writing. *New York* magazine reported on the social meeting, and how the baby "drooled beguilingly through the lunch on Miss Bird's lap."

So here was Afeni, once teetering on the brink of an eternity in prison, now flicking through invites from prestigious universities and lunching with fashionable friends. It was a respite she'd earned, but one that was never going to be a long-term option for a woman with her activist spirit. When Tupac was just a bundle in her arms, Afeni took him to see the Nation of Islam's expressive future leader Louis Farrakhan speak at the 168th Street Armory in the Washington Heights community of Upper Manhattan. In the crowd that day was Billy Garland, Tupac's biological father. The paternity might not have been entirely certain, but upon spotting Garland, Afeni marched right up to him, placed the baby in his arms, and declared, "I think you want to meet your son."

Soon the young mother settled in the Bronx and took a position as a paralegal at the South Bronx Legal Services at 579 Courtlandt Avenue. She loved the job—in contrast to her attempts to hold down stable employment before joining the Panthers, Afeni stayed in the role for a decade, reengaging a passion for tenant rights she'd displayed during her days as an organizer of rent strikes. But things got particularly personal when she became involved in a case relating to her old girlfriend, Carol Crooks. The two had remained close after ending their romantic relationship. But as Afeni enjoyed the admiration of liberal academia, Crooks was running a heroin distribution ring in Downtown Brooklyn. It was a harsh existence and, in 1972, Crooks shot dead an associate who, she claimed, tried to blackmail her. Crooks pled guilty to first-degree manslaughter and was sent upstate, to the Bedford Hills Correctional Facility, to serve up to fifteen years.

Crooks's incarceration proved hellish as she became the victim of sadistic prison guards with evil impulses, running their tiny universes with few checks and little accountability. The worst of her troubles began on the morning of February 3, 1974, when she awoke suffering from a splitting headache. Panicked, Crooks sought medical assistance from an on-duty guard who, like all the inmates and full-time staff at Bedford Hills, was a woman. When Crooks's request was denied, she attempted to push past the stationed sentry. The ruckus alerted a group of four additional guards standing nearby, who quickly surrounded Crooks. A fight broke out, limbs tangled with limbs, bodies contorted into skewed forms. Despite being outnumbered, the tough Crooks got the better of her opponents.

The warden, Janice Warne, determined that the situation warranted support from nearby men's prisons, Sing Sing and Green Haven. About half an hour after the fight, an armed cabal of male guards arrived on the scene. As the rest of the inmates were kept under lockdown, eight of the men entered Crooks's quarters and beat her with clubs and belts. They wrapped her battered body in a sheet and dragged Crooks across the snow-covered prison courtyard to the solitary confinement cells. When the prisoner refused to comply with orders to strip naked, the men forcefully ripped her clothes from her body. Crooks was tossed into a cold, dank cell with only the pain for company.

For the fight with the female guards, Crooks was convicted of three counts of felony assault, sentenced to an additional two to four years in prison, and condemned to solitary confinement until the expiration of her now potentially nineteen-year prison sentence, a punishment too cruel to comprehend. Facing this oblivion, Crooks managed to get word out to Afeni. Hearing that her friend had been left to fester in solitary, she went to one of her colleagues at South Bronx Legal Services, Stephen Latimer. The young prisoners' rights attorney had just been part of a successful lawsuit filed on behalf of seven inmates awaiting trial in the Brooklyn House of Detention that challenged the conditions under which they were being held, and agreed to investigate the Crooks case and the abuses occurring at Bedford Hills.

Latimer arrived at the women's prison and observed that Crooks was still in her solitary cell. He agreed with Crooks's claim that she was being kept in subhuman conditions precisely because of the debilitating effects it had on inmates. Latimer filed a complaint in the Southern District of New York arguing that his client was given inadequate process before the prison extended her time in solitary. The court issued a preliminary injunction ordering Crooks be released from solitary confinement while it considered her case. The lawsuit set a precedent by establishing the right of all women at Bedford Hills to due process before being sent to solitary. After five months, Crooks was sprung from perdition in July and sent back into the general population.

It made Crooks a hero in the facility. Few cons, after all, could claim they took on the system and won. But within the near-sovereign fiefdoms that exist within the borders of prison walls, this is a dangerous status to hold. There is only so much protection people in suits on the outside can provide. And what happened next, Crooks believed, was revenge for her victory.

On August 29, 1974, an inmate reported to staff that Crooks had hit her in the mouth. In response, Crooks was told to return to solitary confinement. This time, she demanded notice of the prison's allegation against her, which she believed the court had deemed a requirement before any transfer into disciplinary segregation. Instead, male guards from other prisons were summoned once more.

A sense of dread must have been palpable as the force approached Bedford Hills. The collect-call pay phones in the cellblocks went dead; klieg lights outside illuminated. The men entered the cellblock through an emergency stairwell in the rear of the building and made their way toward Crooks's cell. In desperation, Crooks attempted to barricade the door, but the guards pushed their way in. The beating started immediately. Crooks was thrown down half a flight of stairs, pulled into a station wagon where more guards continued the assault, and dragged back to solitary confinement, where she was again left naked.

The brutal nature of the beating sparked rumors among the rest of the prisoners that the male guards had killed Crooks. The next morning, they approached administrators to question the legitimacy of these actions and demand an update on Crooks's condition. Warden Warne assured the women that she would respond to their concerns. No answers were forthcoming. Instead, that night the prison instituted an early lockdown.

With questions left unanswered, the women refused to return to their cells. The rebels were led by Crooks's lover Cidney Reed and fellow inmate Dollree Mapp, a fifty-year-old half-Black, half-

Cherokee woman who some years earlier had picked up the reputation as "the Rosa Parks of the Fourth Amendment" for refusing
to let police search her home without a warrant, now in Bedford
Hills on a conviction for drug possession. Quickly outmaneuver-
ing prison staff, about two hundred prisoners seized control of two
buildings and an adjacent recreation yard. The women demanded
proof that Crooks was alive, phonelines be reconnected, and that
friendly lawyers and the press be allowed to enter the prison. The
sudden nature of the seizure meant that some guards found themselves trapped inside with the prisoners. The rebels fought to hold
their territory from prison authorities by using tear gas canisters
the male guards had left behind. Officials responded by using water
cannons, and after midnight, the inmates opted to peacefully relin-
quish control of the buildings. The uprising became known as the
August Rebellion.

Once more, Crooks's allies did what they could on the outside.
From October 1974 to April the following year, Afeni worked to
break the story to the public: she sent out press releases, called up
women politicians looking for support. The rebellion moved back
to the courts. Crooks and some of the other prisoners brought a
class action suit against the Bedford administration. The inmates
won, leading to greater enforcement of the Fourth Amendment due
process rights for incarcerated people and an award of $127,000.
The inmates used this fund for educational and training programs,
word processors, and funding for legal services. And with the last
of the money, the women of Bedford Hills threw themselves an ice
cream picnic party in June 1983. Carol Crooks was released later
that year.

Hearing of hardship endured by her former comrades must have
become a regular feature of Afeni's life. The Panthers were fractur-
ing; the momentum of the New Left had long been snuffed out.
Tupac's childhood was cast in the light of a failing revolution. As
a small boy, his playmates included the sons of Abdul Majid, an
ex-Panther who'd wind up in jail for killing a cop in Queens, and
Twymon Myers, the Black Liberation Army soldier and fugitive on
the FBI's Most Wanted list, killed in the Bronx in 1973 during a

shoot-out with the Feds and New York Police Department. And when he was a little older, Afeni punished mischief by making her son read *The New York Times* out loud, from front to back. Maybe she felt that time-out just didn't mold a mind.

Afeni's home life during these years rarely achieved stability. It often fell on Gloria Jean to put up her sister and nephew. This suited Tupac just fine; he loved goofing around with his cousins. And in Gloria Jean's husband, Thomas "T.C." Cox, there was a stable grown-up male presence in his life. Another father figure emerged when Afeni's close relationship with her comrade Mutulu Shakur fostered a romance between the two.

Mutulu was already a parent to a son almost four years older than Tupac. The boy was born Maurice Harding but became known by all as Mopreme Shakur. Mopreme's parents were just seventeen years old when he was born. With both ill-equipped for child-rearing, he was sent to live with his mother's family in North Carolina, returning to New York at age five. Back in the city, Mopreme became acquainted with a father he barely knew. He first laid eyes on Tupac when Mutulu walked over to him with the one-year-old in tow. "This is your brother," he said with no sense of ceremony. "Hold his hand."

Like his new stepbrother, Mopreme was raised to be a dissenter. One of his first chores upon returning to New York was to hang up posters around the city that read "Fuck the Pigs." The boy did what he was told without fully understanding what the words meant.

Soon enough, the family grew. Afeni and Mutulu welcomed a daughter, Sekyiwa, in 1975. But as serious as Mutulu was about the struggle, this proverbial rolling stone had a devil-may-care attitude toward romantic relationships. His union with Afeni ended soon after Sekyiwa's birth. Still, Mutulu was never far from their door.

Tupac's search for a father figure proved to be a lifelong endeavor. Mutulu certainly saw himself as the man who came closest to fulfilling the role. In 1997, from behind prison walls, he penned "To My Son Tupac," a poetic piece doused in grief for his fallen stepson. "The pain inflicted which scarred your soul, but not your spirit, gave force to rebellion. Many couldn't see your dreams or understand your nightmares. How could they, Tupac? I know your love and understand your passion. But you knew of your beginning and saw your end . . . racing toward it."

And Billy Garland, Tupac's biological father? Well, he later claimed to have been in his son's life until about 1976 or '77. If true, it's fair to assume contact was minimal.

An apartment in historic Harlem, the mid-1970s. The children played exuberantly, zigzagging around adults like learner drivers maneuvering through traffic cones, or Jim Brown around fullbacks. The grown-ups talked about grown-up things, like the struggle for Black determination. It was December and the home was decorated for Kwanzaa, a weeklong winter festival that honors African American culture.

Every day, the family living here passed through a front door decorated with a poster that displayed two flags: on the left, the U.S. flag, Old Glory, thirteen stripes and fifty stars. "You're the emblem of the land I love," George M. Cohan used to sing. "The home of the free and the brave." On the right, a flag of three solid colors: red, black, and green, the banner of the Pan-African movement.

Underneath the flags was a question: "To which nation do you belong?"

This was the sight that greeted Akinyele Umoja and his comrade Kamau Umoja upon visiting the home of Afeni and Mutulu Shakur. Akinyele had first come across the couple when he was just nineteen years old, at a meeting at a Los Angeles church that was seeking to establish an acupuncture clinic to help people overcome heroin addiction. He'd been invited to the meeting by one of his mentors, Mamadou Lumumba, previously known as Kenny Freeman, the man who had once comforted Bobby Seale after the death of Malcolm X.

Afeni and Mutulu had journeyed west as representatives of Lincoln Detox. After being introduced, Akinyele was struck by Afeni's humbleness and good nature. He wondered, *Was this really the same Afeni Shakur he'd been reading articles about in the* Black Panther *newspaper? The woman who was one of the Panther New York 21 politi-*

cal prisoners? The hardened revolutionary who stood up and represented herself against the state of New York in court and won?

So when Kamau invited Akinyele to join him on a visit to the Shakurs' New York home on a cold December night, he jumped at the chance to spend more time in their company. Upon arrival, Akinyele found the apartment to be a quaint and nurturing space. The couple spoke as their children played in the background, and he listened attentively—they may have only been a few years older than him, but Akinyele knew these veterans had rich experiences in the struggle.

But that poster. It stood out to Akinyele not just because of its striking message, but because it was developed by his own organization, House of Umoja, a revolutionary nationalist collective formed to promote Black self-determination. With America in the midst of celebrating its bicentennial as an independent republic, the group had started what they called its "anti-bicentennial campaign."

"Our slogan was, 'We have nothing to celebrate,' and we would talk about the continuation of white supremacy, police state violence, political prisoners, economic disparities, all the stuff that's still going on today unfortunately," Akinyele told me years later. "So we created this poster for the campaign. It was posing the question to the Black community, 'To which nation do you belong?'"

In asking people to reflect on their national identity, House of Umoja was drawing on Pan-Africanism, a movement that attempted to create a sense of kinship among all people of African descent, and to restore to them what colonialism and slavery had stolen. It informed groups like the Black Panthers and the revolutionary movement Republic of New Afrika (RNA), which drew very directly on the experience of anti-colonialists, going as far as mobilizing the language of an internal colony—that is, oppression and exploitation within the borders of the United States.

Pan-Africanism emerged in the context of Jim Crow and the realization across the Americas that the abolition of slavery had not produced equal rights or citizenship but rather new forms of racial hierarchy. At the same time, there was the Scramble for Africa, a period of rapid imperial expansion across the continent. This moment produced what W. E. B. Du Bois called "the color line," a set of societal and legal barriers that segregated people of color from white people. Its existence facilitated an interest in building and fostering solidarity between parts of the African diaspora.

In America, Pan-Africanism manifested as a bold plan to establish a new Black nation within America's borders. In 1968, at a convention in Detroit, the Republic of New Africa (the earlier name of the Republic of New Afrika) proposed a new Black homeland in the South. The RNA saw itself as a state in being, with "consulates" set up in major American cities, such as New York and Los Angeles. And like the Panthers, it had a penchant for flashing guns in public. The organization's slogan was "Free the Land." Yet the idea of a Black nation in the South goes as far back as the 1920s, when the Communist International, in its advocacy of self-determination for all nations, floated what was called the Black Belt thesis—the idea that the Black Belt of America's South, the states where plantation slavery had been most dominant and where African Americans constituted large proportions of the populations, could be the basis of a Black nation-state.

The history of the South held a particular importance to the RNA. It's a space where Black Americans had large pluralities, if not majorities, of the population, and had played a central role in shaping the economy. But looking forward, the organization wanted a place where there'd be land to work. There was an agricultural imaginary to their plan.

And the Pan-African flag itself? Those solid red, black, and green bars are an early-twentieth-century construction. There was a racist minstrel song called "Every Race Has a Flag but the Coon." Its lyrics goaded African Americans by listing national emblems—Ireland's harp and shamrock, China's dragon, etc.—while pointing to people of African descent's supposed lack thereof. There were various attempts to address this absence, but the red, black, and green flag was put forward by the Marcus Garvey–founded Universal Negro Improvement Association and African Communities League (UNIA-ACL), and so is associated with Garveyism. This new banner was part of the 1920 Declaration of the Rights of the

Negro Peoples of the World, which states, "That the colors, Red, Black and Green, be the colors of the Negro race."

African Americans may identify with both descriptors, but the House of Umoja poster at a minimum invited them to consider to what extent and at what capacity. *To which nation do you belong?* One where all people of African origin, on every continent, are united, self-sufficient, and proud? It also invited an examination of what the American flag represents. The Weathermen would say it's the emblem of "a worldwide monster, a country so rich from its world-wide plunder that even the crumbs doled out to the enslaved masses within its borders provide for material existence very much above the conditions of the masses of people of the world." Akinyele Umoja could even break it down color by color: "White stood for white supremacy, the red stood for the blood suckers, and blue stood for blue-blood elites, who are the capitalist class."

The 1996 song "Got 2 Survive" by Young Lay featuring Ray Luv, Mac Mall, and 2Pac reveals the friction inherent in honoring the flag of a nation that was failing to deliver its promised freedom, justice, and liberty to all: "Now how could I pledge allegiance to a racist-ass flag," raps Mac Mall, "when the rollers at my do' with a .44 mag?" Similarly, on 2Pac's "Words of Wisdom," from his first album *2Pacalypse Now*, he raps: "Pledge allegiance to a flag that neglects us / Honor a man that refuses to respect us." A quarter of a century later, this rejection of the American flag as a form of pro-test intensified when NFL quarterback Colin Kaepernick refused to stand for "The Star-Spangled Banner." "I am not going to stand up to show pride in a flag for a country that oppresses Black people and people of color," he explained. Taking the knee has become a symbolic gesture in solidarity with the Black Lives Matter move-ment and broader anti-racist activism.

The poster offers a microcosm of the righteous ideology Tupac was raised on, his parents' unfinished revolution fusing itself to his bones. You can point to the demands of destiny to explain the icon he became, but sometimes images like this are burned into the sub-conscious. Like many Black men of his generation, Tupac grappled with being a person of African descent in America—but unlike most, there was an eloquence in his portrayal that clearly revealed the weight. Some of the tension of Tupac's life was him trying to complete a circle that couldn't be squared: his own identity.

There's a story of Tupac, ten years old, being asked by a minister what he wanted to be when he grew up. Without hesitation he said, "A revolutionary."

By triumphing in her trial, Afeni had escaped the tentacles of authorities determined to destroy her for being a member of the Black Panther Party. But she wasn't willing to abandon the fight against the FBI just because she had been one of the lucky ones. Not while comrades who'd fallen to the surreptitious serpent still languished in jail or in exile. She and Mutulu served as coordinators on the National Taskforce for COINTELPRO Litigation and Research, formed to expose these government attacks and to free some of those thrown in jail under its watch. Listed on the group's advisory board was a professor at MIT named Noam Chomsky.

"We wanted, on the one hand, to inform people how the government was working," recalled Jeffrey Haas, a lawyer with the task force, "and at the same time, wanted to build support for political prisoners because their cases were questionable about how they came to be convicted, what provocations existed, how was the evidence tampered with, how was the evidence obtained. So the whole idea was to arm the movement with the awareness of COINTEL-PRO and also to build support for political prisoners."

The Shakurs were crucial drivers of the task force. One of Afeni's primary goals was to secure the release of Geronimo Pratt, the Black Panthers' former deputy minister, imprisoned on a disputed first-degree murder conviction. After Pratt asked for Afeni's help, she journeyed to California with her infant son, who'd play with toys on the floor as mother and lawyers discussed details of the case.

Afeni acted as the task force's spokesperson and would organize panel discussions that she herself would sit on. Haas remembered attending one such panel in New York before driving with Afeni and Mutulu to a second engagement in Washington, D.C. Time was passed by the couple asking questions about his work representing the family of Fred Hampton; Mutulu described his work treating drug addiction through acupuncture. "They were pretty charged, I guess they were pretty hyped up," recalled Haas. "And, I think, pretty worried about what was going on and what was happening to the movement."

Mutulu Shakur was born Jeral Williams on August 8, 1950, in Baltimore, Maryland. His father painted houses for a living, but skipped out on the family when the boy was just three years old, leaving Jeral's devout Christian mother, Delores Porter, to raise both her son and younger daughter, Sharon, on her own. Further hardship struck the following year when Delores lost her sight. Three years later, the family sought greener pastures in South Jamaica, Queens. Though still a child, Jeral took on the responsibility of obtaining access to basic but vital social welfare to assist his mother. The difficulty he faced navigating the system hardened his attitude toward the state.

The relocation brought Jeral into the orbit of some of the key players of the East Coast's strengthening Black nationalist movement. He grew up around members of the Nation of Islam as Malcolm X's profile was rising—the NOI even had a distribution center for its newspaper, *Muhammad Speaks*, in Jeral's neighborhood. By the time he was in junior high, Jeral and his friends were accepting organized rides to Temple Number 7 in Harlem, to hear Minister Malcolm speak.

Jeral was fifteen years old when Malcolm was assassinated, but the neighborhood wasn't short of wise elders to guide him. He soon found a mentor in Herman Ferguson, a prominent member of Malcolm's Muslim Mosque Inc. and, later, his Organization of Afro-American Unity. Ferguson brought Jeral into his newly established Black Brotherhood Improvement Association (BBIA) and its affiliate group, Revolutionary Action Movement. He even introduced Jeral to his Jamaica Rifle and Pistol Club, formed to train Black residents of Queens in how to use weapons. Ferguson fed Jeral's mind with the writings of Kwame Nkrumah, Frantz Fanon, Mao Tse-tung, and Marcus Garvey. So when Ferguson and fellow BBIA member Arthur Harris were charged with conspiracy to murder integrationist leaders Roy Wilkins and Whitney Young, it was Jeral and Abdul Majid (then going by the name Anthony Laborde) who organized a rally of support. In October 1968, Ferguson and Harris were convicted by an all-white jury and sentenced to three and a half to seven years in prison.

Jeral joined the Republic of New Afrika, adopted the Sunni Muslim faith, and upgraded his name to Mutulu Shakur. That he became known uptown by the same righteous surname as Afeni was no coincidence—it was adopted from Saladin Shakur, Lumumba and Zayd's father, who, as he had done with many young men in the neighborhood, became a kind of spiritual mentor to Jeral. As for "Mutulu," that name was bestowed upon him by none other than Robert "Sonny" Carson (also known as Mwlina Imiri Abubadika), an activist who coordinated public protests of the school systems during the 1960s and '70s. He wrote a popular autobiography, *The Education of Sonny Carson*, which was made into a 1974 cult movie.

Despite his youth, Mutulu was made a member of the Provisional Government of the Republic of New Afrika. He attended the convention in Detroit that proposed the new Black homeland in the South. But the New York streets remained his home ground of activism. During the bitter Ocean Hill–Brownsville teachers' strike of 1968, Mutulu and Majid kept the neighborhood kids busy by lecturing them on history, politics, and culture.

For Mutulu, traversing so many organizations as a very young man was a higher education, instilling both a sense of charity and mutiny in his mind. But he found a calling to serve that would trump all others. Heroin had infiltrated this slice of urban America, overwhelming its residents like a biblical tide. The drug was at the time rampaging its way through the Bronx, leaving a trail of the debilitated and dispossessed, and Mutulu subscribed to the belief that it was administered as a way of chemically enslaving people of color in poor neighborhoods. For victims, he saw two cures: education and alternative medicine.

In 1970, Mutulu took a job at Lincoln Detox as a political education instructor, a role he excelled in. That same year, he was introduced to acupuncture by famed Japanese American activist Yuri Kochiyama, who'd gone from suffering internment during the Second World War to joining the civil rights movement and organizations such as the RNA. Mutulu was quickly convinced by the theory that acupuncture could be used as an alternative to methadone in getting people to kick heroin. By 1976, Mutulu had earned doctorates in acupuncture from the Montreal Institute of Traditional Chinese Medicine, where he was trained by Oscar and Mario Wexu. At some point he began prefixing his name with "Dr." and would casually go by the name Doc. Eventually, he became Lincoln Detox's assistant director.

Working alongside Mutulu was Weather Underground affiliate Jennifer Dohrn. "The view at Lincoln Detox was that flooding the community with heroin was a form of control," she recalled. "And the only way to combat it was to get people off of drugs, get people jobs, and give them a sense of understanding that this wasn't random, it wasn't that you were weak or it wasn't an individual thing—I mean it did affect the individual, but it really was a process of wiping out a community with drugs."

Mutulu believed strongly in Lincoln Detox, but the setup faced an onslaught of skepticism and aggression. As Dohrn explained, "FBI and police absolutely hated that they had Mutulu, the Black Panthers, Mickey of the Young Lords, and me of the Weather People running this program—a leadership that was funded by the city."

A report to Mayor Ed Koch by a special health advisory panel depicted the entire hospital as rife with internal and political controversies, with Lincoln Detox one of the building's major sources of conflict. Anonymous hospital and corporation officials told *The New York Times* they were afraid to intervene in management failures of the detox program because of fear that there would be reprisals—when the Health and Hospitals Corporation threatened to cut its funds in 1975, a group from the program showed up at the corporation's offices at 125 Worth Street and raised all kinds of hell. Windows were smashed, furniture was turned over, and the proposed reforms were quickly forgotten.

By 1978, Lincoln Detox had attracted the ire of one Charles E. Schumer, the chairman of the assembly's Subcommittee on City Management and Governance and future Senate majority leader. On a snowy November morning, Schumer stood at the entrance of the hospital and pronounced that "over the past eight years, the program known as Lincoln Detox has compiled a well-documented record of millions of dollars in unsubstantiated payrolls costs, over-billing for patient care and other egregious management failures.

"Despite public knowledge of these matters, the Health and Hospitals Corporation has continued to finance the program out of city funds because the state drug program agency cut off state funds to the program in 1973."

The clinic was finally shut down by Koch and Lincoln Hospital on November 29, 1978. Many of the expelled chose not to disappear with it, but rather move on to new acts of resistance.

Mutulu Shakur maintained a full schedule. There was his work exposing COINTELPRO. He had patients who trusted him in their recovery from drug addiction. He had his women—there were always women—and he had his children. But underneath the good doctor's exterior, it was revolution that stirred his soul. Being a humble clinician of the people could not satisfy him—Mutulu yearned to be a general in the war on this racist, imperialist empire called America, a war that had fallen dormant since the mutinies of the early 1970s. It was in 1976 when he started tinkering with the idea of resuming the armed action of the Black Liberation Army. But revolutions require funding, and in these situations, you can't simply apply for a grant from the Carnegie Corporation.

By now, Afeni's exiled Panther comrade Sekou Odinga had slipped back into the country, reemerging with a steelier bent and undimmed sense of purpose. Upon his arrival on home soil in the spring of 1973, Odinga began raising money by hitting banks. "I couldn't even tell you how many there were," he told author Bryan Burrough in the book *Days of Rage: America's Radical Underground, the FBI, and the Forgotten Age of Revolutionary Violence*. "At least ten before 1976. Connecticut, New Jersey, mostly New York." But when the crew he'd been working with dispersed, Odinga re-established connections with Mutulu, an association that went all the way back to when Mutulu was about thirteen years old.

In late 1976, Mutulu debuted his new group of insurgents. Its initial goal: to expropriate cash—that is, to take money from those who amassed wealth by exploiting the people with the purpose of using it to finance the resistance. They were tactics that evoked the Bolsheviks, who used secret police organization the Cheka to forcibly seize the property of the bourgeoisie and nobility. With Raymond Oliver and Chui Ferguson, two associates from Lincoln Detox turned quasi-soldiers, the trio targeted an armored car outside of Mellon Bank in Pittsburgh. Odinga, not yet convinced by the group, sat the job out, contributing only by allowing Mutulu to use his apartment as a hideout.

Odinga's reservations proved oracular. The scene was absurd, a complete comedy of errors. One guard fainted upon seeing Mutulu and Ferguson flash their pistols. Attempting to handcuff a second guard who'd stepped out of the armored truck, Ferguson, previously one of Mutulu's acupuncture patients, suffered a back spasm, causing him to unintentionally fire a round. Cops descended on the scene. Oliver was tackled to the ground; Ferguson suffered another convulsion. In the chaos, Mutulu managed to slip away. Oliver and Ferguson served short prison sentences but never gave up Mutulu's name.

It was an inauspicious start, but with Odinga talked into the fold, the group would be drilled into a far more effective crew. Mutulu recruited fellow RNA member and Vietnam veteran Tyrone Rison to join his crusade, while Odinga reached out to one of the men he trusted from previous jobs, Larry Mack, a Panther 21 member who'd spent the duration of the trial in Algeria. Mutulu also connected with the May 19th Communist Organization, a group of mostly white female militants who'd graduated from the Weather Underground and longed for a new assault on American imperialism and racism. In support of Mutulu's "primary team" of gunmen, they'd form the base of the group's "secondary team" in charge of logistics such as securing safe houses and driving escape cars. Mutulu also called the clan his "white edge."

The actions of Mutulu's revolutionaries are often attributed to the Black Liberation Army. But the group had its own name. They simply went by "the Family."

During an eighteen-month period beginning in May 1977, the group pulled off three jobs across three separate New York boroughs, netting about $22,180—a decent haul, but hardly a sum to put them in the pantheon of legendary stickup men. Cops initially didn't know they were up against a new revolutionary sect, believing these were the actions of common criminals. Unlike the Black Liberation Army or the Weather Underground, the Family didn't telegraph its ideology; there was no Ten-Point Program. Its existence was entirely covert.

Such secrecy raises the question as to what exactly its intentions were. It's likely that Mutulu needed cash to keep his medical facilities open to the public, and may have been funneling money into the RNA. Moreover, FBI files claim that he and other members of the Family had picked up the expensive habit of using cocaine—stupendous amounts, if you're inclined to believe the FBI. *Days of Rage* reports that Mutulu kept his drug use from Odinga, who considered substances as counterrevolutionary, and the white women, who may have questioned their loyalty if they thought the expropriated money was going into the pockets of dealers. As the robberies continued, group members started to wonder about the direction the Family was heading. "We felt that just robbing Brinks trucks or guards or banks wasn't totally what we were about," Rison said during a trial in 1987. "It was time to do something that was totally political."

That something was a serious act of revolutionary resistance: busting Assata Shakur out of prison.

The plan was bold but unsophisticated. On his visits to the Clinton Correctional Facility for Women in New Jersey, where Assata was being held, Odinga couldn't help but notice that security was comically lax. Liberating his caged comrade wasn't going to require *Escape from Alcatraz* levels of finesse, he deduced. And so on November 2, 1979, Odinga arrived to see Assata like he had before. Only this time, he hid a .357 Magnum against his spine.

During visitations, guests were shuttled in a van from a registration building to South Hall, the maximum-security unit, which housed seventeen inmates. While no fences surrounded the prison, a fifteen-foot-tall chain-link fence penned in South Hall.

Having dropped Odinga off, prison guard Stephen Ravettina was informed via radio that more visitors were waiting. Pulling back up to reception, Ravettina stepped out to chat to another guard as two men entered the van, one in the passenger seat and the other in the back. Ravettina climbed back in and they began the short journey to South Hall. As the shuttle reached the fence, one of the men pulled out a pistol and pressed it against the guard's head. It was Mtayari Sundiata, a former youth worker in the Ocean Hill–Brownsville section of Brooklyn and Republic of New Afrika supporter who'd done time himself after getting into a shoot-out with police. Noticing that the guard was glancing at his radio, Sundiata cooly advised, "You don't wanna do that."

Inside, Odinga and Assata were reunited. Only one guard separated them from Sundiata and the other man, Winston Patterson, a Family member from Washington, D.C., only recruited the night before to replace Larry Mack, who opted out. That guard was an elderly woman named Helen Anderson, affectionately known to inmates as Mama A, who was perched behind glass and tasked with buzzing people into the facility. Odinga fancied that the armor-piercing bullets in his Magnum would penetrate the booth, but there was no need to test the theory. He held a stick of dynamite up against the glass and Mama A buzzed him out just as the second group, still holding Ravettina at gunpoint, were coming in.

The crew handcuffed the guards and ushered them into the van. Patterson took the wheel, driving over the hilly terrain, into a school next to the prison, where they had two cars waiting: a blue compact and a white Lincoln Continental. Emerging from one car was Marilyn Buck, who'd made her reputation years earlier as the only white member of the BLA. Buck had been imprisoned on two counts of purchasing ammunition using false identification, but had been on the run for two years after failing to return to prison after being furloughed. Back on the streets, she joined the May 19th Communist Organization and started assisting the Family.

Just as the group were busying themselves by changing license plates, up pulled Mutulu Shakur in a blue van. The crew drove away in the various vehicles, leaving behind both the prison's van and the guards. Roadblocks were set up, but they eluded police. The Family had pulled off their biggest coup yet.

Sekou Odinga would later plead not guilty to the jailbreak, but in 2016, he asserted his pride in having been involved in the action.

"I have no contentions on that at this point. I was found guilty of it. I don't—if anything, I'm proud to be associated with the liberation of Assata Shakur. So, since they found me—I did plead not guilty to it, if that's what you're asking me. I pled not guilty to it in the court case. But at this point that I've done the time, I don't have no contention on it any longer. I'm proud to be associated with the liberation of Assata Shakur."

Assata eventually left the country, taking up long-term residence in Cuba, under Castro's protection. More so than any other BLA soldier, Assata has become an icon of dissent, lauded among the left as a true revolutionary who chose direct action over passive activism. "Assata Shakur Is Welcome Here," a slogan that emerged just days after her escape, has become a mantra among those left behind in America, dreaming of her unfinished revolution and the day she can return that will almost certainly never come.

Breaking Assata out of prison without a shot fired was in line with how the Family operated. Until this point, the group had not used fatal force in any of its operations. On one expedition in February 1980, to take an armored car in the northern New York suburb of Greenburgh, Family members snatched one of the couriers, handcuffed him, then beat him in front of a second guard still inside the truck in a vain attempt to persuade him to open the door. "Go ahead, kill him," the guard shouted defiantly. "I don't give a damn." The Family refused his direction. It's only when they retreated to a safe house in Mount Vernon that they realized the courier's keys could have opened the door.

The absence of fatal force changed on June 2, 1981. The group trailed a Brink's armored truck into a busy shopping center parking lot in the North Bronx, where the guards were to deliver cash to the Chase Manhattan Bank's Bivona branch. The plan was much the same as it had been on previous jobs: ambush the guards, bind them with handcuffs, secure their weapons, make off with the money bags.

At 10:45 a.m., the truck made its scheduled stop and the Family's primary team got the signal from lookout Judy Clark. The couriers were going about their business when Mutulu screeched up in a station wagon. Out into the morning rain stepped a heavy unit of Sekou Odinga, Mtayari Sundiata, Tyrone Rison, and former Panther and BLA member Kuwasi Balagoon. As planned, they approached the Brink's truck and ordered everyone to freeze. But guard William Moroney chose not to comply. Instead, he shouted "Hit it!" to the driver and the truck began to pull away. The team opened fire. Moroney was wounded and on the ground when Rison approached him and fired a fatal shot. (In court, Rison gave the explanations that the guards had resisted commands and the confusion had caused his M16 automatic rifle to fire several shots in their direction.) The hail of wild gunfire shattered the windows of a nearby liquor store. Another courier, Michael Schlachter, was hit three times but survived his wounds. The third security guard, Frank Rogers, working his first day on the job, was not injured. The Family clambered back into the station wagon and Mutulu accelerated away from the bloody scene. Once clear, the group switched into cars driven by May 19th member Susan Rosenberg and, after that, Clark. Police initiated a large-scale manhunt across the Northeast to catch the group, but their efforts were in vain. The Family got away with $300,000.

It was a tragic outcome. And, on reflection, it may have served as a crucial psychological step—a broken barrier—leading to what was to follow.

In 1980, Mutulu and his new wife, Makini Shakur, moved to a renovated Harlem brownstone at 245 West 139th Street. The address also served as the headquarters of the Black Acupuncture Advisory Association of North America (BAAANA), co-founded by Mutulu two years earlier to continue his work in the community following the closure of Lincoln Detox. The facility was never awash with money. Mutulu believed it should be a community service, and if his clients could not pay, well, they could not pay.

Meanwhile, in the doctor's secret life, he needed to placate Odinga, who was always uneasy about drug use in the Family. Mutulu assured his comrade that the money from their next job would go toward a crusade of great revolutionary consequence: a bombing campaign on New York police precincts. Or, if Odinga and Rison wished, they could walk away with enough money in their pocket to retire. Mutulu planned this action for months, the kind of big score jaded villains plan in noir fiction that will secure their futures. It would go down in modern scripture as the 1981 Brink's robbery. Mutulu dubbed the job "the Big Dance."

That's right, *the Big Dance*—Mutulu could not have conceived of a name more alluring. It was fit for a robbery that would capture the public imagination as a kind of modern-day O.K. Corral fable swathed in gun smoke, cordite, and blood. But the Big Dance also serves as an intersection in the stories of many different radicals and radical organizations. It's a crucial happening in this age of revolutionary violence. Mutulu intended the Big Dance to be a move of substance. And so it was.

I wonder how Mutulu said goodbye to Tupac and Sekyiwa before leaving them to embark on each mission of expropriation. Were they aware that the slightest procedural error, a minor warp in the mechanics of his plan, and Mutulu would not be coming back? Was his goodbye in silence, with a lingering embrace? Or did he include some wise words, lest it be his final opportunity to pass on a lesson? In whatever way Mutulu bid the children farewell prior to October 20, 1981, he would not see members of his family without hindrance until 2022, when he was released from prison.

The location of the job: Nanuet, a hamlet in the town of Clarkstown. It's the archetypal suburban escape from the big city—*the* big city, as Clarkstown rests less than an hour's drive away from Manhattan. Residents enjoy lower crime rates and more family-friendly open spaces, while living within reach of the metropolis. Center to the community was the Nanuet Mall, opened in 1969, where locals could browse superstores Sears and Bamberger's (later purchased by and rebranded as Macy's).

At 3:35 p.m., a Brink's armored truck made a regularly scheduled pickup from one of the Nanuet Mall stores. Starting their journey at 7:30 a.m. in Newark, New Jersey, the three guards had already made eighteen stops that day and were winding down. Emotions were a little heightened and the vibe a bit different. It was due to be the trio's final ride in a fifteen-year stint of working together before Peter Paige was transferred to a new route.

The guards had no idea that tailing their truck was a rented 1981 red Chevrolet van carrying the Family. Behind the wheel, Mutulu had been disappointed to see a relatively small bag of money being picked up at the previous stop, the Chemical Bank in Nanuet. Twitching in the back were a group of men—among them Chui Ferguson, Kuwasi Balagoon, Mtayari Sundiata, and ex-BLA soldier Solomon Bouines (formerly known as Samuel Brown)—armed with an arsenal that included pistols, a shotgun, and an M16 automatic rifle. Each clutched his own ski mask, crucial appendages for what was to come. By the time they reached the mall, the balaclavas were on, their prize ready to be plundered.

Waiting until the truck's final pickup to strike had obvious benefits—cash would be at its most plentiful. But there were additional risks. Traffic back to New York was worsening as the afternoon got late, escape routes were clogging up. The crew knew their window was narrowing. And they were missing one key soldier.

Sekou Odinga had never liked the plan. Perhaps it had been a sense of duty to his comrades that had pushed him into going along on several previous attempts to pull off the Nanuet robbery, all of which had been either aborted or foiled when the truck failed to show up. Eventually, the nagging doubts got the better of Odinga and he dropped out completely. "The plan actually made sense," he later said. "But it had to go perfectly. If just one thing went wrong, they were dead, and they had no backup plan. There was only one way in and out of that town, the highways, and they were going to use the highways. It was stupid."

At Nanuet Mall, the decision rested with Mutulu on whether the moment was finally right to strike. On the commander's urging, Balagoon stepped out of the van and casually walked to a nearby bench, exchanging small talk with a woman waiting for a bus as he surveyed the scene. The crew watched on as Paige, a forty-nine-year-old father of three, and his partner, Francis Joseph Trombino, rolled their pushcart from the mall to the truck. This time, it was loaded with three bulging bags, no doubt causing Mutulu's eyes to narrow as he gazed on. As Paige and Trombino reached the rear of the truck, guard James Kelly, sitting in the front of the vehicle, pressed a button to unlock the door. Trombino lifted one of the three large bags and hurled it into the back.

This was it. With a shock of sound, the red Chevy screeched up and three men in masks clambered out from the back. What happened next is almost always depicted as a wild, unprovoked duck hunt on startled guards by crazed attackers. This is disputed. Whatever the case, the armed men did open fire, their guns lightning in their hands as they squeezed the triggers. One Family member, brandishing a shotgun, ran to the front of the truck and fired two blasts directly at the bulletproof windshield. Kelly ducked, but the strength of the blasts knocked him unconscious. Simultaneously joining the raid from the bus stop, now flashing a pistol, was Balagoon. Another Family member opened up with an M16, striking Paige in the neck, arm, and chest. The guard bled to death in seconds. Trombino managed to get a shot off before he was hit in the shoulder. The round all but severed the limb. "I've got no arm!" he screamed. Though Trombino would survive, he never fully recovered the use of his left hand.

After the short firefight had quelled, the foot soldiers, Mtayari Sundiata among them, dashed to the back of the Brink's van. The crew grabbed six blood-smeared money sacks. Haul total: $1.6 million, though whether it was in haste or because of the sheer weight of the loot, the group left $1.3 million behind.

As the van sped away, Kelly regained consciousness. He exited the truck and found the badly injured Trombino. Cradling Trombino in his arms as bystanders approached the terrible scene, Kelly just repeated, "They shot my friends! They shot my friends!"

Though the assailants had worn masks, Kelly told arriving officers that he believed they were Black males.

The crew raced to their rendezvous point, across the Tappan Zee Bridge, at a rear loading dock of an abandoned Korvette department store, about a half-mile east of where the robbery had occurred. Waiting for them were Judy Clark in a tan-colored Honda and Marilyn Buck in a white Oldsmobile. And in a rented orange-and-black U-Haul truck sat two more white associates. The woman was a celebrity radical and member of a dynasty of left wing lawyers, activists, and thinkers. Her name was Kathy Boudin, former member of the Weather Underground, one of two survivors of the Greenwich Village townhouse explosion eleven years earlier who had fled the scene and been evading authorities ever since. Sitting next to her in the rented U-Haul was David Gilbert, a fellow Weather Underground veteran and wanted man in Colorado on assault and possession of explosives charges who'd joined Boudin in living off the grid. The couple had become parents during their time underground, and so needed to drop their fourteen-month-old son, Chesa, off with a babysitter that morning before driving the U-Haul to the pickup spot.

It was here that a crucial error occurred, the kind of error that Odinga had feared. Mutulu stopped the van a hundred feet short of the predetermined spot. It took the waiting comrades some time to spot them. When Gilbert finally did notice the van, he decided to pull up to the vehicle, rather than wait. The group quickly loaded their weapons and money sacks into the U-Haul, but the new rendezvous position put them in view of a single house on the unpaved lane. Watching on from the living room window was a startled college student working on a school assignment, who immediately called the Clarkstown police. "I just saw something strange happen behind Korvettes," she told the dispatcher. Though the student didn't get the license plate, she told police that the group had left in a U-Haul with a tan Honda following.

The information hit the police airwaves, finding its way to young officer Brian Lennon as he pulled his police cruiser across the single-lane entrance to the New York Thruway at Route 59 to form a roadblock. When Lennon stepped out of his vehicle, a shotgun in hand, three vehicles had already lined up in front of him. The first was the tan Honda. But Lennon's attention immediately went to the U-Haul a couple of cars behind. As he pointed his shotgun at the truck, Officer Waverly Brown and Sergeant Edward O'Grady pulled up in two Nyack police cars, with Detective Arthur Keenan following.

Spotting a white couple behind the windshield of the U-Haul put doubt in the cops' minds—dispatch had told them to be on the lookout for Black men. This was Mutulu's plan in action—to put his white edge in view. They were tactics that went all the way back to the Black Liberation Army, which would send Buck to obtain guns and ammunition so they'd be harder to connect to Black militants. As the couple stepped out of the truck, the woman bristled at the sight of Lennon's shotgun. "Tell him to put the gun back," she shouted toward the approaching O'Grady. Boudin's face may have been featured in many newspapers and FBI posters over the years, but it went unrecognized by the cops in front of her. Believing they had the wrong truck, O'Grady told Lennon to put his weapon aside. Lennon clambered back into his patrol car. *False alarm*, he thought. But Keenan wanted to be sure. He began poking around the back of the U-Haul, inquiring into what cargo lay within.

Inside the vehicle, the group quietly checked their clips. The sense of brotherhood that bonded them together for such a high-risk mission must have felt especially tight, only overwhelmed by the thought that, in mere seconds, they could be riddled with bullet holes. It was burned deep into the Family's ethos not to be taken by the enemy. That didn't leave a lot of options.

The silence was broken by Sundiata: "Well," he said, "let's get it on. It's on now."

Suddenly, the door flew open and the men emerged from the back. Once more the sound of gunfire rang out in suburbia. Sundiata was hit, but the round was stopped by his bulletproof vest. "If it wasn't for this vest," he later said, "I'd be dead now."

The cops, significantly less equipped for this kind of combat, weren't so lucky. Brown was shot and fell to the pavement. One of the masked men then walked over to the officer, took aim, and shot him with a 9-millimeter pistol, killing him. O'Grady managed to get six rounds off before needing to reload. He was shot with an M16 and later died on an operating table. Keenan too was hit, but managed to duck behind a tree and return fire. Lennon, still in his cruiser, tried to exit out the front passenger door, but O'Grady's slumped body had wedged it closed. Witnesses later identified Bouines as the gunman armed with the M16 who caused much of the damage, though investigators came to believe it to be Chui Ferguson.

When the crack of the shoot-out had subsided, the group scattered. Some made it to the front of the U-Haul van. As it pulled away in haste, it took fire from Lennon as he aimed his shotgun from inside his police car. Others carjacked a nearby motorist. Bouines, along with David Gilbert, who'd been driving the U-Haul, made it to the tan Honda driven by Clark. It proved a false savior. Attempting to escape, Clark lost control of the car and crashed. As cops descended on the vehicle, they noticed Clark reaching for something on the back seat—a pistol. But Clark was overpowered before grasping the sidearm and all three were taken into custody. As the only Black man arrested that day, Bouines would suffer terrible beatings at the hands of white jailers.

Watching on from the white Oldsmobile when the shooting started, Buck had attempted to draw her gun, but in the haste of the moment, accidentally shot herself in the leg. Bleeding and in pain, she clambered back into the Oldsmobile as Sundiata made it to the vehicle to escape the scene. He dismissed Buck's suggestion of letting her drive while he traveled in the trunk to avoid police: "I'll take my chances up front."

Chui Ferguson ran into the woods, where he spent a whole day and a half hiding out before making a phone call to the Family requesting his extraction. A spiritual soul, Ferguson passed the time by offering a prayer of thanks. "Praise the ancestors for the trees," he repeated. It's possible that Mutulu was with him too. Whatever the case, the mastermind escaped the chaos.

Meanwhile, off-duty corrections officer Michael J. Koch, just happening upon the scene of the shooting in his camper van, noticed a white woman fleeing on foot. Instinct told him she was no bystander, and so Koch chased her down. "Move and I'll blow out your fucking brains," he yelled, pistol drawn. When arrested, she gave her name as Barbara Edson. It wasn't long before her true identity came to light: it was Boudin, who'd had the wits to insist Lennon put away his shotgun, finally in custody after a decade on the run.

A few hours passed. Kamau Bayete, an associate of the Family, later testified that he received a telephone call from Sundiata, asking him to come to the group's safe house in Mount Vernon. "I recall him saying to me that people were hurt and he was hurt,"

Bayete said, "and he needed me to come up to his place to take care of some people, and he also said that someone would be coming around soon to bring me up there."

Bayete hightailed it to Mount Vernon with Panther 21 member Jamal Joseph, a woman named Iliana Robinson, who would later be put on trial for the robbery, and a second woman he knew as Ginger. "I'm all right, but I almost got killed," Joseph reportedly told Bayete in the car. Upon their arrival, Sundiata opened the door, clutching a 9-millimeter automatic. Buck was lying on a couch with her self-inflicted bullet wound. Bayete cleaned the injury and helped carry Buck out of the house to a van that was driven by Sekou Odinga, who had also arrived.

Within a day, cops discovered the safe house. By then, the Family had bolted, but not before the suspicious building superintendent had jotted down a few of their license plate numbers. It was that piece of information that made cops happen upon Sekou Odinga and Mtayari Sundiata driving through Queens in a Chrysler LeBaron two mornings later. Spotting the law on his tail, Odinga put his foot on the gas. The scene became incredible. When cops tried to sideswipe the LeBaron on its right-hand side, Sundiata rolled down his window and fended them off with pistol fire. Odinga's driving became increasingly desperate; after a twenty-minute chase, the car suffered a tire blowout. Abandoning the vehicle, the Family members opened fire once more before seeking refuge in a construction company yard. Sundiata was shot and killed—Odinga later claimed that his comrade was executed while lying face down on the ground. Cops poured into the area and found Odinga hiding under a van. Aware of his own 9-millimeter semiautomatic pistol, the soldier momentarily considered choosing, for better or worse, the way of the gun. Instead, he uttered the words "I give up." And with that, this dyed-in-blood revolutionary's globe-trotting quest for Black liberation was over.

Why the extreme violence of the Brink's raid? With grand re-creations, TV show *The FBI Files* depicted the gunmen as merciless, striking hard and fast with no regard for cherished human life. This has been the common narrative, denied by the likes of David

Gilbert, who has said, "The story of the combatants charging out shooting at the Brink's guard is a pure propaganda creation" and that "the only fire by revolutionaries that day was in response to a clear threat of fire."

The Brink's robbery wasn't just one of the bloodiest engagements of this era of revolutionary violence, it triggered its collapse. Militarism receded. The veterans were dead, in jail, on the lam, mentally scarred, addicted to drugs. The Family splintered. Judy Clark and Marilyn Buck, the latter left walking with a pronounced limp after taking that round to the leg, returned to a bombing campaign as part of the May 19th Communist Organization until finally being arrested by the FBI four years after the Big Dance.

As for Mutulu, he skipped town, leaving behind his ten-year-old stepson, Tupac, and the rest of the family. Continuing to evade capture, Mutulu was placed on the FBI's Ten Most Wanted list. Finding him was now a priority of every G-man in the country.

Despite this, Mutulu would sneak back into the neighborhood so he could wave at his children from a distance. About checking in on Tupac, Mutulu recalled, "When I would feel he needed me, I'd do whatever I had to to get there, even if it was just so that he could see me—and he'd wave, so happy."

Continuing their search, FBI agents would approach Tupac at school to discern if he had seen his stepfather.

"He had to keep secrets," Mutulu later said.

Candidate Kurt Schmoke on the campaign trail for mayor of Baltimore, Maryland, 1987

6

I AM SOCIETY'S CHILD

CRUCIAL IN UNDERSTANDING Tupac Shakur is knowing that he grew up in the rubble of 1960s radicalism. As a boy, he was raised to hold true to the core tenets of the Black Panthers, yet the group's failures—whether caused by its own weaknesses, or the unrelenting pressure of the FBI offensive—left an ash cloud from which he could not escape. Afeni Shakur was among the orphaned children of the revolution for whom the adrenaline and excitement of the Panthers' peak descended into sadness and pain. The last battles still needed to be fought—not least the quest to free incarcerated comrades. But letting go of the hope or expectation of a sudden and transformative change for Black people—the realization that any gains would only be incremental—must have festered in their souls. During Tupac's childhood, the language of reformism from his elders likely shifted subtly from talk of a beautiful future to the past tense discussions of lost glory days and bitter regret.

For Afeni, stability had collapsed into dust and tears. Mutulu was on the run. She'd lost her job as a paralegal, possibly because of her connection to one of America's most wanted. And the desperation deepened when Afeni once again began seeing Kenneth "Legs" Saunders. It was during this rekindling of their relationship that Legs introduced Afeni to crack cocaine. "That was our way of socializing," she later said. "He would come home late at night and stick a pipe in my mouth."

Crack, a hellish thing. Cheap, highly addictive, and quick to enter the bloodstream, it induces a psychological dependency in users that dwarfs most other drugs. Crack mutates a person's makeup. It does not just compel, it enslaves. Afeni's addiction would engulf her for years, repressing this once brilliant young activist and driving her to a nadir she'd describe as "the pit of the garbage can, underneath the corroded bottom of the garbage can, where only the maggots live."

Afeni's misfortune was not hers alone. Such was the extent of the drug's infiltration of America's poor and disenfranchised communities in the 1980s, and its ability to cruelly distort an addict's appearance and personality, descriptors like "crack fiends" and "base heads" becoming common parlance. These years were dubbed the "Crack Era" as media frenzy reached hysteria. And with the War on Drugs being waged with cultish dedication by its most fervent believer, Ronald Reagan, the government's primary tactic to suppress crack use was jail time. Inevitably, sentences were disproportionately handed out to Black people.

The government's insidious hand in the Crack Era was eventually exposed. After Congress blocked the financial support of a Nicaraguan right-wing rebel group known as the Contras in its opposition to the Marxist government, the Reagan administration, obsessed with stifling the spread of communism, began secretly selling arms to the Iran government in order to supply millions of dollars and weapons to the Contras, and, it's claimed, tolerated drug trafficking to the United States as long as it supported its cause.

Afeni sought to move the family out of New York City to the comparatively tranquil surroundings of White Plains, a suburban city twenty-five miles north of Manhattan. With Gloria Jean and her family, the Shakurs moved into a five-bedroom house in a largely Jewish and Italian neighborhood. Tupac adjusted to his new life relatively well. He enrolled in White Plains Middle School and earned some money by doing the most wholesome of American adolescent jobs—he was a paperboy. But the relocation didn't last a year. With much of her money being spent on crack, Afeni couldn't afford her portion of the rent, and so with her children she returned to New York, where the family slipped further into poverty.

When possible, they found temporary lodgings in the homes of old comrades. Many former Panthers were scattered across America's prisons, fugitives from the law, or enlisted in new clandestine organizations. Others attempted to piece together something resembling a normal life. Transitioning into this new existence was difficult without the same support network or sense of purpose they had previously enjoyed. Sometimes, it was a homeless shelter shielding Afeni, Tupac, and Sekyiwa from the grim, cold New York nights.

With his home life chaotic, Tupac tried to disappear into the arts. An attraction to poetry was displayed at age eleven, when he penned a collection of haikus and illustrations as a gift for four of Afeni and Mutulu's jailed comrades: Jamal Joseph, Chui Ferguson, Sekou Odinga, and Bilal Sunni Ali. Sketched out in pencil on clear white paper, it could pass at first glance as typical childhood scribbles, but upon closer inspection, these pages reveal that Tupac was being raised with an awareness of these men's beliefs and suffering.

"This is dedicated to my family who are imprisoned for trying to build a better nation for me," the booklet begins. "Stay strong."

There are poems that lay out Tupac's appreciation for sunsets and oceans—the kind of thing you'd expect an eleven-year-old to write. Yet others deal with Black self-determination, faith, and escapism. He signed the booklet, "Tupac Shakur. Future Freedom Fighter."

When Tupac was twelve, his cousin Scott introduced him to the 127th Street Repertory Ensemble, an accomplished Harlem acting troupe established to amplify Black stories. Not many kids were part of the group, and at first Tupac mostly observed the other actors, occasionally taking part in a drama scene or improv sketch. But it was with this group that he mastered a drama that proved crucial to his young artistic life: Lorraine Hansberry's *A Raisin in the Sun*. Tupac was handed the role of the mischievous Travis in a performance at Harlem's legendary Apollo Theater in 1984. The show was organized as a fundraiser for Reverend Jesse Jackson, who had hopes of becoming America's first Black president. Jackson spoke for an hour at the intermission, igniting fears backstage that the crowd wouldn't have the stamina to stay until the end of the play. These concerns proved unfounded. Tupac's performance received a rapturous reception. "The night of that show, something clicked onstage," recalled Levy Lee Simon, who played Travis's father, Walter Lee Younger. "When I was on the stage with him you could feel the electricity and feel the audience just focus in on him, and he was brilliant. He was *brilliant*. When he came out for curtain call the audience just went crazy."

Simon described a knuckleheaded boy who loved playing pranks and cracking jokes, "a bundle of energy." But that megawatt smile masked what was going on outside the safety of the ensemble. Seeking respite from a transient lifestyle, Sekyiwa would accompany her brother during rehearsals at the Apollo. Within the historic 125th Street venue, a monument of Black excellence, the siblings could enjoy the free food and temporary shelter. When members of the company chipped in some money for Tupac's birthday, he used the funds not to treat himself, but to buy groceries for the family.

Tupac also performed in *A Raisin in the Sun* over the summer at Walden School, a private institute in Manhattan. But his time with the group was cut short. Maybe too much had happened in New York that weighed on Afeni's heart. Maybe she thought she could outrun her addiction. But the decision was made to seek new pastures for her and her two children. There'd be no Eden to abscond to. Instead, a fresh start was sought three hours away, in Baltimore, where her aunt Sharon on her father's side agreed to take the family in. So, in 1984, when Tupac was thirteen, the family left New York.

By this point, Legs was in prison for credit card fraud. Upon arriving in Baltimore, Afeni phoned him in jail to check in. A voice on the other end of the line broke the news. At age forty-one, Legs had died of a crack-induced heart attack. The news wounded Tupac, who within the framework of this imperfect, absent man had attempted to manufacture some kind of father figure. "I miss my daddy," he told Afeni.

Pilgrimage sites on the hip-hop landscape don't get more imposing than the Enoch Pratt Free Library. This concrete mausoleum stands on Cathedral Hill, north of downtown Baltimore, in the cultural Mount Vernon neighborhood, exuding a mood of scholarly importance, a monument to human enlightenment. The lobby is vast and beautiful, adorned by looming pillars and decorative greenery. Journey farther within and the library feels like a real masterpiece in symmetry, with spotless halls and bookshelves laid out almost impossibly straight across both wings, like an architectural Rorschach test.

As the years passed after Tupac's death, and the magnitude of his legacy became apparent, there were maneuvers within Baltimore to ensure that the city is considered an essential part of the story. A 2016 article in *Baltimore* magazine titled "Tupac Was Here" attempted to solidify his links to Maryland's biggest city. The piece revealed that some of a teenage Tupac's "handwritten verses now reside in the Pratt's Special Collections archive, alongside works by H. L. Mencken and Edgar Allan Poe," connecting him with two of Baltimore's greatest writers and most famous sons. In early 2023, I journeyed to the library hoping to see these pages. But my initial attempts were foiled. Turned out, "Special Collections" means appointment only.

"Can I make an appointment?" was the natural next question to section librarian Debra Elfenbein. She accommodated my request.

I arrived at the Special Collections office a little early the next day to view the material, stepping into a solemn, scholarly-looking room—appropriately pristine and practically dustless—and I was surprised to see that Elfenbein had already carefully laid the pages out on a table for examination. Maybe because, by this point, I'd spent a year thinking about Tupac Shakur, or maybe because he's a figure who commands a certain sense of historic gravitas, the moment ignited a jolt in my chest. *These are pages he handled; his pen actually hit this paper.* Only a small percentage of dead human beings can evoke this feeling. No matter how many times you see a person through a screen or hear recordings of their voice, there's something personal about sharing the same physical space with something they created or an object they cherished. Time doesn't dull that sensation—in fact, it heightens it. As years pass, the more impressive it is to see surviving artifacts. Elfenbein showed me both the original pages and some perfect copies, all protected by plastic.

Despite this shield, I passed on touching the original notes, too anxious about adding even a minor crease to the precious parchment.

The library has been in possession of Tupac's pages since 1985, long before they really meant anything to the larger world. (It's impressive, really, that a member of staff even had the notion to root them out of the archives.) Tupac had been in Baltimore for about a year when he spotted a splashy flier with the signal "Calling All Rappers!" The advertisement encouraged anyone under the age of eighteen to write and perform a rap about the Pratt Library to win a cash prize. Lyrics needed to be submitted to organizers in advance—"No Profanity Allowed," of course. And so Tupac, with his friend Dana "Mouse" Smith, a local kid and skilled beatboxer, created "Library Rap." Tupac wrote the lyrics out in black pen on a piece of lined notebook paper that now is preserved in the institute, alongside an original flier advertising the competition.

Semifinals took place in a smaller branch in the Enoch Pratt Library network and the two boys breezed through. There was just one snag: they didn't have a ride to the final. Fortunately, event organizer Deborah Taylor, fond of the pair and impressed with their talent, offered to pick them up from Tupac's home herself. Her faith in them proved to be well-placed—Tupac and Mouse took first place.

Looking through Tupac's lyrics thirty-seven years later, I wondered where in the building the event took place. Elfenbein had no idea, and I worried that this was a detail that could be lost to history if someone didn't memorialize it. Fortunately, knowledge soon entered the room. It was Special Collections secretary Davetta F. Parker, a forty-nine-year veteran of the library. She told me the event was in Wheeler Auditorium, a two-hundred-plus-capacity meeting room located on the third floor.

"It was the kids that were doing the judging," Parker recalled of the event. "We had three people and they were asking the kids to clap," she said, beginning to applaud herself, "and the one who gets the most claps wins.

"That was the start, right there," she said of Tupac's musical voyage. "It started upstairs."

Equipped with new information, I made a stop at Wheeler Auditorium. An event was in progress, meaning it was just a quick peek at the midsized seated venue with an elevated stage. I can see why performing there would be a big deal for kid rappers. Later, I reread the lyrics that Tupac penned and tried to picture him and Mouse igniting the room.

"Yo' Enoch Pratt, bust this!" the young rapper shouted to the crowd, using an expression he'd later resurrect on one of his biggest hits, "I Get Around." From there, he urged Baltimore's kids to sign up for library cards, stay in school, and work on their course credit. Like most early hip-hop, the lyrics and rhyme patterns were rudimentary—"Enoch Pratt it's your birthday, so why don't you listen to what I say / Because reading and writing is important to me, that's why I visit the Pratt Library." But "Library Rap" was fun, it fulfilled the brief, and it captured fourteen-year-old Tupac's burgeoning love for rapping as a form of expression. Baltimore, it would transpire, would be crucial in progressing his love of not just rap, but the arts. The rapper, actor, and thinker that we know could not have come to be without this detour.

Arriving in the city in 1984, a year before the library performance, the Shakur family moved into the first-floor apartment of a brick row house at 3955 Greenmount Avenue in the small, impoverished North Baltimore neighborhood of Pen Lucy. It was the home of Sharon's daughter, Lisa, and her son, Jamal, who, fortuitously, were preparing to move. Once the apartment was the Shakurs' alone, Tupac slept in a small bedroom, while a converted dining room served as Afeni and Sekyiwa's dormitory. These days, the building is something of a sacred site for fans. Neighbors regularly spot them wandering the street, iPhones in hand, trying to locate it.

Tupac was enrolled at Roland Park Middle School for eighth grade. Immediately, the out-of-towner attracted the attention of his classmates. Kids bristled at the New Yorker with the unusual name, mouth full of braces, and lopsided Gumby haircut. And what, they wondered, was up with his pants? Thin, blue, and baggy, they looked like surgical scrubs, with staples visible across each hem as a makeshift way of making them fit.

The new kid didn't stand out just because of his threads and name. He possessed a certain profundity that seemed strange to his new classmates. On his third day of school, students were assigned by a music teacher to recite an original poem. No one took the homework seriously—except for Tupac, who presented a piece that detailed his love for a girl. "It was a masterful consideration of the finer nuance in the relationship between love and beauty, true beauty, and how the latter had set ablaze the former," wrote classmate Darrin Keith Bastfield in his memoir *Back in the Day: My Life and Times with Tupac Shakur.* "So well thought out and skillfully presented was this unmatched piece that not even the most ignorant and defiant attempted to satirize or ridicule."

As Tupac settled into Baltimore, hip-hop was expanding from his native New York into the rest of America. Tupac wasn't the only kid enthralled with the sounds and style of this new culture. In September 1984, destiny dictated that he take a seat next to Dana "Mouse" Smith on the bus home from school. Mouse was in a hurry: radio station WEBB's *Rap Attack* show started at four p.m. and he always rushed to catch the start of it. The pair struck up a conversation and Mouse, who'd often lead chants of the latest jam among his schoolmates at Roland Park, asked if Tupac was into hip-hop. Proving he wasn't just saying yes for the sake of it, Tupac kicked a rhyme on the spot. Smith later learned the rap wasn't original—it was actually lifted from a song by New York rapper Kurtis Blow that hadn't yet made it to Baltimore. Perhaps Tupac cunningly calculated this.

A friendship was immediately formed. Tupac wasn't superpopular in the neighborhood; Mouse was often questioned about his association with the new kid, why he hung around such an odd-looking transplant. But Mouse recognized the talent and the passion, and their mutual interest in hip-hop blossomed into musical collaboration. At some point, Tupac assumed the name of MC New York, holding tightly his birthplace as he formed his artistic identity. Every day, he and Mouse honed their act at playgrounds, a local rec center, or at their homes. One playground had a large plastic bubble with a metal pole in the middle for kids to slide down, offering a sheltered area for neighborhood hustlers, but also some interesting acoustics. For two Black boys, though, just being out in public brought the risk of being hassled by cops. A caged-in basketball court was one of the law's favorite spots to shake down random kids—once they made their move it was difficult for their targets to escape. On one particular day, Tupac was the one caught inside. Cops forced him to take off his shoes during a search. It was an early run-in with police but not his last or most violent.

A reward for Tupac and Mouse's endeavor came in February 1985, when they scored a gig supporting rap group Mantronix at the Cherry Hill rec center in South Baltimore. For two precocious amateurs, this was a boon. From New York, and signed to Sleeping Bag Records, Mantronix were pioneering a blend of hip-hop and electro funk. The group were three months away from putting out a debut album that would find its way beyond rap circles and into the respected British rock publications *Melody Maker* and *NME*. And it's not as though Tupac and Mouse would be warming up just a handful of early arrivals. Their set was to be tucked in after a performance by Just-Ice, another rising New York emcee of whom Mouse was already a fan.

The duo, alongside their DJ for the night, a slightly older local artist named Buddha, looked on as the visiting grandees set up from the side of the stage. When they first spied the leader of the group, Kurtis Mantronik, they got a surprise: "Yo, Mantronix white!" (He is, in fact, half Jamaican, half Syrian.) But his turntable skills were like nothing they had ever seen before, a reminder if they needed it that they were in the company of major league talent.

This was the prime era for old-school hip-hop, when the message rarely veered from one's propensity to party, electronic percussion tested the sturdiest beatboxes, and disciples dressed in robes designed by Adidas. For the night, the rec center was transformed into an outpost of Planet Rock. After Just-Ice and his beatboxer DMX (not to be confused with Earl Simmons, the growling Ruff Ryders rapper who also went by that name) smashed out their set in style, it was Tupac and Mouse's moment. Backed by Buddha, and announced as the Eastside Crew, the two young teenagers let their dreams play out in real life. They opened with "N***a Please," a song they'd written about a smooth-operating ladies' man, Tupac rhyming and Mouse providing a slow drumbeat he only broke from to yell the title. Their stage generalship needed refining—rather than really work the space, the two friends stayed close to each other, as if tied together by string—but the boys acquitted themselves with pride.

The Baltimore Tupac knew had a way of puncturing such innocent scenes. The event was temporarily suspended when, sometime before or after Tupac and Mouse's set, someone in the hall fired a gun.

In the crowd that night was the promoter who had brought Mantronix to perform in his native Cherry Hill: Virgil Simms of Sleeping Bag Records. Tupac had been eager to meet Simms. The connection came through a man in the neighborhood named Roger, who had industry ties and served as something of a mentor to the boys, even driving them to the show that night. It was Roger who got Tupac and Mouse on the bill in the first place. "We don't do that for anybody, unless you know somebody, and Roger we knew," Simms told me.

He remembered the crowd's reaction to the boys' performance as lukewarm, but he saw a lot in the young act to admire. "Nice-looking kid. And he had star quality," Simms said of Tupac. "Back then, you had to have a stage presence, and they had good stage presence."

In the show's aftermath, a meeting at the local radio station WEBB was set up. Tupac had been putting it around town that Simms loved the group and wanted to sign them. Simms told me he was "somewhat" interested, but in the end the whole thing fizzled. For one, Afeni wasn't about to let her thirteen-year-old son link up with some industry merchants she didn't know anything about.

With their aspirations stifled—for now—Tupac and Mouse prepared for high school. While Mouse went to Northern High, the zoned school for the neighborhood, Afeni sent Tupac to Paul Laurence Dunbar High. But Tupac couldn't settle there. He largely kept to himself, drafting love letters to a girl named Averil. Some were juvenile and unsophisticated. "I love you so much, and I would like for us to become closer," he scrawled before spelling his name out phonetically for her convenience. (Oddly, he describes his name as Puerto Rican and himself as one-quarter Puerto Rican.) In another letter, the language was more grown-up: "With every beat of my humble heart I think of you. I daydream about kissing and caressing your graceful body. My body aches to be loved and to be joined with yours." Both letters end with Tupac asking Averil to write back to him.

His time at Paul Laurence Dunbar High didn't extend beyond a year. Soon the opportunity arose to apply for the Baltimore School for the Arts (BSA). Getting in was based entirely on potential in the arts—grades did not factor into admissions. For the audition, Tupac reached into the past and performed a scene from *A Raisin in the Sun*, this time as Walter Lee, the father of the character he had previously excelled as. For weeks he ran lines with Mouse as his stand-in costar, again and again, perfecting the piece. When the day finally came, he wore a hat and sport coat to invoke the character. The audition lasted less than five minutes, but staff quickly recognized he had a gift. "The empathy, the mimetic instinct, the emotional connection, the vulnerability," theater department head Donald Hicken later said. "He had all of that."

The faculty may not have realized the ordeal Tupac had gone through as he walked through the doors of BSA. As he approached the entrance, a carload of white strangers without warning shouted the N-word in his direction. It was drive-by racism that echoed what Afeni had experienced in Lumberton three decades earlier.

Never deterred, in September 1986, Tupac enrolled at the school.

The American high school possesses its own mythology. It's rooted in the iconography of 1950s rock 'n' roll cool and the muscle cars, milkshakes, and male greasers. It winds its way through to *The Breakfast Club*, Marty McFly, and Kelly Kapowski. Such idealized images were once screened in my home in Ireland via the portals of VHS tapes and Nickelodeon. These starburst counterpoints to our relentlessly gray "school daze" looked like a different existence.

The escort on my visit to the Baltimore School for the Arts in 2023 was Becky Mossing, head of the theater department, BSA class of '88 alumna, and childhood friend of Tupac Shakur. Pinned to the wall of Mossing's shared office, in its original packaging, was an action figure of the character Reva Sevander from the *Star Wars* TV show *Obi-Wan Kenobi*. To the teachers, it's a mold of Moses Ingram, another BSA graduate.

"I just had a student in here crying. Because she's a freshperson," said Mossing, using a term the administration prefers to "freshman." "Our spring break starts at the end of school tomorrow. So she got homework and was like, 'I don't want homework during spring break.'"

They're not like me and my childhood classmates, these kids. They are not forced into conformity; they're not going to get in trouble because their uniforms are incomplete, or shoes don't achieve required levels of formality. Those sweaters, shirts, and slacks were the perfect visual motif for my Irish Catholic school's chief tactic: to suppress our individuality and impoverish our imaginations. For us, 2Pac and the rappers of his generation offered something of an escape. We'd sneak headphones on when we could, or assemble in someone's living room at a nearby home during lunch break to listen to CDs: Wu-Tang Clan, Dr. Dre, Nas. Yet for Tupac, escape was encouraged—no, required—at BSA. Teachers wanted him to disappear into other realms.

As Mossing and I roamed the halls, I saw students hanging around, sitting on the floor, loitering in classrooms unattended. "Do kids here get a lot of leeway?" I asked. She insisted they don't. Fair enough. But it bent my brain when one entered her office with no purpose but to tell the faculty a joke.

Entering BSA as a sophomore, Tupac moved to a school where there were no sports teams or jock culture. For a sensitive, artistic kid, it was a haven. Freshmen and sophomore students began their day with arts classes. For Tupac, this meant lessons in diction, articulation, movement, voice, and acting. After lunch, there were academic classes, including social studies, English literature, math, and science. In students' junior and senior years, it switched to academic classes in the morning and arts in the afternoon. Arts classes adjusted to include musical theater, classical texts—Shakespeare, Molière, Ben Jonson—and more performance-based work.

Despite the workload, Tupac found time to write for himself, scribbling poetry, thoughts, and ideas in a notebook. Sometimes, in homeroom, the kids would sit in a circle and share what they'd written. In these moments, BSA offered Tupac space to read his verses and receive validation of his talent. Mossing would listen on and think, *Holy fucking shit, when did he have a moment to write that? How would he ever think of something like that?*

Tupac's interests veered from Shakespeare's *King Lear* and *Hamlet* to van Gogh. He empathized with van Gogh's inability to be understood in his own lifetime. But Shakespeare? Well, Shakespeare hit home. For the rest of his life, Tupac would regularly observe parallels in the playwright's work with the world around him. "I love Shakespeare. He wrote some of the rawest stories, man," Tupac told the *Los Angeles Times* in 1995, positing that *Romeo and Juliet* was "some serious ghetto shit. You got this guy Romeo from the Bloods who falls for Juliet, a female from the Crips, and everybody in both gangs are against them. So they have to sneak out and they end up dead for nothing. Real tragic stuff.

"And look how Shakespeare busts it up with Macbeth. He creates a tale about this king's wife who convinces a happy man to chase after her and kill her husband so he can take over the country. After he commits the murder, the dude starts having delusions just like in a Scarface song. I mean the king's wife just screws this guy's whole life up for nothing. Now that's what I call a bitch."

As an actor, Tupac was malleable. He could synchronize his body, his voice, his form in a manner that was graceful and free-flowing. Teachers would give him notes and he'd immediately make the adjustment. "I think it was one of the reasons he was such an incredible rapper," said Mossing. "You could say, 'Here are the ideas, rap about them,' and he would. He could just take all of that in and make it mean something and make it rhyme so brilliantly. He just had that ability to synchronize everything fluidly, immediately. He just had this brain that just worked so quickly. He was brilliant in that way. I was always astounded by that ability to think that quickly."

Tupac enjoyed sliding into characters. One he named Redbone, a drunken old man who'd stumble around, slurring words.

Tupac could spend several days performing as Redbone, so much so that his refusal to break character would eventually grate on friends.

Social groups at BSA skidded across racial divides. About half of the school was white, a sharp contrast to the mostly Black circles Tupac was raised in, and students talked openly about what it meant to be members of their race in America. Darrin Keith Bastfield observed that, at times, Tupac acted a little differently around white people, as though he was striving to prove his intellectual nature to them. Perhaps he was aware of the potential for racial biases and, consciously or unconsciously, felt motivated to prove them wrong. But he was popular around school, comfortable in all crowds, and recognized as being a magnetic talent. During one prom, he hardly left the dance floor. But he was also private. Of course, Tupac couldn't hide his socioeconomic status—coming from Greenmount Avenue had certain connotations, reinforced by the fact that he never wore expensive clothes. He spent many a lunch break in the library, and not just because he was a ravenous reader. Bastfield realized that it was because he didn't want the other kids to notice that, like Afeni at a performing arts school years earlier, he had no lunch money. Word got around that his mother had been a Panther, but most kids knew nothing of Assata, or Geronimo, or Lumumba. Whether he wanted to forget, or whether he wanted to fit in, Tupac said little of the family tree of revolutionaries from which he sprang.

Sekyiwa was forced to contend with the sheer otherness of her parentage when her school organized a field trip to an FBI office. Mindful of her family's conflicts with the bureau, she precluded herself from the visit. But when her classmates returned, they informed Sekyiwa of the photograph of her father, Mutulu Shakur, that decorated the FBI's walls as a wanted fugitive. "You look just like him," Sekyiwa was reminded.

On what appeared like it was going to be a lean Christmas Day at 3955 Greenmount Avenue, there was a knock on the door. It was the principal of Sekyiwa's school. Charitable levers had been pulled to provide the Shakur family with turkey, cheese, beans, butter, and other treats. Tupac got a pair of cheap boots as a present. He'd later refer to it as his best Christmas memory.

Poverty influenced Tupac's socialism. A constant thread in his political ideology throughout his life would be a deep resentment of wealth inequality. Personal experience was channeled into organized political activism when he began dating a white girl with reddish hair named Mary Baldridge, who studied in BSA's dance department. Mary's father, Jim Baldridge, was director of the Communist Party in Baltimore. Though he was once a navy man, by 1969 Jim had resolved to resist the American war machine, and he and his wife, Margaret, were arrested for defacing recruitment posters for the Vietnam War. A year or so later, Margaret was involved in the struggle to free Angela Davis. These parents fostered the Red spirit in their daughter. After an enlightening trip to Cuba, Mary founded the Baltimore chapter of the Young Communist League, and through her, Tupac became a member.

On June 16, 2019, the day that would have been Tupac's forty-eighth birthday, the Communist Party USA offered its best wishes. "Happy birthday to our brother and comrade," the party's official Twitter account posted. Accompanying the text was an image of a very simple membership card filled out in scrawled handwriting. "This is his Young Communist League membership card from when he lived in Baltimore, Maryland." Furthering the links to its most famous alumnus, the Young Communist League branch in Baltimore has been named the Tupac Shakur Club in his memory.

As a member, Tupac attended meetings with Mary, discussing ideas for a more just and equitable society. They also joined the Yo-No anti–gun violence campaign, run by influential local activist Truxon Sykes. Tupac's connection to Sykes came after Sekyiwa befriended a girl who appeared to be his daughter. In fact, they weren't related at all. The girl's mother had asked the community leader if he could look after her for a couple of hours and he obliged. Two years passed by and still the mother had not returned. Nonetheless, Sykes continued to honor his word, becoming the girl's guardian. He became a mentor to Tupac too, schooling the boy on the inner workings of gentrification and police corruption.

Tupac and Mary's political interest extended to electoral politics and the 1987 Baltimore city mayoral election. In Democrat Kurt Schmoke, the father of fellow BSA student Gregory, Tupac found a Black politician who reflected his worldview. Alongside Mary, he'd go door-to-door, informing potential voters of Schmoke's progressive program, which included staunch criticism of Reagan's War on Drugs. At a town hall meeting, Tupac spoke about poor people in his community—people who couldn't even afford to have the windows on their homes repaired—and the drug dealers who drove Mercedes and wore thousand-dollar suits and Rolex watches. "If you're a kid growing up, and you're taking a look at those two situations, who do you think the winners are?" Tupac asked the audience. Schmoke won that election and spent twelve years in office.

Tupac had been raised by Afeni to be politically minded, but it must have been thrilling for him to start to prove himself as an independent political activist and thinker, partially facilitated by Mary Baldridge, whose white activist background gave him a fresh perspective.

Socially, Tupac was a regular attendee at parties thrown by Becky Mossing, who came from a middle-class Jewish background. The Mossing household had a basement with a pool table and access to the woods next to the home, a space for BSA kids to hang out, smoke pot, and drink alcohol. Sometimes the parties would go so late the Metro would stop running, and everyone left behind would be allowed to sleep over.

Mossing remembered one particular party where Tupac and friend Gerard Young (who'd go on to have a successful career in music as DJ Ge-ology) wanted to spin records. Deeming the record player in the basement to be insufficient, they inquired about the really good piece of kit upstairs in the family living room. It was Tupac who entered into conference with Mossing's father to bring the record player downstairs. The request was granted. Gerard left early, but Tupac spent the night. When Becky woke up the next morning, Tupac was gone, but she found the record player was back upstairs in its rightful place, plugged in and ready to use, like it had never been disturbed.

The layout of the BSA building has changed since Mossing and Tupac were teenagers. The school has grown to swallow up alleyways where kids in her day would sneak cigarettes. But most notable is a small box theater that's been called the Tupac Amaru Shakur Theatre, being prepared during my visit for a production of *Rent*. A large sign outside the theater, in the school's main hall, announces who funded its creation: Jada Pinkett Smith.

The close friendship that Tupac and Jada (then just Pinkett) formed at BSA is one of the most combed-through aspects of his adolescence, the world demanding a classic Shakespearean romance between two talented teens whose destinies would diverge as adults, one's life path a doomed highway of trouble and infamy that led to a violent death, the other's a glitzy rise to the peaks of American celebrity. (If Tupac is the school's most famous alumnus, Jada is the second most famous.) Truth is, though their bond was tight, it was never romantic. Like Tupac, Jada was from a rough neighborhood and had a mother who struggled with addiction—in her case, heroin. The Panther cub schooled Jada on the fallen party and on Malcolm X; they would talk about "making it," Tupac assuring Jada that she had star quality.

There's a clip of the pair miming to DJ Jazzy Jeff and the Fresh Prince's 1988 single "Parents Just Don't Understand" that pops up online from time to time. "Oh, Kings Dominion," said Mossing when I asked about it, remembering a local amusement park. "We used to go there all the time." The footage was recorded in a booth where you could pay to make your own music video. Tupac, lithe and skinny, is seen wearing a black vest, with Jada in a tomboyish T-shirt, shorts, and sneakers. They mime the lyrics, manically jerking their bodies to the music. It's a goofy rendition, two kids half pretending they're superstars, half just being silly. That they selected a track by Jada's future husband, Will Smith, adds a whole other level of fun to the video.

Also in their circle of friends was John Cole, who dated Jada for a time. A white boy from BSA with a passion for visual arts, John grew close to Tupac. Contrasting backgrounds proved no obstacle to their friendship. John too had grown up without his biological father around, and like Tupac, he cared little for macho bravado. Tupac began spending much of his time at John's family home in the upper-middle-class neighborhood of Bolton Hill, an escape from his own house, where Jada discovered he slept on a mattress with no sheets and even meals could be in scarce supply. When the opportunity arose to move with John to an apartment rented by John's older brother, Tupac grabbed it. Perhaps it was the excitement of independence, or maybe the weight of living under the same roof with his mother and her addiction pressed down too heavy on Tupac. Whatever the case, Tupac and John were happy to take the apartment's two couches. But when John and his brother eventually moved out, Tupac was left with the one remaining roommate, Richard, an older, free-spirited white guy who dug music. To stay, Tupac was expected to stump up $350 a week, and so he worked busing tables and washing dishes at an Inner Harbor restaurant.

Mossing showed me BSA's dance studios. Tupac's lean, muscular physique made the school's dance department eager to use him, and he took part in recitals of Stravinsky's ballet *The Firebird*. Even off the clock, he'd frequently sneak down to check out the girls. And Tupac loved girls. By all accounts, he was a libertine teenager who boorishly enjoyed their attention. But he was also capable of extreme tenderness, particularly through the written word. In that manner, his teen years predicted his musical output, swerving from loutish to tender, misogynistic to loving.

It was the dance studios where Tupac, Bastfield, and Gerard Young sought to recruit some participants to star in their drama skit performed with rapped dialogue titled "I Wannabe Your Man" for the school's annual Spring Fever showcase. The piece cast Tupac as the jock and Darrin as the nerd who eventually wins the girl. But they didn't get past the audition stage. So the next day, Tupac and Mouse, by now a BSA student too, tried out with a song titled "Babies Having Babies," a social commentary on teen pregnancies that predicted one of 2Pac's most celebrated songs, "Brenda's Got a Baby." It was a progressive piece, with the boys taking turns on the mic, probing society's tendency to condemn young pregnant girls, encouraging the use of contraception, and calling out absent fathers. Though still a kid himself, Tupac's compassion blossomed alongside his artistic talent. He was already savvy enough to recognize rap as a way of capturing and pushing back against the grim inequities of the world.

Tupac's awareness of the injustices heaped on poor communities, in Baltimore and beyond, was noticed by the staff at BSA. "He lived in a very rough part of town," Donald Hicken recalled. "He had a real clear, I guess you'd say, revolutionary perspective on the world." But the Spring Fever organizers were no more impressed with "Babies Having Babies" than they'd been with "I Wannabe Your Man." Tupac finally made the cut by performing a section of *A Raisin in the Sun* with some of the other theater students, again as Walter Lee Younger—a signal in his young life that his motivation to make art was going to, at times, bump up against the politics of respectability. Still, the fruits of Tupac, Mouse, Young, and Bastfield's friendship and musical interests culminated in the formation of a rap group, Born Busy. The friends made rough tapes in 1987 that are considered Tupac's first recordings, including an a cappella version of "Babies Having Babies." "We rapped, wrote our stuff, and worked every day," said Bastfield. "Our songs spoke about loyalty and friendship. We were big on that."

One day, Richard Pilcher, principal acting teacher at the school, heard that Tupac had been raised to believe white people are the devil. Dubbing the white man the devil was generally not Panther doctrine but a practice of the Nation of Islam. White people can get tetchy about this, but if you are religious and believe in the devil and his ability to manipulate what happens on this planet, and white people had orchestrated so many evils on your people, why wouldn't you come to the conclusion that they are his tool? The concept was likely not drummed into Tupac in a spiritual sense, but he was no doubt exposed to the idea.

The language of his upbringing could rattle the sheltered among BSA's student body. Mossing, with embarrassment, remembered yelling at Tupac for using the N-word. Decades on, it's his response to her illegitimate complaints that she finds noteworthy. Cornering him in the BSA lobby, Mossing insisted, "I don't like you using that word. That word is derogatory. I have a visceral reaction to that word. I don't want you using it."

"I'm taking that word back," replied Tupac. "I'm using it to empower me."

It's interesting to me that in her pursuit of describing the Tupac she knew, Mossing would tell a story in which she is so clearly the villain. "It's awful that I said it," she explained, "but it was 1986, and I was this young, innocent, privileged white girl, like, what the hell do I know? . . . I was this little immature [girl]. What did I know in that moment? And clearly [I had] not deeply understood where he had come from. But to his credit he said, 'I won't use it around you.'"

One of the expressions Mossing kept reaching for to describe BSA during our conversations was "safe space." Thinking about my visit, and the comforts enjoyed by the student body, I wondered if the middle-class art kids in Tupac's peer group could possibly have grasped some of the realities from which he required shielding. In February 1986, seven months before he began life at BSA, Tupac's stepfather, Mutulu Shakur, now thirty-five years old, was finally arrested in Los Angeles. It took over two years for the case to wind its way through the court system, but eventually Mutulu and Marilyn Buck—also a fugitive until her capture in a diner in Dobbs Ferry, New York, in 1985—were found guilty in federal district court in Manhattan of eight charges relating to the 1981 Brink's robbery, several more robberies, and the 1979 prison escape of Assata Shakur.

To prove Mutulu was the leader of the well-drilled group and Buck as crucial to its secondary team, the prosecution presented one hundred witnesses. None were more devastating to the defendants than their former comrade Tyrone Rison, who admitted having committed many crimes in his time with the Family, including a killing. He pleaded guilty and received a twelve-year sentence.

Mutulu was sentenced to sixty years; Buck was handed fifty years. The judge, Charles Haight, described them as "gifted and capable people who crossed the line into deadly violence that mocks compassion." Both defendants remained defiant to the last. Buck, wearing a floral print dress, told Haight she was committed to battling "the malignant cancer of racism." She was already serving fifteen years in prison on other convictions and under indictment with six other people in Washington for a series of protest bombings, including the May 19th Communist Organization's 1983 bombing of the U.S. Capitol.

"I am not guilty of any criminal act," said Mutulu, dressed in a gray suit, to the applause of his supporters in the courtroom. "I am a freedom fighter."

About a week before Mutulu's arrest, Lumumba Shakur was found shot to death in his home in New Orleans. He had moved to the city as a single father raising twins and was making a living by importing African goods. "It took the ambulance something like forty-five minutes to come," claimed Jennifer Dohrn, who attended Lumumba's funeral.

The proximity of Lumumba's death to his own arrest sparked notions in Mutulu that the two were linked. Said Dohrn, "A lot of people thought, well . . . I never knew if it was a personal thing that happened and he was shot, or if it was a political thing."

In 1988, Tupac's progress at BSA came to an abrupt halt. With his junior year coming to an end, the boy cried in the office of the theater department's Donald Hicken as he delivered the news: he was leaving town with his mother and sister. Hicken, too, was disappointed. He had already mapped out Tupac's senior year, which at BSA is dedicated to technique development through rehearsals and performances. Hicken offered to find a host family so the student could stay for his senior year, but Tupac declined—he just couldn't become separated from his family. Tupac left Baltimore that summer and journeyed west, to California, the fabled state that he'd absorb into his burgeoning artistic identity.

A voice-over tries to make sense of what we're witnessing. "On the other side of the Golden Gate Bridge from San Francisco," says veteran newsman Edwin Newman, "a woman can buy the services of two nude masseurs." On-screen is the client, lying naked on a table, peacock feathers being stroked across her body. This woman, Newman explains, has paid $180 for a four-hour service that includes being bathed, cradled in a hot tub, and massaged.

"How could I be so lucky?" the woman asks, eyes shut so she can fully experience the sensation of the ornate plumes, a symbol of decadence, being carefully swabbed across her skin.

So begins *I Want It All Now!*, a 1978 television documentary focusing on a strand of people living in Marin County, California, and their affluent, hedonistic lifestyles. Newman's reporting captures the then-popular Human Potential Movement, a belief system that professes to help people achieve happiness, creativity, and fulfillment in their lives. But despite the wealth and picturesque setting, *I Want It All Now!* goes to great lengths to expose Marin County's sad underbelly. A high divorce rate is used as an excuse to ask kids leading questions about their parents' breakups. The suicide rate is said to be twice the national average—the Golden Gate Bridge providing one such method of carrying out a Bay Area seppuku. Because as one interview subject sees it, when people realize they can't find happiness in paradise, they're bound to be driven to the edge.

Invisible in *I Want It All Now!* are Black people. "There are people here who are poor, and a few who are Black," says Newman. "But for the most part this is a golden ghetto by the Golden Gate— white upper-middle-class people who seem to have it all."

Perhaps Newman's observations would have been somewhat different if he'd traveled to the southern tip of Marin County, to Marin City, a pocket of urban poverty and towering housing projects, where Tupac Shakur would move a decade later. No mention of his history in Marin City passes without stating its nickname: the Jungle. Yet a second alias has also appeared in the media: the "gilded ghetto," a reference to the wealth that surrounds it.

Marin City rose during the Second World War, when neighboring Sausalito evolved into a huge shipbuilding center. As many as seventy-five thousand workers were employed to build the boats, many of them Black people recruited from the South. Five decades later, Marin City was a mostly Black community in a county that was 90 percent white. A 1992 article in the *Los Angeles Times* revealed it had no supermarket, doctor, post office, or public school—though you could always get a bite to eat at the hot dog stand. Marin City's unemployment rate was nearly ten times the county average. One-quarter of its two thousand residents lived below the poverty line. Crack cocaine was everywhere.

Tupac and Sekyiwa were initially sent to Marin City while Afeni temporarily stayed put in Baltimore. For a time, they resided at the home of Geronimo Pratt's wife, Ashaki, and their two children, Hiroji and Shona, just eight miles from San Quentin State Prison, where Geronimo was held. When Afeni finally did show up months later, it was with nothing but a suitcase and purse. She had abandoned the rest of the family's possessions to once again start over.

To continue his eduction, Tupac enrolled at Tamalpais High School, in nearby Mill Valley. It wasn't a specialized arts institute like BSA, but he clung to his artistic practice. At the school, Tupac performed in Chekhov's *The Bear*. Teacher Barbara Owens also asked him to take the title role in a production of Shakespeare's *Othello*, the intelligent and confident military leader, but as a Black man, an outsider in Venice. So impressed was Owens with Tupac's reading of a scene where Othello considers killing Desdemona that she paused the performance. "I want you all to remember this moment," she told the class. "You will never ever, in your lifetime, hear Othello as well as you just heard it now."

Tupac volunteered to appear in an original play penned by a student teacher to honor Martin Luther King Jr., but the second of three performances had to be cancelled when he failed to turn up. When the young actor finally did manifest, he gave various excuses to his seething costars. Scene partner Liza was told that a fight had broken out at a bus stop after a white man had called another passenger the N-word. Rather than board his bus, Tupac came to the Black man's aid. Whatever the case, Tupac was allowed to star in the final of the three shows, which moved from Tamalpais's own theater to the Marin Civic Auditorium. This time, Liza met Tupac ahead of time and didn't let him out of her sight.

During his time at Tamalpais, Tupac gave an on-camera interview to documentary filmmaker Jamie Cavanaugh. The project was intended to chart the lives of urban youth over the course of a decade, though Tupac appears to only have taken part in this one sit-down conversation. The opportunity was important to him—he quit his job at a pizza place when the boss refused to give him the time off to participate. The interview is regularly held up as evidence of Tupac's beyond-his-years consciousness and wisdom. The baby-faced student, wearing a black tank top, discusses, among many other things, the scourge of poverty, the uneven structuring of society, and the weaknesses in the American education curriculum. "There should be a class on drugs," he asserts. "There should be a class on sex education. A real sex education class, not just pictures and diaphragms and unlogical terms and things like that." Close-up shots display Tupac's long, effeminate eyelashes—a feature that, years later, would betray the hardened masculine image he attempted to construct.

One day, David Smith, another of Tupac's drama instructors, brought his guitar on campus. The student asked if he knew "Vincent," Don McLean's delicate, beautiful acoustic ode to van Gogh. "That's my favorite song," Tupac declared. Smith asked if he would sing along, but Tupac insisted he was no singer. In fact, his musical chops were largely concealed at Tamalpais—Smith knew him for about six months before discovering he was a rapper. Clearly not feeling the same artistic liberation as he did at an arts school like BSA, and facing economic pressures at home, Tupac dropped out just shy of graduation.

Creatively malnourished, Tupac sought out figures in the local rap scene. A talent like his crashing into a relatively small corner of California could not go unnoticed, and he soon formed a friendship with Ryan D. Rollins, a military brat and burgeoning emcee who had spent his high-school days copying Run-DMC's famous dress code. It was Rollins who told Tupac to drop the moniker MC New York and go with his real name. Tupac liked the idea, but with the alteration of changing the first syllable into the number to form 2Pac. It would adorn many platinum-selling albums.

With Ryan and a couple of other local kids, 2Pac started the clique One Nation Emcees. As if to manifest their own success, the boys acted as if they were already pretty big-time, even ordering special jewelry bearing the group's initials, ONE.

There was Kendrick Wells, who, being from Sausalito, enjoyed a relatively comfortable upbringing compared with that of his friends in the Jungle. Interested in the growing West Coast hip-hop scene,

Wells started hanging out with local rappers and organizing parties. His girlfriend would tell him about a kid she was acting in plays with who could also rap. Tupac, in turn, was aware of Wells by reputation. "We finally met at a house party in Novato, California, and we knew each other as soon as we seen each other," Wells remembered. "He didn't know what I looked like and I didn't know what he looked like. But somebody said, 'That's Tupac,' and they described him with the Gumby haircut, and I guess I had been described to him before too, but as soon as we locked eyes we knew who we were."

Tupac had already lived away from his mother in Baltimore, and now that he was older, he asserted his independence even more. Charles "Man Man" Fuller, a friend who would later become his road manager, arranged for Tupac to stay with his brother. There was also a stint living in an apartment with Wells, Rollins, and a few others. "I was broke, nowhere to stay," Tupac later said. "I smoked weed. I hung out with the drug dealers, pimps, and the criminals. They were the only people that cared about me at that point. And I needed a father—a male influence in my life, and these were the males. My mom, she was lost at that particular moment. She wasn't caring about herself. She was addicted to crack. It was a hard time, because she was my hero."

There was an excursion to Los Angeles, where Watani Tyehimba, a politically active friend of Afeni's, invited Tupac to spend a few months volunteering with youth programs in sprawling South Central. But it was upon his return to Marin City that Tupac's fortunes swiveled when he connected with a young backup dancer turned concert promoter with a penchant for poetry.

The specifics of Tupac and Leila Steinberg's connection depend on what source you put your trust in. It's said that Tupac had heard of Steinberg and was eager to meet her. Another account claims Steinberg was aware of the recent East Coast transplant by reputation. Their first encounter may have been in a park, or on the grass outside Bayside Elementary School in Marin County, but when Tupac came across Steinberg, she was reading Winnie Mandela's *Part of My Soul Went with Him*. One telling of the story has his opening line as being cordial ("That's a good one. It really moves well"). Another has it slightly antagonistic ("Give me a break. What do you know about Winnie Mandela?"). Whatever the case, a conversation was struck up. In the most fanciful version of the story, Steinberg, a single mother of three little girls, offered Tupac lodgings in her Sonoma County house by the end of the conversation, and he, in turn, appointed her his manager.

A crucial connection came when Tupac met Ray Luv and DJ Dize (pronounced "Dizzy"). Like Tupac, Ray came from a home blighted by addiction, but while Afeni had managed to just about cling to her relationship with her children, Ray had been alone since he was fifteen. The trio formed a group called Strictly Dope.

With rap not yet generating an income he could live on, Tupac turned to selling drugs. It was a cursed thing to do, antithetical to the teachings of Mutulu Shakur and the radicals of Lincoln Detox, and difficult to understand given that Afeni was still struggling with addiction—Tupac and his mother battled when he accused her of lying to him about her drug use. But his stint as a neighborhood drug pusher was short-lived. "We knew very quickly that that was not going to be our way out," Ray Luv said in the 2023 documentary series *Dear Mama*. "Because capitalism requires that your empathy level is relatively low. And his [Tupac's] empathy level was a little higher than most people. He didn't believe in hurting or killing Black people. So if a person is smoking crack with their daughter or their son, he's not gonna recover from that."

Through the haze of addiction, Afeni would still speak to Tupac and his friends, passing on her hard-earned knowledge. "The number one thing you have to focus on is to survive," she'd tell them. To Rollins and Wells, Afeni's drug problems were discernible, so it was easy for them to deduce why Tupac never seemed to want to go home.

Shortly after moving to Marin City, Afeni began visiting a male friend in prison and, during one of the visits, she became pregnant. Cursing her carelessness, Afeni resolved to have the pregnancy ended. But complications with her uterus meant she struggled to find a clinic that would treat her. Afeni was passed on to different medical centers, none of which could, or would, provide the care she needed. Desperate to terminate the pregnancy, Afeni drastically increased her use of crack, expecting that the drug would eventually kill the fetus. Day and night she smoked the terrible substance, damaging her mind and body, without achieving the desired effect. Learning of her sister's plight from her home in New York, Gloria Jean was horror-struck. To stop this dreadful situation, she told Afeni she'd take the baby in, but Afeni could not contemplate such a scenario. Finally, five months into the pregnancy, she found a clinic that would perform the abortion. The procedure went off without complication, but the scars left on Afeni's soul were devastating.

Leila Steinberg's experience in the music industry was limited, but her belief in Tupac was absolute, and opening doors for him became her highest business priority. When necessary, she would fill the role of chauffeur, driving Strictly Dope around to bookings at high schools, bars, clubs—anywhere they could hone their craft. Contact was made with Atron Gregory, manager of a rising rap collective called Digital Underground. "Sure, send me a videotape," Gregory responded to Steinberg's pitch. Without one pre-prepared, Tupac recorded an impromptu performance in front of Steinberg's house, with no audience. Gregory received the footage and was struck by the burgeoning rapper's undeniable talent.

Gregory introduced Tupac to Digital Underground's leading man, Shock G. Like Tupac, Shock hailed from New York but spent some formative years in Tampa, Florida, where he likely absorbed the region's taste for humorous, buck-wild party rap. Relocating to Oakland, Shock formed Digital Underground, a conglomerate of funky freaks with him as the nexus. Biz Markie might have been rap's clown prince, but Shock was a fellow royal.

Their first meeting came when Shock was perched at the mixing board, working on the group's debut album, *Sex Packets*. Suddenly, he peered upward and saw Tupac looming over him, ready to rap on the spot.

"You want me to do it right now?" Tupac asked. Shock was taken aback by the bout of impatience. It reminded him of the scene in *Scarface* when Tony Montana enters a small apartment to buy cocaine and quickly becomes restless as the deal stalls.

The pair retreated to a piano room and Tupac kicked a few

rhymes. "Pac's diction impressed me that I could hear what he was saying," Shock later said. "But he still had that, you know, Chuck D/KRS-One/LL *clarity* about his words. It didn't have that Oakland kind of curly-fry drawl that that [Too] $hort and E-40 had. At that point, he was talking about real goofy hip-hop stuff. One of the songs was called 'The Case of the Misplaced Mic.' He busted something like that and then he busted something that was more political. I hit Atron like, 'He's good, he's good.'"

So Shock thought Tupac was cool, but not so cool that he was immediately going to usurp some of the rapping talent already in the collective. This included Shock himself, who would veer between rapping in his own persona and, by using a wackier voice and donning a fake nose and glasses, that of his alter ego, Humpty Hump. Tupac would have to pay dues as a roadie and backup dancer, which meant learning the humpty dance, a jelly-hipped new move the group hoped would power the single named after it.

"Yeah, I'll do it," said Tupac. "Anything. That's hot. I'll do anything to get out of here."

Tupac was now in the company of professionals. And Shock's "Humpty Dance," his bass-heavy Iliad of sexual escapades in the bathrooms of fast-food restaurants, was a hit. Digital Underground were blowing up, and Shock was prescient enough to see that this kid bouncing up and down doing the humpty dance onstage—so simple a move that it took me, a rhythmically challenged creature, all of two minutes to master it from YouTube—had star quality. Not least because the women who showed up at their shows would buzz around him, his pretty features and undeniable swagger like a porchlight onstage.

Gregory was still working to get his client a solo deal, but interest was in short supply. And Tupac hadn't quite determined if entertainment would be his ultimate calling or whether the time had come to follow his forefathers. "He took a trip to Los Angeles, when he came back, he was all inspired," said Wells. "He was like, 'I'm going to lead the Black Panther Party, the new Black Panthers.' I'm like, 'OK, whatever, let's go get some bitches.'"

Being out west gave Tupac proximity to one of the men often referred to as his godfather, Geronimo Pratt, locked up in San Quentin. During one visit, the boy pitched a big idea: restarting the Black Panther Party.

Pratt was surely impressed by Tupac's audacity and directed the Panther cub to the New Afrikan People's Organization, and founding member Akinyele Umoja, who had graced Afeni and Mutulu's home all those years before. Part of the group's activity had been to support Pratt while he was incarcerated. As the years ticked by, his case attracted a broad range of supporters, including politicians, activists, and celebrities who contended that Pratt was framed by Los Angeles Police Department and the FBI. He was finally freed in 1997 when an Orange County superior court judge ruled that prosecutors at Pratt's murder trial had concealed evidence that could have led to his acquittal.

For Tupac, an additional pull toward a new revolutionary organization in the Panthers' image occurred when Watani Tyehimba moved to Atlanta. From his new base, Tyehimba called a meeting of young people from all over America to initiate a new youth organization called the New Afrikan Panthers, which would be a component piece of the New Afrikan People's Organization. In the summer of 1989, Tupac, who had recently turned eighteen, attended the meeting in Tyehimba's Atlanta home. The question of who among them would be officers of this new organization was raised. Tupac immediately put himself forward as chairman.

"It took everybody by surprise," recalled Umoja. "Because he was being very assertive, very bold, and very excited about trying to play the role of chairman of this organization."

During a break, Umoja took Tupac to one side to make sure he understood the role. "OK, that's a lot of responsibility," Umoja remembered telling him. "So if you do this, you can't be getting drunk out on the street. You gotta avoid being in a lot of fights. If you're the chair, you're the representative of the group, so a lot of the image of the group is going to depend on you and your personality."

In that moment, the pair's bond was solidified.

Among the group's first tasks was to sell copies of the New Afri-kan People's Organization's newspaper, *By Any Means Necessary*, at the Atlanta University Center. Tupac was excited about the task. Like Huey Newton years earlier, Tupac wanted to interact with young people on campus, to speak directly with students from institutes such as Morehouse, Spelman, and Clark. When every-body else called it a day, Tupac insisted he wanted to sell more newspapers, so Umoja took him to a jazz festival, where despite his enthusiasm, the patrons proved less receptive to revolutionary literature.

Meanwhile, a story was breaking in Virginia Beach, at a Labor Day weekend college party known as Greekfest. For several years the event had attracted students from historically Black colleges and universities and had grown steadily more popular, leading to increasing hostility from locals. Overzealous cops began enforcing curfews and arresting attendees for petty offenses such as jaywalk-ing and playing loud music. On September 3, the fed-up students took to the streets, chanting Public Enemy's "Fight the Power." Rioting erupted. Across two nights of violence, more than one hun-dred stores were looted or damaged. About fifty people were injured and hundreds were arrested. The National Guard was deployed; its shock troops could be seen dramatically marching past the shat-tered storefronts touting machine guns. The damage was estimated at $1.4 million.

This followed the killing of sixteen-year-old Black youth Yusuf K. Hawkins in the Brooklyn neighborhood of Bensonhurst a little over a week earlier. Yusuf and three Black friends were walking through the largely Italian neighborhood to look at a used car for sale when they were surrounded by a group of bat-wielding whites amped up on having just watched the movie *Mississippi Burning*. One of the figures drew a gun and Yusuf was shot multiple times in the chest. He lay bleeding in the street, one hand clutching a Snick-ers bar he'd bought in a local store, the other holding the hand of a neighborhood woman who'd come to his aid.

With both incidents in the national news, the burgeoning New Afrikan Panthers held a meeting at the Atlanta University Center.

A video with news footage was screened. As chairman, Tupac spoke about the incidents and the importance of building a Black youth movement. The meeting was open to all students, who asked questions that Tupac struggled to answer.

"He looked over at me to help him and I said, 'Nah, if you want to be chairman of this organization brother you better handle it,'" laughed Umoja. "But I remember that incident, or that event, made him have a lot of respect for those college students in the Atlanta University Center."

It was also during this trip to Atlanta that Tupac appeared on Bomani Bakari's radio show on WRFG to promote the New Afrikan Panthers, discuss its spiritual connections to the original organization, invite listeners to an upcoming meeting, and take phone calls from the public. He spoke with the eloquence and passion that would make his interviews as relevant to many disciples as his music in later years, covering, among other topics, the blessing of Afeni giving him a name that did not bear the mark of a slave owner. "When my mother gave me Tupac, I felt as though she literally liberated me at birth, cut the ties off me at birth, and set me free, you know, set me on the path to righteousness."

Throughout his Atlanta odyssey, music stayed on Tupac's mind. On the way to one of the meetings he discussed with other New Afrikan Panthers his desire to strike a deal away from Digital Underground's label, Tommy Boy. Still, it's impossible not to conclude that the trip had a powerful effect on him. Flanking Tupac on every side were like-minded young people. The air was thick with righteous intent; the only language spoken was Black power. "He wanted to show [people], 'Look, we're still not free as a people, we're still colonized, and we need to challenge things,'" said Umoja. "That was a theme that really continued throughout his music, right? So that was the connection there and that was the connection that he would see the Black Panther Party of the sixties and seventies was engaged in too."

Tupac returned to Atlanta the following February. This time, he spoke and performed for the Kemet Fraternity at Morehouse, and at another event for students at the Atlanta University Center.

He had rung in the New Year in the faraway setting of Japan, on tour with Digital Underground. But it was during this trip that he announced he was resigning as chairman. Music was becoming a greater part of his life. He could no longer divide himself.

"I think it was something he wanted to do, it was like something that was part of his blood, his heritage," said Wells on Tupac's activism at the time, "but the music was his dream."

Shortly after Tupac's resignation, Umoja offered to give him a ride. Once inside the privacy of the car, Umoja told Tupac he wasn't going to let him out until he was straight about the reasons for him stepping down as chairman. The young man explained how the support he felt in Georgia was not mirrored back home. His mother was on drugs and he'd been selling drugs too. Tupac was contemplating getting on public assistance to ensure their survival. Umoja didn't have a lot of disposable income, but feeling sorry for the young man he was so attached to, he palmed Tupac whatever little money he could.

Umoja discussed Tupac with his wife. The couple agreed that he could return to Georgia, stay between their home and Tyehimba's house, get a job, work toward his GED, and focus on his music career. A female student at Spelman even gifted him a ticket so he could return. But a few weeks later, Tupac called in the middle of the night, clearly distressed. "He was really upset with his situation," remembered Umoja. "And so we just said, 'Man you need to get on that plane the next day and come out here, you've got that ticket, come on.' He probably was drunk, you know, it was late at night. So, I didn't hear from him for a few weeks and then he called me and said everything is going to be all right."

These phone calls appear to be a feature of Tupac's early years out west. They were desperate dispatches sent out to friends and allies all over the country, but words let him down when he needed them most. By the 1988 to '89 academic year, Becky Mossing was a student at New York University. While Tupac's path seemed crooked at every turn, his old BSA friend was fulfilling the life path her circumstances dictated would always be hers. One night that winter, her phone rang shrilly at about two a.m. (eleven p.m. California time). It was Tupac.

"Did I wake you up?" he asked. Mossing immediately recognized something was off about Tupac's energy.

"What's wrong?" she replied, shaken from her slumber.

"I woke you up. I'll call you back," he promised before hanging up. It was the final conversation Tupac and Mossing ever shared.

To keep tabs on Tupac, Umoja also remained in touch with Leila Steinberg. He'd send her copies of his organization's newspaper for Tupac to sell. "She called me a couple times and she was really interested in helping Pac. She thought some of us were a positive influence on him," said Umoja.

Tupac, meanwhile, was trying to sign with Eazy-E's Ruthless Records, but ended up instead becoming a full-time member of Digital Underground. "That was the turning point. He said he signed with Digital Underground and things were better for him, they were going to take care of him, he didn't have to worry about a place to stay, something to eat, all that type of stuff," said Umoja. "And he was going on tour with them. Every now and then we'd get a call."

Tupac decided to fully throw in with Digital Underground, a gig that included humping sex dolls onstage. Seeing photos of him performing in nothing but leopard-skin underwear, it's tough to imagine how someone could be further from chairing a revolutionary Black Power organization. But like the teenager who wrote "Library Rap" back in Baltimore, Tupac understood this was a job and what that job required.

In the summer of 1990, the group Tony! Toni! Toné! released the single "Feels Good." It featured what was at that point still a relatively new phenomenon: a rap verse in a pop-R&B song. Recruited to perform the short segment was a rapper named Mocedes, but to those who knew him, he was Mopreme Shakur, Mutulu's biological son.

After his father disappeared into the underground, Mopreme lost contact with Afeni and the family. Eight years slipped away until Mopreme, now living in Oakland, received an unexpected letter. With stepmother and son back in touch, an invitation was extended to Mopreme to join Afeni and her children for Thanksgiving 1989 dinner. Tupac was excited to see his lost stepbrother again.

Predictably, they bonded over their rap music dreams. Around six months later, "Feels Good" hit the top 10 of the Billboard Hot 100 chart. Tupac was thrilled with Mopreme's achievement and would remind the members of Digital Underground of their connection whenever the song came on the radio.

Soon, he got his own big opportunity to shine on a record. In January 1991, Digital Underground released the single "Same Song," 2Pac's recording debut. West Coast to its bones, the track features James Worthy–sized handclaps sampled from a Parliament track, with some sleazy organ play. 2Pac's verse is short, and he keeps things appropriately light: "Now I clown around when I hang around with the Underground / Girls who used to frown say 'I'm down' when I come around." "Same Song" appeared on the soundtrack to the forgotten comedy *Nothing but Trouble*, and was released with a video that saw Digital Underground go suitably wild. Both Shock and his alter ego Humpty Hump run around dressed in various costumes; 2Pac enters dressed as an African king. One of the movie's stars, Dan Aykroyd, and Eazy-E both show up for kicks. MTV rotation was assured.

On the road, Tupac enjoyed himself like a young man who was experiencing the first flickers of fame. His partying became so anarchic that his roommate, group member Chopmaster J, couldn't take it anymore. "Pac would invite everybody back. So we're like, 'No, Pac, we just invite the girls.' So everybody is up in the room," he told *Rolling Stone* years later. "That's Pac being a pied piper type of dude. He was a guy for the people. But for me, I had had enough of that and felt as though I deserved my own room. Because it just got too wild."

Digital Underground was a vehicle, a means to an end. The paychecks allowed Tupac to rent a one-bedroom apartment on MacArthur Boulevard in Oakland; he'd no longer have to crash with friends or at Steinberg's house. But while Tupac was living it up with the group, Gregory was shopping around solo music of a totally different persuasion. In 1989, 2Pac recorded the song "Panther Power," its title an obvious summoning of the energy of his parentage. He dubs the American Dream a "calculated scheme," harking all the way back to slavery, the failed promises of emancipation, through to modern racism, capitalism, and other evils. Tupac picks apart the struggle with precision. He was reaching artistic maturity and returned to the idea crystalized at BSA that hip-hop could facilitate a political and social message. With "Panther Power," he made clear that the message would be of his roots.

On the morning of August 22, 1989, Huey P. Newton was shot three times in the head in West Oakland, killed in a crack cocaine deal gone bad. The gunman was in his twenties and a member of the prison gang the Black Guerrilla Family. Newton's limp body was found lying in a pool of blood, staining the streets where he first began his life as an activist for the downtrodden years earlier. Tupac attended a memorial for Newton and penned a poem dedicated to him titled "Fallen Star." But the descent of this particular celestial body had begun years before his death.

Murdered at age forty-seven, Newton outlived his hero Malcolm X by eight years, but it was time not best used. After the split with Cleaver and curtailment of the Black Panther Party at the will of America's power structure, the group realigned its borders by returning to its Oakland origins. There was a momentary spark in 1973 when Bobby Seale ran for mayor of Oakland as a Democrat, receiving the second-most votes in a field of nine candidates. But the soul of the Panthers finally fractured in Newton's penthouse apartment, where he banished Seale from the party by ordering his six-foot-eight, four-hundred-pound bodyguard to beat his old friend with a bullwhip. "You have violated the trust of the party," Newton raged. "You are no longer chairman . . . In fact, I no longer want you in this party."

It was a cursed thing to do, and indicative of Newton's later life, which became a litany of court cases and criminality. In 1974, he was charged with the terrible murder of a seventeen-year-old sex worker. Sure he would never receive a fair trial, Newton fled to Cuba for three years before returning to face the charges in 1977. He was still able to command huge support; fifteen hundred people showed up at the airport to welcome him home. Newton was tried twice on the murder charge, both trials ending in mistrials with the juries deadlocked in favor of acquittal. The charges were finally dismissed in 1979. Not for the first time, Newton had stared at a murder rap and walked away free. Still, a fresh start was not grasped. The ex-Panther took to drinking two quarts of cognac a day; cocaine, heroin, and Valium were his drugs of choice. He had attended an addiction program in 1984, paid for by the comedian Richard Pryor. Newton finally did go to prison: nine months in San Quentin Prison on a gun charge; a further six months for misappropriating $15,000 in public money intended for a school that the Panthers had once operated.

His demise spared the world any more of Newton's misdeeds, and, as death often does, restored his best image: that of the revolutionary intellectual and daring effectuator. Newton's brilliance will forever outshine his flaws. But he also serves as a convoy for a certain truth: the leaders of movements are often unworthy of the rank-and-file members who dedicate themselves to their cause.

One of Newton's most interesting hypotheses was what he called "revolutionary suicide"—the act of putting one's life in mortal danger in service of the revolution. The inverse, as Newton saw it, is "reactionary suicide," that is, an early death brought about by hopeless social conditions inflicted on the downtrodden masses. To accept revolutionary suicide is not the same as having a death wish, Newton clarified. "It means just the opposite. We have such a strong desire to live with hope and human dignity that existence without them is impossible. When reactionary forces crush us, we must move against these forces, even at the risk of death."

I've thought a lot about these terms in the context of the deaths of Newton and Tupac. On the face of it, both men's demises would appear to be examples of reactionary suicides. Newton died while attempting to feed his drug addiction; Tupac was seemingly a victim of gang violence (though some believe he was the target of a government fearful of his influence). These are symptoms of systemic societal issues, such as poor education and poverty, that afflict America's ghettos. Neither man could claim a death like that of Che Guevara, who was executed by the U.S. military–backed Bolivian forces he was seeking to overthrow. But violent deaths sealed both Newton's and Tupac's reputations as revolutionary icons;

the word "martyr" is often affixed to Tupac's name in particular. To many, their greatness was entwined with their flaws, veering them so close to oblivion that eventually they lost control. Newton and Tupac lived revolutionary lives. Perhaps that's enough to claim a revolutionary death.

There often comes a moment in a parent-child relationship when the dynamic flips—when the parent becomes the one who requires care, and the child converts to caregiver. It's a difficult subversion for the child, stepping into the role of guardian of an elder who nurtured them when they were vulnerable, witnessing the person who once held authority over them become powerless. The language of the relationship changes; the orientation becomes distorted. Once the roles are flipped, they are almost never fully reversed again.

For years, addiction had eroded Afeni Shakur's parental jurisdiction over her children. By late 1990, it had all but disappeared. Sekyiwa was back in New York with Afeni's sister, Gloria Jean. Tupac was nineteen years old and fully pursuing the independence he'd sought since first leaving the family home as a younger teenager in Baltimore. He would check on his mother between his commitments as a rising musical artist, but Afeni's drug use had practically rendered her a dependent who required more than occasional care. Watching his mother's descent, Tupac realized he would have to send her to New York to save her.

Tupac attempted to coordinate the move with Gloria Jean, the child asserting agency over the parent. He told his aunt over the phone that it was his intention to move to New York in the near future too, and maybe he said the same thing to Afeni—the child crossing his fingers and spinning a yarn to help soothe the parent's misgivings because he believes he knows what's best for her. Still, it was not an easy process. Gloria Jean's husband, Thomas Cox, sent Afeni money for a bus ticket—money that ended up being spent on crack.

The child must have known he needed to be more assertive. On a freezing cold December day, Tupac met his mother and her five suitcases at the bus station. He handed Afeni all the money he had, while one of his friends, Mike Cooley, generously bought her a bus ticket and a fried chicken meal. Mother and son said their goodbyes and, finally, Afeni departed California and headed toward the city of her brightest and best days some two decades earlier.

The cross-country odyssey was complicated by the bus strikes of 1990. It took several days to complete, draining Afeni of her meager financial resources. Buses broke down at least twice, leaving the passengers stranded in the cold of the Great Basin winter as they waited for replacements. There was some mercy in the Denver bus station, where the Salvation Army gave Afeni hot soup and blankets. Charity was harder to come by on the road, but she managed to talk a white woman in the seat next to her into sharing food by claiming her credit cards were packed away.

At every stop along the way, Afeni called her family, cold, hungry, in tears. Down the phone line, they transported what strength they could.

Finally, on Christmas Eve, Afeni pulled into the Port Authority Bus Terminal. She was tired, she'd lost weight. With the five suitcases next to her, she propped herself up against a pillar, feeling like little more than a piece of baggage herself. Then, coming toward her, Afeni saw what must have appeared through weary eyes to be a messianic sight: Gloria Jean and her family.

"When I saw my family come down the steps, it was the first time I felt human again," Afeni later said. "I had ceased to be or feel like a human being. I didn't know who I was anymore, or even who I used to be. I really didn't. So when I saw them it was like a signal that I belonged. I really did belong someplace, you know. And they loved me, gently, back to health. They took me home, and they loved me. I started to feel human again."

Sobriety was not immediate. Afeni continued to smoke crack. Not wanting to see her sister wandering the streets in a stoned state, Gloria Jean laid down some rules for using the drug in the house, infantilizing Afeni once more.

Salvation came in the shape of a figure from her past. In May 1991, Afeni attended a twentieth anniversary reunion of the Panther 21 in Connecticut, where Ali Bey Hassan and his wife, a white woman named Sue, lived. During her visit to the couple's home,

Afeni caught up with their daughter, Tonya. A recovering addict, she asked Afeni to attend an Alcoholics Anonymous meeting with her. That same night, they went to a second meeting. And Afeni kept returning, meeting after meeting. She dedicated herself to the program, each step taking her a degree closer to sobriety, freedom, and agency, the parent a dependent no more.

Tupac on the set of his first movie, *Juice,* shot in 1991 and released the following year

7

SOMETHING WICKED

YOU'D BE FORGIVEN for accepting the title of *2Pacalypse Now* as simply a snappy play on words—the possibility for 2Pac to fuse his name with Francis Ford Coppola's unforgettable war movie *Apocalypse Now* was right there like low-hanging fruit, so why not take it? But the catastrophic inscription etched onto his debut album's cover is extremely relevant to its content. This was the manifesto of a man who saw America as needing to be destroyed and rebuilt. 2Pac called it the "story of the young Black male" and a "battle cry to America"—or, borrowing a motif from Ice Cube, "America! America! AmeriKa-Ka-Ka." A nation found guilty on all counts.

It's normal for an artist's first album to almost rupture from the weight of hoarded ideas, each one unleashed in case the opportunity to lay down a full-length record never comes again. *2Pacalypse Now* is filled with the most dominant thoughts, notions, and impulses running around Tupac's brain in 1991. It was the most socially conscious full-length album he would ever record; 2Pac's anger was righteous, but, crucially, his fury was not so blinding that he couldn't deliver a clear sermon on how the country had gone astray.

Sessions took place in Starlight Studio in Richmond, California, from March to August 1991. Constructing an insular unit, Tupac was flanked by his Digital Underground brethren, with Shock G, Stretch, and Raw Fusion chipping in with beats. But it was an outsider, Deon "Big D the Impossible" Evans, who wielded one of the

most influential hands on the album's sound by providing instru-
mentals for six of the thirteen tracks, including its most famous
song, "Brenda's Got a Baby." Evans had previously asked Money-B
to slip Tupac his beat tape, and the pair later met at a performance
by Raw Fusion, Money-B's side project with DJ Fuze, in Berkeley.
It's fair to assume Tupac was impressed.

In hindsight, we know that 2Pac did not step into the arena
fully formed. Musically, *2Pacalypse Now* was rudimentary for its
time. There are lots of hard-hitting music samples, deep record
scratches, some pitch-shifted vocals, but it sounds dated compared
to, say, the kaleidoscopic weirdness of A Tribe Called Quest, who
were in the middle of recording their classic second album, *The
Low End Theory*. And 2Pac's flow can be a little ragged at times,
his song craft not yet fully matured. This, I would wager, is the
album made during his life that the average fan is least likely to
reach for when they casually feel like throwing on his music. But
2Pacalypse Now is a fireball of energy that never lets up. There are
zero sunny singles to bounce to, no bright moments to release the
constant tension. Sitting next to Public Enemy's reckoning and the
emotional weight of the emerging hood movie genre, epitomized
by John Singleton's revelatory film *Boyz n the Hood*, *2Pacalypse Now*
is 2Pac's unvarnished, blood-in-the-mouth depiction of Black male
reality in the early 1990s.

Securing a record deal had not been a straightforward task.
Atron Gregory had banged on numerous doors and shaken various trees in the pursuit of a company that would see the potential
in his client that he knew to be there. Even Digital Underground's
label, Tommy Boy, declared it wasn't interested in the group's latest
member as a solo artist.

Seeking alternate options, Gregory heard about a new label
founded by movie producer and retail empire heir Ted Field and
music engineer Jimmy Iovine called Interscope. The pair had
secured a contract with Atlantic Records, a component of mam-
moth media company Time Warner, for distribution. Responsible
for scouting the talent was A&R man Tom Whalley. There wasn't
much of a hint that Whalley would be interested in a socially con-

scious kid with Black Panther roots when one of his signees, a gimmicky pop-rap group named Marky Mark and the Funky Bunch, scored a massive hit in the summer of 1991 with "Good Vibrations." But when 2Pac's demo tape came into his possession, Whalley loved it. His twelve-year-old daughter loved the tape, too. It was enough to prompt Whalley to request a meeting with Tupac. Soon the young artist was on a plane from Oakland to Burbank, to a dinner at the unglamorous surroundings of the airport Holiday Inn restaurant. As they spoke about his artistry, Whalley was impressed by how articulate the young man was. But it wasn't just his intelligence—Whalley recognized his aura.

"He's so handsome," commented Whalley's assistant after Tupac departed. "Did you see the eyelashes? And the eyes?" On August 15, 1991, Tupac inked the contract. He was an Interscope artist.

The world's first view of this future superstar was through prison glass. The music video for "Trapped," 2Pac's inaugural attempt to achieve MTV rotation as a solo artist, places him in jail. We witness 2Pac, shooting dice with his crew when Oakland police cruise by, the "Protect and Serve" sign on the side of the squad car ironically on display as bodies go sprinting in all directions to escape its viewpoint. In the narrative, 2Pac is one of the unlucky ones caught and carted away to the penitentiary. The prison scenes are presented in stark black and white. "They got me trapped," 2Pac spits down the phone on one side of the visiting room's prison glass. On the other side is Shock G, who gives his retort, "Uh-uh, they can't keep the Black man down."

"Trapped" did not manifest in 2Pac's brain. In fact, it came from some of Ray Luv's discarded lyrics that 2Pac rescued from a garbage can and used as a jumping-off point. The title points to American society's entrapment of Black men. 2Pac's perceptions are pessimistic: happiness on the streets is impossible, convicts are coming out of prison in worse condition than when they went in, cops are not to be trusted. "Tired of being trapped in this vicious cycle," he raps. "If one more cop harasses me, I just might go psycho." From there, 2Pac's words eviscerate overbearing street cops and the brutality they rain down, before hinting at violent uprising: "One day I'm gonna bust, blow up on this society." For a former dancer and hype man, it was a startling about-face; for a first single, it was a hell of a gambit.

It's impossible, though, to grapple with the content of *2Pacalypse Now* further without examining what was unfolding some four hundred miles south just as recording was getting under way. It was a happening that would set the discourse around racial profiling and police brutality, not just in the mind of one young rap artist, but across America.

The night of March 2, 1991, began unremarkably for Rodney King, who would soon find himself at the center of one of the most infamous incidents of police brutality in United States history, one that would send a blast wave through Los Angeles that would reverberate from coast to coast. King, twenty-five years old at the time, visited a friend's home in suburban Los Angeles to watch basketball over forty-ounce bottles of Olde English 800. It was after the game that King had a notion: he and his two friends, Bryant "Pooh" Allen and Freddie Helms, should go cruising for girls. And so the three men jumped into King's car, a white two-door Hyundai Excel, and journeyed west down the 210 freeway, toward a desperate destiny.

Rodney King's name has since come to exist as a byword—a verbal shortcut taken by pundits when making a point about police brutality, a late-night talk show host punch line, simply the name of an incident that needed to be overturned or avenged. That you can't see Rodney King's face in the grainy videotape that would define his life adds to this sense of him as an emblem of historic pain. That the most widely circulated photographs of King see his face heavily bruised and swollen strip his character away further. And he never went by the name that would end up on the lips of commentators and activists anyway; King's family always called him by his middle name, Glen. But King had a life before becoming this symbol, a life of common problems.

Born in Sacramento, Glen moved to the foothills of Altadena with his family when he was just two years old. His father, Ronald, was a heavy drinker who took his anger out on his son before ending up in an early grave. Glen began drinking too, in junior high school. There were run-ins with authorities. In 1989, he robbed a store in Monterey Park, attacking the store owner with an iron bar before fleeing the scene with two hundred dollars. He was caught, convicted, and sentenced to two years in jail, serving one. It was just two months after his release that King embarked on the doomed voyage that would end in a severe beating, while the lens of amateur videographer George Holliday's camcorder looked on.

Though King's drive would become a defining moment in LAPD history, the first cops involved were the California Highway Patrol (CHP) husband-and-wife team of Tim and Melanie Singer. Patrolling the freeway at about 12:40 a.m., Melanie saw the headlights of King's car approaching at high speed in her rearview mirror. King, presumably having spotted the patrol car, slowed after he passed it. The CHP unit exited at an off-ramp, but returned to the freeway behind the Hyundai, by which point King had increased his speed once more. Melanie Singer clocked the car at 110 to 115 miles per hour (later, some questioned whether a Hyundai Excel can reach those speeds) and up to 85 miles per hour on residential streets after it exited the freeway at Paxton Street.

As one of King's passengers, Helms, slept through history, Allen urged King to pull over. But King ignored both Allen and the flashing lights and screaming sirens of the highway patrol car, prompting Tim Singer to radio for help. It wasn't long before the LAPD joined the pursuit.

The chase wound to the corner of Osborne Street and Foothill Boulevard in Lake View Terrace, where King stopped at a red light. When the light turned green, he pulled through the intersection and came to a stop. About ten minutes and 7.8 miles had passed since the CHP unit first spotted the Hyundai. At this point, an LAPD unit radioed a Code 6, signaling that the chase had concluded. In response, the LAPD radio transmission operator (RTO) broadcast a Code 4, notifying all units that "additional assistance is not needed at the scene" and indicating that any officers not already present "shall return to their assigned patrol area."

Yet eleven additional LAPD units, including a helicopter, with twenty-one officers arrived at the end-of-pursuit scene. At least twelve cops showed up after the Code 4 was broadcast. Several had no convincing explanation for why they were there, according to the report of the independent commission that examined the case in depth later that year. Take the five officers from Foothill Station, for instance, who abandoned paperwork at the end of their shift to make their way in two separate cars to the scene *after* the Code 4. The report states that one of these officers told district attorney investigators that he did so "to see what was happening."

With the Hyundai having come to a stop, Timothy Singer used a loudspeaker to order the three occupants out of the car. Discovering that he couldn't be heard over the blare of the sirens and helicopter, Singer stepped out of the police cruiser and yelled out at the top of his voice. Allen and Helms made a swift exit from the right-hand side, lying down on the ground so Singer could approach. King's actions are disputed. According to officers at the scene, he initially refused to comply, and when King finally did leave the Hyundai, he did not follow directions and instead reentered the vehicle before coming out once more. Yet in a statement to the press on March 6, 1991, King insisted he had followed orders to exit the car. Allen told investigators that King responded to the initial command, but neglected to unbuckle his seat belt, thus requiring him to sit down again to undo it before finally freeing himself.

Regardless, King eventually emerged from the Hyundai. Feeling the situation was safe, Melanie Singer began to walk toward him, gun in hand, intending to perform a "felony kneeling" procedure to take him into custody. But as she drew within five or six feet of King, Singer heard a voice: "Stand back. Stand back. We'll handle this."

The command belonged to Stacey Koon, a forty-year-old sergeant and commanding LAPD officer at the scene. The LAPD are instructed not to approach a suspect with a drawn gun, so Koon felt compelled to stop the CHP officer. "Had she proceeded, either she was going to shoot Rodney King, or he was going to take her gun away and shoot her," Koon later stated in his book *Presumed Guilty*. His intervention was crucial to what was to follow.

Koon ordered four LAPD officers—Laurence Powell, Timothy Wind, Theodore Briseno, and Rolando Solano—to surround and "swarm" King. Powell and Briseno jumped on his back, causing

King to stand up in response. For this apparent resistance, Tasers were deployed. There were arguments on how effective the electroshock weapons proved to be, but for certain they did not fully incapacitate King.

This was the point that George Holliday, a thirty-one-year-old manager of the Hollywood office of a national plumbing company, turned on his Sony Video 8 Handycam CCD-F77. Holliday had been awakened by the noise of a helicopter and the sound of sirens. Though groggy from sleep, he could see everything out the bedroom window of his second-floor apartment in Lake View Terrace, ninety feet from the action.

As the lens zooms in, King is seen rising to his feet and taking a couple of quick steps—Solano later called it a "lunge"—before being struck by Powell's baton, putting the suspect down immediately. As the camera rediscovers focus, Taser wires can be seen coming from King's body. Powell hits King several more times with his baton. The videotape shows Briseno moving in to try to stop Powell from swinging, with Powell then backing up. King rises to his knees; Powell and Wind continue to hit him with their batons. Briseno later described Powell's flailing as "out of control."

Koon subsequently acknowledged that he had ordered the baton blows, directing officers to hit King with "power strokes" and to "hit his joints, hit his wrists, hit his elbows, hit his knees, hit his ankles." Finally, after fifty-six baton blows and six kicks, officers swarm in and place King in handcuffs and cord cuffs, restraining his arms and legs. King is dragged on his stomach to the side of the road to await arrival of an ambulance.

Of course, there were excuses. For *The Washington Post*, veteran journalist Lou Cannon wrote a piece sympathetic to the cops that pointed to their fears that King might have been on PCP (he wasn't), something that police dreaded as it seemingly made suspects impervious to pain and gave them extra strength. Cannon argued that the Holliday video lacked the context of what had happened before he started rolling, and the incredible claim that Koon didn't realize he was being backed up by so many officers.

Photos taken of King three days after the incident show his face severely swollen and marked, his body bruised, his eye rolling around the socket like a red marble. The beating, he said, had left him feeling like "a crushed can."

Holliday didn't immediately know what he had on tape. The next day, he used the same camcorder to film both the Los Angeles Marathon and a wedding he attended. But the beating gnawed at his conscience. Two days after the incident, Holliday called Foothill Police Station to let the LAPD know that he had the tape, and it might be of interest to them. Met with indifference, he reached out to CNN's Los Angeles bureau but nobody took his call. Now more determined, on Monday morning, March 4, Holliday personally dropped by local news channel KTLA, who instantly recognized the video's importance. Producers brought a copy of the tape downtown to LAPD headquarters in the Parker Center. Senior officers were stunned by what they saw, but there was little time for them to maneuver. The first story of the King beating ran at 10:15 p.m. on KTLA that night. CNN, which had an affiliation agreement with KTLA, finally picked the recording up. And once it was on the air, it stayed on the air. "Television used the tape like wallpaper," said Ed Turner, executive vice president for CNN.

By Wednesday, March 6, the tape had transformed King into an international symbol of police brutality. It ignited millions of Americans who had not understood—or had naïvely refused to accept—the reality of racially motivated police brutality until they were able to observe it with their own eyes. Here was long overdue evidence of what the Panthers had sought to protect themselves from.

"The beating was not the aberration," said Reverend Jesse Jackson. "The videotaping was the aberration."

Police brutality colors *2Pacalypse Now* blood red. On "Soulja's Story," 2Pac inhabits the character of a fifteen-year-old driver being chased by a police cruiser. When the kid finally pulls his vehicle over, it's to entrap one of the cops in his web. "Remember Rodney King?" the boy cackles at the approaching officer before drawing a pistol and fatally firing.

The album is full of such fantasies that reflected the anger the

King tape had brought to the surface of Black America. On "Violent," 2Pac envisions himself beating a cop who tries to frame him. On "Young Black Male," rapping in a more double-time flow than he'd later favor, he admonishes authority figures who assume he's a crook or drug dealer simply because he fits the title description. It's angry and it's visceral, but it's also eloquent. The message is clear: the promises of Lady Liberty do not apply to men like Tupac Shakur.

2Pac's words were not pure fiction—he was drawing from fresh experience. In the original liner notes to *2Pacalypse Now*, he claimed that "I Don't Give a Fuck" was a direct response to Digital Underground getting accosted by the San Francisco Police Department. "They put guns to our heads," they read. "Right after getting nominated for a Grammy: 'Shut up or we'll blow you away!' Two hours later, I'm in the studio session and this is what came out. I'm talking some true shit here."

If accurate, the SFPD case was underreported, with few other details ever revealed. But the song tells you all you need to know about how the incident made Tupac *feel*. "I Don't Give a Fuck" opens with his phone ringing off the hook with friends calling to tell their latest stories of police harassment. 2Pac places himself in the back of a cop car, forced to listen to the officers bragging about their misdeeds. From there, he starts firing verbal barbs in all directions: the cabdrivers who'll swerve to pass a Black passenger in favor of a white one, the Grammys and other award shows that "pimp us like hoes, take our dough, but they hate us though." He mentions the ongoing Gulf War, evoking Muhammad Ali's refusal to fight in Vietnam: "And now they're trying to ship me off to Kuwait? / Give me a break, how much shit can a n***a take?"

Undeniably, though, the most lasting song on *2Pacalypse Now* is "Brenda's Got a Baby," a painful dispatch from the ghetto that relays the short life of a preteen girl. Over solemn guitar plucks and the harrowing wails of singer Dave Hollister, 2Pac, in one long, single verse, follows Brenda as she's molested by her cousin, impregnated, and abandoned. Strung out on the street and having turned to sex work to support herself, Brenda is murdered. 2Pac describes the trauma of her giving birth on the bathroom floor: "She didn't know what to throw away and what to keep / She wrapped the baby up and threw him in a trash heap."

"Brenda's Got a Baby" was penned after Tupac came across a newspaper story while in New York shooting the movie *Juice*. The pages laid out the harrowing tale of a twelve-year-old girl in Brooklyn who threw her newborn baby boy down a trash chute. Two maintenance men heard the infant's cries just as they were about to start the motorized compactor. He was eventually rescued by a police sergeant who crawled into the space with a flashlight. With umbilical cord still attached, the baby was taken to Brookdale Hospital, where he was treated for hypothermia.

"When this song came out, no male rappers at all anywhere were talking about problems that females were having, number one," Tupac said in 1995. "Number two, it talked about sexual abuse, it talked about child molestation, it talked about families taking advantage of families, it talked about the effects of poverty, it talked about how one person's problems can affect a whole community of people. It talked about how the innocent are the ones that get hurt. It talked about drugs, the abuse of drugs, broken families . . . how she couldn't leave the baby, you know, the bond that a mother has with her baby and how . . . women need to be able to make a choice."

2Pacalypse Now is not 2Pac's most famous album. It didn't produce his most successful singles, and it wasn't made during his greatest musical time. But the period did produce what is by a distance Tupac's best-known film performance.

Ernest Dickerson had come up as a cameraman for Spike Lee but always retained an ambition to be a director himself. A dream project was to shoot *Manchild in the Promised Land*, a 1965 autobiographical novel that chronicles author Claude Brown's adolescent years living in Harlem poverty during the 1940s and '50s. Those influences were eventually funneled into his directorial debut, *Juice*, co-written by Dickerson and Gerard Brown, which captured the same cold Harlem streets in the 1990s.

Tupac plays Roland Bishop, one of four high-school friends try-

ing to find their place in the world, whose quest for street credibility ends up corrupting his soul. The shot of Bishop surprising
friend Q (Omar Epps) as he closes his locker door is the most lasting image of Tupac in a film; the subsequent soliloquy probably his
most potent: "You're right. I am crazy. And you know what else? I
don't give a fuck. I don't give a fuck about you. I don't give a fuck
about Steel. I don't give a fuck about Raheem, either. I don't give
a fuck about myself." It could almost be the outline of how Tupac
would eventually see himself; years later, he'd tell a magazine that
Bishop had never truly left him. Tupac would make other movies,
but never would a character get in his bones like Bishop.

How he nabbed the role was more luck than design. Money-B
had an audition for the movie and Sleuth Pro, Digital Underground's road manager, suggested Tupac go along too. Dickerson
himself spotted this fascinating young man in the waiting area. An
impromptu approach was made and Tupac found himself reading
for the part of Q and, after further discussion and some light prep,
Bishop. The latter role was offered to Tupac immediately.

"The thing that he came with, that he understood about Bishop,
was the pain that forces Bishop to make the decision that he makes,"
Dickerson told *The Root* in 2017. "It's easy to come in and act ballis-
tic and go crazy in front of the camera, but to have a depth, to have
a reason for that, that was the most amazing thing about Tupac
because he brought that in his audition, and then later on we found
out that Tupac had actually trained as an actor at the Baltimore
School for the Arts," he added. "So he was a young, trained actor
already, and he created a character that I believed in."

Tupac was eager to stress that *Juice* is "not a hip-hop movie,"
but "a real good movie that happens to have hip-hop in it." Yet rap
is undeniably in *Juice*'s blood. One of the first images you see is a
record bearing the logo of esteemed hip-hop label Def Jam as Q
works his bedroom decks in the hope of becoming a DJ. Though
it fits into the 1990s hood movie canon, alongside *Boyz n the Hood*,
Menace II Society, *New Jersey Drive*, and *South Central*, it plays more
like a thriller, chilly and dangerous.

Tupac's performance established him as a screen actor of both
star quality and adaptability. As Bishop, he had to be good-natured

and likable, using that million-dollar smile as a tool of disarmament. But like an uptown Travis Bickle, he morphs into a young man whose ability to reason has short-circuited under the pressure of the city, provoked to murder by the meanness of it all.

There are flaws to *Juice* should you be looking for them. It's undeniably heavy-handed—Bishop goes from knuckleheaded kid to serial murderer in a matter of days. And the romantic subplot involving Q and a more mature woman is given only a couple of scenes and doesn't really go anywhere. But the central idea that street credibility is a potentially tragic pursuit is a powerful one. When we see a clip at the end of the four friends before their descent, it's a reminder of what's been lost.

With a little bit of success came a desire within Tupac to assert ownership over his work. Making the most of being back in New York, the young star and his crew hit the streets of Manhattan. Tupac was beaming, happily kicking his rhymes as he strutted the boulevards of the city. But his mood dimmed when he came across a newsstand selling bootleg copies of Digital Underground tapes. To Tupac, this was nothing less than thievery. The scene turned tense as he aggressively demanded payment for the transgression. "I want my money, I want my tape, and I want it now," he yelled. "You're taking money out of my pocket."

Tupac left with no cash but delivered a warning to the proprietor: keep stealing from him and the whole newsstand was coming down.

During his days as Digital Underground's roadie, Tupac desired just two things for himself: to rap on a record and be in a movie. By the fall of 1991, he had one of each waiting to be released, a breakthrough just like he dreamed it. But then an incident occurred that would alter his trajectory and reframe his mindset. Though he'd already proved himself an adept at social commentary, any semblance of belief that he was a witness to, and not a participant in, the AmeriKKKan nightmare fully collapsed.

In occurred on October 17. Tupac was at the intersection of Seventeenth Street and Broadway in downtown Oakland. About to enter the Union Bank, he was stopped by two cops. They were officers Alexander Boyovich and Kevin Rodgers, they were white, and the crime they purported to have observed? Jaywalking.

The cops requested to see his ID. Words were exchanged. Tupac accused the cops of having a slave-master mentality.

"Master?" Rodgers replied. "I like the sound of that."

Suddenly, Tupac was violently thrown onto the concrete. He was choked, cuffed, and, when sufficiently softened up by the beating, thrown into the back of a squad car and hauled off to jail. Battered and bruised, Tupac was left in a cell for seven hours, the pain and the shock for company. Heartbreakingly, being in captivity meant he missed the MTV premiere of his first single, "Trapped."

The police brutality depicted in Tupac's writing had proved to be chilling prophecy. The attack wounded him, not just physically—his face was left marked and puffy—but psychologically. Tupac almost certainly suffered from post-traumatic stress disorder. His hair began falling out in clumps—the iconic shaven-headed image he cultivated was partially down to necessity. It was a weight on his soul that dragged him to a bleak nadir.

Tupac hired John Burris, a local attorney who'd doggedly been pursuing Boyovich and Rodgers for what he deemed multiple incidents of misconduct and seen this case as potentially a high-profile opportunity to finally bring about their demise. In Tupac, Burris sensed a young man of strong will burdened by a social structure that had rendered him a victim at the hands of these two men ostensibly empowered to serve and protect him. With the charges against Tupac quickly dropped, Burris prepared a civil lawsuit against the Oakland Police Department seeking $10 million in damages.

"The main dollar sum was really more to dramatize the conduct, not so much the value of the case," Burris explained to me. "At that point in time, we were trying to dramatize police brutality and what it meant. And so, a large dollar figure brought attention to the case itself. But it wasn't like the case had the value of a ten-million-dollar case, okay? That was a strategy on my part."

Tupac wasn't required to appear in court for the civil trial. Still, when the opportunity to settle for $42,000 arose, he took it and moved on with his life. Burris was satisfied that the case was resolved with a spotlight on the two officers' brutal nature. Boyovich and Rodgers ultimately left the department. "They should have been fired," rued Burris.

In the meantime, the album was stirring controversy. *2Pacalypse Now* was released on November 12, 1991, eight months after the King beating, and it soon attracted the rage of the establishment. Ice-T and other rappers were making powerful enemies, but this was the album that Vice President Dan Quayle called on Interscope to withdraw. A Texas state trooper was shot dead in April 1992 by a nineteen-year-old suspect whom police pulled over; he was allegedly found to be listening to the album on the tape deck of a stolen truck. "There's no reason for a record like this to be released. It has no place in our society," said Quayle.

Like his Shakur forebears, Tupac had attracted the ire of the American ruling class—a feud he was not going to shirk. As criticism rained down on him like machine-gun fire, Tupac's renegade inclinations grew. And the influence of the Rodney King case, of a people seeking justice for centuries of tyranny and subjugation, would only intensify.

"Burn, baby, burn": Los Angeles revolts following the 1992 acquittal of the LAPD officers who beat motorist Rodney King.

8

A THUG LIFE LESS ORDINARY

I N THE SPRING of 1992, Tupac Shakur was on the set of his second movie, *Poetic Justice*. It was directed by John Singleton, fresh off the hit *Boyz n the Hood* and armed with twice the budget. The lead was one Janet Jackson, making her big-screen acting debut. On paper, it was an obvious opportunity for Tupac to expand his pop culture presence.

Movie sets exist in bubbles—that is, until the outside world insists that they don't. On April 29, in the middle of Tupac's shooting schedule, four Los Angeles cops were acquitted by a Simi Valley court of the savage beating of Rodney King. Fury over the jury's decision transformed the city into a battlefront. Not far from the courthouse, production on *Poetic Justice* came to a standstill as the cast and crew gathered around a small black-and-white screen to watch the chaos. What they witnessed was footage shot at Florence and Normandie, the South Central intersection not far from Watts, a focal point of the unrest that news media heavily focused on. Most notably, a white truck driver, Reginald Denny, was grabbed out of his vehicle and attacked by four Black assailants. One hurled a brick at the helpless Denny's head as a helicopter news crew swirled overhead, documenting the brutality.

"I gotta go down there!" screamed Tupac. Singleton, who'd earlier journeyed to the courthouse after hearing the verdicts on the radio, forbade the request. Instead, his actor was dismissed from the set and told to go to his hotel room to cool off. But when the crew checked on him an hour later, he had vanished. Singleton later heard stories of Tupac driving down Wilshire Boulevard shooting out windows.

"At least he came back to work," Singleton joked twenty-five years later.

Ice Cube called the police helicopters "ghetto birds," beasts of steel and light that patrolled South Central neighborhoods nightly, peering into every dark corner with voyeuristic indecency. "At night, I see your light through my bedroom window / But I ain't got shit but the pad and pencil." The choppy sound of rotary blades offered a rhythmic pulse over the firing of handguns and automatic weapons below. Residents had to get used to the racket if they ever hoped to achieve a state of slumber.

War zone conditions were the result of decades of urban mis-management, heavy-handed policing, and systematic racism. Street crime, police brutality, and crack cocaine engulfed more lives every day. "South Central" had become a national byword for metro-politan decay. The Crips and Bloods, deadliest of enemies, were recognized around the world as exemplifying the most violent ten-dencies of street gangs; the Crips' penchant for blue apparel and the Bloods' preference for red, dueling hues from the moment kids can create a cognitive link between fingerpaints and the words used to describe them, defined the concept of gang colors.

Straight out of the Jordan Downs housing project of Watts was Aqeela Sherrills, a member of the Grape Street Crips, but one who'd left the area in the late 1980s to attend Cal State North-ridge. Off the block, Sherrills grappled with mixed feelings about street life. His gang-member brethren had been like a surrogate family to him, but so many members of that family had been cut down in what Sherrills had no doubt was a war that was raging out of control. "I lost thirteen good friends in 1989 alone," he told me. "Military conflict? Yeah, people had high-power weapons. I watched one of my partners get cut in half with an AK-47. When I say war, I mean it was war. And the numbers basically show it." True enough, in 1992 alone the reported number of gang-related homicides in L.A. County was 803. To contextualize that figure, the United States suffered a total of 383 fatalities during the entire Gulf War.

For Aqeela Sherrills, the situation could no longer be tolerated. He came together with his older brother, Daude, and several other Watts residents with gang connections to explore the possibility of brokering a peace. The result of their efforts was the Watts Treaty, a four-year process of hazardous negotiations that took place mostly outside the view or interest of those beyond the territory of the gangs. Because, as the group saw it, neither the government nor law enforcement had any real interest in stopping the killings happening in the neighborhood. Cops, after all, had a financial incentive to keep the violence going due to the income they were generating via overtime pay and the formation of specialized gang units and task forces. Said Aqeela, "We had to take strategy in our own hands."

It had to happen in historic Watts, the neighborhood underneath those famous steel towers that resemble something like a Gothic cathedral or post-apocalyptic cityscape, depending on what angle you look at it from. Incredibly, the seventeen interconnected architectural structures were designed and built solely by one man, Sabato Rodia, an Italian immigrant, between the years 1921 and 1954.

As Rodia constructed his masterpiece, the surrounding area was changing irrevocably. Prior to the 1920s, Watts was in line with the broader demographics of Southern California: its citizens were mostly white or of Mexican ancestry. When postwar migration caused the African American community to mushroom, Los Angeles responded by building several large housing projects in Watts between 1942 and 1954. The area soon had the highest concentration of public housing in the United States west of the Mississippi River. By the early 1960s, these projects were almost entirely Black.

The resettled families couldn't escape the racism they had attempted to flee. Soon Watts was segregated all but legally. The area became socially isolated, economically repressed, and publicly neglected. Communities were overcrowded, dilapidated, suffered high unemployment, and sat under the watch of an abusive police force. These were viselike conditions. It was only a matter of time before the neighborhoods cracked.

On August 11, 1965, at 116th Street and Avalon Boulevard, twenty-one-year-old Marquette Frye was pulled over on suspicion of drunk driving with his brother, Ronald, in the passenger seat. Soon after, their mother, Rena Frye, arrived at the scene from her nearby home to scold her sons and ask the officers if she could take the car—her husband, after all, needed it to drive to work. As a crowd gathered, a scuffle broke out between the cops and brothers. Mrs. Frye, five-foot-nothing if that, jumped on one officer's back. No sooner had she been dragged off than the charged-up Rena leaped on another patrolman. All three were taken to jail.

Residents considered the Frye arrests as indicative of the type of police misconduct that was rampant in the area—there were even rumors that an officer had kicked a pregnant onlooker at the scene. Their disgust ignited six days of civil uprising that became known as the Watts Riots. Thirty-four people died, with coroner's inquests into thirty-two of the dead finding that twenty-six were justifiable homicides, most at the hands of the LAPD and National Guard. Dr. Martin Luther King Jr. was warned not to visit—people were in no mood to hear his spiel on nonviolence. But he ignored the advice and arrived to what he described as "occupied territory" due to the presence of the National Guard. "After visiting Watts and talking with hundreds of persons of all walks of life," King later wrote, "it was my opinion that the riots grew out of the depths of despair which afflict a people who see no way out of their economic dilemma."

King left with major doubts that the white community was in any way concerned. True enough, just days after the riots began, Los Angeles police chief William H. Parker, a monumental presence in the department's history who became a hate figure in Black communities, rejected the suggestion that his department's failure to address allegations of police brutality had charged the tension. In his blinkered mind, the riots could have been avoided if police had not been handling the area's Black populace with "kid gloves."

When rioting failed to produce tangible change, the next response in Watts was the formation of gang culture. To the younger residents of the housing projects, gangs offered protection, hierarchy, respect, and, with the expanding narcotics trade, money. Selling drugs incentivized gangs to protect what they perceived as their territory. Borders and battle lines were drawn. Gang violence in Watts steadily increased throughout the 1970s and '80s. By the time Nancy Reagan was spearheading the "Just Say No" campaign in 1984, gangs were practically militarized. Pistols, submachine guns, and AK-47 assault rifles were among their arsenals. The most brutal tactic was the drive-by shooting—a phrase that became associated with Los Angeles more than any other city on the planet.

Aqeela remembered Markham Middle School sitting right next to railroad tracks that served as a border between different gang dominions: Crips, such as his own Grape Street set, to the east and Bloods to the west. "We traded a lot of bodies over the years, you know what I'm saying? If you can imagine that, like, I was terrified to go into the Nickerson Gardens as a kid. Terrified. Not so much so in the PJs [Imperial Courts housing projects], because we were both Crip neighborhoods, but I had family over there [in Nickerson Gardens]. I wouldn't go over there by myself. Please, man. Because people had gotten killed over there for just being over there, and vice versa."

Attempts to broker peace were as common as they were futile. In 1989, Louis Farrakhan invited gang members to a summit at a downtown hotel he called "Stop the Killing." The Nation of Islam claimed that gang members agreed to suspend all potentially murderous activities on that day. But lasting change proved elusive.

Then came the Watts Treaty, the precious fruit of a grassroots process, a small miracle in an area conditioned to not believe in such things. All its major architects were, or had previously been, gang members from Watts's four major housing projects: Hacienda Village, Imperial Courts, Jordan Downs, and Nickerson Gardens. They quickly surmised that achieving peace in a single swoop across the whole of Los Angeles would be impossible. But if these four projects could be united, it could inspire similar truces across the city.

The peacemakers retained the support and counsel of former National Football League player turned actor Jim Brown, who facilitated conversations through his community development program, Amer-I-Can. Early treaty meetings even took place in Brown's own home on swanky Sunset Plaza Drive. As many as four hundred people from across the city were summoned to Brown's house, with a Nation of Islam security team frisking everyone as they came through the door. Gangsters shed tears as they told stories of fallen friends to the attending Farrakhan. More meetings were held at Masjid Al Rasul, a mosque in Watts led by Minister Mujahid Abdul-Karim, a respected figure in the community. Discussions were tense. Gang members were often across the table from enemies responsible for the deaths of their friends. Many were paranoid about being set up. "The idea of retaliation was very much on the minds of every gang member," said William J. Aceves, the Dean Steven R. Smith Professor of Law at California Western School of Law. "And so it was simply getting them to recognize that you've got to let it go—you've got to let that past go." Reconciliation was the chief aim, though smaller issues also needed to be untangled to help facilitate it. "One of the big ones at the time was colors," explained Aqeela Sherrills. "You could literally get killed for wearing red or blue."

As these meetings advanced, it dawned on the group that if lasting peace was ever to be achieved, it required a formalized text. Daude Sherrills's interest in history led him to consider using an international peace treaty as a template. Because if the war between Crips and Bloods was analogous to a military conflict, it required a diplomatic solution—a ghetto entente cordiale. Daude asked fellow activist Anthony Perry, who later changed his name to Rasheed L. Muhammad, to draft the document. Perry paid a visit to the Von KleinSmid Center at the University of Southern California to investigate its collection of international legal documents. He soon came across the 1949 armistice agreement between Israel and Egypt to end hostilities in the 1948 Arab-Israeli War. If Perry required any more convincing of the document's suitability, its main architect was Dr. Ralph Bunche, a Black American diplomat from Los Angeles. Bunche had attended both Jefferson High School, which was just a few miles away from Watts, and the University of California, Los Angeles (UCLA). Using the armistice agreement as a basis, Perry, with help from Daude Sherrills, produced what was called "the Multi-Peace Treaty–General Armistice Agreement."

In addition to the treaty, Daude wrote a separate document, United Black Community Code, to serve as a code of conduct for gang members. "I accept the duty to honor, uphold and defend the spirit of the red, blue and purple [color of the Grape Street Watts Crips]," Sherrills wrote, "to teach the black family its legacy and protracted struggle for freedom and justice."

The text added extra weight to four years of dialogue. By 1992, Aqeela could feel peace getting tantalizingly close. Neutral-ground meetings had been successful, but there was one thing that had still never been attempted: negotiations in hostile territory.

On April 26—three days before the Los Angeles riots—a delegation of a dozen Grape Street Crips led by the Sherrills brothers drove two miles south from the Jordan Downs housing project to Imperial Courts, where their PJ Crips rivals resided. The final destination was a local gym, where talks would continue.

"This was the meeting that we finally went into the enemy's territory after months of meetings," said Aqeela. "We were like, 'Hey, we've talked to everybody, we've talked to the shooters, every conversation has been had, the only thing that hasn't happened is we haven't gone into each other's territory and see what happens.'"

Picture the scene. Upon arrival, the Grape Street Crips could hear the warning calls ring out: "All the cats from Jordan Downs over here!" Soon, the figure of Tony Bogard, a senior PJ Crip, emerged, ushering his guests to step into the gym for the conference. A fearsome presence in the neighborhood, Bogard was a quintessential gangbanger with a growing rap sheet when, in January 1990, while standing in the doorway of his stucco bungalow, a high-powered military-style rifle put him on a life-support machine. Bogard made a deal with God: if he lived, he would turn peacemaker. And here he was, ready to settle that debt.

Younger gang members waited outside the gym as their elders, many of them high-ranking gang leaders, got down to business. Soon Don Gordon, a member of Grape Street Crips fundamental in the work toward peace, switched on some music. Suspicion faded away for hugs and handshakes.

As word began to spread outside about the impending peace agreement, excited young guys from the Imperial Courts began approaching Aqeela.

"Man, you all with it?" one asked. "You all with the peace?"

"Yeah, we with it!" Aqeela replied.

For Aqeela, this was the moment the treaty became reality.

The next day, Jordan Downs returned the hospitality by welcoming PJ Crips into the neighborhood. Only this time, the two Crip sets were joined by gang members from Nickerson Gardens, a Bloods neighborhood. "There were people there who'd never been in Jordan Downs and literally lived four blocks away," said Aqeela of his guests that day. On May 3, the day before the Los Angeles riots ended, the Pirus Bloods of the Hacienda Village housing project became the fourth Watts set to enter the accord.

The Watts Treaty is an underreported story, part of the neighborhood's murky history, obscured by the insular nature of its creation. As such, it's prone to inaccurate claims and inflated myths. For one, it's regularly said that the treaty was signed by representatives of four gangs in a mosque on the eve of the Los Angeles riots. This meeting appears to be a fabrication. In fact, the treaty itself was never signed with much sense of ceremony. "It didn't happen that way," confirmed Aqeela. "People signed the documents at different times."

Aceves actually judges the importance of the Watts Treaty as having little to do with the actual text. He sees it as an emblem of peace, rather than a pact that required men to ink their names to become enforceable. "There really wasn't an official signing. I think the treaty metaphor is quite accurate, certainly in terms of the document itself. The articles that they referenced, the inspiration behind it was clearly treaty based, and the document itself incorporated treaty language. In terms of the actual signing, I think it was more informal."

There was a significant event that happened the day before the riots, though: about two hundred Crips and Bloods attended a Los

Angeles City Council meeting to inform elected officials of the treaty and their intention to bring other gangs into the fold. They were met with funny looks from the bemused politicians. Yet once the uprising broke out, the city contacted the coalition for help. And despite the lack of respect shown to them at the meeting, they worked to suppress the violence and looting.

By the time the riots raged, graffiti in Watts had announced the truce. Over the next few weeks, Bloods and Crips held exuberant beer-soaked unity parties, tearfully toasting the suspension of hostilities. As lawlessness gripped the rest of the city, the treaty stood firm. Property damage in Watts was comparatively modest during the riots, and though there were three deaths, it was the police alone that were responsible.

In 1992, Tupac moved to Los Angeles, a rising rap stronghold with which he would become closely associated. He too became motivated to work with the gangs on fostering positive change. As Watts partied to honor peace, he was preparing his own manifesto. Developed with Jamal Joseph and, from within prison, Mutulu Shakur, it was a twenty-six-point code of ethics for gangsters to live by, a Bushido code for South Central to bring honor and nobility to gang life, a common framework that would alleviate the lifestyle's more destructive—more fatal—aspects. They dubbed their reformist text the Code of Thug Life.

Tupac's attempt to broker his charter is easily conflated with the Watts Treaty, a movement he was not involved in. "It [the Code of Thug Life] was something that I'd heard about vaguely," Aqeela told me. Like the Watts Treaty, this maneuver to bring some kind of order to L.A.'s gangs was carried out beyond the gaze of the city's politicians, authorities, and administrators. Reporting by Ben Westhoff in his 2016 book *Original Gangstas: The Untold Story of Dr. Dre, Eazy-E, Ice Cube, Tupac Shakur, and the Birth of West Coast Rap* revealed that representatives of the Grape Street Crips, PJ Watts Crips, Bounty Hunter Bloods, and Hacienda Village Bloods agreed to abide by the Code of Thug Life at one of the picnics that happened in the wake of the riots. "These were summits, raucous parties, and family picnics all in one," wrote Westhoff. "Despite some fights breaking out, resulting in the appearance of a police heli-copter, the involved parties agreed to abide by Thug Life." Tupac himself was not present at the event, but his counsel is said to have been crucial.

In the fog of the neighborhood's undocumented history, how much of this story is fact and how much is folklore is difficult to discern. It's entirely plausible to me that some gang members—impressed by Tupac's artistry and celebrity, and respectful of his Panther lineage—did agree to adhere to his code at one of the post-treaty picnics.

Whatever the case, the Code of Thug Life probably wasn't as directly responsible for reducing gang violence as the Watts Treaty proved to be. What is undeniable, though, is the glimpse we get into Tupac's beliefs as a unifier of the underprivileged, a statesman of the projects. Tupac was a proud Panther cub who'd once tin-kered with the idea of restarting the party. But as the 1990s moved on, he began to blend his roots with a new ethos. Here he was, summoning the spirit of Huey Newton and Bobby Seale's origi-nal Panther manifesto by laying out in clear language a guide to live by. But while the Panthers' Ten-Point Program envisioned a restructuring of society, Tupac's plan was tailored for those living outside of such structures: it was penned for the gangbangers, the outlaws, the thugs. As such, it eschewed the Ten-Point Program's righteous, authoritative eloquence for the unpolished language of the streets. As the first line of the code's preamble reads, "Someone must dare put the street life back on track, because it is clear to anybody that can see—that the hustling game has gone stark rav-ing mad." Tupac seemed keenly aware that in the 1990s he'd have to evolve the Panthers' principles. The Code of Thug Life repre-sented this evolution.

The Code of Thug Life is not a sophisticated document. Many of the twenty-six points are repetitive, while others are vague or obvious to the point of being meaningless—it's easy to picture a gang member glancing at rules about not snitching and respecting old people and saying, "Sure, I'll sign up to this." It can feel in places like it's playing to a glamorous, cinematic ideal of what a gang-ster is, rather than difficult realities. But at its heart, the Code of

Thug Life preached self-governance. Of course it did. Tupac's own mother had fought off the cloak-and-dagger tactics of authorities empowered by the state to destroy her; he himself had experienced police brutality firsthand. In the shadow of such beasts, short-term tangible change to a community needed to come from within.

The Code of Thug Life asserts that Tupac's societal theories were largely shaped by realpolitik—ending gang violence was going to be difficult, so first try to eliminate the deaths of innocent bystanders; you won't stop drug dealers, so stop them selling to pregnant women. If collapsing the system feels too big, maybe thriving within it is the only option. That is to say, you make the best of the proverbial cards you are dealt.

Some have eviscerated the initiative. In their book *Tupac Shakur: The Life and Times of an American Icon*, Tayannah Lee McQuillar and Fred L. Johnson III say that the Code of Thug Life "wasn't the mother of all bad ideas, but it came close," criticizing its outlook that Black people should simply better endure their community's disintegration—if Thug Life forbade carjacking friends, did that mean stealing from strangers was absolutely fine? It's fair commentary. But Thug Life asserted Tupac's belief that being an outlaw was how you struck back against America for imposing such conditions. It meant embracing the notion of being a thug, taking a word often used to stigmatize and denigrate and wearing it with pride.

The Code of Thug Life came and went, and is a relatively small component in Tupac's story. "Thug Life," however, became a huge part of his ethos and legacy. Moving beyond the code, he started using it more as a catchall expression for different aspects of what it is to be a Black man in America. He'd later declare it an acronym: "The Hate U Give Little Infants Fucks Everybody," the idea that the vicious cycle of racism and oppression ends up folding back on society. And in 1994, 2Pac formed a group also called Thug Life with Mopreme and three other artists he'd grown close to: the Rated R, Macadoshis, and Tyruss "Big Syke" Himes, a deep-voiced Inglewood Crip who'd become one of 2Pac's closest collaborators. The collective put out their one and only album, *Thug Life, Volume 1*, that September.

The expression "Thug Life" and Tupac are inextricably linked—

he had it inked across his abdomen in huge lettering. But Thug Life is often misunderstood as simply the surface-level glamorization of criminality. To be certain, he wished to claim the word so over-used to smear him and other Black men. But Thug Life went much deeper. "I don't consider myself to be straight, you know, militant. You know what I'm saying? I'm a thug," he said in 1994. "I'm a thug. And my thug comes from . . . my definition of thug comes from half of the street element. Straight street hustling. And half of the Panther element. Half of the independence movement. Saying we want self-determination. We want to do it by self-defense and by any means necessary. That came from my family and that's what Thug Life is. It's a mixture.

"When I say 'thug' I mean, not criminal or someone that will beat you over the head, I mean the underdog," he explained. "I mean someone who goes out there and succeeds who has overcame all obstacles."

Similarly, Tupac had a partiality for identifying as an outlaw. The word is typically defined as a synonym for fugitive—the Weather Underground had been outlaws. But Tupac felt he met the historic definition of a person deprived of the benefit and protection of the law. It's natural he would come to embrace this term too.

Thug Life would go on to become a meme. The internet is filled with cell-phone-recorded clips that typically begin with people, often small children, using profane language, followed by a sudden freeze-frame as a gangsta rap song kicks in and the words "Thug Life" appear on-screen. The idea is that living a Thug Life means threatening people, copping an attitude, being belligerent as a default. It was antithetical to Tupac's interpretation, returning "thug" to its lowest terms.

The treaty's impact was as immediate as it was unprecedented. There are plenty of raw numbers to support its success: gang homicides in L.A. County fell from 803 in 1992 to 399 in 1998; drive-by shootings were cut by one-third between 1991 and 1993. This is not eradication, of course: in 1994, Tony Bogard was tragically killed at the Imperial Courts housing project; the rush of shootings in Compton in the days after Tupac's murder is widely attributed to the Bloods, with which he'd been affiliated, seeking retribution against Crip compatriots of the men it blamed for the killing. But anecdotally, South Central became a better place to live. Families separated by gang conflict were united. In August, the only funeral home in the neighborhood, the Ashley-Grigsby Mortuary at Century Boulevard and Central Avenue, told the *L.A. Times* it had not scheduled any gang rites since the treaty took hold.

"It felt like [we were] burying our own kids because, literally speaking, they are our kids," said operations manager Betty Edwards. The truce was "so beautiful," she added. "God has his hand in this."

The peacemakers' theory that an agreement among the projects of Watts would lead to broader peace proved correct, with truces being made in Compton, Long Beach, and Pasadena, among other areas. "When Watts reached its peace treaty, it created a domino across the city," said Aqeela.

"I think it was a real good thing to get people to stop looking at their brother like he was the enemy automatically, just based on whatever location he was from or what color he had on," reflected rapper Big Tray Deee, a former Crip. "And it kind of broke the ice that needed to be broken for the interactions to start taking place. And once that did, a lot of the murders decreased."

As the years went by, the impact of the Watts Treaty began to subside. Gang leadership began to retire; some were killed. They were replaced by new members without the same connection to the treaty and so less likely to respect it. "Because so much of the treaty was about forgiveness and letting go of the past, when new members came in, they had none of that to go on," said Aceves.

Still, its impact can't be ignored. Who can know how many lives were saved because these activists managed to step on the hose of gang violence?

"If the truce ends tomorrow," resident Roosevelt Williams told the *L.A. Times* in August 1992, "I'll be grateful for the little peace we did have."

For a year, Rodney King kept his head down. District Attorney Ira Reiner had determined there was insufficient evidence to prosecute King for any crime related to the pursuit that resulted in his beating. Reiner did, though, announce that he would seek indictments against the officers from a grand jury. Within a week, the jury—after watching the videotape and listening to testimony from King and others—returned indictments against Sergeant Stacey Koon and Officers Laurence Powell, Theodore Briseno, and Timothy Wind. And so King waited for his wounds to heal and for justice to be served.

It would be the perception that the same prejudices that guided the baton blows existed in the legal system that ultimately turned huge sections of Los Angeles into ash. Rebelling against police brutality had happened before, most notably in Watts. But many Black Angelenos held out hope that in the 1990s, with this racism caught on modern cameras and beamed out to the whole country, there would be accountability. Finally.

They had fresh reasons to be skeptical. Two weeks after the King beating, Latasha Harlins, a fifteen-year-old Black student, walked into Empire Liquor Market and Deli on South Figueroa Street. Latasha's grandmother had warned her that the store was quick to accuse local kids of shoplifting, but being just five minutes away from her home, it was an ideal place to stop. And besides, all Latasha wanted was a bottle of orange juice, which she picked up and stuffed into her backpack. Watching on was middle-aged Korean-born merchant Soon Ja Du, who immediately concluded that Latasha was stealing. The accusation was made; Du grabbed Latasha's sweater. The girl reacted by punching Du in the face and darting for the shop door. But before Latasha could make it to the safety of the street, Du had picked up a handgun. The trigger was squeezed and, from a distance of about three feet, Latasha was shot in the back of the head. Police found two dollars in her lifeless hand. The killing was caught on the store camera. That November, a jury found Du guilty of manslaughter, yet Judge Joyce Karlin sentenced her to five years of probation, no jail time.

To local activists, the leniency of the sentence was a bitter blow. The Du case exacerbated long-simmering tensions between Korean merchants and their Black customers, and, by extension, both L.A. communities. The shooting death of Lee Arthur Mitchell in June

1991 by store owner Tae Sam Park in South Central had sparked a boycott of all Korean-owned stores. But Latasha stirred emotions. Every Black parent in L.A. saw this little girl die. And for what? Orange juice and because of the color of her skin.

Besotted with the case, 2Pac referenced Latasha in multiple songs for the rest of his life. On "Hellrazor," which didn't receive a release until after his death, 2Pac cries, "Dear Lord if ya hear me, tell me why / Little girl like Latasha had to die." From there, he describes the tragedy in brutal detail ("She never got to see the bullet, just heard the shot") before collapsing into despair: "Now I'm screamin' fuck the world."

While 2Pac's lyrics tended to focus on the tragedy of Latasha's death, his sensitive soul wilting at the sadness and pointlessness of it, Ice Cube's writing captured the rising animosity between L.A.'s Black and Korean communities with his trademark fury. To understand these tensions, listen to his controversial song "Black Korea." The narrative follows Cube as he is hassled by distrusting Korean store owners while trying to buy a forty-ounce bottle of malt liquor. Cube confronts the entrepreneurs, first threatening them with a boycott ("So don't follow me up and down your market / Or your little chop suey ass'll be a target / Of the nationwide boycott") and then arson ("So pay respect to the Black fist / Or we'll burn your store, right down to a crisp"). It was incendiary—the National Korean American Grocers Association even tried to convince malt liquor company St. Ides to drop the rapper as their spokesman— but Cube didn't guide what was to come, he merely captured why it happened.

Back in the courtroom, there was a legal struggle to pull King's trial out of Los Angeles County. Judge Bernard Kamins denied the defense's motion that claimed L.A. could not produce an untainted jury. But in what was likely crucial to the outcome, the California Court of Appeals unanimously granted the change of venue. The court also found cause to take the case away from Judge Kamins entirely when it learned of a message he sent to prosecutors stating, "Don't panic. You can trust me." The case was reassigned to Judge Stanley Weisberg, who, in November, okayed the predominantly white and conservative Simi Valley as the venue. The jury assembled consisted of ten white people, one Hispanic, and one Filipino American.

As part of his opening statement for the prosecution on March 5, 1992, Deputy District Attorney Terry White played the Holliday footage in its entirety. It wouldn't be the last time jurors were asked to watch the infamous tape.

On April 29, 1992, the seventh day of jury deliberations, the jury acquitted all four officers of assault and acquitted three of the four of using excessive force. The verdict came at around three p.m.; less than three hours later, L.A. began to burn.

Outside the courthouse, mutiny was immediately palpable. County sheriff's deputies had to protect Stacey Koon from angry protesters as he made his way to his car. John Singleton, who was in the crowd at the courthouse, predicted, "By having this verdict, what these people done, they lit the fuse to a bomb."

Despairing members of the Black community gathered in churches. First African Methodist Episcopal Church, the oldest Black congregation in Los Angeles, became a magnet for politicians, religious leaders, and parishioners who wanted to process the jury's decision. Among them was Mayor Tom Bradley, who in an earlier statement had made it clear where he stood: "The jury's verdict will never blind the world to what we saw on the videotape."

But the uprising was happening on the streets. Unlike the 1965 Watts Riots, the conflagration that took hold after the King trial wasn't constrained to a single neighborhood and was not restricted to Black Angelenos. It did, though, ignite at Florence and Normandie, which the *Los Angeles Times* would call the riot's "ground zero." There sat Tom's Liquor, its inventory fueling the anger. The situation soon became so dicey that cops advised one another to stay clear.

Radio stations stopped playing music shortly after the verdict to cover the fallout. Listeners called in to report what they were seeing around the city and vent their frustrations. One caller phoned up his local radio station to simply repeat the rallying cry of the Watts Riots: "Burn, baby, burn."

Filmmaker Matthew McDaniel grabbed his camera and began shooting at street level. His footage would become the ultra-low-budget documentary *Birth of a Nation*—the title an obvious take on D. W. Griffith's 1915 silent movie about the American Civil War and the rise of the Ku Klux Klan. In the most moving scene of McDaniel's film, a man begins preaching to onlookers, asking them to disregard material things to start their own businesses. He calls them "Africans," pointedly omitting the "American" from the signifier. His attention soon turns to a small boy.

"Hey, I'ma tell you right now. If-if-if I have to die today, for this little African right here to have a future, I'm a dead motherfucker."

Dr. Dre later took the clip and placed it at the start of his song "Lil' Ghetto Boy."

Being chauffeured through the city by his father was future Dre protégé and Tupac disciple Kendrick Lamar. From the vehicle, the four-year-old could see the smoke billow. Soon Kendrick's dad, Kenny, pulled up outside an AutoZone outlet, returning with four boosted tires. This was the kind of out-of-control looting that was occurring throughout the city. As the older Lamar told *Rolling Stone* in 2015, "We were all taking stuff. That's the way it was in the riots!"

Looting, as we understand it in a contemporary context, is spontaneous wealth redistribution. It's a temporary small-scale reversal of the balance of power; the root cause is enforced poverty. But it also represents the breakdown of a key societal structure: the concept of ownership, whether goods or property. In confusion and disorder, proprietorship is revealed to be an entirely man-made concept, weak at the tendons, given strength only if the people choose to abide by it.

"Then we get to the house," Kendrick added to his story, "and him [Kendrick's dad] and my uncles are like, 'We fixing to get this, we fixing to get that, we fixing to get *all* this shit!' I'm thinking they're robbing. There's some real mayhem going on in L.A. Then, as time progresses, I'm watching the news, hearing about Rodney King and all this, I said to my mom, 'So the police beat up a Black man, and now everybody's mad? Ok. I get it now.'"

In the center of the storm, *Time* journalist Sylvester Monroe witnessed one young Black man who seemed to manifest everything that was happening in the city. The man was shouting at the police in front of a burning building: "Burn, baby, burn! How you like me now, Mr. POLICEMAN!" Not even a shotgun pointed in his face could convince the man to stand down.

"Oh no! You gonna shoot me, Mr. POLICEMAN! I bet you wanna give me a Rodney King type ass-whipping, don't you, Mr. POLICEMAN!"

Monroe wrote, "As I watched the city burning that night in what would become the worst unrest in U.S. history—more than 50 dead, 2,000 injured, and nearly $1 billion property damage—I couldn't help but think how much I identified with the young man screaming at the police officers. His screams echoed decades of pent-up anger and frustration over the use of excessive force by police officers against black victims, not just in Los Angeles, but all over the country."

Into the pyre landed Tupac Shakur. The rage he'd bottled on *2Pacalypse Now*—and the rage of so many rappers, particularly those from the same streets that were now burning—had proved prophetic.

New York rap legend Kool G Rap remembered meeting Tupac for the first time during the riots, confirming John Singleton's stories of his actor riding around the city streets shooting guns. Amid the chaos, only a couple of people recognized either of the two stars. "Everybody was just so bugging out and doing their own thing so much, they didn't notice no Pac or G Rap at that time," he said. "Pac was expressing his sense of anger for the verdict. He was shooting out store windows, shit like that."

Tupac wasn't there as a celebrity. He wasn't there as a peace-maker. This was the closest he'd touched the Weathermen's Days of Rage; squint his eyes and he could imagine himself in Eldridge Cleaver's vision of the masses rising up in violent defiance. There was no intention that a domino effect would occur, toppling city after city, government after government, until the White House fell. It was just fury. But to be part of that message was not *nothing*.

The looting stretched into the next day. It was a calmer loot-ing, seemingly done opportunistically rather than in anger. By this point, Koreatown's business owners were done feeling helpless. They armed themselves and started to guard the buildings. The image of gun-toting Koreans on rooftops became a defining image of the riots.

On Friday, May 1, the third night of unrest, President George H. W. Bush made himself seen. Appearing on TV, he claimed to be disturbed by the King verdict, but these assertions came with the message that he would use "whatever force is necessary to restore order." It was a heavy-handed response. Two thousand riot-trained federal officers were deployed to Los Angeles to join the three thousand National Guard troops already stationed there. Among them were Border Patrol agents, who searched for undocumented migrants whether they took part in the riots or not. By the end of the uprising more than 20,000 law enforcement officers and soldiers had arrested 16,291 people.

In Bush's mind, the riots were not about social justice or equity in the eyes of the law; this was criminality, plain and simple. "What we saw last night and the night before in Los Angeles is not about civil rights," he said. "It's not about the great cause of equality that all Americans must uphold. It's not a message of protest. It's been the brutality of a mob, pure and simple."

It was also the day Rodney King was presented at a press conference, apparently with a prepared statement. "People, I just want to say, can't we all get along? Can't we all get along?"

Amid relative calm, Tupac found himself back in the city a week later. In footage shot in what appears to be a local park, he agreed to speak to Swedish TV, giving them a pointed encapsulation: "I hate to say I told you so, but I told you so."

Tupac's absconsion from the set of *Poetic Justice* wasn't just an emotional reaction to what was happening in Los Angeles. Throughout the shoot, he was a challenging talent for Singleton. The young actor admired the director, no doubt about that. On a location scout during preproduction, he sat in the van next to Singleton, discussing *Boyz n the Hood* and what he thought made the movie so special. (The director's first choice for Tupac's role in *Poetic Justice* was actually *Boyz* star Ice Cube, who turned it down after disagreements over the script.) One part in particular struck Tupac: the scene where Furious Styles, played by Laurence Fishburne, takes his son, Tre, to the beach. The father's bond with his child tightens when, during the drive home, an old soul number comes on the radio: "O-o-h Child" by the Five Stairsteps.

Suddenly, Tupac started singing the song: "O-o-h child, things are goin' to get easier / O-o-h child, things will get brighter . . . / Someday, we'll walk in the rays of the beautiful sun / Someday, when the world is much brighter." The scene had stirred something within the young man eternally seeking a father-son connection.

"I loved that song, man," Tupac told Singleton. "That shit meant a lot to me."

Recognizing the opportunity in front of him didn't quell Tupac's unruly side. There were days he'd get high in his trailer, or arrive to set hours late, or get irritated by the crew. But the performance he delivered was more mature and polished than even his electric turn in *Juice*.

Poetic Justice is, quintessentially, a great American road movie, taking viewers on a tour from Los Angeles to NorCal. It centers on hairdresser and South Central resident Justice (Janet Jackson), who writes poetry to deal with the pain of the murder of her boyfriend (portrayed by A Tribe Called Quest's Q-Tip). Tupac plays Lucky, a postal worker and young father dealing with a lot of common problems. The pair grow close on a long drive to Oakland with Justice's friend Iesha (Regina King) and Iesha's boyfriend Chicago (Joe Torry).

Dawn Gilliam served as script supervisor on *Poetic Justice*. Encountering movie stars was part of her job; still, Tupac's aura stood out to Gilliam as something special. "We would go to dailies, and I remember seeing a scene that he had done," she said. "He was mesmerizing on-screen."

That his core cast members jelled must have delighted Singleton. Jackson even asked the director and her costars if they wanted to go to see instrumental rap band the Roots perform, and they all hung out as friends. The intimacy of the group's working relationship meant that Torry and King quickly observed that Tupac was a young man burdened. He often acted jittery, and when he removed his hat, they saw that clumps of his hair had fallen out. It wasn't until later that Torry heard about the beating he'd taken from police and put the pieces together.

Poetic Justice also starred one Maya Angelou, who featured in the scene when the group crash a family reunion barbecue in a park. Her presence on set was undeniable. "That's everybody's grandmother; that's everybody's teacher," remembered Torry. "That's this character that you heard of in school." Angelou wasn't impressed with Tupac's foul mouth, and on their second day working together, watched on as he and another young man squared up to each other like they were going to fight. It was enough. She pulled Tupac to one side.

"Do you know how much you are needed?" Angelou asked him. "Do you know what you mean to us? Do you know that hundreds of years of struggle have been for you? Please, baby, take a minute. Don't lose your life on a zoom."

In Angelou's arms, Tupac began to weep. She led him to a little gully near the shoot, his back to the crew to keep the tears private.

Back in her trailer, Angelou was visited by Janet Jackson.

"Dr. Angelou," she shrieked, "I don't believe you actually spoke to Tupac Shakur!"

"Darling," she replied, "I don't know six-pack."

"I had never heard of him," Angelou recalled years later. "That wasn't in my world."

Tupac was so moved, he called Afeni to describe the moment. Afeni, in turn, wrote Angelou a thank-you note. And Tupac ensured his behavior was always respectful around Angelou thereafter.

If Angelou was like a grandmother to the young cast, she still had her favorites. Torry's experience with her was markedly different from Tupac's. After Angelou had showed a soft touch with Torry's costar, he had the notion to share some poetry with her as she was talking to Jackson. "Shut up young man," yelled Angelou when interrupted by the comedian. "You're not here to entertain me." *Whoa*, thought Torry. *Give me the same talk you gave Tupac.*

Tupac, too, showed himself capable of compassion. That same reunion scene features Dawn Gilliam's then-thirteen-year-old daughter as an extra. Gilliam had recently trimmed the girl's damaged hair into a tight do, and the other kids on set teased her about her new look. It was Tupac who came to the girl's aid, telling her that Afeni too wore her hair in a short Afro and that it was beautiful. He even let the girl listen to some of his forthcoming music in his Jeep.

Toward the end of production, on the morning of what was supposed to be his day off, the producers decided that they would shoot publicity stills and called Tupac to the set. Ticked off by the change in schedule, he arrived with his crew and began screaming, "I can't take this shit. Y'all treat a n***a like a slave." Having stormed off to his trailer, he released his anger by slamming his fist through a window.

Poetic Justice wasn't received with the same rapture as *Boyz n the Hood*, and Tupac didn't associate with the role of Lucky in the same way he did Bishop in *Juice*. It was like the character's DNA was amalgamating with his own: the more successful he became, the more the Bishop ideal tightened itself to his bones. Chaos was taking hold.

August 22, 1992, was a warm, sunny day in Marin City—the kind of weather the tightly knit community was no doubt praying would grace its annual music festival, one of the oldest events of its kind organized by African Americans in Northern California. This particular year would also mark Marin City's fiftieth anniversary. It was a bright spot on the calendar in a poor neighborhood that had too few opportunities to celebrate.

Joining the festivities was one of Marin City's most famous sons, Tupac Shakur. Flanked by a group that included Mopreme, the star guest posed for photographs and signed autographs with residents of the community he once called home. But the atmosphere grew cold when, his lawyers would later claim, Tupac was confronted by a group who had been greatly offended by supposedly derogatory statements about Marin City that he had made in a television interview. Arguments escalated to a brawl. It was later claimed in court that Tupac pulled a .380 Colt automatic handgun during the ruckus. He was then struck by rival rapper Demitrius Striplin, causing him to fall to the ground and drop the weapon.

The stricken Tupac sought help from Mopreme: "Get the gun, get the gun!" In the ruckus and confusion, shots were fired—three to six of them, police claimed. One hundred yards away, a six-year-old boy named Qa'id Walker-Teal was pedaling his bicycle at a school playground when the gunfire rang out. A bullet struck Qa'id in the forehead, killing him.

The stepbrothers and their crew ran to their car but took a wrong turn and ended up in front of a sheriff's substation, where they were confronted by an angry mob pointing at Mopreme and shouting, "He's the one!" When they did finally make it to their Jeep, locals descended on the vehicle, smashing one of the windows and reaching inside in an attempt to seize the slender Tupac. Sheriffs soon arrived at the scene, guns drawn, and the group were arrested. In nearby bushes, investigators found Tupac's gun. Mopreme's driver's license was also recovered close by. Though all were detained and questioned, none of the group faced any charges.

A wrongful death lawsuit was filed by Qa'id's parents against Tupac and Mopreme accusing them of responsibility. It was three years after the tragedy when a Marin County Superior Court finally saw the case. During the proceedings, Tupac's lawyer, Dennis Cunningham, pinned responsibility on Striplin and his friends, saying it was the "attackers whose actions caused the shooting."

"Bad on him for allowing his gun to be in that place," Cunningham said of his client, but "it was a mob scene and it was nasty . . . Somebody fired the gun over the heads of the advancing crowd that was going to do them harm."

The case ended up being cut short. After just two witnesses, both Marin City police officers, took the stand to testify—and despite indications from Qa'id's parents' attorney that she was prepared to call twenty-nine witnesses—the lawsuit was settled.

Four years after losing her son, on the day of Tupac's death, Qa'id's mother, Ocita Teal, was approached by *The New York Times*. The grieving parent was unable to reply when asked by the reporter whether she had forgiven the rapper. Instead, Teal stared into the distance for a few moments, grimaced, apologized, and walked away.

Ingrid Casares, Madonna, Sting, and Tupac attend a book party for Gianni Versace's *Designs* at Barocco in New York City, 1994.

9

NIGHTMARES

ICONS TYPICALLY HAVE origin points, a traceable event that chroniclers can isolate as the moment in time when they went from simply being famous to something beyond. Michael Jackson moonwalked across the stage at *Motown 25* to the grinding, electro-slap funk of "Billie Jean." Marilyn Monroe felt a breeze. Dr. Martin Luther King Jr. declared that he had a dream. With Tupac Shakur, the beginning of the legend is less clear. If anything, his importance maintained an upward trajectory after his death, until a true mythology took shape. But I can identify the moment when Tupac first *looked* like a superstar—the moment when he began to resemble the strongest image he'd leave behind.

"I Get Around" borrows a title and theme from the Beach Boys' sunny 1964 single. One of the original visions of surf's-up 1960s California, Brian Wilson and Mike Love's composition is often interpreted to be about promiscuity, a reading strengthened when you read some of Wilson's unused lyrics: "Well there's a million little girls just waitin' around / But there's only so much to do in a little town / I get around from town to town."

Almost three decades later, 2Pac wasn't interested in burying his song's horny overtones. The 1993 "I Get Around" is about a young knucklehead who likes girls, plain and simple. Over a Shock G beat with the producer's trademark smooth 'n' funky snap, 2Pac describes his pager blowing up with communiqués from young beauties eager to hook up. His rapping is relaxed and full of mischief; Shock G and Money-B provide verses because this is a party and parties need esteemed guests. "I Get Around" became 2Pac's first true solo hit single, and one of the songs I'm most likely to throw on at a get-together if the moment demands some of his music.

There's also the video, which follows 2Pac as he wakes up in a mansion having slumbered with several women, just in time to welcome the homies to party once more. It was shot in the good Malibu weather; the sun smiles on the revelry as countless guests carouse on the grounds of the estate, no storyline to complicate the joy and jubilee. "The funnest day of my life," reflected Money-B. "It was like we had a party and we shot the video within our breaks."

But it's more than that. "I Get Around" is when much of the 2Pac image became calcified. Banished were the grayscale tones of previous videos, with a 1990s rap star emerging in living color. The socially conscious rapper was displaced by a paragon of MTV appeal. The baby-face features of Bishop from *Juice* had melted away, replaced by more striking handsomeness. You see 2Pac's chiseled torso, the Thug Life tattoo in full view. The sunny climate firmly positioned the transient young man as straight West Coast. And when he raps the line "And I'll be there in a jiffy / Don't be picky, just be happy with this quickie," it's with an almost cartoon character–style run around the mansion's tennis court—elbows out, fists tight to his chest—the glint in his eye sparkling brightly. This is the fun 2Pac of many people's memories.

The urbane, neck-snapping beat came from Shock G himself. The producer had promised to share some music when, during a break in his *Poetic Justice* schedule, Tupac visited Digital Underground's tour bus in Atlanta. Seizing a copy of *Billboard* magazine to check the charts, Tupac grew frustrated that *2Pacalypse Now* was floundering behind his old group's second album, *Sons of the P*. "Well, if I could get a beat like 'Kiss You Back,'" Tupac argued, referencing Digital Underground's boppy hit single. Perhaps it was at that moment he realized that he needed tunes with radio appeal to sit alongside his more impassioned message records. And so Shock gifted him the "I Get Around" instrumental, which 2Pac turned into a wondrous banger. "Still clown with the Underground, when we come around," he raps, showing loyalty to the crew who assisted his come-up. Yet it was clear that 2Pac was accelerating far beyond what Shock G et al. could ever hope to be.

There is always a slight surprise when you see him, isn't there? A jolt. Memory never seems to do Tupac justice. The greatest icon hip-hop ever produced is also its most aesthetically perfect man. This, of course, is no coincidence. It would be ridiculous to deny that beauty bolstered both Tupac's fame in life and symbolism in death. You can say the same for Che Guevara and Bob Marley, similar icons, similarly beautiful.

Many people who knew Tupac have told me much the same thing, rendering the observation trite to the point that I hesitate to repeat it. But here goes . . . They describe the magnetic pull he exuded, relying on clichés like "it factor" to describe that hard-to-define quality that four versions of the movie *A Star Is Born* convinces us is innate in certain special human beings. This quality is intangible, yet unmissable. If Tupac had never rapped a bar or appeared on a second of celluloid, he still would have been a luminous presence, capable of igniting love and lust, envy and reverence.

"I Get Around" was released as a single in the summer of 1993, just in time to kindle barbecues. Nothing would be as innocent again. By Valentine's Day 1995, Tupac's home was not a mansion, but a prison cell. His mind had traced the decor of many courtrooms; that toned physique bore the imperfection of bullet wounds. "I have headaches," he told *Vibe* as he stewed in prison. "I wake up screaming. I've been having nightmares, thinking they're still shooting me."

This was the psychological trauma of the previous eighteen months, not even escapable in sleep.

The business brains with a vested interest in 2Pac must have approved of the radio-friendly vibes of "I Get Around," but they didn't love everything the rising star was doing. Tupac spent much of 1992 working on his second album, eventually settling on the title *Troublesome '21*. Soon enough, he discovered the sharp edge of breaking bread with a behemoth corporation. Time Warner, rattled by politician-led controversies surrounding *2Pacalypse Now*, refused to sign off on the follow-up due to its content. *Troublesome '21* was eventually scrapped.

Salvaging what he could from the burned-down house, 2Pac assembled *Strictly 4 My N.I.G.G.A.Z . . .* Though a compromised product, it nonetheless built on the same hard-hitting sounds of his debut. Again commenting on the times, 2Pac revisits themes of police brutality, Black nationalism, and the urgent need to fight the powers that be.

One figure of power looms over *Strictly* above all others. Since inserting himself into the discourse, the figure of Dan Quayle had played on 2Pac's mind, begging to be addressed on record. Whether he was genuinely irked by the vice president or simply saw him as a useful vessel to further his own notoriety, 2Pac used *Strictly* to draw attention to Quayle's condemnation. The two-minute track "Pac's Theme" is just a repeated audio snippet of Quayle's criticism of *2Pacalypse Now* ("There is absolutely no reason for a record like this to be published. It has no place in our society.") mixed with clips from a Tupac interview over a beat. Even the title of the track feels like a taunt toward Quayle: "Pac's Theme," the artist taking his enemy's words and wiring them into his own anthem.

The ghastly figure of Quayle is returned to throughout the album. 2Pac teams up with Ice Cube and Ice-T on the thunderous "Last Wordz," a song that matched the grisly yet politically incisive work Cube was doing at the time, evidence that 2Pac, at this point in his development, was still happy to contort himself to match other artists' styles. He again hits out at the vice president, suggesting that Quayle should be spending more time curing the ills affecting Black America than attacking a young rap artist: "Dan Quayle, don't you know you need your ass kicked? / Where was you when there was n****s in the caskets?" And on "Souljah's Revenge," he declares Quayle clueless to the plight of young Black men, before closing the song by looping on repeat one of the lyrics from *2Pacalypse Now* that caused so much controversy: "They finally pulled me over and I laughed / Remember Rodney King and I blast on his punk ass (I hear ya!)." The message is clear: 2Pac regretted nothing.

"The Streetz R Deathrow" (not a reference to his future label, Death Row Records) compares inner-city living to waiting for execution. 2Pac takes the role of a child whose father has abandoned the family. With his mother powerless to control him, the boy commits a murder. "I'm startin' to lose my hair 'cause I worry," 2Pac raps, no doubt a reference to his own alopecia, brought on by the violence he suffered at the hands of police. As if to punctuate the fact that he was arriving at his peak, the title track charts his ascent up the music industry, as sinister forces wait to kick him back down again: "Since I wear a lot of gold, they plot."

Musical and lyrical maturity intersects on "Keep Ya Head Up," 2Pac's tribute to Black women, especially single mothers, and one of his most enduring songs. By 1993, as the reach of rap music expanded, fears circled in Black feminism that misogyny was becoming one of its core tenets. Not helping this degeneration was a lack of women's voices in the genre. In a lengthy interview with Ice Cube in 1991, former Black Panther Angela Davis felt compelled to probe the rapper on his use of misogynistic words: "What do you think about all the efforts over the years to transform the language we use to refer to ourselves as Black people and specifically as Black women?" Davis asked. "How do you think Black feminists like myself, and younger women as well, respond to the word 'bitch'?"

2Pac could be just as loutish in the studio booth as Cube, but "Keep Ya Head Up" offered something of an ointment. The chorus features singer Dave Hollister interpreting one of 2Pac's favorite soul numbers, the Five Stairsteps' "O-o-h Child," as the rapper himself ponders men's propensity for violence and resentment against women. Breaking briefly from the theme, his feelings on American imperialism are also summed up: "They got money for wars, but can't feed the poor." It's a lyric that's been clipped many times in the years since to display the artist's wisdom, so simple yet so obviously apparent.

"Keep Ya Head Up" includes another one of 2Pac's most celebrated lyrics: "I think it's time to kill for our women / Time to heal our women, be real to our women / And if we don't, we'll have a race of babies / That will hate the ladies that make the babies / And since a man can't make one / He has no right to tell a woman when and where to create one." It's not 2Pac's most sophisticated piece of writing—he rhymes "babies" with "babies," "one" with "one"—but as an unashamed pro-choice message, it's potent. American music, not just rap but across all genres, has avoided the topic of abortion despite its permanence in the political discourse. Here, 2Pac firmly declares his position.

Reproductive rights—eternally a crucial battleground for leftist activists and their reactionary conservative antagonists. It's interesting to look back on the Black Panther Party and the dim view it took of loosened legislation that gave women greater control over their bodies. In April 1970—one year after the Panther 21 arrests and three years before abortion was decriminalized in the United States with the Supreme Court's decision in *Roe v. Wade*—New York legalized abortion up to the twenty-fourth week of pregnancy and at any time the mother's life was at risk. One of the Black Panthers' chief remits was the improvement of health care in Black communities, yet the response to this liberalization of abortion laws was to publish an article by New York member Brenda Hyson that claimed it was a victory for "the oppressive ruling class who will use this law to kill off Black and other oppressed people before they are born." The Panthers' position was that voluntary abortion would "turn into involuntary abortion into compulsory sterilization," a view with recent historical weight as sterilization was forced on as many as seventy thousand women in America during the twentieth century, most of whom were poor women of color. A belief in eugenics meant this process often took place in psychiatric facilities and prisons, but many doctors also sterilized women (especially Black women) without consent immediately after they gave birth. With the expressed aim of reducing the number of children born into poverty, some expectant mothers were told that the only way they could give birth at a specific hospital was if they agreed to sterilization, or that if they did not consent to the procedure, their welfare benefits would be cut off.

At the core of the Panthers' theory was the belief that raising a child comfortably is often beyond the resources of poor women and, therefore, they have "little practical ability to exercise their theoretical freedom of choice." And so, the availability of abortion is no mitigation for the economic factors that often drive such decisions.

It's difficult to say how much popularity this position had within the rank and file, a huge proportion of which were women. Black Panther Cleo Silvers remembered the New York abortion legislation occurring during the middle of the Newton-Cleaver feud, which dampened the possibility or will for internal discussions on policy direction. Denise Oliver-Velez viewed the position as simply reflective of the gap between the Black working-class plight and white feminism. "The white movement tends to look at it in terms of just abortion. We were looking at reproductive rights as the right to be able to have your child, and for your child to have a roof over their head, food, and health care. And, at the same time, saying you have as much a right to have an abortion. We make it very clear that reproductive justice was about justice for children to be born and survive, particularly because of the uninformed step [of the] sterilization of women. So, it was your right to be able to birth your child or decide not to have one. Two-sided, which I think was a much more balanced approach than simply focusing on abortion."

Abortion has never been a major concern of rap music, a symptom of males setting the agenda. There have been a few fully formed songs about abortion, such as New York rapper Jean Grae's "My Story," released in 2008, a profound and impactful depiction based on her own experiences. But the most famous is surely "Keep Ya Head Up," for the quality of the song itself and the brevity of 2Pac's message. In a recording career that's sometimes criticized as duplicitous, 2Pac's support of reproductive rights was consistent. On the vibey urban soul of "The Good Die Young," released posthumously, he raps, "A woman's tryin' to make decisions, we should leave 'em a choice."

The song given the critical task of being *Strictly*'s flagship single was "Holler If Ya Hear Me," unrecognizable from the never-to-be-officially-released version of the song that 2Pac recorded for *Troublesome '21*. His original vision is a lightning shock of threats to kill crooked cops, warnings to outgoing Los Angeles police chief

Daryl Gates to move to another state, and a direct reference to Malcolm X's speech "The Ballot or the Bullet." The minister had dismissed the fecklessness of nonviolent action, summarized by his painting the image of protesters "walking around here singing 'We Shall Overcome.'" Almost three decades later, 2Pac flippantly chants the civil rights anthem before encouraging weapons training. No doubt hearing this recording of "Holler If Ya Hear Me" caused many heads to explode at the Time Warner offices.

The version that did find its way onto *Strictly* resembles the original only in its title. The record was completely re-produced—it now samples Louie Ramirez's "Do It Any Way You Wanna," adding a mean 1970s funk edge—and the language is less shocking. Despite it being prominently placed as track one and the album's lead single, it didn't appear on the mammoth-selling two-disc *Greatest Hits* compilation released after 2Pac's death, an indication of how far it had slipped down his pecking order of hits.

"Holler If Ya Hear Me" was accompanied with a video as hard-hitting and political as "I Get Around" was playful and carefree. The clip follows a young kid—seemingly a boy, but in a twist ending, revealed to be a girl—who slips into the street life after witnessing her father's death, the relentless cycle of chaos and violence laid bare. 2Pac appears in the video, but he and the girl don't interact. Instead, he serves as a narrator to the scene, inhabiting the same world without affecting the story.

Once more, the suits ran interference. Interscope asked that an alteration be made to a sequence that sees a menacing figure emerge from the shadows and shoot a patrolman as he sits in his squad car. Director Stephen Ashley Blake dutifully re-edited the piece so the cop only gets startled.

For filmmakers, this kind of tug-of-war with creatively clueless executives is not a rare occurrence. Blake's most desperate struggle, though, was with the young star himself. It was the second day of the two-day production and work was set to take place at a shooting range in Compton. Tupac was there with his entourage, except when he wasn't. At one point, a member of the production staff was tasked with journeying to a Roscoe's Chicken and Waffles in Hollywood to retrieve him. The situation turned dangerous and the mood more sinister when one of Tupac's entourage shot a live round at a target while the crew was busy working.

Another flash point occurred toward the end of production, when Tupac insisted that a change be made to a planned shot of a group of armed men sitting at a table in the range. Blake intended the table to be in the background, with Tupac sitting in the extreme foreground. Now, the star wanted to be sitting at the table itself.

Blake was taken aback. This made no sense to the internal logic of the video—Tupac could not become entangled in the narrative. The director desperately explained that the concept demanded that the two separate entities did not overlap in space.

"Well, he got furious about that, and he just went on a huge, huge, huge rant," remembered Blake. "He insisted that this was his production. And then he actually proceeded, with some of his guys, to chew out my crew, and he condemned the fact that half of my crew was white. It was just a huge explosive tirade. And it was a scary tirade—again, one of his guys had just fired a live round, a live weapon, within yards of our crew members. So, it was very, very tense. So tense that under any other circumstances, I would have shut down the production then and there."

Blake did everything to resist that extreme. "The previous day had been phenomenally successful, and the second day also was phenomenally successful. The footage was just spectacular. I interacted with Tupac and we really had a great kinetic interaction on camera, I was getting some stunning performances from him, and I didn't want to cancel the job."

An impromptu meeting was held in a back alley so that Tupac, one of his people, Blake, and a producer could rescue the situation. If not, the star would be out of there, and Blake would be left with an unfortunate hole in his film. In the end, the director created a scenario in which 2Pac could sit at the table without jeopardizing its concept. "We set up a circular dolly track around that table, so that we could spin [the camera] around him three hundred and sixty degrees very, very rapidly, like a race car. And we had an overhead light I brought in; we had the light swinging around. What I ended up doing was converting what had been planned, which was a static shot or a still shot, into a very fast-moving kinetic shot. So it then came back to a performance-esque video with the guys sitting around Tupac as sort of a context."

With all the footage in the can, Blake needed just one more element: snippets of an interview with Tupac to bookend the video. A few days after the tension of the shoot, both men met at Afeni's house with a tape recorder. They spoke in the living room at length about social justice issues relevant to the song and video. But Tupac grew frustrated by the rhetorical questions Blake was asking—stuff like "How do you feel about these wrongful deaths?"

"What do you mean?" asked Tupac, irritated. "Am I affected by this? Of course I am. Why are you even asking me this question?"

"Pac, we're just asking you so we can get it on tape. That's it," Blake recalled saying. But the questions continued to infuriate the rapper and the conversation soon flatlined.

It's at this point that Afeni stepped in. "Listen, Stephen, let's ask him if he'll go into a bedroom and put the audio recorder there with a microphone and just let him rant into the mic." So Blake set up the equipment and Tupac, with no prompts, duly smashed the intro and outro.

Interscope soon nixed the audio that closes the video with Tupac saying, "Revolution is the only way," an insanely overcautious demand, one last strike at their star's artistry. Other decisions that affected *Strictly* seem equally odd. It's unlikely that "Nothing but Love"—a song originally included on *Troublesome '21* that sees 2Pac pay homage to his time in Oakland—would have upset the label heads, but it was deleted anyway. "Nothing but Love" would eventually receive an official release on the posthumous album *R U Still Down? (Remember Me)*. To consider *Strictly* a compromised product is the only conclusion.

If there was any lingering frustration, 2Pac could console himself with the fact that "I Get Around" and "Keep Ya Head Up" were his first platinum-selling singles. Released back-to-back, they reflected the duality—some say contradiction—of his music. But the more 2Pac appeared in the news, the more a particular descriptor seemed to stick to him: gangster rapper. A morality war on rap music accused of glorifying violence and criminality was being waged, and 2Pac was a favorite target of conservative pundits. But

2Pac's early music did not engage with the same gangster illustrations as, say, that of N.W.A., Above the Law, or MC Eiht. His music touched on the social conditions in which gangs bloom, without judgment or favor. The gang life was not his life, and Tupac was an observer, not a fantasist.

"When did I ever say I was a gangsta rapper?" he groused. "Is Frank Sinatra a gangsta singer? Is Steven Seagal a gangsta actor? What is that? That's such a limited term. Marlon Brando is not a gangsta actor, he's an actor. Axl Rose and them are not gangsta rock and rollers, they're rock and rollers. So I'm a rapper, this is what I do. I'm an artist. And I rap about the oppressed taking back their place. I rap about fighting back. To me, my lyrics and my verses are about struggling and overcoming, you know? . . . I make it uncomfortable by putting details to it. It might not have been politically correct but I've reached somebody; they relating to me. They relate to the brutal honesty in the rap. And why shouldn't they be angry? And why shouldn't my raps that I'm rapping to my community be filled with rage? They should be filled with the same atrocities they gave to me."

Strictly 4 My N.I.G.G.A.Z . . . confirmed that 2Pac was one of the princes of the advancing West Coast hip-hop world. But the East Coast was striking back with a new rush of inventiveness. Kool G Rap and Rakim had filtered into Nas, the Wu-Tang Clan, and one particular artist who'd be remembered as the greatest from his city to ever do it.

When Buddha-sized Brooklynite Christopher Wallace stepped on a plane to Los Angeles in 1993, he had a to-do list of precisely three items. Two of his objectives involved sampling the city's famous fast-food institutions: Fatburger and Roscoe's Chicken and Waffles. The third was to see Tupac Shakur.

For Wallace, Tupac was a man not just to be admired, but emulated. The twenty-one-year-old was emerging out of the Bedford-Stuyvesant neighborhood as the fresh hope of New York rap, a vaunted virtuoso who would oust Los Angeles and restore Gotham's position as hip-hop's holy city. The stage name he took was as large as the persona he was crafting: the Notorious B.I.G.

But the bodega kids, then and forever more, would more typically call him Biggie Smalls. He arrived out west with a hot debut single called "Party and Bullshit" to his name and the company of the man who had signed him to his first label, Uptown Records, Sean "Puffy" Combs.

The hookup came from the kind of figures that make the entertainment world tick: interns and drug dealers. After Biggie and Puffy arrived in L.A., it was Uptown intern Dan Smalls (no relation to Biggie) who reached out to a guy he knew who supplied Tupac with weed. As Biggie and Puffy pulled up to their hotel in Studio City, Tupac was already waiting outside in his convertible. "Yo, what else you gotta do today?" he asked. All plans would have to be canceled. "Let's go to my house," suggested Tupac. And so a small crew that included Dan Smalls, rapper Greg Nice, and Biggie's stylist Groovey Lew headed to their host's abode.

The group disappeared into a dimension that was part music video, part childhood fantasy. After sharing some weed and freestyle verses, Tupac pulled out a green army bag filled with handguns and machine guns. Each member of the group seized one of the (unloaded) weapons and started fooling around in the backyard like little kids with plastic toys.

"While we were running around, Pac walks into the kitchen and starts cooking for us," Dan Smalls later said. "He's in the kitchen cooking some steaks. We were drinking and smoking, and all of a sudden Pac was like, 'Yo, come get it.' And we go into the kitchen and he had steaks, and French fries, and bread, and Kool-Aid and we just sittin' there eating and drinking and laughing. And you know, that's truly where Big and Pac's friendship started."

Much like legendary baseball sluggers and lost mid-Atlantic continents, the meeting of Tupac Shakur and Christopher Wallace is prone to myth. One story goes that they first got together when Tupac invited Biggie to the set of *Poetic Justice*. However, loyal Biggie auxiliary Lil' Cease has spoken of his mentor returning home from a show in Maryland to support "Party and Bullshit" in early 1993 with a tale of how Tupac had introduced himself at the show and the pair hung out. If true, evidently they hit it off: The way

Biggie told it, at eight a.m. the next morning, he answered a knock at his hotel room door to reveal Tupac with a bottle of Hennessy, ready to keep the celebrations going.

Whatever the truth of their initial union, Tupac and Biggie became fast friends, then dangerous rivals. It's impossible not to consider their lives as adjacent; both intertwined like thick grapevines. Tupac and Biggie's rivalry would heavily color both men's careers and legacies. Each serves as a yardstick of the other's greatness, as brilliant rivals tend to do.

It was a connection built from their recognition that the other was an elite rap artist. But the differences were also huge. You could barely slide a piece of rice paper between Tupac Shakur the man and 2Pac the rap persona, but Christopher Wallace was not the Notorious B.I.G. Unlike Tupac, young Christopher enjoyed a relatively stable childhood, nothing like the bleak vision he presented in his music. He was raised by Voletta Wallace, who, as a young woman, emigrated from Jamaica to New York in the hope of cornering off her own section of the American dream. Her son enjoyed the unconditional love of a woman who worked hard to shield him from the hazards that dwelled right outside their Fulton Street door.

As a teenager, Christopher became frustrated by an education system ill-equipped to engage a child of his intelligence. He was also bedazzled by nice things, and the local hustlers who loitered on Bed-Stuy's corners offered the means to make a living. At seventeen years old, Christopher dropped out of high school and began running up a rap sheet. In 1989, he received five years' probation for weapons charges and would later spend nine months behind bars after being arrested in North Carolina for dealing crack cocaine before finally making bail. Voletta may not have been able to totally shelter her only child from the allure of the hustle, but her influence—coupled with the timely intervention of a hungry young music executive in Puffy, who instantly recognized the superstar potential of the amateur rapper with a baritone that sounded forged in a furnace—probably saved Christopher from being totally consumed by an unlawful existence. Biggie signed to Uptown Records, where Puffy worked as an A&R man and record producer. He may have had an eagle eye for talent, but Puffy's frequent clashes with his boss, Andre Harrell, and other Uptown executives eventually got him fired. Undeterred, Puffy took Biggie and the artist's half-completed album with him to his new venture, Bad Boy Records. It would become one of the era's true hit-making factories.

Tupac spent much of 1993 living a rap star existence. In March, he strutted into the Soul Train Awards wearing an appropriately flashy double-denim outfit and beanie hat bearing the words "Thug Life," and actress Rosie Perez as his date. The child of Puerto Rican immigrants, Perez was a heavily accented Brooklyn beauty who'd parlayed her dance skills into memorable roles in movies such as *Do the Right Thing* and *White Men Can't Jump*, becoming oft referenced in rap verses forevermore. But before that, she'd been a backup dancer for artist Heavy D and first crossed paths with Tupac as he toured with Digital Underground.

Tupac and Perez made a striking couple, and their entrance was diligently snapped by photographers. But the night led to a connection with a woman whose stardom overshadowed even a zeitgeist figure like Perez: Madonna. Offered a chance to be set up with Tupac, the material girl didn't pass. As Perez recalled years later, "I went to the Soul Train Music Awards . . . and then Madonna comes over and looks at me, and she goes, 'Girl.' I said [to Tupac], 'She wants to meet you,' and he goes, 'Hook that up.' And I hooked it up, and I was very happy about it."

The union of Tupac and Madonna could have yielded one of the era's true pop culture power couples. Instead, both resolved to keep the relationship discreet. At least relatively—about a year after the Soul Train Awards, an amped-up Tupac showed up to Snoop Doggy Dogg's rehearsal for a *Saturday Night Live* performance, excitedly announcing that he'd soon be joined by his "rich bitch." *OK, whatever,* Snoop's team thought. To their amazement, the "rich bitch" turned out to be none other than Madonna. But as far as public perception, Tupac is not associated with Madonna and Madonna is not associated with Tupac. Yet being thirteen years older than Tupac and of significantly more experience in the public eye, Madonna would prove a person of strength in his life when the walls began to cave in.

His celebrity ever strengthening, Tupac went on *The Arsenio Hall Show* that July as a speaking guest for the first time. Kicking back on Hall's famous sofa, Tupac acted giddy throughout the tête-à-tête, immaturely talking about the pleasure of kissing Janet Jackson on the set of *Poetic Justice*. Through the goofiness, though, he could be enlightened. "The masses, the hungry people, they outweigh the rich," he told Hall. "So as long as I appeal to the hungry and the poverty-stricken people, it's all good, I'm going to have a job for life. It's these rich people who are worried about fooling the poor people."

"See, I get a feeling there are two Tupacs," observed the talk show host. "You're this kind, sensitive, friendly guy . . . yet you're involved in so much controversy."

Hall spared his guest the potential discomfort of going into specifics, but both men knew that Tupac's life was in an increasingly violent spiral. In March, while traveling to a television studio to record a segment for the show *In Living Color*, Tupac and road manager Charles "Man Man" Fuller scuffled with a limo driver who complained about them smoking weed in his car. Both were arrested, with all charges later dropped. The following month, at a show in Lansing, Michigan, Tupac was accused of swinging a baseball bat at the head of a local rapper. He pleaded guilty seventeen months later and was sentenced to ten days in jail.

It was around the same time that Tupac was involved in a brawl with Albert and Allen Hughes, the talented twin brothers who, as directors of some of his early music videos, had been critical in the development of the rapper's image. It was a fallout born of artistic divergences. The Hughes brothers had asked Tupac if he would star in their first movie, *Menace II Society*, a nightmarish vision of life in South Central Los Angeles that eclipsed even *Boyz n the Hood* in its violence and fatalism. Tupac was cast as Sharif, a former delinquent whose conversion to Islam inspires him to become a better man. Such was the filmmakers' faith in their star that they accepted his recommendation that Jada Pinkett play the lead female character—her first major role in a movie. But after two days of table reads, Tupac was having a hard time understanding the character, and his frustration manifested in juvenile behavior that was derailing the whole production. "Tupac, why are you acting like a bitch?" Allen eventually asked in protest. Soon enough, the star stormed out. He later heard on MTV News that there was no chance he'd be allowed back on the project. The role instead went to Vonte Sweet.

Tupac stewed over reports that he'd been fired for not knowing his lines and being unprofessional, the anger in him building. Then, in April 1993, he visited the set of rapper Spice 1's music video for "Trigga Gots No Heart," a song that appeared on the *Menace II Society* soundtrack. It brought Tupac face-to-face with the Hughes brothers once more.

Insults were exchanged. Tupac swung a balled fist at Allen— characterized by Hughes as a sucker punch as he walked away. It triggered the rapper's crew to pile in, beating the filmmaker bloody as Albert made a run for it. The incident was sufficiently serious for the Hughes brothers to file assault-and-battery charges against Tupac.

Days before his appearance on *The Arsenio Hall Show*, Tupac admitted to the assault on *Yo! MTV Raps*. "They fired me but did it in a roundabout punk snitch way. So I caught them on the streets and beat their behinds. I was a menace to the Hughes brothers and it ain't over." Host Ed Lover tried to make light of the situation by putting his hand on Tupac's mouth to shut him up. Really, the experienced broadcaster was trying to stop any statements that could incriminate his guest.

As his profile rose, Tupac's friendship with Biggie blossomed. The pair would inevitably get together when Tupac was in New York. So eager was he to impress the younger and less successful Biggie, Tupac even pulled through Fulton and Washington in a white stretch limo to pick up his friend for a show.

They were also connecting artistically. At the Budweiser Superfest in October, the pair shared a stage with Big Daddy Kane. Flanked by the more experienced stars, Biggie unleashed what would go down as a legendary freestyle, beginning with an inventory of his armory: "I got seven Mac-11s, about eight .38s / Nine 9s, ten Mac-10s, the shits never end," his husky voice showing impossible dexterity.

With money starting to flow in, 1993 was also the year Tupac purchased a house, selecting Lithonia, Georgia, as the place to make a home he dubbed "Thugz Mansion." Likely inspiring the choice of location were Afeni and Gloria Jean, who had both settled into new lives in nearby Decatur. But a fresh movie deal also afforded Tupac more time in the city of his birth. That October saw production begin on *Above the Rim*. The film was part street saga and part sports drama, and Tupac was cast in the villainous role of Birdie, a local drug dealer fixated on seeing his neighborhood's basketball team win at all costs. It was during his research for the role that a key character entered the Tupac story. His name was Jacques Agnant, but the various street hoods and celebrity figures in his circle called him by a different moniker: Haitian Jack.

Tupac was first intrigued by Agnant when he spotted him at a Manhattan club. He was confidently sipping champagne in the company of beautiful women, and there was something to the man's bluster. To a young actor, this was like uncovering a real-life Blaxploitation hero. Even that name, "Haitian Jack"—it deserved to be in the movies. None of what impressed Tupac meant much to Biggie, to whom Agnant was well known. Biggie even warned his friend to keep his distance. It didn't matter; Tupac followed his curiosity.

"I'm glad I met you when I did because it really helped with that character I was working on," Tupac told Agnant.

"You got something from me?" he replied.

"Yeah, man. Just your swagger, the way you handle yourself, how everybody's always around you. That was important for me to see that that happens. That people gravitate to a gangster."

The filming of *Above the Rim* mostly took place around Harlem. One curious kid attracted to the set was Ayize Jama-Everett. About three years younger than Tupac, he was a CBGB enthusiast who dug Bad Brains and Fishbone, not the rap music that features throughout *Above the Rim*. Still, the movie was shooting around the corner from his mom's job, so he and a bunch of his friends went down to check it out.

When he got there a voice called out, "Yo, Ayize!" It was Tupac. "You're Ayize?" he inquired.

"Yeah."

"Do you know who I am?"

"Um. Of course I do."

"Okay. Cool."

That was it, interaction over, leaving Ayize and his friends perplexed as to how this famous movie star knew him. It wasn't until years later, when Jama-Everett had grown up and Tupac was dead, he discovered the connection. Through the imprisoned father he barely knew, Mutulu Shakur, Ayize and Tupac were stepbrothers. Jama-Everett went on to become a successful writer specializing in science fiction. How Tupac recognized him that day, we can only speculate.

Halloween 1993. Commencing at sundown, America was its annual Imaginarium of ghouls, hexes, and all associated sorcery, and Tupac Shakur was floating on air. Work on *Above the Rim* was going smoothly; he'd just released a new single that would soon become his second to go platinum. In quiet moments, he surely drew great satisfaction from his achievements, while pondering just how steep this upward trajectory he found himself on would prove to be. But a journey to Atlanta saw everything he'd worked toward put at severe risk. Such a hazard would have been avoidable had Tupac thought it best to mind his own business—if swerving past trouble was something in his makeup.

It took place after a show to celebrate homecoming at Clark Atlanta University, where 2Pac was the main attraction on the bill that included local group P.A. (Parental Advisory). The performance was going off without a hitch until an argument with security about smoking weed caused him to cut the show short. Tupac and his entourage, among them his cousins Billy Lesane and Dante Powers, left the school to celebrate in his room at the Sheraton

Hotel. He took a spot in the front car of a motorcade of about six or seven vehicles.

As the chariots pulled off into the night, thirty-three-year-old Mark Whitwell, his younger brother Scott Whitwell, and their two wives had just finished their own celebration. Scott's wife had passed the bar exam, and so the couples toasted the achievement at a local hotel. But their festivities turned into confrontation when the group tried to cross the street and, they would later say, were nearly struck by a car. The driver, who was a Black man, clambered out of his vehicle and an argument broke out between him and the two brothers, who were white. The bickering soon became a brawl.

It was at this point that Tupac and his entourage arrived on the scene. Peering at the ruckus in the distance, they saw a fight was happening. As they drew closer, the picture became clearer: two white men were working over a Black man in the middle of the street. And so Tupac stepped out of the car, to lead the rescue charge. Not apparent was that the Whitwell brothers were actually off-duty police officers.

Upon seeing Tupac approaching, Mark Whitwell quickly drew a pistol and pointed it right at him. Unfazed, Tupac responded by pulling up his shirt to bare the large Thug Life tattoo on his abdomen. "Thug life, motherfucker, shoot!" shouted the famous rapper. Suddenly, Mark Whitwell stepped forward and used the butt of his gun to smash Tupac's car window. Seeing the glass break, the brothers turned to run. As they fled, Tupac demanded one of his entourage hand him his 9-millimeter Glock. Sensing it was a bad idea, nobody responded to the request. But with his target escaping, Tupac reached into the car himself to retrieve his gun. In what must have been a ridiculous scene, he took to one knee like an expert military marksman and fired three shots at his targets, now about forty feet away, before placing the weapon on the tarmac.

Billy Lesane reached down and picked up the pistol. "You missed! You missed! I know you missed," he insisted.

"Nah, I got him, I got him!" replied Tupac.

He was correct. Two of the bullets struck the Whitwells—Mark was shot in the stomach and his brother in the buttocks.

Seemingly unperturbed by the shooting, Tupac and his entourage returned to his hotel room, threw on some music, and escaped into a more blissful dimension, like nothing had happened. But the calm didn't last. Hours later, Tupac was arrested and charged with two counts of aggravated assault. The Whitwell brothers were treated at Grady Hospital and released the next day. Tupac pleaded not guilty and was released on a $55,059 bond.

What a story this was—a rap artist previously embroiled in controversy after one of his fans shot a cop had now shot two cops himself. The news media did what it could to solidify these links. The *New York Times* report noted that "some of Mr. Shakur's best-known lyrics describe young black men as targets of police violence and discuss gang members shooting police officers." The Quayle beef, of course, was also mentioned in the copy.

Members of his inner circle must have believed this was the end of Tupac. A Black man in America had shot two white police officers. But the Whitwells turned out to be imperfect representatives of their profession: they'd been drinking before the confrontation; and even more controversially, the gun pulled on Tupac had been stolen from an evidence locker. In the end, prosecutors dropped all charges against Tupac after finding that he had acted in self-defense.

To seek parallels between historical figures of similar ilk is natural. Sometimes, they're apparent. Tupac's actions in Atlanta strongly invoked one of his heroes and spiritual forefathers, Huey P. Newton. The Black Panthers' co-founder had once emptied a clip into a police officer and escaped conviction. Tupac, albeit unknowingly, had turned his weapon on cops and gotten away with it. It can be tempting to believe in destiny, set paths from which one cannot deviate. More likely is when men are of the same energy, some things are bound to happen. Though it's unlikely Newton ever walked out of a courtroom the way Tupac swaggered out, bobbing up and down, arms flailing, when he found out he had no case to answer to. Tupac always seemed to walk fast and loose, no time to waste. But *that walk*, captured on camera—so defiant, so ridiculous. It's the strut of a man who knew that firing rounds at the law usually ends one of two ways: prison or death. That Tupac exited the court as a free man just strengthened his notoriety.

Tupac's increasing propensity for violence during this period is a difficult thing to understand. The theater kid had by now developed a taste for using his fists, baseball bats, even pistols. It's likely that the less serious punch-ups with drivers and music video directors made him increasingly ambivalent to confrontation, culminating in the Halloween shooting. This personality transformation is perhaps most simply down to Tupac's lifelong tendency to absorb the characteristics of people in his sphere. As more hardened figures entered his world, he allowed his character and image to move in that direction.

Oakland rapper Too Short recognized this trait in Tupac early on. It was as though a different Tupac presented himself every time they met. And so Too Short consciously avoided introducing him to the gangsters in his circle, lest Tupac try to emulate them. "I wouldn't do that to him," Too Short explained years later.

In Los Angeles, it was a different story. "When Tupac got to L.A., and they let him get around," Too Short said, "he was going ten thousand miles an hour."

Two weeks after the Atlanta shooting, Tupac was back in New York to continue work on *Above the Rim*, and that meant being back in the presence of Haitian Jack. Both men were part of an entourage that, on the night of November 14, attended Nell's, a club on West Fourteenth Street that had opened in 1986 on the site of an old electronics store, described by *The New York Times* as "a scene of decadent Victorian elegance, a small space that had been converted—with deft use of wood paneling, beaded chandeliers, tufted velvet sofas and Oriental rugs—into what seemed the drawing room of a somewhat dissolute English aristocrat."

Under the lights and music, Tupac was introduced to a nineteen-year-old clubgoer who had managed to gain entry to the VIP section. A first-time attendee at Nell's, she sipped champagne, enjoying the surroundings and the celebrity company. This was Ayanna Jackson, the woman who would accuse Tupac Shakur of rape.

For years, Jackson was an indistinct figure in her own story. Few details of her life outside of her relationship with Tupac were known; her words were seen only in court reports and a statement released to the hip-hop press that did not reveal her name. But in February 2018, Jackson, then forty-four years old, sat down for her first on-camera interview with YouTuber DJ Vlad, a persistent chronicler of people whose lives intersected with Tupac's, and spoke candidly about those few days in New York.

Jackson and Tupac's depictions of November 14 to 18 rarely snap perfectly into line, making it difficult to chronicle with certainty. What there's no dispute about is that on that first evening there was an attraction. Jackson remembered, "When I first met Tupac, he kissed me on my cheek and made small talk with me. After a while, I excused myself and started to walk to the dance floor. When I felt someone slide their hands into the back pocket of my jeans, I turned around, assuming it was my friend, but was shocked when I discovered it was Tupac."

The two started to kiss. In a "dark corner" of Nell's, Jackson is said to have performed oral sex on him. She described this moment as Tupac pushing her "head down" where, in a three-second encounter, she came into contact with his penis. Much would be made of this by Jackson's detractors, who wished to paint her as a certain *type* of woman—this is to say, sexually unprincipled, and therefore not to be trusted. Whatever the truth of what happened in the shadows of the club, the incident didn't offend Jackson. "It was all in good fun. I was not upset about it, no, not at all."

Soon, the possibility of taking things more private came up. "Do you want to leave?" asked Tupac. "Let's hang out."

The two exited the club, drove to Tupac's hotel in a white BMW, and had consensual sex. Jackson stayed for a few hours, but with Tupac having a five a.m. call to work on *Above the Rim*, they parted early the next day.

Jackson told DJ Vlad that the pair hung out several times over the next few days. She'd typically receive a call from Charles "Man Man" Fuller to inform her that Tupac was requesting her presence. A car would be sent. These meetings, Jackson said, were not always sexual, and continued until the night of November 18—four days after they first met at Nell's—when the summons brought her to Tupac's hotel room. Jackson bought a new dress for the occasion. (The hangouts between the night of their first meeting and

November 18 are not mentioned in the statement Jackson wrote before Tupac's death outlining her side of the story.)

Jackson got to the hotel suite where Tupac and several other men were hanging out—a fact not disputed. According to Jackson, after twenty minutes or so, she went with Tupac into the bedroom to give him a massage, positioning herself on top of him, fully clothed, as he lay down. Some time passed. The door opened and Jackson was hit by noise and light. When she turned to look toward the door, she said, Tupac grabbed the back of her head, wrapped her braids around his hand, and turned her head back toward him. "I'm looking at him face-to-face, and I hear people talking and I hear people saying, 'Oh look at her' and 'Her ass is fat,'" she told DJ Vlad. "I'm looking at him dead in his eye, and I'm like, 'What's going on?' And he's saying to me he's like, 'Relax baby, these are my boys. I like you so much I decided to share you with them.'" The men Jackson identified were Haitian Jack, Fuller, and a third man who is usually assigned the name Trevor. (A man named Nigel is sometimes described as being present. In her interview with DJ Vlad, Jackson said she believed this to refer to Haitian Jack.)

Jackson kept trying to lift her head up, but, she said, Tupac still had her hair wrapped around his hand. The men who had entered the room began to rip off her clothes. It was at this point—struggling for her freedom and telling Tupac no—that, Jackson said, Tupac raped her. (In 1994, she wrote, "My lips and face came crashing down hard onto his penis, he squeezed the back of my neck, and I started to gag.") She then described slipping into something akin to an out-of-body experience, during which time Tupac left the room and some of the other men present proceeded to rape her. When she came to, Fuller was there, apologizing to her, but he was not, Jackson clarified, one of the men who raped her. (Nonetheless, Fuller would end up facing the same charges as Tupac.)

In an interview with *Vibe*, Tupac broadly painted the same picture, but insisted he did not rape Jackson, and instead "froze up."

"So we get in the room, I'm laying on my stomach, she's massaging my back. I turn around. She starts massaging my front. This lasted for about a half an hour. In between, we would stop and kiss each other. I'm thinking she's about to give me another blow job.

But before she could do that, some n****s came in, and I froze up more than she froze up. If she would have said anything, I would have said, 'Hold on, let me finish.' But I can't say nothing, because she's not saying nothing. How do I look saying, 'Hold on'? That would be like I'm making her my girl.

"So they came and they started touching her ass. They going, 'Oooh, she's got a nice ass.' Nigel isn't touching her, but I can hear his voice leading it, like, 'Put her panties down, put her pantyhose down.' I just got up and walked out the room."

Jackson described being left alone in the room with Fuller, who, seeing her in a hysterical state, tried to calm her down. Jackson retreated to the bathroom, where, she said, Fuller attempted to placate her, saying, "You know what happened with Mike Tyson?," referring to the former heavyweight champion who was at the time in prison for rape. "Pac doesn't need that."

After leaving the hotel room, Jackson did everything women who are victims of rape are told to do. She summoned the security officers, who called the police. Tupac, Fuller, and Haitian Jack were arrested. Press snapped Tupac being taken in a hotel in a black leather zip-up vest and handcuffs.

Shielded in a Meridien Hotel robe, Jackson was taken to St. Luke's Hospital, where a rape kit examination was performed.

Unlike the Atlanta shooting, which was dealt with swiftly, it would be a year before Tupac stood trial for what happened at the Meridien. Being an accused rapist hurt his career—John Singleton was forced to roll back his decision to cast Tupac in his movie *Higher Learning* before filming started. (In an act of great symmetry, Singleton replaced Tupac with Ice Cube, who had been his first choice for Tupac's role in *Poetic Justice*.) But he continued to pore over new music and speak to the media.

On March 8, 1994, Tupac made another appearance on *Arsenio Hall*. "It bothers me so much, you know what I'm sayin', to go through my life, and everything I did in my life, coming out of a family and a household with just women, to get to this point to have a woman sayin' I took something from her," he said.

Two days later, the sentence came down for the assault on Allen Hughes: thirty days in jail and thirty months of probation.

Throughout the ninety-minute sentencing, as his lawyer and the prosecutor argued back and forth, Tupac mostly sat in silence.

Above the Rim hit cinemas in March 1994. It's a solid enough street basketball flick, neither as raw and from the gut as *Juice*, nor as effective a showcase for Tupac's acting ability as *Poetic Justice*. Six months later, though, another wholly cinematic piece set in New York was released. Blurring the lines of fact and fiction, it depicted Brooklyn's tough Bedford-Stuyvesant neighborhood through the eyes of an ambitious young hustler. But rather than capturing the city on camera, it was a masterwork committed to tape. Writer, director, and star of the piece was the Notorious B.I.G., who drew upon his experiences as a low-level street criminal and dreams of large-scale success to conceive the concept of his debut album, *Ready to Die*, utilizing his vivid lyrics and unparalleled rap ability— not only is *Ready to Die* one of the greatest rap albums of all time, it's also one of the greatest *rapped* albums of all time—to execute his vision. Biggie's tale voiced the plight of young Black men living in Brooklyn's neglected neighborhoods in a manner so uncompromising it sounded practically aired from behind enemy lines.

It was in this climate that Wallace spent his adolescence, submitting to the "everyday struggle" that seemed fated for someone born into his life circumstances. This would prove key to the worldview he laid out on *Ready to Die* with such clarity. Following its protagonist from the cradle to the grave, the album is epic in its scope, scale, and execution. Born to the sounds of Curtis Mayfield's classic *Super Fly* soundtrack (released in 1972, the year of Wallace's birth) and raised by dysfunctional parents during the development of hip-hop—which is depicted in a visceral three-and-a-half-minute opening skit titled "Intro"—the album goes on to chart Biggie's rise from two-bit stickup kid to the lofty heights of the criminal underworld and the violence that takes him there, eventually winding to a death at his own hand.

While there are plenty of breaks in the chaos for women and weed, *Ready to Die* is a raw, unflinching record, violent to the point of being uncomfortable. Yet like so many silver screen antiheroes, Biggie is a gripping character—his charm, exuberance, and sense of humor seemingly at odds with his stone-cold willingness to do terrible things if necessary. Wallace even went as far as to liken himself to his cinematic heroes, calling himself "the Black Frank Wright," referring to the ruthless mob boss in maverick filmmaker Abel Ferrara's urban classic *King of New York*.

However, performing under his Biggie Smalls guise allowed Wallace to inhabit a character that would let him ponder what might have been. The Voletta Wallace who worked tirelessly to both educate herself and provide for her son is not Biggie Smalls's mother. That much is clear on the intro track, which features a heated domestic dispute between Biggie's parents that highlights the difficult nature of his upbringing. The mother is portrayed as an unhinged, irresponsible young mother—a world away from the strong woman whose sternness cast fear in the local young ruffians who sometimes hung around her son.

So "Intro" isn't an accurate depiction of Wallace's childhood, but rather an early indication that Biggie Smalls's story is not totally autobiographical. Voletta herself has spoken on numerous occasions of the real Christopher versus his alter ego in her laudable work on keeping her son's legacy alive in the years since his death in 1997. Still, had Wallace not been afforded the opportunity to lay his vision on wax, there's every chance he would have lived it out on the streets, and, such is the stated presentation of the album, it cuts to a greater truth.

There is no happy ending for Smalls, who fulfills the album's title by taking his own life in the final seconds of the record. Biggie may have been ready to die, but for Christopher Wallace it was the start of his creative birth.

Indictments were entered on sex abuse, sodomy, and weapons charges relating to two guns found in the hotel room. By the time Tupac went on trial a year later, the case against Agnant had been severed after his lawyer argued that only Tupac and Fuller had been charged with the weapons offenses and so the indictment was improperly joined. The prosecutor did not oppose the motion and the judge granted it. To Tupac, the whole situation was outrageous. It stirred a suspicion in his mind: *Was Haitian Jack a government informer?* It was an accusation that, once he heard it, Agnant would strenuously deny.

Tupac's trial began in November 1994 at the New York Supreme Court in Manhattan. Assistant District Attorney Melissa Mourges's opening arguments attempted to strike the jury with an unvarnished depiction of what Tupac and Fuller were being accused of: "They set her up. She never knew what hit her. She thought she was there to be with him and while [they were] kissing, three other men burst in. They held her. They raped her. They terrorized her. They took turns sodomizing her. And when it was over they held her until she stopped crying."

Defense lawyer Michael Warren, a former SNCC member who'd known the Shakur family for years, retorted by questioning Jackson's credibility, describing her as "starstruck" and bringing up the alleged oral sex that occurred at Nell's. "It is our position that this woman is highly incredible," he said. "What we have here is a woman who was infatuated with Mr. Shakur. Don't be fooled by emotions displayed on the witness stand."

Lurking in the courtroom was actor Mickey Rourke, Tupac's costar in the movie *Bullet*, shot in 1994 and released two years later. "Anytime you're in the public eye, you are at an automatic disadvantage," said Rourke, even though in these cases the opposite tends to be true. The trial went on for the next three weeks. Jackson, granted anonymity by the court, only appeared to testify.

"No matter what happens, innocent or guilty, my life is ruined," Tupac told reporters outside the court on November 29, 1994, as the trial was winding to a conclusion. "Because when they say— whatever they say in this verdict, y'all are not gon' make it front page news. It won't be bigger than me, no matter what. All that you wanna hear is that he's guilty, he's in jail, the reign of terror is over, the outlaw's gone. That's what they wanna do. So I'm starting to think I don't know which story to read. I don't know if this is, you know, about Black and white, and loud and quiet, or is it about me and this girl? 'Cause if it's about me and this girl, c'mon, we shouldn't even be here."

. . .

November 29 was a Tuesday. Tupac Shakur likely wondered if it would be one of the last days he knew as a man without a sexual assault conviction next to his name. But financial struggles trumped all other considerations. An offer had come through associate James "Jimmy Henchman" Rosemond to record with rapper Little Shawn, an artist on Bad Boy Records and ally of the Notorious B.I.G. Tupac's demand of $7,000 for the guest appearance was agreed on.

Potentially facing a twenty-five-year sentence, Tupac must have thought that this could be his last recording session for a generation, the death of everything his fans understood the artist 2Pac to be.

Tuesday had ticked into Wednesday by the time he reached Quad Recording Studios on Seventh Avenue, more than an hour behind schedule. Rosemond had grown irritated by Tupac's lateness: "Where you at? What aren't you coming," he tersely paged. "I'm coming, man. Hold on," the artist answered.

As Tupac and his three-man entourage walked toward the building, they clocked Bad Boy artist Lil' Cease, waving them in from an upstairs terrace. The group shuffled past at least one Black man estimated to be in his thirties, wearing army fatigues, a hat pulled low over his face. Inside the lobby, Tupac scanned another man in camouflage apparel, reading a newspaper at a desk in the entranceway of the office building where Quad is located. *Biggie's bodyguards*, thought Tupac, though their failure to acknowledge him seemed odd. Shaking the notion off, Tupac pushed the button to call an elevator.

Suddenly, the man got up from the desk as one, maybe two, of his accomplices came through the door. These were no bodyguards but a stick-up crew. The men stalked Tupac and his squad to the elevators, pulled out guns, and yelled, "Give up the jewelry, and get on the floor!" Most of the group cowered at the cold steel. But while his friends moved to lie on the gray stone floor, Tupac stood tall. Just like he had stood up to the armed cops in Atlanta, he began cursing the holdup men. Only this time, he suddenly lunged for one of the guns while simultaneously reaching for a pistol he kept in his front pocket.

Triggers were squeezed; four shots pierced Tupac's flesh. One of Tupac's entourage, Freddie "Nickels" Moore, was hit once. The robbers grabbed $45,000 worth of jewelry from their victims, but somehow missed Tupac's diamond-encrusted gold Rolex. Suddenly, one of the elevators' doors opened and there stood two startled teenagers, Lil' Cease and rapper Nino Brown, who'd come down to greet Tupac. "Get the fuck back in the elevator," the men ordered. The pair obeyed and immediately headed back upstairs, to inform Biggie.

Before running off, the assailants made sure to get a few more licks in, pistol-whipping and kicking the defenseless Tupac as he lay on the floor bleeding. Full of adrenaline, the wounded Moore attempted to pursue the assailants before collapsing in front of a strip club next door. The others clambered into one of the elevators and headed up to the eighth-floor studio, where they saw about forty people, including Biggie and Puffy. Though badly hurt, Tupac was lucid enough to sense the energy of the room was amiss.

"Nobody approached me. I noticed that nobody would look at me," he later said.

The NYPD descended on the scene. Among them were Officers William Kelly, Joseph Kelly, and, soon after, Craig McKernan. All three had been involved in Tupac's arrest at the Parker Meridien. In a city of 35,000 cops—the largest police department in the United States—this was undeniably strange.

"Hi, Officer McKernan," Tupac sputtered, greeting the man who had just testified at the rape trial.

"Hey, Tupac, you hang in there," McKernan responded warmly as paramedics secured him to a stretcher for his unplanned journey to Bellevue Hospital.

With the patient laid out on the gurney, the EMS team had to awkwardly prop him upright to get him into the elevator. Once downstairs, McKernan was among those who helped carry Tupac outside, where they passed a waiting photographer. "I can't believe you're taking my picture on a stretcher," the star groused, flipping off the shutterbug.

At Bellevue Hospital, doctors discovered that, by good fortune, Tupac had been hit by low-caliber bullets. "Had it been a high-caliber missile, he'd have been dead," Dr. Leon Pachter, chief of Bellevue's trauma department, commented. Unable to stop the bleeding, Pachter made the decision to operate. At 1:30 p.m., a team of more than a dozen doctors began work on a damaged blood vessel in Tupac's right leg.

Informed of the shooting, Afeni flew in from her home in Atlanta, arriving to the hospital before Tupac had awoken from surgery. Back in the city, she called her old Panther comrade Denise Oliver-Velez, still living in New York, to ask if she'd be willing to take Tupac in. Oliver-Velez was surprised to hear from Afeni— they'd been in touch only sporadically over the years. Nonetheless, she agreed to the request. As things turned out, Oliver-Velez's help was not required after all. Instead, the actress Jasmine Guy would provide Tupac a sanctuary.

At four p.m., Tupac was rolled out of surgery. At 6:45 p.m., against doctor's advice and general common sense, he checked himself out of the hospital. But not before Afeni authorized an unexpected visitor to be allowed access to Tupac. When the stricken star first saw the man through blurry eyes, he wondered if he'd died and entered another spiritual realm. Impossibly, the figure in front of him appeared to be his double. But Tupac soon realized that there was no supernatural element to this phenomenon—in fact, their mutual likeness was very easy to explain. The man was Billy Garland, his biological father.

The father-son reunion had little time to ferment. Escaping the hospital, the heavily bandaged Tupac was wheeled out the back door, fighting through a crowd of reporters covering one of the biggest stories in town.

The men and women responsible for Tupac's fate were completely unaware of the defendant's plight. For the previous three days, the jury had been sequestered, living in a cockroach-infested Holiday Inn near Kennedy Airport, severed from the outside world, as their civic duty demanded.

The deliberations had been a shambles. Things began simply enough. Immediately, the jury dismissed the gun charges. Jackson's description of the weapons she'd seen were inconsistent with those entered into evidence, making it an easy decision. Jurors had even felt the guns had been planted.

When it came to the alleged rape, there was little alignment. An elderly right-wing Catholic member of the jury became convinced that Jackson had expected Tupac to marry her, and that his actions constituted a betrayal. Even when a younger woman tried to explain that women did indeed have casual sex outside of marriage, the elderly woman wouldn't hear it. Juror Richard Devitt couldn't believe what he was seeing. "Had it not been for her," he recalled, "we would have acquitted on all counts. She would not back down an inch, she wouldn't concede a single point."

Devitt also alleged that an older Jewish woman was so eager to get to her condo in Florida before the weather in New York got too cold that she'd swing to guilty or not guilty based on the majority. He also claimed to have noticed that a younger male juror would regularly excuse himself to go to the bathroom. As deliberations dragged on, the young man became agitated and eager to wrap things up quickly. Devitt deduced he was a crack addict who'd run out of drugs.

So Tupac rolled into the courtroom—literally. Before his entrance, the jury had been told that his appearance—sitting in a wheelchair with his left wrist wrapped in gauze, his bandaged head and leg covered by a Yankees beanie hat, and wearing a black Nike jogging suit—had nothing to do with the case they'd been asked to cast judgment on. Still, as he was wheeled in, surrounded by members of the Nation of Islam for security, startled jurors nudged one another in surprise.

Just showing up had been an act of pure defiance. It was December 1, a mere two days after the shooting. Tupac sat through the morning court session before his right leg went numb. Perhaps feeling his point had been made, he left and quietly checked into Metropolitan Hospital Center on East Ninety-Seventh Street under the alias Bob Day.

As he got comfortable in the medical center, the verdict came in. Tupac and Fuller were convicted of felony sex-abuse charges for groping Jackson but acquitted of the more serious charges of forcing her to have oral sex with him and his friends, and of weapons charges.

"The mixed verdict," reported *The New York Times*, "seemed to suggest a compromise by the jurors." It was an astute observation. Most jurors felt Tupac had not been in the room at the time of the rape, but there were two holdouts: the old Catholic woman and another elderly woman. Facing the prospect of a hung jury, the group settled on a compromise that none felt reflected reality. The defense did not dispute during the trial that the defendants groped Jackson's buttocks and had oral sex with her. And so in its verdict, *The New York Times* pointed out, the jury essentially found that the former had been a crime but the latter had not.

Nonetheless, when a recovered Tupac faced sentencing the following February, it was with hard words. "This was an act of brutal violence against a helpless woman," said Justice Daniel P. Fitzgerald. He called Tupac the "instigator" of an "arrogant abuse of the victim." Then the sentence came down: Tupac Shakur was sentenced to one and a half to four and a half years in prison.

About a month later, it was time for Tupac to begin his sentence. Before the long ride to prison, Afeni and Gloria Jean visited him at the apartment of Jasmine Guy and found an awful sight: Tupac sitting on the couch in tears, clutching a rifle, with "Fuck the World" scrawled across his face. He entertained the impulse to simply flee rather than turn himself in. But if you run, you run forever. Mutulu was caught. Sekou Odinga was caught. Eldridge Cleaver had ended his own exile. Assata remained in the wind, severed from anything in her homeland she might have still felt an affinity for. These were the possibilities.

Darker thoughts dilated. Tupac laid out a desperate plan: friends would drive him somewhere away from the city, he'd smoke a lot of weed, and then, by his own hand, he would enter the hereafter. "Tell Mutulu that one of us got away," Tupac instructed those in the room.

No. In the end, Tupac chose the six-by-nine-foot pen provided with compliments by the New York State Department of Correction.

Tupac Shakur was convicted of sexual assault. Barring an unlikely posthumous legal exoneration, that conviction will remain next to his name. Yet Tupac's icon and reputation have remained resilient to this wretched truth. It's not so much omitted from the narrative of his life but often treated as an unfortunate moment in the story, an obstacle to overcome, another case of a powerful man simply getting caught up by an attractive woman—in essence, a modern retelling of the story of Eve and the fall of man.

While writing this book, I was walking through Dublin City when I saw an adorable little girl, maybe five or six years old, wearing a stylish white Tupac sweatshirt. It struck me as strange that her parents would dress their child in the image of a man who'd been convicted of sexual assault. One of two things had to be true: they either did not know about the conviction, or it didn't preclude Tupac from appearing in their daughter's wardrobe. Either way, it laid bare to me just how much his popular status has survived the biggest crisis of his life.

How can this be? Undeniably, the nature of the sentence in many people's minds offers some wiggle room—being found guilty of first-degree sexual abuse for "forcibly touching [a] woman's buttocks" doesn't reflect the weight of Jackson's harrowing story of gang rape. And much has come out about the trial to cast doubt on the verdict, not least that most of the jury were reluctant to convict Tupac of *anything*. Casual observers might wonder if Tupac had done something so terrible, how was he free to be murdered and not languishing in prison?

In a post–Me Too world, we're still grappling with if and how we reframe the legacies of dead celebrities who were accused or convicted of terrible things. Their reputations have been less susceptible to ruination than those of the living. It would appear that the old saying "Don't speak ill of the dead" remains a powerful one.

To understand the safeguarding of Tupac's reputation, we must consider the historical context in which his conviction occurred. Tupac lived in a nation where Black men have long been smeared as sexual deviants and rapists, typically framed in a manner that depicts them as a disproportionate threat to white women. This has frequently been used to justify the maintenance of a status quo that keeps Black people subservient to whites. As an on-record piece of evidence, you can look to the year 1900, when Senator Benjamin

Tillman, former Democratic governor of South Carolina and white supremacist, said on the Senate floor, "We of the South have never recognized the right of the Negro to govern white men, and we never will. We have never believed him to be equal to the white man, and we will not submit to his gratifying his lust on our wives and daughters without lynching him. I would to God the last one of them was in Africa and that none of them had ever been brought to our shores."

Such predatory Black male tropes have been used to justify racist violence. Take the lynching of Will Brown in 1919 with no trial and on extremely dubious evidence. The Tulsa race riot of 1921—when white Oklahomans burned and bombed a prosperous Black section of the city—began after Black teenager Dick Rowland was accused of attacking a white girl in an elevator in the building he worked in as a shoeshiner. (One theory is that Rowland accidentally stood on the girl's foot and, recognizing the danger he was in, fled when she screamed.) The Rosewood massacre of 1923, in Florida, was also sparked by an accusation of rape. And most famously, fourteen-year-old Emmett Till was abducted from his bed and murdered for allegedly wolf-whistling at a white woman. Even Tupac's lawyer, Michael Warren, had previously represented three defendants in the Central Park Five case, which saw five Black and Hispanic boys, aged between fourteen and sixteen, found guilty and jailed for a rape they did not commit. Tupac's accuser might have been Black, but many saw his takedown as AmeriKKKa using one of its favorite weapons against a potent, influential Black man. Some point to the misdeeds of white music icons—white rock 'n' roll of the 1960s and '70s essentially created a gaggle of predators and deviants—and ask why their reputations seem so bulletproof.

There are the theories—Tupac was set up, Jackson was a plant, and so forth. There's a tendency to draw a circle around every controversial incident in Tupac's life and attribute it to lurking governmental forces. It's tempting to believe in the continuity of authorities targeting Tupac like they did so many of his Panther forebears, and if you lived through Emmett Till, the murder of Fred Hampton, and any other travesty of justice experienced by Black people, anything seems possible. Jackson herself believed that authorities would not have put the same effort into the case had the accused been a relative nobody. That the sentence Tupac received for the crime he was ultimately convicted of was disproportionate is undeniable.

I don't blame anyone who deems Tupac Shakur a poisoned figure, or who can't listen to one of his songs without considering the charge. The oft-put-forth idea of simply separating the art and the artist is undeniably appealing but insufficient when artists put so much of themselves into the art. How do you reconcile that someone as wise as Tupac, someone with his feminist leanings, could potentially have a monstrous streak? Really, it's personal, and the truth is that I don't have good answers as to how much asterisking we do. Should every Tupac song played on the radio or MTV have a note attached about his conviction, like old racist cartoons?

Two weeks after Tupac's sentencing, Jackson filed a civil suit seeking $10 million in compensatory damages and $50 million in punitive damages. The courts ruled that in doing so, she would have to waive the anonymity she received in the criminal trial. The suit was settled out of court, after which Jackson disappeared from public scrutiny, perhaps insulating herself from the hostility that circles women accused of bringing about the downfall of more powerful men. In her interview with DJ Vlad, she had oddly little knowledge of the legal fates of the men convicted of sexually assaulting her, but perhaps that was because she managed to move on quickly to live a life not dominated by her worst moments.

One thing to be certain of is that Tupac was never the same following the charge. In prison he dealt with feelings of both remorse for his role in Jackson's abuse and paranoia over the potential that he was a victim of forces trying to destroy him. How far these feelings tipped toward one direction no doubt depends on how guilty he was—or, perhaps more accurately, how guilty he *felt*. How much of Jackson's trauma did he feel culpable for? These emotions would have time to percolate in a prison cell. Forbidden thoughts on nervous nights in Clinton Correctional Facility, a prison that shares the name of a president who carried 83 percent of the Black vote, circled the mind of Inmate No. 95-A-1140. Figures from a celebrity life pinged into Tupac's brain. *Were Biggie and Puffy complicit in the Quad Studios shooting? Were they loyal? How many lifetimes had he lived since "I Get Around"? Is the price for getting your palm prints on unbelievable highs to suffer shocking lows?*

Yes, he was sure of it now: the Quad Studios shooting had been a setup, and the Notorious B.I.G. was the man controlling the skies.

It's hard to envisage what the release of 2Pac's third album, *Me Against the World*, did for his mood. It debuted at number one, making him the first artist to top the album charts while serving a custodial sentence—an achievement that must have tasted bittersweet.

To the fans who bought the album on the day of its release, there was a sense that 2Pac was speaking to them directly from his cell. There are moments when he muses about getting shot and sent to prison. These were prognostications—*Me Against the World* was mostly recorded before either occurred in real life. It raises the question: Did 2Pac foresee his demise or will it into existence?

"This album was made before I went to jail, before I got shot, and all I'm talking about is going to jail and getting shot," said Tupac. "So it was a prophecy. So when the album comes out and then you hear about what's really going on in my real life, I mean, I don't have to say I'm keeping it real, you could listen to the music and go, Whoa he said that . . ."

It had been over two years since the release of *Strictly 4 My N.I.G.G.A.Z . . .* and 2Pac had spent much of that time preparing new music. Soundcastle Studios in Silver Lake, Los Angeles, was one of his favored laboratories, where he worked, shirt frequently off, bandanna frequently on, Hennessy readily available. At Soundcastle, Tupac had one rule: all guns were left on a table upon entry.

There is no listed executive producer on *Me Against the World;* by now Tupac required no guiding hand. Collaborators invited into his inner sanctum didn't always know if they were working toward a specific project, and the same sessions yielded the group album *Thug Life, Volume 1* as Tupac searched for the right alchemy for each set. For his own solo record, he toyed with the title *Fuck the World*.

"Pac was definitely like our coach in the studio," Thug Life rapper Big Syke later said. "He was the most inspiring cat I ever been around in my life. So I was like a sponge with him, everything that I could soak up from this cat, I had to."

Work took place in New York when necessary. Local producer Easy Mo Bee was asked to come to Rucker Park to work on music as Tupac filmed *Above the Rim*. In Tupac's trailer, Mo Bee played a beat that reworked Roger Troutman's classic 1980s robo-soul "Computer Love," spliced with the unserious vocal croons of rapper Erick Sermon ("Heeeey . . . Haaaaay," from the Redman song "Watch Yo Nuggets") into a smoky, soulful beat. That track ended up being the love affair saga "Temptations." It was around the same time that Mo Bee produced a rare Tupac and Biggie collaboration, "Runnin' from tha Police," though the song wouldn't receive a release until 1995, when included on a compilation album celebrating the Million Man March.

Me Against the World was 2Pac's most lyrically sophisticated album yet, right from his opening bars on the dark and hazy "If I Die 2Nite." It's a masterpiece of alliteration as the rapper shows the kind of vocal dexterity traditionally valued on the East Coast. And this, for certain, is an East Coast–leaning 2Pac album, encapsulated by "Old School," an ode to the pioneers of New York rap.

"Old School" was produced by Soulshock & Karlin, two transplants from Denmark who'd pitched up in America in the hopes of becoming big-time rap producers. They scored an early victory by producing a significant amount of Queen Latifah's second album, *Nature of a Sista'*. After hearing "I Get Around," Soulshock noted 2Pac as a dream rapper to work with. The duo asked their manager to deliver some of their beats to him. Just a few days later, Soulshock was driving down Sunset Boulevard when he got the call with some feedback: 2Pac loved the beats and had invited the producers to work with him in a studio. Elation soon melted into uncertainty when it dawned on Soulshock that maybe Tupac didn't know they were white. Concerned, he told his manager to communicate to Tupac's people that they were Danish boys, and if Tupac didn't want them around, so be it.

Hours later, Soulshock received a call. It was Tupac himself.

"I know who the fuck you are, motherfucker," the rapper declared.

Soulshock was bemused. How did this celebrity artist he dreamed of working with know who he was? Tupac asked him if he remembered DJing at Digital Underground shows a few years earlier.

"Who do you think put up your turntables when you're DJing?"

Soulshock couldn't believe it—Tupac was the roadie who had set up his equipment.

"Get your white ass down to the studio and let's do this," instructed Tupac.

All other plans would have to be put on hold. Soulshock & Karlin arrived at Soundcastle that night ready to work. Upon seeing the number of guns being placed on the table, Karlin decided to bail.

Soulshock lined up a beat and Tupac vibed to its New York feel. To build the verses, he asked everyone in the studio on who had been to the city and what were their lasting memories of it. Funneling their input into his verse, he wrote "Old School."

"And at one point he doesn't get it right and he just smashes the mic stand into the window between him and I," remembered Soulshock. "There wasn't a window after that. But [he was] still laughing . . . Joy is really the word I wanna use, even though it was intense."

Soulshock & Karlin also produced the song "Me Against the World," recorded at the Record Plant in Hollywood. Afeni came by the studio that day, ensuring everyone was on their best behavior. As well as serving as the title track for *Me Against the World*, the song was included on the soundtrack to the Will Smith and Martin Lawrence cop movie *Bad Boys*. The beat samples Isaac Hayes's classic cover of Dionne Warwick's "Walk on By," a hip-hop producer staple, but almost unrecognizable in this form. Soulshock's girlfriend at the time was singer Puff Johnson, who freestyled the vocals, while guest verses came from Yafeu Fula (aka Young Hollywood) and Malcolm Greenidge (Big Malcolm) of Dramacydal, a new group that Tupac himself had been mentoring. Tupac's connections to Fula were deep-rooted: his father was Sekou Odinga, comrade of the Shakurs, imprisoned on convictions relating to the liberation of Assata Shakur and the 1981 Brink's robbery. Fula's mother was Yaasmyn Fula, a friend of Afeni's and fellow Panther.

Tupac and Yafeu had played together as children, both raised in revolution.

On an album that values the aesthetics of the East, the clearest West Coast joint is "Heavy in the Game," produced by the Bay Area's Mike Mosley. Constructed out of humming synths and a fat bass line, it's the song here most likely to slide onto a tape of 2Pac's later work with ease. I'm also partial to "Can U Get Away." With a Frankie Beverly sample, it's as syrupy a beat as 2Pac ever rapped over, inspiring him to write a song about rescuing a woman from an abusive relationship. ("Can U Get Away" is rumored to be about TLC member Lisa "Left Eye" Lopes, whose relationship with football player Andre Rison became the stuff of tabloid intrigue.)

Also R&B-inspired is closer "Outlaw," which came together as a fortunate accident. After hearing a demo tape sent to him by Moe Z MD, Tupac flew the producer to New York to work on some songs.

"I like most of the tracks on there, but there's this one on there that's at the end," Tupac told him.

"Oh, that's a R&B track that I had left by accident," replied Moe.

"Well it's a rap now, n***a," insisted Tupac. The beat became the mournful "Outlaw," on which 2Pac muses on death over the sound of gunfire.

The most impactful song on *Me Against the World*, though, was "Dear Mama," a son's ode to his mother and Black single mothers in general. Appropriately, "Dear Mama" crosses generations by sampling Joe Sample's 1978 "In All My Wildest Dreams." And for the song's hook, singers borrow from the 1974 song dedicated to mothers, "Sadie" by the Spinners. 2Pac details their shared struggles: poverty, drug addiction, his defiance of authority, and they put it all behind them, ending each verse with the message "You are appreciated."

In a crucial passage, 2Pac asserts, "And even as a crack fiend, Mama / You always was a Black queen, Mama." "Dear Mama" is a song that touches hearts not because it takes the position that all mothers are perfect and must be lionized, but that the parent-child connection coded in utero onward can withstand anything. It's a song that will continue to draw tears from boys whose own mothers represent the purest relationship in their lives, and the women who allow themselves to acknowledge the hardships they faced while raising children.

With *Me Against the World*, Tupac had his first classic album, and right on time. Since the release of his previous full-length, numerous rap masterpieces had been unleashed, the bar being pulled further and further skyward. Tupac had stardom, but not every great rapper makes a great album. With *Me Against the World*, he enjoyed new critical and cultural cachet.

2Pac did not participate in the video for "Dear Mama," or any other videos released to promote *Me Against the World*, for that matter. As the streets embraced his music and message, the man himself was pacing a cell. Having initially been held at Rikers, Tupac was moved to Clinton Correctional Facility in Dannemora, a tiny town in upstate New York, just twenty miles shy of the Canadian border. Cold and isolated, the institution is known to the men forced to roam its corridors as Little Siberia.

Not wanting to show any weakness, Tupac refused the offer of protective custody and instead joined the prison's general population. "We didn't have any problems out of Tupac," said a staff member not long after his arrival at Dannemora. "He was sweet as pie, there were no signs of him being a thug." Still, concern among the correctional officers about the ruckus a celebrity might cause eventually forced him into segregation. "Inmate Shakur is well known Rap Singer," a prison official wrote in June 1995. "He is a very high profile inmate and in light of such is victim prone. He is being approached for autographs, and has become the focus of undue attention. His fame and background could possibly make him a likely target for extortion."

Like any prisoner attempting to better themselves, Tupac was a ravenous reader. He consumed *The Art of War* by Sun Tzu, and the work of the *Poetic Justice* costar who had left such an impression on him, Maya Angelou. In September, Tupac wrote to a fan in England, claiming he was kept in his cell twenty-three hours a day because of his own disobedience. A list of music he was into at the time included Aretha Franklin, Sarah McLachlan, Jamiroquai,

Counting Crows, Sade, Prince, and Dionne Farris, the latter of which he also shouted out in an interview he gave while locked up: "Different types of music calms my soul. Dionne Farris, she really got me through a lot of this stuff."

One day, while loitering in the yard, Tupac was approached by a white convict roughly his age. The man was an unassuming kind of figure, nothing like the hardened criminals that made up much of the institute's population. But this exterior masked his notoriety. It was Joey Fama, imprisoned for the 1989 murder of Black teenager Yusuf K. Hawkins, the crime that had sparked a meeting of the New Afrikan Panthers in Atlanta that, as chairman, a young Tupac had led. In fact, Tupac had been so moved by the killing that he had penned a poem to the boy's mother. "But Mrs. Hawkins as sure as I'm a Panther / with the blood of Malcolm in my veins / America will never rest / if Yusef dies in vain!" Now he was sharing an address with the man convicted of being the gunman of the group that ambushed Yusuf and his friends that night.

Fama at first hid the specifics of his sentence to Tupac. It was the productive civil rights activist Reverend Al Sharpton, who had led protest marches after the murder of Yusuf, who told Tupac who Fama was when, during a visit, Tupac revealed he'd met a prisoner who blamed Sharpton for his conviction. Still, the pair appear to have been on courteous, even friendly, terms. Both denied the crimes they were accused of—Fama did not dispute he was present at Yusuf's killing, but maintained he was not the triggerman—and shared a distain for the media's coverage of their cases. Tupac told Fama about the plight of Assata Shakur, and they played on the same team in football games in the yard.

Prison can be a gruelingly repetitive existence, but there was one day a bit different from all the others, a moment of romance in Little Siberia. On April 29, Tupac married a woman named Keisha Morris in a short civil ceremony. Serving as witnesses to the union were Tupac's cousin, Billy Lesane, and one of Morris's friends, Pauline Elder.

A relationship had developed between the couple when Tupac was still a free man. On one date night, they went to the movies to see *Forrest Gump*, witnessing its narrow-lensed view of the Black Panthers and their seemingly imprecise anger at whitey. (Tupac had actually auditioned to play the soldier Bubba in the multi-Oscar-winning movie but lost out to Mykelti Williamson.) A camp counselor and student, the petite, pretty Morris appeared of a different universe than her infamous boyfriend. Yet she stuck by Tupac's side during the trial, rushed to the hospital after he was shot at Quad Studios, and visited him in prison regularly, bringing with her Newport cigarettes, notebooks, and a cheap RadioShack cassette tape player so he could listen to music. Meanwhile, he penned seductive letters to a fan named Angela Ardis and kept in touch with Madonna. "The only person who had my back was a white woman," he wrote in a letter to Kendrick Wells about the pop star. The marriage to Morris was later annulled.

On Labor Day weekend, Tupac received a visit from Wendy Day, the founder of the nonprofit Rap Coalition. Since helping to organize the Fruit of Islam to act as security for the wounded rapper as he was wheeled into the courtroom, Day had kept in correspondence with Tupac. But when guards told the prisoner that a white woman had come to visit him, his mind immediately thought, *Madonna*. So when he first spotted Day, he couldn't hide his disappointment.

"Damn, I just drove eight hours to visit," she reminded him.

"No, no, no. I didn't mean it like that," Tupac insisted.

"He had a really great sense of humor and I loved to laugh," said Day years later. "So we were kind of riffing back and forth off of each other."

Day recalled how close the guards sat to their table. "I think they were bored and it amused them that they could listen in on this rapper's conversations, but they were very close to us. I mean, they were four to six feet away."

Moments of relief eased bouts of misery. There were the nightmares. Tupac would wake up in the middle of the night sweating and screaming, memories of the Quad Studios shooting rushing to the surface. Soulshock remembered Tupac phoning into a session the producer was having with Dramacydal when he was still on Rikers Island. "I'm not good. This is fucking hell," Soulshock remembered Tupac complaining. Still, the artist asked for a mic to be switched on, and duly smashed out an intro to the track they were working on. (Soulshock believes the song was never released.)

Tupac needed a way out, and the possibility presented itself when the court decided he could be freed pending his appeal, with bail set at $1.4 million. Where was he going to get that kind of cash? Tupac might have had a hit album, but legal fees had drained his resources. Interscope was open to the idea of putting up the money to get its star out of jail, but parent company Time Warner, unwilling to be seen as having anything to do with springing a convicted felon, blocked the move.

As fate had it, a former NFL defensive end turned music mogul named Marion "Suge" Knight was willing to broker a deal. All Tupac had to do was sign a makeshift handwritten contract Knight put in front of him during a visit. The prisoner agreed, and the wheels to release him were put in motion.

Knight being the face of the deal was enough to calm the higher-ups who actually wrote the check. "I imagine Tupac himself thought Suge bailed him out," recalled Interscope's then head of business affairs, David Cohen. "But the truth is we and Time Warner put up the money. I mean, look . . . I was definitely part of bailing out Tupac."

Just nine days before Tupac left prison, O. J. Simpson discovered he would not be spending the next few decades of his life examining the inside of a cell. The verdict came in his trial for the murder of ex-wife Nicole Brown Simpson and her friend Ronald Goldman: acquitted.

Played out in front of cameras, it has a legitimate case for being considered the trial of the century. But the effects were most keenly felt locally. In Los Angeles, the trial deepened the still-open wounds of the Rodney King beating and L.A. riots, becoming a wedge issue that skewered a racial divide, furthered by the racism of the LAPD being center of the defense team's strategy. Detective Mark Fuhrman became a symbol of police bigotry after tapes were played of him, with a heavy use of the N-word, describing various incidents of brutality. Defense lawyer Johnnie Cochran, a legal legend by the end of the trial, condemned Fuhrman as a "lying, perjuring, genocidal racist"; even prosecutor Marcia Clark had to concede that her witness was the "worst LAPD has to offer." Juror Carrie Bess admitted she voted to acquit for a singular reason: payback for King.

As the realization that he was a free man dawned on Simpson, he glanced over at the jury leaving the courtroom and saw Black juror Lionel Cryer with a first in the air, proudly completing his service with the Black Power salute.

Tupac Shakur was released on October 12, 1995. As if to completely cleanse himself of the experience, he left all his personal possessions in his cell. Waiting at the prison gates were Afeni's Panther comrade Yaasmyn Fula, Big Syke, and a white limousine, to chariot them to a nearby motel, where champagne, Alizé, and weed were plentiful. Tupac's tolerance levels would have been shattered by his imprisonment, so it wouldn't have taken him long to feel the familiar buzz. But the motel was just a short-term sanctuary. Immediately, he flew to Los Angeles and resumed his cause with new allies and fresh armaments.

"Come to Death Row": Tupac with label mogul Marion "Suge" Knight, 1996

10

WINTER IN AMERICA

MARION "SUGE" KNIGHT is typically portrayed as an uncomplicated figure—a man of a singular image, with a singular purpose. Anyone vaguely familiar with the Tupac Shakur story understands the character of Knight to be an amalgamation of Sonny Liston and Tommy from the movie *Goodfellas:* a ferocious, uncompromising, cigar-chomping behemoth who'd sooner snap a man's clavicle than be on the bad end of a business deal. That the name "Suge" comes from the nickname "Sugar Bear," bestowed on him as a child because of his sweet nature, seems like the stuff of bad Mafia fiction. But in his heyday, Knight had an aura that appeared beyond belief.

Tales of his short run in the music industry have become the stuff of gangster rap lore. There is the story of the white rap music executive who went missing for forty-eight hours. When he did finally surface, the executive claimed amnesia, but there were whispers of Knight having him kidnapped in broad daylight as he obliviously stood at an ATM. Or the rumor of Knight becoming so frustrated by a journalist's inquests, he held the scribe up against the office piranha tank with a plain offer: restart the interview with better questions, or risk being skeletonized.

Then there was the case of Lynwood Stanley and George Stanley Jr. The names probably don't mean much to you, but the brothers inadvertently helped shape L.A. gangster rap history when, in 1987, as members of the New York trio HBO (Home Boys Only), they backed out of recording a song with Dr. Dre titled

"Boyz-n-the-Hood." The distinctly West Coast lyrics, penned by Ice Cube, just didn't compute in their East Coast minds. Frustrated that the session might fizzle, Dre asked Eric Wright, head of burgeoning label Ruthless Records, to jump on the beat. As it turned out, Wright's high-pitched voice and street-cool attitude was the perfect complement to Dre's synthesized bass and hard drums. "Boyz-n-the-Hood" fashioned Wright's Eazy-E persona and sowed the seeds for L.A.'s defining gangster rap group, N.W.A.

But this was five years later, in July 1992. Dre was now a superstar producer, and Lynwood and George were just a couple of artists in his orbit, hoping that if they hung around the Good Doctor for long enough, he'd ask them to record a track once more.

At the offices of SOLAR Records—an early base of operations for Suge Knight's burgeoning empire—Lynwood had the temerity to use Knight's phone, infuriating the goliath.

"Say, Blood," said Knight, "don't be on the phone."

"Don't be coming at me with all that gangbang shit. I'm not from L.A.," Lynwood unwisely replied.

George intervened, and the two artists retreated to the building's cafeteria, where Lynwood could instead use a pay phone. It proved to be no sanctuary. Knight stalked his victims with a pistol in hand. With the gun drawn, he proceeded to beat the brothers bloody. The assault continued in a studio area, where celebrity artists Dr. Dre, Snoop Doggy Dogg, the D.O.C., and others feebly looked on before Knight ushered them out of the room.

Terrifyingly alone with their assailant, Lynwood and George were ordered onto their knees. When Lynwood refused, Knight fired a round into the air and demanded his victims take off their clothes. To end the ordeal, Knight, his blood chilling another degree every minute, re-created a scene from *Goodfellas*. He seized Lynwood's wallet, studied his ID, and gave the half-naked pair a choice: leave and forget about the incident, or members of their family would be killed. The threat didn't stop them from going straight to the police, who quickly arrived at the office. Nobody would give a statement about what happened to the Stanley brothers; the only evidence was the bullet fired from Knight's gun, which investigators found lodged in the wall. It was enough to get him convicted on assault charges and put on probation when the case finally wound its way through the legal system in 1995.

I repeat these stories to make one thing clear: if Tupac needed to be tough to make it out of prison intact, he needed similar steel to be an artist on Suge Knight's Death Row Records.

Knight was only six years older than Tupac, but the small and slender artist looked like a boy in his presence, seemingly always peeking out from behind the hulking frame of a man who loved wearing extravagant suits that suggested he was older than his years. Knight is often considered the wrong boss for Tupac at the wrong time, an accelerant that caused the troubled artist to burn out of control. If you discard the music 2Pac created during his Death Row tenure—of such a high quality that it sealed his artistic legacy—then this is observably true. What Tupac the man needed in his life was a calming presence. Instead, his eternal search for a father figure brought him into the clutches of a six-foot four-inch, 315-pound sphinx with gang connections.

Not everyone can be as naturally gifted as Tupac Shakur, but in 1990s America, an iron will could take you some of the way, and Suge Knight was nothing if not a man of focus and determination. Unlike Tupac, the West Coast had always been his home. Knight's parents, Marion Sr. and Maxine, were among those who left the South—in their case, Mississippi—for California in search of a better life. Marion Sr., a truck driver before the relocation, became a custodian in UCLA's housekeeping and laundry departments, while Maxine worked in an electronics factory. On April 19, 1965, their third child, Marion Jr., was born in a downtown Los Angeles hospital. Four years later, the couple hoped to complete their own vision of the American dream by purchasing a two-bedroom house in Compton.

The Compton of the 1960s was not the urban war zone that would be depicted by N.W.A. two decades later. For their hard-earned capital, the Knights believed they'd be acquiring a piece of suburban bliss. But, just as had happened in the Bronx, when Black families moved into the neighborhood, the Caucasians moved out, taking with them the businesses, jobs, and infrastructure investment. Racism meant insurers charged extra fees to the new Black population. Unemployment grew; poverty levels increased. The rise of the Crips and Bloods gangs in the 1970s, the crack epidemic, and LAPD chief Daryl Gates's paramilitary approach to policing began to erode the social fabric of Compton and broader South Central Los Angeles. Suge grew up as the gangs were becoming more territorial, doctrinal, and violent. That he ended up friendly with the local Tree Top Pirus, a Bloods sect, was simply a consequence of his address.

Though wily enough to stay on the right side of the local gang members, it was sports that interested young Suge. Marion Sr. had been a high-school football star, and his son inherited some of that talent. From 1983 to 1985, Suge lined out for El Camino College, later transferring to the University of Nevada, Las Vegas, where he played for a further two years. Knight was good enough to enter the National Football League draft but went unselected. He eventually made two appearances in the NFL by scabbing for the Los Angeles Rams during the 1987 players' strike. Nobody fucked with Knight the music mogul, but as a replacement player, he and his teammates had to withstand the striking Rams pelting eggs at the team van as it made its way to practice. The incident became so heated that the picketers began to rock the vehicle; offensive tackle Robert Cox went a step further, shattering one of its windows with his bare hands.

Returning to Los Angeles after his short stint as a professional athlete, Knight became immersed in the music industry by working security for stars like Bobby Brown. But the Comptonite's ambitions were larger than stopping groupies from getting to the self-proclaimed King of Stage, and in 1989, he established a music publishing company. There was an early boon when one of his clients, Mario "Chocolate" Johnson, claimed that he was the man behind much of rap pop-tart Vanilla Ice's early oeuvre, including the mega smash single "Ice Ice Baby." Legend has it that Suge and his goons burst into Ice's suite at the Bel Age Hotel, seized the diminutive star by the ankles, lowered him over the balcony, and threatened to let go unless he gave up the rights to "Ice Ice Baby." The rapper himself has denied the story in different ways, from claiming Knight didn't threaten him at all to describing his own bodyguard being reduced to tears after the room invaders pulled out a gun and intimated that they'd throw the rapper off the balcony if he didn't sign what they wanted him to sign. Whatever the truth of the matter, Knight left with the signature he wanted and an enhanced reputation of being a fearsome man to have in your corner.

Building on these early skirmishes, Knight resolved to be the head of his own label. A crucial relationship was fostered with Dick Griffey, an industry veteran and founder of SOLAR Records, best known for its pop-disco releases of the late 1970s and '80s, who agreed to provide office space and a studio to record in. An early investor in Knight's musical activities was Michael "Harry-O" Harris, who through various business moves was eventually omitted from the picture. There wasn't much Harris could do about it, sitting in a prison cell for drug trafficking. He wouldn't, in fact, be released until 2021, when, after thirty-three years inside, he received a presidential pardon from Donald Trump. (In some small recognition for his role in the company, Dr. Dre thanked him in the liner notes for his debut solo and Death Row's inaugural album, *The Chronic*.)

His early entrepreneurial endeavors brought Knight into the circle of young artist Tracy Curry, who went by the D.O.C. A hit solo album released in 1989 on Ruthless Records titled *No One Can Do It Better* appeared to set the native Texan up for rap stardom, until a car accident crushed both his larynx and his dreams. Nonetheless, the D.O.C. remained a valuable songwriter and potential core component of any ambitious enterprise. More important for Knight, though, was that the connection gave him access to the man who had produced *No One Can Do It Better*: another Compton native who had searched for something greater than the gangs, Andre Young, better known as Dr. Dre. (It's fair to say that Dre was a better music-maker than Knight was a football player.)

Knight's timing could not have been better. Both Dre and the D.O.C. were unsatisfied with Eazy-E's stewardship of Ruthless Records and loyalty to business manager Jerry Heller, a Jewish industry veteran. Ice Cube had already left N.W.A. and Ruthless in 1989 due to a royalties dispute, and Knight wanted to examine

Dre's contract to see if his grievances were also legitimate. When Ruthless refused to provide the paperwork, Knight forced his way into the company's offices and riffled through filing cabinets until he found what he was looking for. Shaken by the threat of Knight, Heller hired an armed bodyguard and began a routine of driving home each day via a different route.

Upon examining the contract, Knight vowed to secure Dre's release. The way Knight engineered the acquisition of Dre, the D.O.C., and singer Michel'le would become a point of contention. Eazy-E claimed in court that he signed the release contracts under duress when, during a meeting between the two, Knight ushered a couple of mean henchmen into the room and threatened to beat Eazy with pipes and baseball bats. Knight said this never happened, yet by the end of the meeting, the documents had been signed and the power balance in Los Angeles had shifted.

From this maneuvering, the entity known as Death Row Records emerged. Listed as the four original founders were Griffey, the D.O.C., Dre, and Knight. A distribution deal was reached with Interscope, who settled with Eazy by agreeing to pay Ruthless Records a percent of Dre's production revenue. It opened a curious scenario where the records Dre was releasing that dissed Eazy were actually generating income for his former groupmate.

As the ink dried on the contracts, Knight maintained his links to the Mob Pirus. At times, Death Row's offices at 8200 Wilshire Boulevard resembled a Bloods social club, with gangsters roaming halls decorated in appropriately scarlet and ruby hues.

Suge Knight's Piru connections set the tone at Death Row, but they were indicative of the gangster boogie that had dominated Los Angeles rap since the late 1980s. The city had initially built on early hip-hop's electro-bop sounds but added its own sense of style: glitzy leather, glam-rock eyeliner, sequin suits, Prince in general. It couldn't have been more different from the gang violence devastating the areas where many of the artists came from.

In search of something fresher, more real, was Dr. Dre. He'd already indulged in the garish hip-hop scene as part of the group World Class Wreckin Cru, where his talent stood out like a luminous fresco on a drab gray wall. "I hadn't seen that in any Black artist in the last two hundred years," World Class Wreckin Cru's manager Jerry "Swamp Dogg" Williams Jr. told me.

For his next endeavor, Dre joined forces with Eric "Eazy-E" Wright, Ice Cube, Arabian Prince, MC Ren, and DJ Yella to form N****z Wit Attitudes, or N.W.A. The group did more than anyone to shift hip-hop's tectonic plates from New York—where the *hip-hip-hop-a-you-don't-stop* sounds of the old school were simultaneously being banished by the harder content of the likes of Boogie Down Productions and others—to the West Coast. For a global audience, N.W.A. cemented South Central Los Angeles's image of young Black men with Jheri curls and baseball caps, cruising down Crenshaw in six-four Impalas, screaming, "Fuck the police!"

When Dre deserted Ruthless, tearing down the remnants of N.W.A. with him, a wounded Eazy-E popularized the term "studio gangsters" to deride his musicophile former groupmate as a wannabe outlaw. The lines were clearly drawn: it wasn't enough to be a rap artist who simply portrayed what was happening on L.A.'s mean streets like a talented actor—your connections, your activities, had to be 100 percent legit. Otherwise, you were a phony.

Over a long career, Dre has cultivated the reputation of a cerebral studio loiterer, a man entirely wrapped up in his music and the constant striving for sonic perfection. But in his Death Row days, he was also a hard-partying celebrity routinely accused of assault. For a time, Dre's rap sheet was constantly extending: In August 1991, he pleaded no contest to charges he viciously attacked MTV personality Dee Barnes. Dre was fined $2,350 and placed on two years of probation. Over a year later, he pled guilty to battery of a police officer and was convicted on two additional battery counts stemming from a brawl in the lobby of a New Orleans hotel. For this he spent thirty days under house arrest. And in June 1993, Dre pleaded no contest to battery charges stemming from an assault that left producer Damon Thomas with a broken jaw.

In the middle of it all, Dre's Calabasas home caught fire during one of his raucous pool parties. Dousing the blaze left two firefighters with minor injuries. Dre claimed the fire was down to an electric fault, and maybe it was. But it was indicative of the inclination he had at the time for chaos. As he told the *L.A. Times*, "1992 was not my year."

Through the madness and shame, Dre fashioned his solo debut and Death Row's inaugural album, *The Chronic*. In one funky swoop, it banished his status as N.W.A.'s man behind the music and established him as a star name in his own right. Whether or not Dre invented G-funk music is disputed—Above the Law's Cold187um is often considered its father. What's harder to argue is that Dre was the one who found the perfect alchemy by bolstering the throwback P-funk samples on which G-funk was built with live instrumentation. *The Chronic* has buzzing synths, sour whistles, guests using patois vocals, distinct L.A. gangsterisms, and plenty of weed smoke. In his N.W.A. days, Dre had declared, "I don't smoke weed or sess / 'Cause it's known to give a brother brain damage." On *The Chronic*, he reinvented himself as a connoisseur of the sticky-icky, hosting a rolling smoke session that invited Death Row's growing bullpen: Daz Dillinger, Jewell, Kurupt, the D.O.C., RBX, Nate Dogg, the Lady of Rage, and Dre's latest protégé, a gangly, theatrical Long Beach bohemian who selected the stage name Snoop Doggy Dogg.

A hip-hop Snagglepuss with an Iceberg Slim aura, Snoop possessed a certain joie de vivre unlike anything else the West had seen before. Though barely out of his teens, Snoop was entrusted by Dre to appear on the majority of songs included on *The Chronic*, including its star-making summertime cookout classic, "Nuthin' but a 'G' Thang." On the back of its success, Death Row plotted Snoop's debut album, *Doggystyle*, with the D.O.C. tasked with mentoring the still-young rapper. "We would stay up to two or three in the morning at his house, playing video games and drinking beer," Snoop later recalled. "Then we'd go off and write rhymes and record them on cassette and deliver them to Dre the next day."

Doggystyle is one of the greatest party records ever made. Yet behind the revelry, Dre had worked on the album obsessively, often to the chagrin of Snoop himself, who didn't always share his partner's fastidiousness. As Snoop found his own ideas shot down, Dre was conducting session musicians for hours on end to find the right loop. Inevitably, the release of *Doggystyle* was put at risk of delay.

"The very last night, [Interscope's] Jimmy Iovine came to the

studio because he was like, 'We gotta turn this in right now,'"
remembered Nanci Fletcher, a singer on the album. "They had all
these warehouses up, waiting to print the album. We did all the
skits in like that same day, all the skits on that album, we had to rush
through that."

Desperate to get the record to the pressing plant, Knight and
Iovine loomed over the shoulder of mixer Chris "the Glove" Taylor as he perfected the final track. "They told me that it would cost
them $42,000 for every hour that it went over," said the Glove.
"They had trucks lined up, and they were waiting to ship it."

The process paid off. *Doggystyle*, like *The Chronic* before it, sold
and sold, and G-funk became the de facto sound of the West.

All the while, Death Row staff were required to be ambivalent
about the violence that underpinned its operations. Not even the
company's offices on Wilshire Boulevard, adjacent to its partners at
Interscope, were spared such brutal scenes. Anyone Knight thought
was trying to cheat him would be dragged into a storeroom and
beaten.

Tired of the sadism was Dre's own stepbrother, Warren G, who
made some crucial contributions to *Doggystyle*, but dreamed of
being the man whose name adorned the front cover of platinum-
selling albums, not the credits. In a bout of impatience, Warren
told *The Source* that he "made" Death Row, only to call the magazine a few days later, asking it not to run the quote. His claim was
printed anyway, and soon the rumor around the Death Row office
was that for this indiscretion, Warren had suffered a threatening
late-night rendezvous with a gun-toting unit of Bloods.

A party was planned to launch Snoop's album on November 22,
1993, the eve of its release. For the occasion, Death Row went predictably big by hiring a luxurious 165-foot yacht. Passengers were
instructed to board the vessel from beachside suburb Marina del
Rey; Coolio and Queen Latifah were among the celebrities on the
guest list. But the scene quickly fell apart. Tensions grew as security
attempted to slowly board passengers through a narrow gangway
that could accommodate only one person at a time. Dozens ended
up being refused entry; fights broke out on land and sea. On board
the yacht, Knight's crew ended up whaling on some of Warren G's

friends. It was all too ridiculous for the ambitious rapper. He quietly cut a deal with Def Jam and, powered by the single "Regulate," his debut album *Regulate . . . G Funk Era* became a mega-smash, leaving Knight to ponder what had slipped through his fingers.

Suge Knight cut a flashy figure. With the threads, the bulk, the fearsome presence, the CEO was impossible to miss. But Knight felt comfortable as a facilitator of talent, an executive who made things happen for the artist, and, in the end, collected his princely fee. He was not a man to make unwarranted noise that would make him the focus of attention.

On August 3, 1995, however, Knight was front and center. It was the night of the second Source Awards, an event inaugurated by the magazine to recognize excellence in rap. It took place at the Paramount Theater in New York, bringing Death Row onto distant soil. With his entourage, Knight accepted the award for Soundtrack of the Year. The label had produced the music for Tupac's movie *Above the Rim*, gathering an impressive set of tunes from many of its own artists, plus the likes of R&B group SWV and 2Pac himself. In his speech, the towering Knight encouraged artists who were unhappy with their labels to come to his kingdom. "Any artist out there that want to be an artist and want to stay a star, and don't have to worry about the executive producer trying to be all in the videos, all on the record, dancing . . . come to Death Row!" he yelled. It was a thinly veiled jibe. The audience knew that his acidic words were directed at Sean "Puffy" Combs, who was known for tripping the light fantastic when his artists were shooting their MTV clips. In the crowd that night was music journalist Michael A. Gonzales, who after Knight spoke immediately told his girlfriend they were moving to seats closer to the auditorium exit, in case things kicked off.

The barbs continued to fly. As Dre was accepting his award for Producer of the Year, Snoop, part of the crew who'd accompanied Dre onstage, became agitated by the crowd ("The East Coast ain't got no love for Dr. Dre and Snoop Dogg?"). Puffy tried to deescalate the situation, but not without showing his hometown allegiances ("I live in the East, and I'm gonna die in the East").

Even Atlanta's OutKast got booed, and one-half of the group, André Benjamin, whom the world would come to know as André 3000, rose to the bait ("The South got something to say!"). It all prompted the Roots' sage-like drummer Questlove to reflect years later that "the '95 Source Awards was a funeral in hip hop's history."

The East Coast–West Coast feud didn't start at the Source Awards. Still, the event represented an intensification of the animosity that was brewing. It's entirely probable that Knight sensed the rising tension between the two edges of the hip-hop nation, and that the stature of his label, which already traded on a sense of menace, would increase with an all-out war. It's also highly likely that Puffy's brand of flashiness simply stuck in his craw.

Nanci Fletcher, who sang on dozens of classic Death Row records, took a dim view of Knight's attacks on Puffy. "Suge was jealous of him, period," she told me. "Because Death Row only had hip-hop. They didn't have R&B like Puffy. He had Mary [J. Blige], Faith Evans, Jodeci—they excelled at everything. They knew how to groom their artists better. Puffy just had a flair for knowing what looked good, what sounded good, and how to dress. The guys in L.A. weren't into fashion like that. We're just not like the Harlem guys. The New Yorkers have always been able to dress better and just had more style. So, there was a jealousy thing there. And I think Suge got Tupac out of jail because of that. He knew it was perfect for him."

Tupac was still languishing in prison when Knight delivered his benediction at the Source Awards, but his own problems with the two key figures at Bad Boy, Puffy and Biggie, had germinated at the Quad Studios shooting. And when Biggie's song "Who Shot Ya?" received an official release just a week after Tupac's incarceration, it seemed to reinforce every suspicion. No names are mentioned, but the song casts Biggie as an unsentimental gunman—trifle with him and prepare to get "Swiss cheesed up." The denials that "Who Shot Ya?" is about Tupac have always been strenuous, as have been the denials from Biggie and Puffy that they had anything to do with what happened at Quad Studios. But in Tupac's mind, it was tantamount to an admission.

Knight wasn't always a fan of Tupac. He had considered the

former art school student's tough-guy posturing to be as fake as knock-off Rolexes. But looking on as Tupac made the evening news for shooting cops, ticking off major members of the Republican Party, and becoming embroiled in a high-profile court case that ultimately saw him thrown in jail was intriguing to a CEO who had long realized that controversy sold records to white kids.

Death Row's overtures began before Tupac became a guest of the prison system. Knight came in hard, paying the rapper a cool $200,000 to record just one song, which became "Pour Out a Little Liquor," credited to 2Pac's group Thug Life and included on the *Above the Rim* soundtrack. With work on the track completed, Knight offered Tupac a contract at Death Row, and was surprised when it was rejected. Needless to say, by October 1995, things looked significantly different. Hence the bail money, the hastily drawn-up contract signed behind the walls of Clinton Correctional Facility, and the cross-country flight, straight into the cauldron.

After eight months in the cooler, there was no time to waste. The way *Tupac Shakur: The Authorized Biography* tells it, the rapper left LAX, stopped for some quick shopping at the Beverly Center Mall, and checked into the Peninsula Beverly Hills hotel. After dinner with Knight at a steakhouse in Westwood, he headed to Death Row's favored recording studio, Can-Am in Tarzana, eager to repay the company's investment. But as soon as he started to rap, the exhaustion brought on by the whirlwind schedule set in, and the slender Tupac collapsed into Knight's giant arms. The bedraggled artist returned to his hotel for much-needed rest. But others have claimed that Tupac immediately went from airport to studio and cooked up "Ambitionz az a Ridah."

I like this version of the story because it suggests "Ambitionz az a Ridah" was bursting to escape 2Pac, manifesting itself at the earliest opportunity. No ring rust had developed during his time away from the studio. Over the slow-motion movement of the piano keys and killer snare, the rhythm of 2Pac's voice is insane—warbling, belligerent, all-around undeniable. But there is also a haunted quality to his performance, complemented by the eerie *ooh ooh* female background vocals. On his opening bar, he encapsulates the duality of being a star in the '90s gangster rap crucible: "So many battle-field scars while driven in plush cars."

All Eyez on Me is the kind of gangster rap record that news reports had always insisted the conscious, politically engaged 2Pac was making—it's tougher, uglier, bloodier, and more macho than anything he had previously concocted. America's Worst Nightmare was uncaged and coming for the pale-skinned persecutor. And on the album's cover is an image of the star with his left hand clutching the Death Row chain around his neck, his right hand held up with fingers curled into the shape of a "W." It was a gesture for all who represented America's Westside, a signal of his allegiances in the coastal war, a hand sign recognized all over the world as represent-ing California rap. Nobody would become more famous for throw-ing it in the air than Tupac Shakur.

Across a series of predominantly G-funk grooves, 2Pac's tales of beautiful women, alcohol- and weed-fueled adventures, the down-fall of his enemies, and the thrill of being out of prison glimmer like a Desert Eagle in the sunlight. Both a reaction and retort to his reputation as a controversial agitator, the notion is unmistakable: *If you keep calling me a gangster rapper, you'll get a gangster rapper.* And, as he croons on his Snoop collaboration, "2 of Amerikaz Most Wanted," "Ain't nothing but a gangster party." Even the title of the song was provocative: Tupac was only free on bail, and Snoop was at the time staring at a murder charge, of which he'd be acquitted the following year.

Like a gray reef shark, Tupac would move between Can-Am's Studio A and Studio B, always restless, never still. After arriving at the studio, he'd often joke around with Johnny J, one of the album's core producers, until a fresh beat finally emerged from the speak-ers. Tupac would then do a little head shake, which would evolve into a dance—a signal to all around that he was feeling the music. With a pen and paper in hand, he'd sit next to the mixing board, sketch out the number of bars he needed to fill as a guide, and begin to write. Nobody would talk to him during this phase, only a cigarette would divert his concentration. After twenty, maybe thirty minutes, Tupac would say, "I'm ready." Then it was into the recording booth, where the necromancy would occur.

In front of the mic, he was in a state of abstraction, his inner impulse pushing him to thump, hiss, rack, stack, or gatling the syllables, depending on what the beat demanded. "Me and my producer Johnny J keep coming up with new songs till people start passing out," he explained. "Then we come back early in the morning and start over. You're going to feel the entire eleven months of what I went through on this album. I'm venting my anger." Johnny J eventually had to tell Tupac that he'd no more beats left—something that gave the artist tremendous satisfaction.

For years Tupac had wanted to work with Dr. Dre. A move to Death Row facilitated that ambition. But the sum of their artistic relationship would be just two songs: "Can't C Me," a trunk-rattling G-funk standard featuring guest vocals from one of the genre's P-funk ancestors, George Clinton, and, of course, "California Love." Their lack of productivity together makes sense, really: 2Pac, the jittering ball of fury who could simultaneously record different songs in different rooms, and Dre, the pathological perfectionist. It was never going to be a wondrous match.

What Tupac might not have known when he first pitched up at Can-Am is that he was only ever going to catch the death throes of Dre's Death Row era. The producer was already preparing his exit, and the signing of this new star did nothing to alter those plans. Tommy D. Daugherty, a house engineer for Death Row, witnessed Dre's frustration firsthand. "Fuck it, I can say it: Dre really didn't want nothing to do with that record [*All Eyez on Me*]. He didn't like it at all that Tupac came to Death Row, which I thought was kind of interesting, 'cause I remember he said, 'That's it, I'm done with Death Row now that Tupac is here.' I was like, 'What the fuck?'"

So, 2Pac and Dre fell short of kindred spirits, but the music they did create together is the sum of their collective talents. "California Love" is probably 2Pac's most recognizable hit. It's strange, then, to consider that it was originally intended to be a Dre solo single, until Knight ordered that his latest signee be added to the final product. (Each rapper's segments were recorded at different times. The ad-libs on the outro might appear to be Dre and 2Pac in discussion but were actually just 2Pac bouncing off Dre's original vocal.) Knight's musical chops are rarely discussed, but his instinct here was immaculate. The Death Row CEO wanted two of his superstars on *that* beat—the starburst of horns and funky piano play was adapted from Joe Cocker's blue-eyed funk hit "Woman to Woman"—bigging up the virtues of their home state at a time when battle lines with New York were being drawn. With a chorus provided by talkbox-voiced alien freakster Roger Troutman of the Dayton funk band Zapp, it was a concoction conceived in hip-hop heaven; Dre's original is rendered flat in comparison.

Released a couple of months before *All Eyez on Me*, "California Love" topped the *Billboard* rap charts. Yet an alternate version ended up on the album, supposedly due to sampling clearance issues. It's typically credited as a remix also helmed by Dre, but the beat was actually orchestrated by two lesser-known producers, Laylaw and D'Maq. Dre liked it so much he stitched together both versions of "California Love" around the same time, leaving the original beatmakers in the dark and, eventually, uncredited. Upon discovering what had happened, Laylaw called up everyone—Dre, Tupac, Knight—to ask where his credit was. None had any satisfactory answers.

A casual attitude to crediting the talent was a problem at Death Row. "It's crazy. A lot of the credits got fucked up back then," said DJ Quik, who produced "Heartz of Men" for *All Eyez on Me*. "It was real bad business going on up there sometimes, and if you didn't go into the office with Roy Tesfay [Suge Knight's assistant] and them and you do your credits, you got screwed. I got fucked. I did a lot of remixing on that record [*All Eyez on Me*], and overdubbing and mixing [that I wasn't credited for]. I made a lot of those records sound a lot better than they did when they came into the studio, and in a real small amount of time. In two days, I remixed like twelve songs."

Similarly, Nanci Fletcher claims she received credit for only a fraction of the work she did on Snoop's *Doggystyle:* "Nobody came to me and asked me about any information for the credits, no business was handled," she said. "I thought maybe they were going to come at the end, 'Okay, Nanci, let's get your info. What song was you on to do paperwork,' *La la la*. Nothing."

With recording on *Doggystyle* completed, Fletcher spotted

Snoop in the studio speaking to Interscope's Jimmy Iovine, who had the masters in his hands and was about to leave. "Something in me was like, *I wonder if he's talking about the credits.* And I was like, *Let me just go over and see.* And I'm glad I did because I went and I was like, 'Snoop, are you giving him credits?' He was like, 'Yeah, Nanci.' I was like, 'Okay, well, can you tell him about the songs I was on?' He was like, 'Oh yeah, fo' sho'.' But he was only in the studio when I did 'Lodi Dodi' and 'Gz and Hustlas.' He wasn't there for the rest of the songs. So even though he probably knew I was on it, but he didn't think, he wasn't thinking. So those are the only two songs he gave Jimmy Iovine my name for. That's why those are the only two songs I have credit for, but I did every song in that album, except for 'What's My Name.' "

From artistic conception to criminal conviction, 2Pac's audience had largely accepted his various mutations. But the fans who had been on the journey with him since *2Pacalypse Now* would surely have noticed his social justice bent is suppressed on *All Eyez on Me*. There is, though, "Shorty Wanna Be a Thug," a portrait of a young man enamored of a life of crime. With the vibe on the day of its recording a little more laid-back than usual, Tupac tried to tap into the mind of a delinquent child. From that seed of an idea, the song came together quickly. "Shorty Wanna Be a Thug" samples Hank Crawford's "Wildflower," which Kanye West would later flip into his even more mournful "Drive Slow."

Further forays into social or politically engaged content include the calling out of presidential rivals Bill Clinton and Bob Dole ("You're too old to understand the way the game's told") and C. Delores Tucker, a civil rights activist who'd been waging a high-profile war on gangster rap. That said, they're baked into "How Do U Want It," a club tune about coming from nothing to living large, with a video starring several porn stars. And on the final minute and a half or so of "Picture Me Rollin'," 2Pac brightens the corners by calling a roll of those in power who'd sought his demise: cops, correctional officers, and the district attorney who prosecuted him, his words intending to invoke the image in their mind's eye of Tupac Shakur living the high life that was always fated to be his.

It was during the *All Eyez on Me* sessions that Tupac assembled his definitive group, the Outlaw Immortalz, often truncated to just the Outlawz. It was a faction built out of various rappers in Tupac's sphere, including artists who'd been in Thug Life and Dramacydal. But he also baptized each with a fresh name inspired by different political leaders. So Mopreme took the name Komani after Iranian revolutionary leader Ayatollah Khomeini; Big Syke became Mussolini. Dramacydal's Yafeu "Young Hollywood" Fula, Malcolm "Big Malcolm" Greenidge, and third member Katari "K-Dog" Cox were rebranded as Yaki Kadafi, E.D.I. Mean, and Kastro respectively. Bruce Edward Washington Jr., a friend of Fula's, took the name Hussein Fatal. And Mutah Wassin Shabazz Beale became Napoleon. They were political figures from all over the ideological map, and the rappers appeared to have little connection to the men whose identities they were absorbing. "When he named me Mussolini, I had to grab a book and read up on this fool," said Syke. Never mind, though: the group showed their collective talents on crew rap classic "When We Ride." It was an early mention of the alter ego Tupac was envisioning for himself: Makaveli.

My least favorite 2Pac song released in his lifetime is "Wonda Why They Call U Bitch." In this brutish piece, he calls out the supposed immoral behavior of wearing skin-tight miniskirts in nightclubs and having casual sex in cars. 2Pac disparages the anonymous woman for becoming the subject of male locker-room sex brags, failing to turn his lens inward and call out the talk itself. The message is that some women are responsible for the misogynistic attitudes that shadow them, unbecoming for the mind that had previously conceived of "Keep Ya Head Up."

Not invited to the sessions that yielded *All Eyez on Me* were Carsten "Soulshock" Schack and his production partner Kenneth Karlin, key producers on *Me Against the World*. The Danes were, of course, desperate to work with 2Pac again—they had the beats ready to go. But the atmosphere around the star had palpably changed, and that was set from the top of his new label.

Soulshock was delighted to accept an invitation from Tupac to attend a show with him at the House of Blues (the producer doesn't remember who performed that night). Upon arrival, he was encouraged when Tupac gave him the usual warm embrace. Knight, however, displayed none of the same affability. At the bar with Tupac and his stone-faced boss, the conversation turned to music, and Soulshock revealed he had cooked up five new beats that could potentially be of use to the rapper.

"Man, did you hear that, Suge?" Tupac shrieked, as if to foster some sort of connection between the two men. Once more, Knight refused to respond.

Also unsettling to Soulshock were the changes he saw in his onetime collaborator. When other patrons pushed past Tupac, he pompously yelled out not to touch him. Soulshock also saw that Tupac had a gun tucked into his waistband. Bemused by the spectacle, he excused himself, exited the House of Blues, and never saw Tupac Shakur again.

Tupac was exhibiting a strong need for Knight's approval, and that meant becoming more acquainted with Bloods. Thug Life had been about unity among gangs, positioning Tupac as a man between factions. On "Fuck the World," from *Me Against the World*, he'd rapped, "I don't give a fuck if you Blood or Cuz [a Crips term of endearment for each other], long as you got love for thugs." Like a chameleon turning red, the more Tupac was in close proximity to Knight, the more he absorbed his Bloods identity.

To Garrick "Numskull" Husbands, one-half of the rap duo Luniz, it was a perturbing development. Driving down Melrose Avenue around the time, he spotted his old Oakland rap scene acquaintance in a black drop-top Rolls-Royce. When Tupac pulled up alongside him, Numskull noticed he was wearing all red.

"What's up, man? What's up with that?" Numskull inquired.

"Man, this is who I fuck with. I'm just fuckin' with the folks," he recalled Tupac responding.

"I hated to see it," Numskull told me years later, "because we always respected him as an Oakland n***a. I mean, I still respect him to this day—I respected him right then and there. But I didn't like it. You know what I mean? And that's what got him killed to me . . . One thing I can say about Pac, he moved around, man. You know, he fucked with everybody. I can say that. But that L.A. shit? That gangbang shit? That's nothing we [people from Oakland] know about. And if we're not from that culture, we're not gonna be accepted in it, no matter what."

In mid-December, Snoop and fellow Death Row artists Kurupt and Daz Dillinger, a duo known as Tha Dogg Pound, flew into hostile territory to shoot the video for their song "New York, New York." In the completed clip, the crew of rappers take giant form and move around the city's skyscrapers, kicking over the buildings of Gotham like three hip-hop *kaiju*. "New York, New York, big city of dreams / And everything in New York ain't always what it seems / You might get fooled if you come from outta town / But I'm down by law, and I'm from Tha Dogg Pound." The lyrics weren't overtly disrespectful, but the message was potent: not only were the West going to talk about the East, they were also going to do it on their own turf. After hearing about these trespassers, an insulted Biggie appeared on a local radio station, telling listeners, "This is our city, and you know the beef we have with these muthafuckas."

Whether on Biggie's urgings or not, someone crept up to the set of the video with a pistol. Sitting in a production trailer, the artists and their entourage were smoking weed and enjoying the downtime when, suddenly, rapper Big Tray Deee thought he heard a shot. *Just noise from the city*, he assured himself as he resumed receiving the blunt from Snoop. Then the sound rang out again. Tray was sure of it now. Like a Secret Service agent, he grabbed Snoop and pulled him to the ground. After a long twenty seconds or so, security burst through the door, ushered the unscathed group into a van, and they took off back to a hotel in New Jersey.

As bullets flew in the coastal war, Tupac nursed his own trauma. The Quad Studios shooting still haunted his waking moments. Even on the set of the video for "California Love," potentially a moment of excitement and satisfaction, he stewed on it. "He told me everything about the Biggie incident, the whole thing, why he didn't like him," recalled Nanci Fletcher. "He was pouring his heart out." Tupac tried to talk Death Row artist the Lady of Rage into dissing Biggie affiliates Lil' Kim and Foxy Brown. But being cool with Kim, and not interested in following the men into battle, Rage gave him short shrift.

Afeni Shakur advised her son that the beef was reminding her of the tactics of COINTELPRO, suggesting that she suspected greater forces were turning these influential Black artists against one another. But it didn't matter. Instead of cooling tensions, Tupac unleashed what is widely recognized as rap's most savage diss track.

You can't underestimate the importance of "Hit 'Em Up" to Tupac's reputation. It's a simple calculation: "Hit 'Em Up" is the most uncompromising rap song ever made, ergo, 2Pac must be the most uncompromising rapper of all time. Like that of a spitting cobra, the venom that had been building in his glands is fully unleashed; the determination to match the impact the bullets had on his body with his words is unmistakable. Biggie allegedly cried when he first heard the song; perhaps it was a sense of sadness he had that his friend had turned on him so unjustly.

Even before the beat is given the chance to kick in, 2Pac began his vicious attack: "That's why I fucked yo' bitch, you fat motherfucker." There is no overture to this statement, so the "why" is never placed on record. But there's no doubt of the woman in question: Biggie's wife, the singer Faith Evans. Despite the ongoing beef with her husband, Evans had agreed to sing on a 2Pac song, which became "Wonda Why They Call U Bitch." Her contributions ultimately went unused, but the two artists were cordial enough to be spotted socializing in L.A. together around the time of the recording. Evans always denied anything more than that happened between her and Tupac, but whatever the case, their acquaintanceship didn't stop Tupac from dragging her into the quarrel: "You claim to be a player, but I fucked your wife," he raps on "Hit 'Em Up." "We bust on Bad Boys, n****s fucked for life."

In the middle of the madness, 2Pac references both the Quad Studios shooting and Biggie's song "Who Shot Ya?," which he considered an acknowledgment of guilt. ("Who shot me? But you punks didn't finish / Now you 'bout to feel the wrath of a menace.") The message was clear: Biggie started a conflict that he didn't finish, and now the hounds of hell had been unleashed.

"Hit 'Em Up" is noted for its particularly savage outro, where 2Pac, the rage eating him from the inside out, drops the hindrance of rapping and just ad-libs threats to numerous East Coast targets, including Prodigy of the group Mobb Deep. "Don't one of you n****s got sickle cell or somethin'? You're fuckin' with me, n***a, you fuck around and have a seizure or a heart attack." It was a particularly insensitive jibe—in 2017, Prodigy, a great rap artist in his own right, did pass away from complications of sickle cell anemia, for which he had been treated since birth. But it was also an insult to anyone whose life had been affected by the condition, including his trusted elder, Panther 21 member Jamal Joseph, whose own son had sickle cell disease.

"I was disappointed," Joseph told me, "but I kind of understand that Tupac was in the whirlwind. We had subsequent conversations where that didn't come up in particular, but he always cared about how [Jamal Joseph's son] Jamal was doing and knew that he was suffering. And there were other people that he knew that had sickle cell anemia. But I knew he was mercurial in terms of his personality, and that he would say whatever he was feeling at the moment, and sometimes without a filter, and sometimes not thinking about it until after he had said something. And he would admit that. He would always talk about that."

A video for the song was shot, featuring the strong image of Tupac and his crew rapping toward the camera in front of a plain white background. Actors were cast to play the roles of Puffy and Biggie. Despite the viciousness of the lyrics, the mood on set was jubilant. At one point, Tupac donned an outrageous wig and did his best Rick James impression.

Many of the key players of the East Coast–West Coast wars occasionally expressed regret that their issues with specific enemies had expanded to, or been interpreted as, a geographical feud. Tupac, too, became interested in the idea of reconciliation. In the spring of 1996, he plotted a coast-fusing collaboration album titled *One Nation*. On the invite list was Brooklyn rap collective Boot Camp Clik. Through their own label, Duck Down Records, Boot Camp had put out some successful underground singles that leaned on classic New York sounds, perhaps tickling Tupac's proclivities.

When the phone call came in, it was almost written off as a prank. Informed that Tupac Shakur was on the line, Boot Camp Clik rapper Buckshot, of the group Black Moon, refused to believe it until he picked up the receiver himself. Buckshot listened to Tupac's pitch. Two days later, the plane tickets were sent. When Tupac's guests touched down in Los Angeles, they were picked up by a limousine and chauffeured straight to the studio.

Tupac's Calabasas home served as a make-do hotel for the artists, with Kastro of Outlawz acting as their driver while Tupac was occupied by a new movie, *Gang Related*. "Some of the rooms weren't furnished," remembered Darrell "Steele" Yates, one half of Smif-N-Wessun, another Boot Camp Clik group. "But we stayed in there. We Boot Camp guys, we slept on the floor. I had a whole room to myself, but like no bed, it was carpet. It was beautiful, though. 'Cause the vibe, the energy in there, was just like we was at our home back in Brooklyn."

Though the project was intended to promote unity, the studio bore some symptoms of the sense of danger that still swirled. Never before had Steele been required to go through a metal detector to simply make music. Once inside, though, things relaxed, with everyone from Snoop to New York legend Melle Mel stopping by.

Through the hustle and bustle, an impromptu meeting was arranged between Steele and Tek, his partner in Smif-N-Wessun, as well as Buckshot, and manager Drew "Dru-Ha" Friedman. Devising ideas, somebody started singing sections of the Bob Marley and the Wailers song "Zimbabwe." Tupac immediately went crazy for it.

"Yo, what's that? Sing that again!" Steele remembered Tupac shouting. "That's the hook right there. White people are gonna be scared." From that kernel, a song was formed.

The Boot Camp Clik worked for about a week and a half on what they thought would be an album released on Tupac's own label and not Death Row, signaling his intent to break with Knight's company when contractually possible. "He even went as far as to say the second volume of *One Nation* should be released on Duck Down Records," revealed Steele. "So, that was super huge for us."

Though the subsequent sessions with his East Coast guests did not receive official releases in the way Tupac intended, his motivation was apparent: bring the coasts together, and do it independently of the Death Row machine. Tupac envisioned his stint on Knight's label as a temporary one. Trying to get money flowing through the turnstiles of Death Row and into his own pocket was a constant source of discord for him. Tupac would regularly be on the phone to the label, seeking payments he felt were his. But he may have underestimated Knight's grip on him.

"His take on leaving Death Row was actually not correct," claimed Wendy Day, who as CEO of Rap Coalition would informally advise Tupac. "It was a three-album deal. He felt that he could just deliver three albums and then leave. And it doesn't work like that. There's actually a time commitment in every contract. And when I explained that to him, he was a little bit disappointed, but he felt that he had a relationship with Suge where Suge would let him go and start his own label."

Hoping to foster business times with Tupac was Gobi Rahimi, who helmed some of his final videos. Holding a dim view of Knight—the CEO was "scary as shit," Rahimi told me—he tried to talk his collaborator into joining him to start a production company. "Selfishly, I wanted to be as connected to him as possible, but I figured if he was owner of a company that was doing his videos, one, he would make money off of his own videos that were recoupable and, two, we'd have less drama with Suge Knight and Death Row."

The palpable anger of "Hit 'Em Up" ran counter to the new serenity of Tupac's private life. In 1996, a relationship bloomed with Kidada Jones, the daughter of legendary music producer Quincy Jones. Kidada was young—she only turned twenty-two in March of 1996—but she accepted Tupac's invitation to move into his house in Calabasas, and the couple planned to be wed.

The Jones family took Tupac to their hearts. It was a remarkable turnaround given that the relationship began with some horrible words. In a 1993 interview with *The Source*, Tupac chastised Quincy for his relationships with white women, asserting that mixed-race unions created "messed-up kids." It was a bizarre thing to say, a sentiment that Tupac did not seemingly repeat before or after that single quote. Quincy Jones was understandably offended by it, as were Rashida and Kidada, his daughters with white actress Peggy Lipton. Rashida Jones (better known now as the star of TV shows such as *Parks and Recreation*) responded with a letter to *The Source* defending her father.

Tupac regretted his lunkheaded words. When he thought he spotted Rashida in a club one night in the aftermath, he rushed to apologize, only to find that the young woman was actually Kidada. Tupac's contrition won her over. Rashida, too, was forgiving: "Once I experienced his sincerity, he endeared himself to me, there was no way I couldn't like him, you know? Just his smile, just who he was was so, he was one of those really transparent people, everything's kind of on the surface, you know? Buzzing."

Further refuge from the chaos of Death Row was found in moviemaking. Tupac's first role post-prison was in *Gridlock'd*, which teamed him with British actors Tim Roth and Thandiwe Newton (credited to her then screen name Thandie Newton) as jazz musicians struggling to access state assistance in kicking heroin. It was a personal project for writer and director Vondie Curtis-Hall, who based portions of the film on his own experiences of trying to get clean in Detroit's punk-rock scene. Despite the potential resistance to hiring an actor out on bail on a sexual assault charge, Def Pictures president Preston Holmes lobbied to cast Tupac, and the actor saw the role as a chance for people to reevaluate his image. "This movie is really about friendship and what unconditional friendship means. I did it basically because it was funny and I never really got to be funny." Alongside two actors in the middle of long and brilliant screen careers, Tupac didn't look out of place.

There is *Gang Related*, a shadowy little neo-noir potboiler, the most underrated movie in Tupac's oeuvre. His casting proved a moment of Nostradamus divination. For what nobody involved in the project knew at the time, and what Tupac did not live to discover, is that its tale of police corruption predicted the Rampart scandal, a catastrophe for the Los Angeles Police Department in which Death Row Records would find itself entangled.

The opportunity to star in *Gang Related* came up fortuitously. The suits above writer and director Jim Kouf coveted Jim Belushi to play the lead role, which chimed with Kouf's vision of the character. But they also wanted to follow the popular trend of recruiting a rap artist to play the second lead role. Kouf had written the part for an actor in the vein of Edward James Olmos, a middle-aged American of Mexican descent. Accordingly, the character's name was Detective Jacob "Jake" Rodriguez, something Kouf decided not to change.

Tupac Shakur was suggested. Kouf knew little about the young star but nonetheless traveled to the recording studio in North Hollywood, where he was working on his album *The Don Killuminati: The 7 Day Theory*. Intrigued by the idea of playing a cop, Tupac accepted the role, joining a cast that included James Earl Jones, Lela Rochon, Dennis Quaid, and David Paymer.

Working with genuine movie stars did not put Tupac on his best behavior. He ticked off Belushi by turning up to the first day of rehearsals an hour and a half late. The veteran screen actor pulled Tupac aside and demanded he behave professionally for the remainder of the project. It was a rocky start to their relationship, but Belushi and Tupac forged an unlikely connection. "We would rap together in the trailer," Belushi recalled. "I kept up with him, you know. I did the original rap on *Saturday Night Live* in 1983, and I told him that. I said, 'I was rapping when you were in grade school, man.'"

Their on-screen chemistry was dynamite. Tupac looked small in stature in a suit that overwhelmed his narrow shoulders, but it worked as a counterpoint to the bombastic Belushi, who must have been impressed by his celebrity rap artist costar throwing everything he had into the role. Shooting a late scene in a bar with Belushi, Tupac insisted on the authenticity of drinking real alcohol. Multiple takes took their toll. Tupac was unable to show up for work the next morning, such was the severity of his hangover.

The pressure of the outside world remained inescapable. Filming on the streets of Los Angeles, Tupac couldn't shake the need to keep looking over his shoulder. Eventually, he pulled aside his bodyguard and raged, "You're not watching my back."

"It was at that point we all thought, *Holy crap, if he's worried about being gunned down on the street while he's making a movie . . .*," director Jim Kouf told me. "So we all started watching his back."

The script demanded Rodriguez meet a bloody demise, murdered in his own apartment by a jilted bookie. But Tupac was reluctant. "He was really nervous about doing the scene where he gets shot," remembered Kouf. "He didn't want to be dead on-screen."

The director made a promise to his actor that he'd get it over with as soon as possible. In the scene, Rodriguez arrives home and, in a fit of frustration, begins destroying the room before realizing the bookie and his muscle are present. He then lunges toward the two men and the fatal shots are heard off-screen. Kouf wrapped up the scene in two takes. The necessary image of Rodriguez as a corpse in the kitchen was handled even more expediently. "We ran camera once or twice and got him out of there," said Kouf.

This discomfort in portraying his own demise perhaps signaled the sense of dread that hung over Tupac in the final weeks of his life, like he was on a path that couldn't be veered from. (Tupac signed on to write the score to *Gang Related* but wouldn't live to complete the work.) Paranoia reigned. A couple of weeks before his death, though he was ostensibly engaged to Kidada, Tupac asked his old acquaintance Numskull if he could bring some girls over to his hotel room at the Montrose Hotel in Hollywood. The Oakland rapper observed him in an agitated state, constantly looking out the doors and windows, watching for the clear and present danger he knew to be there.

It was morbidness that could make way for melancholy. One night, Tupac and Belushi took some quiet time to watch the sun come up after a long night of shooting. Through the fatigue, Tupac broke the silence, looking at Belushi and remarking, "I'm a thug, I prefer the sunrise."

Following the death of Tupac Shakur on Friday, September 13, 1996, debonair reporter Murray Kempton—who, a quarter century earlier, bore witness to a heavily pregnant Afeni Shakur convincing a New York jury that she wasn't a terrorist—wrote in the *New York Post*, "He was a chosen child and a testament to faith no less noble for having a reward no better than this."

Honestly, I didn't think I needed to overly detail the killing of Tupac Shakur, a crime more pored over than the Manson Family murders. Various volumes have been released over the years charting the inadequacies of the investigation; various (conspiracy) theories are regularly posited. But during the writing of this book, one of the most significant pieces of Tupac news in the decades since his death broke. Duane "Keffe D" Davis, a veteran Crip, was arrested and charged with the murder. Sometimes, it's the person you least suspect. Other times, it's the person who gave multiple interviews claiming he participated in the murder, wrote a book detailing the murder, and who is widely acknowledged on the streets to have been involved in the murder. Go figure.

I remember the Mike Tyson–Bruce Seldon fight well. Like so many of Tyson's opponents, Seldon was a beaten man before he ever got in the ring. The look in his eyes after rising from the first knockdown is the most petrified I've ever seen in a professional prizefighter. Seldon was a man totally intimidated by the persistent hunter with the twenty-inch neck in front of him. It's hard to fathom that Seldon went into the fight not as the challenger, but a world title holder in what was a unifying bout, something you can't achieve without a measure of toughness. That was the fear Tyson inflicted on his prey.

Tupac was in the crowd at the MGM Grand in Las Vegas that night—in fact, he'd recorded a new song specifically for his friend's ring walk. I believe the butterfly effect is indisputable fact and have often considered that if Tyson had showed some mercy, or if Seldon had been able to stand up for a little longer, the consequence on the timeline would have been Tupac leaving Vegas safely. Not so. Knockout, round one.

In this timeline, Tupac, Knight, and their entourage left the arena and headed to the MGM Grand's lobby, where they came across Orlando Anderson, known on the streets as Baby Lane, a South Side Compton Crip, unemployed father of three, and supposedly the owner of many 2Pac records. The twenty-one-year-old was just loitering when a member of Suge's posse whispered into Tupac's ear, identifying Anderson as the man involved in the theft of a valuable Death Row gold chain some weeks earlier. Tupac quickly took off in the Crip's direction.

"You from the South?" Tupac asked. Then, paying no attention to passersby or hotel security cameras, he cocked his fist and slammed it into the side of Anderson's head, knocking him to the ground.

A melee broke out; a medallion around Tupac's neck fell to the floor. It was collected by his bodybuilder bodyguard, Frank Alexander, who threw his client to a wall to get him away from the fight. Security guards descended on the scene and broke up the encounter. Tupac, Knight, and their crew immediately left, unimpeded. They made their way to the valet area in front of the hotel, then embarked on the fifteen-minute walk south on the Las Vegas Strip toward the Luxor Hotel and Casino, where the group was staying.

Back in his hotel room, Tupac told the waiting Kidada Jones what had gone down. Also in the room was Alexander, who recalled Jones's excited giggles as she heard about the action. Her fiancé opted not to invite her to his next appearance, at Knight's Club 662. (Kidada has characterized this as Tupac looking out for her well-being. "There's been a fight with a Crip and it's not safe," she quoted him as saying. "You stay here.") Knight was tremendously proud of the club. He was even known to work as a bouncer there himself, and he was eager to get Tupac to make an appearance to help generate a sense of buzz around the place.

Tupac changed from a tan silk shirt and jeans (the second-to-last outfit he ever wore from his own wardrobe would later go on display at a Hard Rock Cafe) into a black-and-white basketball shirt and blue jeans or sweatpants. Much has been made of Tupac's decision not to bring the flak jacket issued to him by Death Row to Las Vegas. Yet his bodyguard Alexander has said it wasn't common for him to be seen in it. "Tupac only wore it one or two times."

What Tupac and Knight didn't know was that Anderson had already rendezvoused with his uncle Keffe D (pronounced "Kee-fee Dee"), who, as he claims in his book *Compton Street Legend*, predicted that Club 662 would be their destination. With a cadre of other Crips across several cars, they pulled into the parking lot and waited for the enemy to show up. After an hour and a half of mostly silence, Keffe D grew irritated. His trip to Vegas was being wasted on the futile scouting of a club parking lot. On his cell phone, Keffe D commanded the other Crips to abandon their surveillance.

"They're taking too damn long," he recalled saying. "Let's get fucked-up. Move out."

As he left the Luxor, Tupac spotted two familiar faces: actors

Omar Epps and Marlon Wayans, his costars on *Juice* and *Above the Rim*, respectively. Delighted that their paths had unexpectedly crossed, Tupac gave the pair a warm embrace. After some small talk, both parties turned to go their separate ways. But as Wayans hopped into a taxi, he noticed Tupac's lingering gaze, as though the celebrity rapper wished he could abandon his commitments and instead join their journey. Not possible. Tupac clambered into the passenger seat of Knight's black BMW with his boss behind the wheel and pulled off into the night.

They briefly stopped at Knight's house, and then it was on to the club. A caravan of cars followed as the BMW slowly inched through the traffic of Las Vegas Boulevard.

Having left Club 662, Keffe D and his crew headed for the Carriage House, a hotel where they'd rented a few rooms. On the way they stopped to buy champagne. Keffe D changed cars, taking the passenger seat of a white Cadillac with Anderson, as well as two friends he referred to in his book as Bubble Up (believed to be Terry Brown) and Freaky (DeAndre "Big Dre" Smith).

Then came a tragic twist of fate. From his seat, Keffe D caught sight of the man he'd been seeking. There he was, the great Tupac Shakur, one of the most famous musical artists in America, sticking his head out of a passing BMW. Bubble Up immediately turned the ignition and rolled the Cadillac back onto the road and into quiet pursuit.

The shooting occurred when the white Cadillac pulled up to the BMW's right side as it was stopped at a red light at East Flamingo Road and Koval Lane. Looks were exchanged. Knight, according to Keffe D, looked "terrified"; Tupac reached for a gun. The triggerman in the Cadillac fired from a rolled-down left-rear window. From the cars sitting powerlessly behind Knight and Tupac, bodyguard Frank Alexander saw the pistol extend out the back window and then a fog of gun smoke as the assailant appeared to empty the clip. Tupac was struck by four rounds fired from a .40-caliber Glock: two in the chest, one in the arm, and one in the thigh.

A desperate Knight made a sharp U-turn, riding on two blown-out tires punctured by bullets as he sped back down Flamingo Road, the other vehicles in the caravan following. Knight made a wide, shaky turn onto Las Vegas Boulevard before eventually col-liding with the concrete meridian, riding up on the deflated front tire and blowing out the other tire in the process. It was less than a mile from the scene of the shooting.

"You hit?" asked Knight.

"I'm hit," Tupac mustered.

With the damaged BMW shipwrecked on the meridian, two cops on mountain bikes were the first to appear. Within minutes, the scene was swarming with officers, who immediately ordered everyone in the convoy out of their cars and face down on the side-walk, including Knight, whose head by now was covered with blood from scalp and neck wounds he suffered after being grazed by a bullet or shrapnel. Tupac, though, was left where he was, obviously too gravely injured to move, his breathing shallow as he passed in and out of consciousness. The cops finally allowed Knight and his associates to stand up just as the paramedics arrived.

"I can't breathe," Tupac repeatedly told the emergency medical personnel as Knight and Alexander lifted him out of the car and placed him on the ground. The response team opened a gurney and wheeled Tupac's limp body into the ambulance. Knight took a seat in the vehicle as it tore away from the scene, sirens blaring, heading for University Medical Center, some three miles away.

I endeavored to visit the site of the shooting as a kind of pilgrim-age, a hip-hop hajj, to see where the culture's greatest icon—the man I'd spent the previous couple of years of my life scrutinizing—met his demise. It was a crusade I opted to do alone. Commencing from my hotel, located about eight miles from the Las Vegas Strip, I approached a waiting taxi that I hoped would be my carriage. The driver was a middle-aged man with long hair and a hippie voice and vibe. Leaning down to speak through the window, I told him the destination: the intersection of East Flamingo Road and Koval Lane.

"What are you trying to accomplish there?" he asked, intrusively.

I knew the truth might seem strange, but there was no time to cook up a lie about this very specific intersection I knew little else about.

"I'm gonna see where Tupac was shot," I said with some light-heartedness in my voice.

"I can show you where Tupac was shot, but where do you want to go from there?" the driver asked, clearly baffled that someone would wish to spend time on this dreary section of road. I told him he could just drop me off.

As it transpired, this cabdriver was very familiar with the shooting. On his way to his job at a hotel just hours after the shots had been fired, he drove right past the spot where the black BMW eventually came to a stop. He noted how unusual it seemed that only one detective car appeared to be present. Politely chatting about it all these years later, he also repeated an unsubstantiated story of the assailants stashing the Cadillac in the parking lot of the Carriage House, with the murder weapon curiously placed on top of the tire, before later returning to move the vehicle to a new destination.

"It's just a road," he told me more than once, probably hoping to cushion any sense of disappointment I might have with the under-whelming scene.

Then, with no sense of grandeur, we were there. And, of course, the driver was correct, it is just a road, surrounded by an unused parking lot, a service station, and various hotels. The core attraction is entirely fan made: two electrical poles that my fellow pilgrims have covered with Tupac stickers and scrawled messages of love and loss. It's a reminder of the deep, personal connection his followers feel toward him that goes beyond music. To be a Tupac fan decades after his death isn't necessarily to be a part of a greater community, like it is to revere a contemporary pop star. People become disciples because they believe Tupac was inherently good, principled, and wise. They believe he was the best of us, and they mourn because the best of us was martyred, right at the intersection of East Flamingo Road and Koval Lane. It desperately needs a permanent, official tribute.

I began walking away from the scene, but took the notion to return to the site for a second look—it had been a long trip to Las Vegas, better to linger on the moment. As I doubled back, I faintly heard the sound of Tupac's voice. The words were impossible to pick up, but those distinct cadences could not be confused. Yes, it must have been him. From the gathered traffic on my left, a car was blaring his music, but I couldn't make out exactly which vehicle or even which song. Sensing that this must mean something, I darted across the four lanes of traffic used by cars traveling in the opposite direction, mercifully empty in that moment, trying to home in on where the audio was coming from. Before I could identify the song or vehicle it was coming from, the traffic pulled away, heading back in the direction that Tupac came from on the night of September 7, 1996. But just as they escaped me, as I stood in the center of eight lanes of Las Vegas asphalt, I finally made out one of the words Tupac was pronouncing. It was, with that familiar sense of both revelry and belligerence in every nuance of his voice, "Westside."

As Knight made a U-turn, the Cadillac carrying the assailants made a right turn on a green light onto Koval Lane and, as far as investigators could figure out, vanished. Keffe D wrote that from where they ended up, they saw two ambulances ostensibly leaving the scene where the BMW had come to a halt. The group ditched their Cadillac and then "popped our bottles and partied like it was any other night."

Upon his arrest, Keffe D was described by authorities as the "ringleader" of the group. Consistent with his own accounts of the crime, he isn't the accused gunman, but in Nevada, you can be charged with murder if you act as an accomplice. In a failed motion seeking bail, Keffe D's lawyers called his tales of the killing, both in his memoir and in interviews, "entertainment" produced for the purpose of making money, and pointed to the denials made by Suge Knight himself that their client had anything to do with the killing.

Keffe D has claimed to be a blood descendant of Nat Turner. Ironically, Tupac spoke in interviews about his admiration for the man who led what's been called the only effective slave rebellion on American soil, and honored Turner with a cross tattoo on his back bearing the words "EXODUS 1831," a reference to the year Turner led the rebellion. Supposedly he wanted to develop a movie about Turner with himself in the lead role.

The years passed. Orlando "Baby Lane" Anderson was killed in a May 1998 shooting in Compton believed to be unrelated to the murder of Tupac. DeAndre "Big Dre" Smith died of natural causes in 2004; the alleged driver, Terrence "Bubble Up" Brown, was killed in a 2015 shooting in Compton. But Keffe D saw middle age. It mellowed him, as aging tends to do, and, at least before his arrest, he appeared to become motivated to reckon with his past and place in history.

"At this point in my life, I can say that I have a deep sense of remorse for what happened to Tupac," he wrote. "He was a talented artist with tons of potential to impact the world. I hate that Tupac's family, friends, and fans, especially his mother, Afeni Shakur, had to go through the pain of losing her son. It's terrible losing people like that; I know that pain too well.

"However, I stand firm on the point that Tupac, Suge Knight, and the rest of those n****s didn't have any business putting their hands on my beloved nephew, Baby Lane. Period. Them jumping on my nephew gave us the ultimate green light to do something to their ass.

"Tupac chose the wrong game to play and the wrong n****s to play with. Suge and them should have done a better job of protecting that dude because they knew who the fuck we were and the kind of shit we were capable of. Tupac may not have known, but Suge and his peeps definitely knew. Tupac was a guppy that got swallowed up by some ferocious sharks. He shouldn't have ever got involved in that bullshit of trying to be a thug."

For six days, Tupac clung to life. His right index finger had been severed. Three bullets had punctured his lung, forcing surgeons to remove it, making ribbons of his tattoos. When Kidada Jones arrived at the hospital, she was informed of how grave the situation was, and handed a bag of bloodstained clothes and jewelry.

Afeni received the cursed call at her home in Georgia. "Tupac's been shot," said friend Yaasmyn Fula. "In Las Vegas. They say it's bad." Afeni quickly boarded a flight and made her way to her son's bedside. Outside University Medical Center, crowds began to gather. Among them was Tupac's biological father, Billy Garland.

For those not fully aware of the severity of his condition, there was often the assumption that he'd be fine. Tupac was too strong, too reliable a survivor, for this to be the end. "I didn't think he would die," said Wendy Day. "He had been through so much and lived that, honestly, it never crossed my mind that he could die. In fact, I FedExed a get-well card to the hospital because I just knew he was gonna wake up . . . He was indestructible, you know?"

Jones spoke to her fiancé tenderly. "Do you know I love you?" she said to him as he lay in a hospital bed. "Do you know we all love you?" The patient nodded. But as Jones turned to the door, Tupac convulsed and slipped into unconsciousness, from which he never woke.

On the afternoon of Friday, September 13, Afeni was informed by doctors that Tupac had suffered a series of heart attacks and needed to be resuscitated. Concluding that her son was ready to leave this world, she pleaded with doctors to let him go.

With his final breaths, this link to the Panthers faded, a flame of past radicalism snuffed out. Forever.

With Tupac cradled between life and death, his loved ones played Don McLean's "Vincent," to allow him to listen to a song that was important to him one last time. "They would not listen, they did not know how," sang McLean softly. "Perhaps they'll listen now."

PART III

HANDS UP:
AFTERLIFE, LEGACY, AND
A FUTURE NOT SET

Jay-Z on the set of "Girls, Girls, Girls," 2001

HOW MUCH A DOLLAR COST?

I T TAKES ABOUT fifteen seconds for the "Make 'Em Say Uhh!"
video to unveil its big set piece. The scene is quickly set: a basketball court appears under near-blinding lights, the beat's off-kilter
orchestral stabs appearing to line up with the penetrating flashes.
There are cheerleaders, a rapturous crowd, enough players decked
out in basketball jerseys to fill the NBA draft. Suddenly, a tank rum-
bles into the arena—not just any tank, one plated in gold, as if it
had just rolled out of King Midas's own showroom. The hatch pops
open and a man emerges. Spitting rhymes on top of the glimmering
war machine, he calls himself the commander in chief and "colonel
of the motherfuckin' tank." His flow is jagged, as if the aggressive
beat is too much to slide smoothly on top of, so he better just go all
out and try to overwhelm listeners by rapping from seven different
directions. That's Percy Robert Miller. That's the boss of No Limit
Records. That's Master P.

And this is one of the most crazy-brilliant crew rap songs of its
era. Released in 1997, the video for "Make 'Em Say Uhh!" is a masterpiece of ostentation that showcases the strength and depth of No
Limit. Four other artists on the label—Fiend, Silkk the Shocker,
Mia X, and Mystikal—are summoned to perform like they're business assets. Leading the collective is hip-hop's ultimate tycoon.
That's Master P.

Perhaps no rapper exemplifies the opportunities of hip-hop capitalism like the Louisiana entrepreneur who built an entertainment
empire from the soil up. If Master P's business acumen is legend-

ary, it's because he put it front and center of his persona. The gold tank was the physical manifestation of the No Limit logo and the ultimate symbol of wealth, success, and power. Because it was never enough for P to have the money, he had to flaunt it. His appearance on *MTV Cribs*, a show that existed to make a spectacle of gross pop-star excesses, is one of the most startling you'll ever see. Filmed in the year 2000, Master P takes us on a tour through his Baton Rouge home, proudly pointing to the marble floors, 14-karat-gold ceilings, an elevator that takes you to a home studio (of course), chandeliers imported from Greece and Spain, ceiling-to-floor oil paintings of P himself, and a security system that makes Tony Montana look easygoing. It's a mansion fit for Tutankhamun. In fact, the design of his bed had been influenced by the legendary pharaoh himself.

Watching *Cribs* in the early 2000s offered a clear indication of the sea change in rap's ethos that had occurred in the preceding decade and has remained a truism ever since: that hip-hop exemplifies the core ideological premise of the United States that every citizen can achieve upward social mobility through hard work and/or smart entrepreneurship. This is further inflated by its leading players often coming from extreme poverty to achieve massive wealth. The narrative of the street rapper graduating to the corner office has become common in hip-hop lore. A handful even became among the richest people in the country. In rap, billionaires aren't just encouraged, they're deified.

The commodification of hip-hop starts early on. I suppose you could, technically, go all the way back to the first rap records, cut for the purpose of putting a few dollars in the artists' pockets. But even in the embryonic stages of hip-hop as a commercial entity, there were some key moments. Kurtis Blow inked a deal with major label Mercury in 1979. That same year, New Jersey's Sugarhill Gang released "Rapper's Delight," the first rap single to sell over a million copies. In 1986, Run-DMC recorded "My Adidas," an ode to the sports brand that led to the first-ever endorsement deal between a musical act and an athletic company. All the time hip-hop was being refined in a manner that appealed to the mainstream. As Jeff Chang writes in his book *Can't Stop Won't Stop: A History of the Hip-Hop Generation*, "The tension between culture and commerce would become one of the main story lines of the hip-hop generation."

As the golden age of rap music progressed, with 2Pac as one of its core diplomats, the records became hugely successful, but the artists' ends were generally kept under wraps. As N.W.A. say on "Gangsta Gangsta" via a vocal sample taken from Boogie Down Productions' song "My Philosophy": "It's not about a salary, it's all about reality." (Though Ice Cube did also use the song to announce, "Life ain't nothin but bitches and money," so maybe "Gangsta Gangsta" is a bit of a Rorschach test on how you interpret N.W.A.'s philosophy.)

In the wake of N.W.A., gangster rap became a dominant strand of mainstream hip-hop. Where you locate the line between capturing the realities of urban living in the USA and hawking a corrosive image of young Black men to impressionable kids, especially captivated white audiences, has been one of the most prominent conversations surrounding hip-hop for over three decades. What's undeniable is that the free markets demanded a proliferation of the gangster rapper image.

But something happens in the 1990s. Capitalism doesn't simply serve as the backdrop that rap, like everything else in America, must operate against—it becomes one of its core tenets. Profit is no longer a happy side effect of making music—profit becomes the point. Money morphs into the ultimate muse, bling a crucial status symbol. Music videos become extremely expensive to reflect the importance of exuding wealth. Hype Williams, a kid from Queens who came up as a graffiti tagger, develops a flashy style of video making that defines the bling-bling era. See Puff Daddy and Ma$e wear shiny suits and levitate in an air chamber in the video for the Notorious B.I.G.'s posthumous single "Mo Money Mo Problems," or Jay-Z partying with a group of models atop a massive yacht in "Big Pimpin'." Brands become important, from what you drink—Rémy Martin, Cristal, "pass the Courvoisier"—to the fashion you rock, all the way up to the high-end art you collect. Such luxuries, of course, are unattainable to 99 percent of people who listen to the music, yet they went crazy for it. The records sold and sold.

The 1990s was a strange era in America. With the Cold War won, there was a feeling that everything a country could achieve had been achieved. This sense of fulfillment was broken by 9/11 and completely shattered by the financial crash of 2008, but for a time, those with a little money in their pockets partied, and a sense of self-absorption seeped from the pores of pop culture.

It's not just materialism and consumerism that became a core part of rap; business sense began to be viewed as a key component of the rap star image. The lines between being an artist and being an entrepreneur blurred into nothingness. To accumulate huge amounts of wealth became cool, particularly if a star could outsmart an industry set up to consolidate power among old elites. Suge Knight was among an early clutch of Black rap moguls to show the potential size of the business, but he wasn't the only one with shrewd instincts. RZA cut a deal with Loud that allowed each member of the Wu-Tang Clan to ink their own solo deals with other labels and raked in the plaudits for his foresight. Jay-Z's rise from street hustler to A-list star was facilitated by business deals so successful, they inspired the famous proclamation, "I'm not a *businessman*, I'm a *business*, man."

For decades, Black artists had been denied an appropriately sized slice of the pie by white record label owners and executives who controlled the structure of everything. This new generation was not going to be quiet about beating the industry with their own ingenuity.

Not content to keep their business dealings low-key, rappers began using their music to brag about their portfolios, which typically grew to include entertainment companies, clothing lines, drinks brands, even venture capital endeavors. They agreed to deals with consumer brands, bucking the tradition of rock music stars who saw "selling out" as poisonous to their reputation. They became capitalists in the truest sense of the word: that is, not just people who support and believe in the principles of capitalism, but those who own the capital, who own the means of production. Roc-A-Fella Records co-founder Dame Dash has advocated for what he calls an octopus strategy—having eight revenues of income. When one company isn't making money, another one is. "The head's always strong, but the legs are expendable," said Dash. "I can cut one off anytime I want, and it will grow back."

The tendency for business and music to intertwine is epitomized by 50 Cent's 2007 single "I Get Money." So raps 50: "I took quarter water sold it in bottles for 2 bucks / Coca-Cola came and bought it for billions, what the fuck?" The lyric references 50 accepting a 10 percent stake in Glacéau in exchange for the rapper endorsing Vitaminwater and subsequently allowing Glacéau to market the grape-flavored "Formula 50" on the strength of his brand. "Quarter water" is a reference to small plastic bottles of flavored water typically associated with impoverished kids, as it cost just twenty-five cents. After the Coca-Cola Company bought Glacéau for $4.1 billion, 50's investment vehicle received a $400 million paycheck and he himself retained over $100 million after taxes. A second version of "I Get Money" was later put out featuring Jay-Z and Diddy (then-moniker of Sean "Puffy" Combs) that was dubbed the "Forbes Remix."

In the wake of Biggie's death, Puffy revamped himself as both Bad Boy Records' flagship artist and one of hip-hop's most prosperous moguls. There's something apt about him taking Grandmaster Flash and the Furious Five's "The Message" and turning it into a money anthem. Released in 1997, Puffy's song "Can't Nobody Hold Me Down" tweaks Flash's original beat into a glitzy glamorama. Over the instrumental, Puffy, one of hip-hop's arch capitalists, gives us the nuts and bolts of his business ("Now with Sean on the hot track, melt like it's hot wax / Put it out, all the stores, bet you could shop that"). His compadre Ma$e, meanwhile, claims to rock Versace silks over a steel V-neck. At one point Ma$e quotes Melle Mel's words "Broken glass everywhere" before completing the couplet with a nod to his own philosophy: "If it ain't about the money, Puff, I just don't care." If you're looking for a clear vision of hip-hop's original message being corrupted, it's this.

"Can't Nobody Hold Me Down" features on Puff Daddy's debut album *No Way Out*, which might just feature the best rap song about money ever made: "All About the Benjamins (Remix)." It's an anthem about the pleasure of blowing money fast. In this world, you order three different main courses not to satisfy your appetite, but because appearances demand it. While Puffy rides around in a Mercedes-Benz with a spoiler, Sheek Louch shows up to describe traveling in a gondola with the gondolier singing Italian music. "All About the Benjamins (Remix)" put the name of the man famous for not actually being a president into the hip-hop lexicon some two centuries after his death.

(Many brands began to dissolve their relationship with Combs when, starting in 2023, he was the subject of a number of sexual misconduct allegations and lawsuits. Among his accusers was his ex-girlfriend, the singer Cassie Ventura. Combs issued a blanket denial of the allegations and settled Ventura's suit outside of court. However, the following year he issued an apology after a 2016 hotel surveillance video surfaced that captured him shoving, dragging, and kicking Ventura. Numerous other lawsuits relating to different allegations were filed in the aftermath. Combs was arrested and indicted in September 2024 on charges of racketeering, sex trafficking by force, and transportation for purposes of prostitution. To all he pleaded not guilty.)

It would be easy to trash the bling-bling era as uncultured, tasteless, and corrosive to traditional hip-hop values. And for sure, we must decry some effects of rap's commodification: N.W.A. fractured as members became dissatisfied with the business side of things, just one example of money not being right skewering rap history. But a lot of capitalist rap proved to be colorful, visceral, and enjoyable. It's hard to deny that watching rappers popping bottles on yachts and flying around in jets tickles certain pleasure centers in the brain, especially when the beats bang, the hooks stick, and the flows are silky.

It's revealing to consider the two visions of Donald Trump that appear in rap history. Of course, you know the latter-day Trump—to show affection for him in any way after 2015 proved toxic to a rapper's brand. But prior to declaring his intention to run for president, he was depicted in rap as a figure of business success, a flashy billionaire bigwig who represented the highest peaks of entrepreneurial excellence. (The vetting of his business record that occurred when he entered the political sphere has shown that reputation to be made of straw.)

Back in 1989, Buff of Fat Boys used their song "Lie-Z" to declare, "Boy, I got money like Donald Trump." A few years later, Houston rapper Scarface described himself as "rolling hard, stackin paper like Trump" ("Money and the Power"). Method Man even put the future president on his second album, *Tical 2000: Judgement Day*. The skit sees Trump leave the Wu-Tang rapper an answering machine message: "Hey, Method Man. This is Donald Trump, and I'm in Palm Beach, and we're all waiting for your album. Let's get going, man—everybody's waiting for this album!" I could go on.

On "FDT" (or "Fuck Donald Trump"), the most brutal and iconic (and catchy) takedown track penned about Trump the politician, Compton star YG acknowledges that Trump was once generally respected by the hip-hop community. "Me and all my peoples, we always thought he was straight," he speaks on the intro. "Influential motherfucker when it came to the business." Only with that acknowledgment can YG and guest Nipsey Hussle's evisceration begin.

One rapper never fooled by Trump's bluster, though, was Tupac Shakur. On the night of Trump's second electoral victory in 2024, a doctored photograph appeared on social media of Tupac wearing a red hat bearing Trump's slogan "Make America Great Again." It wasn't long before it was pointed out that Tupac viewed Trump as the epitome of capitalist greed. "This world is such a . . . 'gimme gimme gimme! Everybody back off,'" he said in an interview. "If you want to be successful, if you want to be like Trump, gimme gimme gimme, push push push push. Step step step, crush crush crush. That's how it all is, and it's like . . . nobody ever stops."

It was an odd quirk of fate, then, that Tupac's name was uttered at what could be considered the birth of Trumpism. It was April 30, 2011, at the White House Correspondents' Dinner. Hawaii had just days earlier released President Obama's original long-form birth certificate, laying waste to questions raised by Trump and others surrounding Obama's eligibility to hold the office. Seizing the moment, Obama preluded his speech with a video of the document pulsing over a patriotic montage of American flags and imagery, with the Hulk Hogan theme song "Real American" blaring in the background.

"Now, I know that he's taken some flak lately, but no one is happier, no one is prouder, to put this birth certificate matter to rest than The Donald," Obama said mid-speech with his comedian-like wit. "And that's because he can finally get back to focusing on the issues that matter—like, did we fake the moon landing? What really happened in Roswell? And where are Biggie and Tupac?" As he sat quietly in the crowd, taking in the mockery, the toxic notion of revenge swirled in Trump's brain.

Bling-bling music was usually about having fun, but it did reflect something deadly serious. Without a revolution looming, capitalism is an attractive vehicle for talented young rappers to escape poverty. Jokes about sports and entertainment being the only routes for Black children born into degenerative cycles of impoverishment are well-worn, but that's because those cycles have been so lasting. Deep within many rappers is a longing to come up in the world, and only working the capitalist system can deliver that dream—they can be one of the lucky citizens who through hard work and talent can beat the very structure that caused the economic oppression into which they were born. There's little talk in rap of destroying the system because artists can't excel in what ceases to exist.

Like Dame Dash said of Cam'ron during the pair's infamous interview with Bill O'Reilly on a Fox News segment about the impact of hip-hop music on Black youth, "If an eleven-year-old were to imitate Cam'ron, what they'd be doing is becoming a CEO of their own company, controlling their own destiny, taking a bad situation and making it good."

Some would call all this the American Dream.

Yet so many are left behind. A 2010 study by the Insight Center for Community Economic Development, based in Oakland, found that the median household wealth for working-age single Black women (eighteen to sixty-four) was only one hundred dollars. For single white women, the figure was forty-one thousand dollars.

Tupac Shakur, too, felt the pull of the corner office. His death came as he was plotting a new phase of his career: running his own media company called Euphanasia Incorporated. If executed correctly, Tupac would use the organization to oversee screenwriting projects and youth outreach programs. He even had business cards printed with the Euphanasia logo: a graphic of a kneeling, masculine angel with a halo, wings, and a gun with a long band of piano keys that encircle the divine figure.

Some might bristle at the idea of the former Young Communist, critic of the very existence of the super-rich, perched at the top of a media conglomerate and wonder if he might have aged into an executor of big business, idolater of the almighty dollar—just another unanswerable confusion in a life of contradictions. For what it's worth, I like to believe that Tupac's rebel heart would have stopped him from becoming a CEO of the worst impulses.

Suge Knight's swift rise demonstrated the potential of rap music as a business in the 1990s, but his empire collapsed under the weight of his strong-arm business practices, lengthening rap sheet, and own hubris (though the man himself contended that authorities' interest in him was driven by racism). The hotel brawl that preceded Tupac's murder saw Knight jailed for violating parole. In any circumstance, it would have been difficult for Death Row to recover from the absconding of Dr. Dre and death of Tupac; with its CEO in prison until 2001, it proved impossible. The company has existed in different forms since, a mere zombie of its former self.

More legal problems followed; bankruptcy was declared. The years drifted by and the music industry left Suge Knight behind. He watched on as Dre took advantage of his reputation as an audiophile by launching headphone company Beats. Its products became ubiquitous, and Dre accepted a lucrative offer for the firm from Apple in 2014, declaring himself "hip-hop's first billionaire."

Then, in early 2015, Knight discovered that *Straight Outta Compton*, an in-production N.W.A. biopic produced by Dre himself, was making heavy use of his own image and story. Angered, Knight decided to pay an unannounced visit to the set in his red Ford Raptor pickup. He evaded security but not Cle "Bone" Sloan, a technical adviser to the movie and former gang member turned activist, who locked horns with the intruder until he left the set. Shortly after this retreat, Knight received a call from Terry Carter, the fifty-five-year-old co-founder of Heavyweight Records known in the industry for mediating beefs. Carter asked if Knight would meet him at the Compton burger joint Tam's to talk over his griev-ances. Minutes later, Knight pulled up outside the restaurant in his pickup, where Carter and at least one other man were waiting for him.

What Knight didn't know was that Sloan was there too. Sloan later claimed he heard Knight bad-mouthing him to Carter. Knight might have been the baddest man in all of L.A. two decades before, but that didn't mean much to Sloan, who, as he himself described, "just popped out like a jack-in-the-box" and began throwing punches at Knight through the vehicle's window. Knight began to reverse, knocking Sloan to the ground. The former Death Row head honcho then put the pickup into drive and moved forward, running over Sloan as he lay on the ground, crushing both of his ankles. Knight continued to surge, hitting the fleeing Carter, kill-ing him.

Three years later, Knight pleaded no contest to voluntary man-slaughter. The judge sentenced him to twenty-eight years in prison: twenty-two years for running over the victim and six additional years because it was Knight's third infraction under California's three-strikes law.

The damage was total; the fall of Suge Knight complete. Left behind was an outline that other music industry entrepreneurs such as Murder Inc. Records' Irv Gotti would aspire to without ever truly matching Knight's fearsome reputation. But by examining two of Knight's contemporaries who prospered as he floundered, we can see how the reach and influence of hip-hop capitalism has continued in the years since Tupac's death.

Master P grew up in the Calliope Projects, New Orleans. The year of his birth is unclear. Some sources cite 1967. A questionnaire he is purported to have filled out at the University of Houston in 1985 stated that he was born in April 1968. But speaking to *The New York Times* in 1998 for an article about his attempts to forge a basketball career with the Fort Wayne Fury, Miller maintained that he did not fill out the document and was actually born in 1970. (In fairness, being the old guy at a basketball tryout is an understand-able reason to lie about your age.)

Percy was raised by parents with a strong work ethic. His father, Percy Sr., was a military man turned security guard, while mother Josie worked in hotels. Despite their grind, the couple and their five children, of whom Percy was the eldest, lived in poverty. When his parents separated, it fractured the whole family. While his other siblings stayed with their mother, Percy and his brother Kevin went to live with Percy's paternal grandparents, who were often required to take various other relatives into a crowded three-bedroom apartment. Keeping busy, Percy attended a nearby Catholic school, made a little money by selling popcorn at the Superdome, and played basketball. Hour after hour he'd practice alone in the dark on the neighborhood courts, always hopeful that the ball in his hand could provide a ticket out of the projects.

For a time, the dream felt within reach. During his senior year, Percy transferred from Booker T. Washington High School to Warren Easton High School and starred as a point guard, averaging eighteen points, nine assists, five rebounds, and three steals. After graduating in 1987, he enrolled at the University of Houston, but an ACL tear destroyed his best-laid plans. In just one example of how college sports makes capital of its athletes with very little interest in their well-being, the NCAA permitted schools to revoke scholarships if injury rendered athletes worthless to them. Miller was forced to drop out during his freshman year. With the avenue of sports blocked off, he headed back to New Orleans and turned to selling drugs.

Calliope Projects would become synonymous with violence. A 2004 article in *The Advocate* attributed decades of unrest to a drug war started in 1987 and the killing of Sam "Scully" Clay, the project's first crack kingpin. Between 1994 and 2004, eighty-eight people were murdered within Calliope's small confines. Miller was one of the lucky ones who cheated death. Fleeing an attempted stickup, he somehow managed to evade the hail of bullets. His partner, Hot Boy, was shot eight times but somehow survived.

Sensibly, Miller packed up with his wife, Sonya, and young son, Romeo, and headed west to Richmond, California, for a change of scene. While there, he studied business administration at Merritt College in nearby Oakland—the same institute where years earlier Bobby Seale met Huey P. Newton. Having received $10,000 as part of a malpractice settlement awarded to his family due to the circumstances of the death of his grandfather Claude on New Year's Day, 1984 (Master P claimed this was due to Claude being given medicine intended for the patient in the bed next to him), he funneled the money into opening his own record store in Richmond in 1989. He named the outlet No Limit Records.

The record store wasn't a huge success, but Miller was able to use the period to study sales trends. He noticed an unfilled demand for more hard-edged gangster rap music. A plan formulated in his mind. Miller didn't have any real musical experience, but he had intimate knowledge of the world that street rappers strived to depict. So he expanded No Limit into a record label, the name reflecting his limitless aspirations. Taking up the moniker Master P, Miller anointed himself the company's flagship artist, deciding that his music would draw from his own life hustling on the streets of New Orleans. An image of a tank became the No Limit logo as a nod to the family's military roots. To see Master P rapping on top of a gold tank years later, you can't help but think he might have lost sight of that.

Enthused by his latest endeavor, P called for his younger brothers. Vyshonn and Corey pulled into town ready to join him on the journey. Vyshonn became Silkk the Shocker while Corey dubbed himself C-Murder, a name P hated but let slide. Kevin had planned to join his brothers, but by this point he was heavily embedded in the streets. On September 25, 1990, he was shot dead by a man sitting in the back seat of an acquaintance's car as he rode on the passenger's side. Kevin's body was found dumped on the edge of Interstate 10. (Years later, rapper Isaiah Rashad honored him by releasing a song called "RIP Kevin Miller" that appropriated Master P's hook from "Weed & Money.")

The Master P story could also have ended in tragedy or imprisonment. In the BET documentary series *No Limit Chronicles* (produced by Master P himself, so very favorable in its depiction), he tells a story about him and his crew getting into a scuffle at a club in Oakland, which culminated in P retrieving a TEC-9 from his trunk and pulling the trigger on one of the men who had crossed him.

The gun jammed once, then again. Fleeing the scene, he immediately drove to a secluded part of the city, pulled the trigger once more, and *prapppp prapppp*.

P's early music was rough and undistinguished, but like an alchemist, he was constantly refining this work. As would be the case throughout No Limit's peak, he began a habit of relentless releasing. Neither his self-produced debut album, *Get Away Clean*, in 1991, or 1992 follow-up, *Mama's Bad Boy*, sold well, but he framed the records and hung them on his workspace walls as if they'd gone platinum, almost willing success to come his way. P's early promotional strategies included handing out T-shirts to homeless people so they'd serve as walking billboards for No Limit, and passing his tapes on to drug dealers, who had the power to influence neighborhood taste.

P's first major success was the 1994 album *The Ghettos Tryin to Kill Me!*, and in particular its captivating title track, which featured a dirty bass line, programmed strings, out-of-tune crooning, and an anxious-sounding P giving an unvarnished depiction of the street life. The following year he uprooted No Limit Records to New Orleans. By 1997, he was based in Baton Rouge. Still, this period out west left a huge imprint on the No Limit sound as the label retained elements of the smooth pimp-funk sound synonymous with the region.

With his records gaining more traction through simple word of mouth, P signed a distribution contract with Priority Records in 1995 that entitled No Limit to between 80 and 85 percent of the profits, as well as ownership of all its masters. It was a shrewd move. Master P's next album, *Ice Cream Man*, hit number three on the *Billboard* album charts. But it also represented a significant stride forward artistically.

P ran No Limit with a machinelike efficiency that defied the ostensibly artistic nature of his business. From 1994 through '97, the label put out twenty-two records; in 1998 alone, that number jumped to twenty-three. (In a way, No Limit predicted a later era when rappers often dropped multiple projects a year, or padded albums out to well over twenty songs, to the benefit of their stream statistics.) It wasn't quantity over quality—most of the records were great, thanks in large part to P recruiting Beats by the Pound to produce the bulk of the label's songs. True to their name, the group cranked out instrumental after instrumental at a pace that matched P's ambitious schedule. Reports of the finances can vary wildly, but in 1998 it's said that No Limit sold 15 million albums and earned $160 million. P was even on the cover of *Fortune*.

No Limit had a loyal audience that loved the music, but nobody would deny that P's business instinct was a core factor of his success. Veteran journalist Charlie Braxton remembered the first time he met Master P. The rapper assumed he was from New York, the center of rap journalism at the time. Braxton told P he actually lived in Hattiesburg, Mississippi.

"Do you know J.J. over at J.J.'s Record Mart?" P inquired.

"Of course I know J.J.," Braxton replied. "The question is how do you know J.J.?"

"He sells records, don't he?"

As Braxton told me years later, "He understood the mom-and-pop retail and their importance in selling records."

P was so convinced that local stores were a key battleground to achieve sales, he would allow them to jump release dates. Back then, albums normally came out on Tuesday, but P would make sure No Limit releases hit small retailers' shelves over the weekend.

"So all the kids in the ghetto would have the opportunity to buy the record," explained Braxton. "And what would they do? They would come back to school on Monday and tell all the little white kids how dope the record was and they were playing the records and whatnot. That would make the white kids run to the record store that Monday evening after school trying to buy the record. So, Sam Goody and Tower would think, 'Wow, there's a rush on the record, people are already buying it,' and they would order more records. He was getting paid on shipping. The more records they ordered, the more money he made."

Years later, P spoke of the need to understand the ground level of his industry. "I tell people, if you get in a business, you need to know everything about your business," he told Jen Rogers in a 2019 interview for Yahoo! Finance's *My Three Cents*. "You need to know what the janitor is doing. You need to know what the guy who's cooking the burgers is doing . . . You need to know what the mail-room is doing. You need to know everything about your business to be successful."

It's impossible to listen to Master P's music without contemplating it as a vehicle for the growth of his own wealth. Because he raps about being rich, yes, but also because every narrative thread you pull on comes back to his business skills. I suspect it's for these reasons that there's a pervasive myth that P isn't a good rapper—that he simply played the role of an emcee to make money. That's unfair to him as an artist. P was never the most technically proficient rapper or elegant writer, but he had charisma to burn. His laid-back southern drawl was an effective instrument, and he could write hooks as sticky as sweet honey ribs.

Naturally, P diversified his business interests. There was his movie company, credit card company, clothing line, and toy line, which included a talking Master P action figure dressed in camouflage.

P never achieved the fame or influence of Dr. Dre or Jay-Z—especially outside of the United States—but he knew his market. He differs from most other famous hip-hop entrepreneurs because he never appeared interested in toning down No Limit's sound for chart traction. The label traded almost entirely in hardened gang-sterisms, its disdain for the mainstream reflected in the albums' art-work. Designed by the legendary Pen & Pixel design studio, the covers all featured garish fonts and images. And still, the records sold like crazy.

A 1998 *New York Times* story described P sitting in his office behind a large oak desk, wearing a pound of gold jewelry and a bulletproof vest. "There ain't no goal to stop at," he told them. "I guess I want to be the ghetto Bill Gates."

So P masterminded one of the most successful enterprises in hip-hop history. His was an almost caricatural display of wealth: Mr. Burns, Scrooge McDuck, choose your own industrialist. He represents the ultimate hip-hop entrepreneur. But as P solved capi-talism, he also fell to its darkest sides. Contract disputes began to puncture No Limit. Beats by the Pound walked in 1999 after feel-ing slighted during negotiations.

Charlie Braxton expressed his own disappointment with how

No Limit conducted business. "Because P was a capitalist, the thing that really disappointed me about him was that he turned around and did the exact same thing that the record companies did. Let's be honest, the record industry is capitalism on steroids.

"When I first met P, what made me, as a southerner, proud was to see an African American kid from the ghetto ascend on his own wits in a place where there is no way for him to survive, the odds are stacked against him, and there's a pistol loaded to his head. He was able to circumvent all that and become successful, and then not only become successful, he placed his company in the business district of Baton Rouge. This is someone who took his homeboys out of the ghetto, placed them all in gated communities, and gave them the deeds to their own houses. So, in that respect, I really respected him, but in the long run, when it was time to actually just pay them their publishing and stuff like that, and let them buy their own houses, he didn't do that. Cash Money [Records, a southern label founded in 1991 that would later become the home of Lil Wayne and Drake], same way, they operate like record companies do. But everybody has to keep this in the back of their mind: They are capitalists. They are imitating that capitalist system that runs throughout the industry."

He continued, "My disappointment again with P and Rap-A-Lot [a label founded in Houston in 1986] is that you know what these young brothers have been through, you've been through that. I'm not saying to give them the store, but give them a little bit more than they normally would, especially when a lot of these artists started in the mud with you."

To understand *Scarface* is to understand the themes that bind gangster rap. Even if your hip-hop knowledge is limited, you're probably aware that Brian De Palma's 1983 movie is treated by rappers as sacred text—so much so that in 2003 Def Jam put out a compilation titled *Music Inspired by "Scarface"*; so much so that Universal Studios had the terrible idea of releasing the movie with an all-modern hip-hop soundtrack, a move blocked by De Palma himself.

Some will say that the movie's over-the-top violence and profound amount of profanity jibes with the grim imagery of gangster rap (or its first cousin, mafioso rap, which takes more influence from mobsters, both real and fictional). This is not untrue. But Al Pacino's Tony Montana is not idolized by rappers for his brutality, but for his ascent up the societal ladder. Sprung from a Cuban prison and shipped to America by Fidel Castro as part of the Mariel boatlift, he lands in Miami fully convinced by the idea of America as the land of opportunity. Entering the drug trade, he parlays steely determination and streetwise understanding of the industry into a personal fortune. Ironically, by the end of the movie, the communist-bashing hell child is denouncing a capitalist society that would allow a bank to charge a man ten points on his own money.

Set in Miami when the city was one of the planet's true pop culture epicenters, when Don Johnson and Philip Michael Thomas's pastel suits were all the rage, *Scarface* traverses a lush, impenetrable urban jungle by the sea. It's a vivid dream of flat, painted backdrops and snow-white sand—a world with its own internal logic, indecent set of morals, drug-fueled sense of excess, and commitment to pop-art beauty. There's a gaudy brilliance to Tony's over-the-top taste as he decorates his lavish trophy mansion with deep-red foyer carpet, gold fittings, and black leather furniture. Writing for *The New Yorker*, celebrated film critic Pauline Kael dubbed *Scarface* "a joke about consumerism (and capitalism)."

Scarface is your classic tale of the rise and fall of a gangster. The highest peaks of the American dream are reflected in the phrase that captures Tony's attention and guides his actions through the movie's latter portions: "The world is yours." It's better to experience the highs of success just for a moment than to live a long life at the bottom.

Plenty of rappers have attempted to present their own crime epics in album form that mirror the narrative arc of movies like *The Godfather, Goodfellas, Casino,* and *Scarface.* Often their music is inspired by lived experience, and for sure the lives of glamorized real-life career criminals such as John Gotti and Pablo Escobar have been pillaged for inspiration too. But the influence of cinema has helped add a narrative thrust. There's the Notorious B.I.G.'s *Ready to Die*, which charts Biggie's Brooklyn street soldier from the cradle to the crypt. Raekwon's *Only Built 4 Cuban Linx . . .* follows two young hustlers—Rae and Ghostface Killah—as they plot one last score. And *The Diary* by Brad Jordan, the Houstonite who took up the rap name Scarface, chronicles a career in crime like pages of a journal, including "I Seen a Man Die," which follows the character as he struggles to adjust after a seven-year bid.

A funny thing happens when you listen to gangster rap and mafioso rap music. Rappers veer from depicting life in the streets to charting the realities of being rappers, sometimes flipping back and forth line to line. They quickly switch from performing as a mobster character to spitting about their experiences in the music industry. It's as if in America being a gangster and being in the record business are two sides of the same coin.

For Shawn Corey Carter, it was the movie *American Gangster* that unlocked feelings buried deep in his soul. When Carter saw an advance screening of Ridley Scott's 2007 movie in the Fifth Avenue screening room in Manhattan, he was, according to *Rolling Stone*, overcome with emotion. *American Gangster* is based on the real-life criminal enterprise of Frank Lucas, played by Denzel Washington, who in the 1960s and '70s rose to become the biggest importer of heroin in Harlem by buying the narcotic directly from a source in Southeast Asia. As Carter stared at the screen, he saw his life in an alternate timeline. The thought stayed with him: What if he hadn't left the drug trade years earlier? What if he'd never become Jay-Z?

It's fascinating to consider the Jay-Z story and its proximity to Tupac. As a disciple of Biggie, Jay had been in Tupac's crosshairs on his first version of "Hit 'Em Up" that was eventually discarded for the more famous edition of the song. Yet he emerged from this bloody saga that shocked America and became one of the nation's most powerful celebrities, richest self-made men, and embodiment of the American Dream. He harnessed the potential of hip-hop that Tupac did not live to witness—and may not have foreseen.

Born in the final month of the 1960s, Shawn grew up in Brooklyn's Marcy Projects. In a 2002 interview with CBS, he recalled the hardship of coming up at the height of the crack epidemic: "Especially in that neighborhood. It was a plague in that neighborhood. It was just everywhere, everywhere you look. In the hallways. You could smell it in the hallways.

"Back then, it was like, I would say it was, like, two things," he added. "It was either you're doin' it or you was movin' it."

Shawn was introduced to the drug business in the late 1980s by childhood friend DeHaven Irby. DeHaven had moved to Trenton, New Jersey, with intentions of playing high-school basketball. Instead, he fell into dealing and reached out to his friend to join the new venture. Irby would later say that Jay "nickeled and dimed, but nothing on a major scale."

Hip-hop was always in the background. Shawn had started rapping from an early age and his interest in music revved up under the tutelage of Jaz-O. His early forays into recorded music included spots on Jaz's records. And as destiny had placed him under Jaz's mentorship, it saw him cross paths with Damon Dash, a party promoter with a flair for marketing. The pair formed a business relationship that would shift the tectonic plates of hip-hop.

Jay got busy recording a debut album. But with the bulk of the record in the can, he couldn't land a deal. So Jay, Dash, and silent partner Kareem "Biggs" Burke pooled their resources and started Roc-A-Fella Records. Like so many burgeoning rap enterprises, they sold music out of the trunks of their cars.

With a buzz forming, the trio inked a deal with Freeze Records, in partnership with Priority. Everything finally in place, Jay dropped *Reasonable Doubt* in 1996, a mafioso rap classic boosted by its gritty realism and cinematic thrust, even replicating dialogue from *Scarface* and the De Palma and Pacino follow-up, *Carlito's Way*. But when Jay felt he wasn't getting paid correctly, he negotiated his release from the label, and, crucially, took the masters with him. Def Jam purchased a 50 percent stake in Roc-A-Fella in the spring of 1997. The deal included a second run of *Reasonable Doubt* on extremely favorable terms. Hit record after hit record followed. Jay grew into hip-hop's most famous A-lister.

In 1999, Jay launched clothing line Rocawear, which sold for a reported $204 million in 2007 to apparel company Iconix. A year after that sale, he launched entertainment company Roc Nation, which by 2019 was worth an estimated $75 million. Like Master P, he embodied hip-hop entrepreneurism, but with a mainstream acceptance that P never cultivated.

In his book *Empire State of Mind*, a full-length treatise on Jay-Z the businessman, Zack O'Malley Greenburg wrote, "His story is the American Dream in its purest form, a model for any entrepreneur looking to build a commercial empire."

As his fame grew, Jay's music sounded even more capitalistic than the relatively gritty sounds of *Reasonable Doubt*. He hired the greatest (and most expensive) producers to make beats as large as New York's skyscrapers and rapped about his life of excess. On "U Don't Know," from the classic 2001 album *The Blueprint*, he brags about his ability to work the market: "That's another difference that's between me and them, hah / I smarten up, open the market up / One million, two million, three million, four / In eighteen months, eighty million more."

The clearest example of Jay pushing his entrepreneurial image comes in the video for his 2003 single "Excuse Me Miss." Decked out in a sharp suit with pocket handkerchief, Jay attends late-night board meetings, enjoys drinks with clients in clubs, and uses his significant wealth to court a woman he meets in an elevator (or not, as it's revealed that their relationship is a daytime fantasy). He even uses the song to plug two of his brands: "50/50 venture with them S Dots kickin' off / Armadale poppin' now, only bring a n***a more," referencing the signature sneaker he's recently put out with Reebok and his brand of vodka. The following year he became president of Def Jam. Among the successes of his three-year tenure was the signing of Rihanna to the label. An infamous split between Jay and his partners Dash and Burke occurred when the trio sold their 50 percent interest in Roc-A-Fella to Def Jam, making the label full owners. As president, Jay retained control of Roc-A-Fella and his masters, essentially ousting his former partners. Their relationship has remained acrimonious.

By 2007, Jay epitomized not just the American dream but American celebrity in the way Frank Sinatra once did. (He'd call himself "the new Sinatra" a few years later on "Empire State of Mind," a song that felt as much like a consolidating tactic as it did a rap single. So embedded in New York culture, it's become a cliché. Jay could dine out on the track as long as New York has sports teams to play the song.) He probably had Barack Obama's personal number on his cell phone. It's impossible to imagine that people who achieve a certain level of fame don't regularly put the question to themselves, "How did I get here?"

Yet there was something about the movie *American Gangster* that unlocked a curiosity for what could have been. Jay's previous album, the overly glitzy *Kingdom Come*, had seen him muse on the number of stamps in his passport, twice reference his boycott of Cristal champagne, and indulge in brand names so high-end that most of his listeners probably didn't get the references. His next record—which he adorned with the only possible title, *American Gangster*—was the antidote. The narrative-driven concept album sees Jay envision his life if he'd remained a drug dealer, while working in commentary on his life not as a crime boss but the music industry kingpin he became, with elements of the movie completing the DNA code. Consider the very first line Jay raps on the album, from the song "Pray": "Look, mind state of a gangster from the '40s / Meets the business mind of Motown's Berry Gordy." Immediately he frames the two sides of himself: the criminal and the music industry player.

So you get "Party Life," which follows Jay on the town as he dines out well. You get "Blue Magic" (presented as a bonus track), named after a potent form of heroin sold by Lucas, where Jay blames Reaganomics for turning him into a "monster" by helping to create the dope game, even referencing the CIA and Contras' cocaine trafficking scandals that punctuated the Reagan presidency. On "No Hook," Jay calls out old friend DeHaven Irby by name ("Fuck DeHaven for cavin', that's why we don't speak / Made men ain't supposed to make statements"). And you get "Fallin'," the end of this gangster's run. But he's also happy to break character on "Blue Magic" by declaring that crime made him the rapper he became, while "Hello Brooklyn 2.0" sees him reveal his gargantuan dream to bring the Nets basketball team to Brooklyn, which, get this, *he actually achieved a few years later*. This lack of dedication to the album's concept may frustrate, but it reveals that in Jay's mind, they are one and the same. Two examples of the American Dream at work.

In 2019, Jay was declared the first hip-hop billionaire with a study of his rise published by *Forbes* magazine, with a preface by Steve Forbes himself. Dr. Dre is not far behind, having parlayed his reputation for being an audiophile into his headphones company Beats, which he sold to Apple in 2014. The presence of mega-rich hip-hop stars completed the culture's ascent to capitalistic heaven.

The problem, from a socialist point of view, is that this entanglement of music with big business places obstacles in the way of people who want to make politically radical music. There's an obvious friction between making anti-capitalist anthems in a capitalist system (remember what Charlie Braxton called the music industry: capitalism on steroids). While the internet promised a flattening of the structure, the bottom falling out of music sales means that only a small percentage of artists can self-sustain. Inevitably, most rising rappers seek to break bread with the capitalist gatekeepers.

In an instance of saying the quiet part out loud, "Moment of Clarity," from his project *The Black Album*, sees Jay-Z openly admit curbing his artistic impulses for commercial purposes: "I dumbed down for my audience to double my dollars." He goes on to admit he'd veered clear of making conscious rap in the vein of one of its biggest proponents because it's less lucrative: "Truthfully I wanna rhyme like Common Sense," referencing the deep-thinking Chicago rapper. "But I did 5 mill', I ain't been rhyming like Common since."

As fate had it, Master P did not have the staying power of Jay-Z. In 2003, No Limit Records filed for bankruptcy. It came one year after *Billboard* reported that P had been forced to sell an unfinished recording studio in Baton Rouge to settle unpaid construction bills and other debts. P once had big plans for the studio, but the contracting disputes slowed construction and, as *Billboard* described, "the studio is now a shell, with unfinished walls and a chain-link fence warning of guard dogs."

Financial trouble has continued to cling to the Master P brand. In 2004, he pled guilty to failing to file a corporate income tax return years earlier. He was later successfully sued for compensation by several members of the crew of his 2007 film *Uncle P* and, after apparently failing to pay the $240,000 judgment, the matter was referred to the U.S. Bankruptcy Court in Los Angeles. Reports at the time found that court documents listed Miller's monthly income at $1,387.

The downfall of the hardened street hustler who appeared to master America is perhaps a cautionary tale that in the Land of the Free, fortune is sometimes built on sand. As for Miller himself, maybe he wasn't totally immune to leftist principles. Speaking to TMZ about the welfare of rappers in the wake of DMX's death in 2021, he mused over the benefits of a hip-hop union.

A demonstrator holds up a placard of Tupac on Hollywood Boulevard during protests over the killing of George Floyd, 2020.

12

SPARK THE BRAIN THAT WILL
CHANGE THE WORLD

1.

The Solomon Islands sit to the northeast of Australia, one of the few speckles of land in the vast abyss of the Pacific Ocean that separates Australasia and the Americas. Six main islands make up the archipelago nation, but if you were to count them all from the perch of the gods, you'd come up with a figure just shy of a thousand. All reside within the Pacific "Ring of Fire." Thus, earthquakes, tsunamis, and volcanic activity regularly rock the region.

The history of the Solomon Islands is soaked in blood, much of it shed by men with no connection to the land. Guadalcanal, the largest of the islands, is known in U.S. military history as the place where the war in the Pacific turned in its favor. Thousands of American and Japanese troops died in the Second World War for control of its shores. Decades after the fighting stopped, filmmaker Terrence Malick depicted the engagement in his soulful film *The Thin Red Line*. Scuba divers have been known to journey to the region for a peek at the wreckage of American ships.

A war it never asked for had knock-on effects for Guadalcanal. When the United States captured a half-built airstrip from Japan, it invited laborers from nearby Malaita, an island just 30 kilometers away and visible on Guadalcanal's eastern horizon, to complete the work. When the foreign soldiers went home, Henderson Field grew into Honiara, capital city of the Solomon Islands, and the Malaitans rose to become the ruling class.

In 1978, the Solomon Islands gained independence from Britain. As is often the case with decolonization, the new maps showed little concern for tribal lines, and a shared sense of nationalism proved elusive for the Solomon Islanders. Many ethnic Guales (who preferred to call Guadalcanal by its Indigenous name, Isatabu) resented the influence of the Malaitans, with whom they shared little, not even a language.

As the twentieth century began to dim, ethnic tensions reached an apex. In 1998, the five thousand men of the Guadalcanal Revolutionary Army (sometimes called the Istambu Freedom Fighters) initiated its uprising. Armed with rifles retrieved from wartime munitions dumps, the rebels ousted tens of thousands of Malaitan settlers, herding them onto overcrowded ferries bound for Malaita. The police were rendered powerless as militants swept the island. The intensity of the rebellion meant that, for a time, a breakup of the country seemed a possibility.

Joining the side of the rebels were the island's youth gangs. In the suburbs of Honiara prowled the West Side Outlaws. Its membership fancied themselves militias but more closely resembled a street gang, with uniforms consisting of high-top basketball shoes, baggy knee-length shorts, and T-shirts with the sleeves torn off. Among the West Side Outlaws' favorite weaponry was the machete. From thatch hut to thatch hut they went, forcibly evicting the Malaitans with their heavy blades. After the dirty work was done, gang members would scribble on walls their calling card and tribute to the martyred soldier who had inspired the gang's name and ethos: "2PAC OUTLAWZ, KILL 'EM ALL."

"Tupac was a man of action," a bare-chested West Side Outlaw in cutoff blue jeans told *Newsweek*. "He wasn't afraid of dying."

"We, too, are outlaws," said another, perched under a tree shade on one of the island's idyllic beaches. "So when outsiders come in and try to boss us around, like Malaitans and the police, we cop a Tupac attitude."

The Solomon Islands were late discovering Tupac—this is a part of the world that didn't receive television service until 1992. It's said that a traveling islander brought one of the rapper's CDs back from

Australia in 1995, which was copied ad nauseam for the new fans. Soon the country was flooded with imported Tupac T-shirts and bootleg cassette tapes. Its only private radio station, ZFM, began getting requests for 2Pac songs. By 1997, the West Side Outlaws had adopted him as their spiritual leader. When police cracked down on the group's marijuana farms, they responded by planting rows of the drug to spell out WEST SIDE on a hill overlooking Honiara.

Sectarian violence between the Guales and Malaitans continued for five years. At least two hundred people were killed and thousands more displaced. This ugly period of their history became known among Solomon Islanders by a rather low-key name: they call it "the tensions."

The West Side Outlaws may have been distinguished by their youth, but no nation engrained the image of the child soldier in Western minds in the 1990s more than Sierra Leone. A gruesome civil war in the West African country began in 1991 with an uprising by the rebels of the Revolutionary United Front, led by Foday Sankoh. Its ideology was a mishmash of Pan-Africanism, Marxism, and Maoism; their rhetoric was that poor people, the people of the land, were being exploited by a rich elite, and the RUF would bring democracy, education, and equality.

Having initially claimed to be militants for the people, the RUF subjected civilians to horrendous cruelty. It became notorious for its use of child soldiers, whom it snatched from villages, handed weapons to, and subjected to radicalizing violence. Sankoh didn't pay his RUF soldiers with any kind of regularity and instead gave them free rein to loot and pillage. This was dubbed "Operation Pay Yourself."

These juvenile fighters were heavily influenced by popular culture. Conflict analyst and writer Marc Sommers has submitted that there were three global icons in particular who made an impression on them: Bob Marley, Rambo, and Tupac. The RUF adopted Tupac's likeness, even wearing T-shirts with his image as a makeshift uniform. He represented a clear vision of how they saw themselves: young Black men dismissed by those in power as a criminal and outcast, fighting back against an unjust system.

In 1997, a faction of the Sierra Leone military called the Armed Forces Revolutionary Council took power. When they were removed from the capital city of Freetown, partly through an intervention by Nigerian forces, the group split further. One faction that emerged called itself the West Side N*****. Boasting as many as one thousand men, and strongest around Masiaka, forty miles from Freetown, its membership was bolstered by men from the Sierra Leone Army, the RUF, and ordinary civilians. Western media would elevate the group to its highest tier of notoriety but not before smoothing out the name to the most audience-palatable West Side Boys.

The name reflected that they did, indeed, come from the west of Sierra Leone, but it also invoked hip-hop's California-representing contingent, of which none was better known than Tupac. Hip-hop fueled their whole bravado. They wore basketball shirts, baggy trousers, and wraparound sunglasses. Many shaved their heads to emulate Tupac's image. They spoke the lingo of rap and saw themselves more as gangsters than rebels. And like Tupac, many had been in jail, at Pademba Road Prison, possibly released during the 1997 coup. The title of 2Pac's song "Only God Can Judge Me" was their mantra.

For the West Side Boys, Tupac was someone who guided their journey, with a story that resembled their own rebel life. In his lyrics, they recognized their own lives—how they were pushed aside from society, and the only way to respond was to fight their own way back.

Many who bore witness to their activities deem the term "rebel" as generous to a group they considered more bandits than soldiers. Especially when their operations were fueled by drugs and "morale boosters"—plastic sachets of cheap gin and whisky. They also had a propensity for shocking violence. "They cut off people's hands, grab whatever they can," a student in Freetown commented. "Wherever they go they kill. Even the military personnel are afraid of them."

Despite this, the West Side Boys saw themselves as embodying "youth revolution" and placed importance on avoiding violence and "being righteous." They were efficient and resourceful fighters too, with leaders who often came from military families. In one notable operation, the West Side Boys captured eleven British soldiers, relieving the well-armed foreigners of their SA80 rifles, pistols, and Land Rovers. Members even showed up to negotiations for their release driving the vehicles they had commandeered. It made the West Side Boys targets for the British media, who turned them into little more than barbarous thugs. Almost no effort was made to understand the feelings of frustration and humiliation behind their radicalization.

"It wasn't just the humiliation of poverty," explained Kieran Mitton, a field researcher on violence and youth marginality who has traveled Sierra Leone, "but specifically young people feeling like the older generation, and certainly those in power, like local chiefs or teachers or university professors, were actively conspiring against them and keeping them away from things that they had a right to access: jobs, opportunities, even marriage."

In the chiefdoms of Sierra Leone, these young men were sometimes denied the right to marry the girl they loved because their rulers would not grant them permission, or they couldn't afford to pay the dowry price. When the war arrived, it presented an opportunity for an outpouring of frustration, even revenge. "There are lots of accounts of these atrocities being targeted against the chiefs, against teachers, against leaders," said Mitton. "A high-school student would go back to his high school and find his headmaster and he would publicly strip him naked and kill him or do something to humiliate him."

The near decade-long conflict that had gripped Sierra Leone appeared to be ending on July 7, 1999, with the signing of the Lomé Peace Agreement. Foday Sankoh, the commander of the RUF, was appeased with an offer of the vice presidency and control of Sierra Leone's diamond mines. UN peacekeeping forces were permitted to monitor the disarmament process. But RUF compliance was inconsistent and sluggish, and by May 2000, the rebels were again advancing on Freetown. With help from United Nations forces,

British troops, and Guinean air support, the Sierra Leone Army, now fighting alongside the West Side Boys, finally defeated the RUF before they could take control of the capital. On January 18, 2002, newly installed president Ahmad Tejan Kabbah declared the Sierra Leone Civil War had finally ended, and the people could finally hope for brighter days.

2.

For a global superstar, Tupac was not particularly well traveled. There was his roadie gig in Japan with Digital Underground, a holiday to Cancún, a trip to Italy toward the end of his life when he accepted an invitation from Gianni Versace to attend his fashion show, but not much else to discuss. There's an equivalence here with Elvis Presley, a fellow American icon, who never left the United States, except with the military. Yet where there is poverty on this planet, the image of Tupac is found. Where there is conflict and struggle, his influence is palpable.

2Pac's music was a potent propellant among the Libyan rebels attempting to oust Colonel Gaddafi in 2011. "When the besieged Colonel Gaddafi recently started hearing 'Me Against the World' booming from rebels' advancing vehicles, one suspects he might have identified with the track himself," reported the *LA Weekly*. One young militant told the paper, "I only listen to 2Pac before going to shoot Gaddafi boys."

Rapper and activist Youssef Ramadan has said that during the Libyan uprising, many saw Tupac as a kind of "sacred man" and drew inspiration from his words. It's an interesting word, "sacred." It suggests that, to these soldiers, Tupac was holy, venerated, like a saint. Similarly, you often hear words like "prophet" used to describe him. There are rappers who have fervent fans, but none attract the same type of reverence. You'd almost believe Tupac was placed here by a higher power to be a beacon to the downtrodden, an example to the freedom fighter.

But why is Tupac the one? His only competition for the position of hip-hop's most recognizable icon is probably Eminem, but

I'm not sure Marshall Mathers's image evokes a strong sense of *anything*. Conversely, Tupac exists in the realm of great pop culture figures whose images radiate a certain concept or purpose. Elvis and Marilyn Monroe represent 1950s American idealism; Bruce Lee conjures a sense of self-discipline. Bob Marley signifies the quest for freedom. In a very surface way, there's something of the Malcolm-Martin duality to the perception of Marley and Tupac. "We used to be into Bob Marley, who sings 'Get up, stand up, fight for your rights,'" said one of Sierra Leone's West Side Boys. "But when we stood up, the police shot at us. Then we became outlaws, like Tupac."

So, there you go. When Marley's famous mantras don't work, you can always shout, "Thug life!"

Tupac's penchant for baring his torso is a reminder of the vulnerability of flesh and bone, renders him ripe for martyring, and brings forth the image of him as a kind of modern-day Jesus Christ. (It's an easy thing for me to recognize. Educated in an Irish Catholic school, for me images of Christ's suffering were like background noise.) Like Jesus, Tupac died young, violently at that, which humanity tends to demand its saviors do.

The Christ juxtapositions were not entirely unplanned. 2Pac is depicted on the cover of his album *The Don Killuminati: The 7 Day Theory* as crucified. The project was completed before his death and released two months after, making it his final true work and form. It is rarely referred to by its full title. Instead, fans call it by the name of the alter ego Tupac released the album under: *Makaveli*.

Tupac created the alias to honor the fifteenth-century Italian philosopher Niccolò di Bernardo dei Machiavelli, who wrote the classic political treatise *The Prince*. With the name change and Jesus-posturing cover, there's a sense 2Pac was attempting to invoke the concept of the Great Man. "The Italians I speak about were truly great men," he explained in an interview. "And I find any great man, Black or white, I'm going to study them, learn them, so he can't be great to me no more. Like, Machiavelli. My name is not Machiavelli. My name is Makaveli. I took it, that's mine. He gave me that. And I don't feel no guilt. All these motherfuckers stole from us forever. I'm taking back what's mine. It's just that they recorded it when he said it. It's probably something he took from us that they didn't let us record."

It's natural to listen to an album completed shortly before an artist dies and sense that the work is shadowed by their death. In the case of *Makaveli*, it's unmistakable. This is a project that sounds haunted. The beats have an eerie, skeletal beauty. The kid with the large, fluid eyes who wrote "Panther Power" years earlier had by now mutated into a man whose aura suggested he'd seen too much. (The Notorious B.I.G.'s second album, *Life After Death*, also released posthumously, feels similarly grim.) On any given day, *Makaveli* is my favorite 2Pac album; that he died right at his peak as a recording artist adds to the sadness. The religious imagery doubles down on the sense of transcendence—Christ died and was resurrected. Tupac died and was now restored to life, through *Makaveli*.

It's not the hit parade of *All Eyez on Me*. Whereas 2Pac's two-disc opus looked outward, by recruiting big-name guests and hit-making producers, on *Makaveli*, he kept the circle tight. Most of the on-mic guests were from his close-knit clique, the Outlawz. Production primarily came from Darryl "Big D" Harper and Hurt-M-Badd, two marginal producers at Death Row, generally relegated to work in what was referred to around the label as "the Wack Room." A smaller squad allowed Tupac to record more furiously. He was determined to finish *Makaveli* quickly, and most of the work was done in a single week. Once more, Hennessy was the fuel.

All Eyez on Me is a party; *Makaveli* is a séance. It's music for Tupac's eulogies that he couldn't have known were soon coming. Except maybe he did.

Despite releasing the album under a moniker, there's little sense that 2Pac is inhabiting a different character. *Makaveli* is just as much a temperature check of the life of Tupac Shakur as any other album he made. Unable to shake a confrontational mindset, his enemies are not forgotten: over a piano motif that sounds straight from a horror movie, opening track "Bomb First (My Second Reply)" is another spray of "Raid on cockroaches" against bitter enemies Bad

Boy Records, Jay-Z, Mobb Deep, and others. Claims that Tupac wanted to quash his various beefs at the time of his death, or that he blamed the media for stoking the coastal wars, are not supported by his own lyrics.

You can't begin to evaluate the album without quickly getting to "Hail Mary." One of 2Pac's true masterpieces came together in ninety minutes, after the rapper ordered his producers to give him "some slow, thuggish shit." The beat's gothic bells invoke religious ruminations: "And God said he should send his one begotten son to lead the wild into the ways of the man," 2Pac announces on the intro, invoking Christ once more. "Hail Mary" also includes a dispatch to former jail mates: "To my homeboys in Clinton Max doin' their bid / Raise hell to this real shit and feel this / When they turn out the lights, I'll be there in the dark." At a listening party, Tupac vibed to every track of *Makaveli*. But when "Hail Mary" played, he escaped into his own world, his arms in the air, still clutching a Hennessy bottle. As Hurt-M-Badd observed, "He threw his hands up in the air like he ruled a nation."

The religious allegories continue on "Blasphemy," which ends with a prayer recited by 2Pac's cousin Jamala Lesane. Watching on during the song's creation was Young Noble, a new Outlawz member, who felt in the presence of something special. "He got real deep on there, and he didn't even know where it came from . . . Dude was definitely sent from up above. I can't explain everything. There's certain shit I don't know."

After the bombastic *All Eyez on Me*, there's evidence throughout *Makaveli* that 2Pac was reengaging with his revolutionary roots. "White Man'z World" is set in a prison and dedicated to his incarcerated elders, "all the real OGs," Mutulu Shakur, Geronimo Pratt, Mumia Abu-Jamal, and Sekou Odinga. Attempting to take ownership of his mistakes, while never losing sight of the institutional discrimination he faced, a more contrite 2Pac apologizes to the Black women whose pain he has overlooked—no specifics. There are snippets from speeches by controversial Black nationalist leaders Khalid Abdul Muhammad and Louis Farrakhan. "The seal, and the constitution," declares the latter, "reflect the thinking of the founding fathers, that this was to be a nation by white people; and for white people, Native Americans, Blacks, and all other non-white people were to be the burden bearers, for the real citizens of this nation."

There's even a highly flammable Bonnie and Clyde fantasy in "Me and My Girlfriend," with his girlfriend firing off a machine gun halfway through. Famously, Jay-Z teamed up with Beyoncé seven years later to record their own version of the track, "'03 Bonnie & Clyde."

It's not all bleak. "To Live and Die in L.A." seizes the revelry of "California Love" and pares it down to the boulevards of the state's most famous city. There are allusions to the riots: "We might fight amongst each other / But I promise you this: we'll burn this bitch down, get us pissed." And, on the third verse, 2Pac declares, "It wouldn't be L.A. without Mexicans / Black love, brown Pride in the sets again," a lyric that would be adopted by Nipsey Hussle years later in the searing anti-Trump song "FDT" as a pushback to the presidential hopeful's scapegoating of Mexican immigrants.

Mostly, "To Live and Die in L.A." reflects the idyllic vision Tupac had for his adopted home—a vision he perhaps hoped he could live in one day, free of the drama and beef: "Gettin' high, watchin' time fly; to live and die in L.A."

3.

Six months after the murder of Tupac Shakur, Christopher Wallace joined him in the hereafter. Like his great rival, the Notorious B.I.G.'s final breaths came far from home. He was assassinated shortly after midnight on March 9, 1997, outside a music industry party at the Petersen Automotive Museum in Los Angeles. Biggie was sitting in the passenger seat of a sport utility vehicle when the gunman pulled up in the next lane in a dark Impala and fired at least seven shots from a 9-millimeter handgun. His early death solidified his perceived spiritual connection to Tupac, but some believe the links to be much stronger.

Police corruption is at the center of many theories regarding Tupac's demise. There is an eeriness to the FBI opening an investigation on Death Row just months before Tupac's death—it had plotted against his Black Panther ancestors, now it was lurking in the background as the most prominent of Panther cubs was murdered. But Biggie's demise became wrapped up in a legitimate scandal that deeply shamed the Los Angeles Police Department. These revelations of impropriety came at the tail end of the 1990s, already a decade of sin from the LAPD. There'd been the Rodney King beating, the Fuhrman tapes, and, following Biggie's death, the divulgence of the bandit behavior of the department's Community Resources Against Street Hoodlums (CRASH) unit. It would go down in the history books as the Rampart scandal.

Police impropriety was evident when it was revealed that as many as six Inglewood officers violated department policy by working off-duty as security in Biggie's entourage. Having witnessed the shooting from a car directly behind the client, one cop pursued the Impala as it peeled off away from the scene, but, hamstrung by a rental that decreased the fuel supply when it breached ninety miles an hour, soon lost sight of the vehicle after it disappeared down a dimly lit side street off Wilshire Boulevard. He left the scene without reporting his observations about the shooting to investigators.

Among the detectives assigned to the Biggie murder case was Russell Poole, a respected investigator who joined the Robbery-Homicide Division in 1996 after over nine years spent as a homicide investigator at the South Bureau and Wilshire Division. Poole later told his story to journalist Randall Sullivan for the true crime book *LAbyrinth*. It was turned into a pretty average movie called *City of Lies* starring Johnny Depp, with Poole depicted as the quintessential ex-cop obsessed with that one case that went unsolved—the murder of Christopher Wallace. True enough, his dedication to the case deeply compromised his standing with his hapless higher-ups, led to his resignation from the LAPD, and even put a strain on his marriage. Poole would not live to see the case reach a conclusion. He died of a heart attack in 2015.

Poole wasn't assigned to the Biggie case until months after the rapper's death, but had already unwittingly entered the Los Angeles rap ecosystem when he was appointed to investigate a moment of road rage that had escalated into a deadly shooting. On March 18, 1997—coincidentally the day of Biggie's funeral in Brooklyn—Frank Lyga and Kevin Gaines got into an altercation when stopped at a red light on Ventura Boulevard. Stern stares and barbed words were exchanged; the two vehicles screeched away alongside each other like two dueling predators. Weapons were drawn and when the smoke cleared, Gaines's vehicle had rolled to a stop at a gas station with the driver dead behind the wheel. What neither man knew during their altercation was that the other was a cop.

Lyga had never shot a person on duty before, let alone killed someone. But he could take comfort in the belief that it had been him or the other guy. This comfort was disturbed when what he felt was a simple act of self-defense rumbled into a scandal. In a post–Rodney King, post–O. J. Simpson city, Lyga, a white cop, had shot Gaines, a Black cop. Lyga was tormented in the media for the killing. The Gaines family, represented by none other than Johnnie Cochran, filed a wrongful death lawsuit against the city of Los Angeles for $25 million. But eyewitnesses and CCTV footage backed up Lyga's story that Gaines had been the aggressor. Concerning Poole was his discovery that off-duty Black officers had scoured the neighborhood looking for witnesses to contradict Lyga, and even applying pressure on them to change their story. His investigation would also find that Gaines was, in just about every way you can be, a bad cop. (The city later settled the wrongful death suit for just $250,000.)

Poole discovered that the green Mitsubishi Montero that Gaines was driving during the altercation with Lyga was registered to Sharitha Knight, estranged wife of one Marion "Suge" Knight. Gaines had struck up a romance with Sharitha and was living with her at the time of his death. That didn't curb his appreciation for her husband. Found taped to the back of Gaines's locker were eight-by-ten glossies of both Suge and Tupac. Poole heard whispers that cops earned big money off-duty working security for Death Row. "Most of them were off-duty LAPD officers, moonlighting for that extra bread," rapper Big Tray Deee confirmed to me years later. And Gaines did not exactly live a frugal life. He wore designer threads and drove a Mercedes. Found in his belongings was a $950 receipt from Monty's, a Westwood steakhouse and popular hangout for the staff at Death Row.

As the Biggie and Gaines investigations churned away that November, armed men pulled off a daring heist at a Los Angeles branch of Bank of America, making off with $722,000. When investigators discovered that an unusually large amount of cash had been delivered to the bank just ten minutes before the robbery, they were immediately suspicious of assistant bank manager Errolyn Romero. Sure enough, one month later, Romero confessed to her role in the crime. Not only had she ensured there was a huge amount of money to be plundered, she secretly ushered the robbers toward the vault. One of the men was Romero's boyfriend and the mastermind of the heist: LAPD officer David Mack. When detectives searched the former track star's house in connection with the bank robbery, they found what one cop called a "shrine" to Tupac. What piqued Russell Poole's interest, though, was the black SS Impala parked next to it, a vehicle that matched the description of the one used during the assassination of Biggie, and the same German 9-millimeter ammunition used in the shooting. Poole was eager to have the car tested by the Scientific Investigations Division, but the request was denied by his higher-ups. In fact, Poole consistently felt hampered by the brass. The reason, he deduced, was that having cops implicated in Biggie's murder could have huge negative consequences, and the LAPD did not want that stone kicked over.

"For the first time in my career I was witnessing a cover-up and an obstruction of justice in the LAPD, and the whole thing was being orchestrated from the highest levels," said Poole. "I knew the chief was behind it, and that Internal Affairs was in on it with him."

Mack was arrested and later convicted of the bank robbery. He was sentenced to fourteen years and three months in federal prison, where he associated himself with the Mob Piru Bloods.

Detectives investigating Mack discovered that two days after the robbery, he hit Las Vegas with two other police officers for a weekend of gambling. The group included his former partner, Rafael

Perez, and Sammy Martin, members of LAPD's specialist anti-gang unit CRASH, part of the Rampart Division servicing communities to the west of Downtown Los Angeles, including Silver Lake, Echo Park, Pico-Union, and Westlake. Its name is derived from Rampart Boulevard, one of the principal thoroughfares in its patrol area.

Perez would become *the* central figure in the Rampart scandal, a cop so infamous he became the basis for Denzel Washington's larger-than-life, *King-Kong-ain't-got-shit-on-me* corrupt detective in the movie *Training Day*. He was first arrested in August 1998 on suspicion of having stolen eight pounds of cocaine valued at more than $1 million from a police evidence locker. As part of a plea agreement for a reduced sentence, Perez agreed to cooperate with investigators. Singing like a bird, he provided information on more than seventy officers, whose sins ranged from drinking on the job to planting weapons on suspects to cover up bad shootings, and including police supervisors who committed corrupt acts or allowed them to occur.

Perez spun a saga of CRASH officers essentially operating as a gang unto themselves. They wore skull tattoos with cowboy hats and poker cards portraying the dead man's hand of aces and eights. The corruption within the Rampart Division became well known within the force, and law-abiding officers transferred out of the division while cops with no scruples requested transfers in. Little was done to curb the corruption because the units were reducing crime in the area.

In addition to reporting the theft of money and drugs, Perez described some of the horrific actions that he claimed police officers in the CRASH unit committed. One example was the police shooting of a man, Juan Saldana, while he was running in an apartment hallway. Saldana fell to the floor, and the officers planted a gun on him to justify the shooting. Officers then fabricated a cover-up story while Saldana bled to death. Other innocent victims were paralyzed or served time in prison on trumped-up charges. These crimes, according to Perez, were celebrated and rewarded by CRASH supervisors.

Because of Perez's cooperation with investigators, he was sentenced to five years in prison and received immunity from further prosecution. Over one hundred convictions were overturned based on his testimony. Yet questions swirled around the reliability of Perez and the saga he spun. He was released from prison in July 2001.

At no point was Biggie's murder ever mentioned in Perez's plea agreement. The only hint of a suggestion of such a crime was when the district attorney made clear to Perez's lawyer, Winston Kevin McKesson, that they would not offer immunity for it. "When Perez decided he wanted to be contrite and he wanted to come forth and talk about what was going on, we had to get an immunity agreement in place," McKesson told me. "And one of the things that the DA kept insisting, 'We're not gonna give him immunity for a murder.' And excuse my French, Perez and I were like, 'What the fuck is he talking about?' And my client said, 'Kevin, there's no murder here.' And so I had no clue as to what he was talking about. So it [Biggie's murder] was a part of the case only to the extent that the immunity agreement that he was going to prepare, that he was going to sign, had nothing to do with Perez's involvement in a murder, separate or apart from police work."

Still, in 2002, based on Poole's findings, Biggie's family brought a wrongful death suit that alleged that Mack and Perez had conspired with Suge Knight to murder the rapper. (Mack and a suspect named Amir Muhammed, who had been accused of pulling the trigger, had long since been cleared of criminal charges.) The suit alleged that, prior to the killing, the LAPD "knew or reasonably should have known" that an atmosphere of violence and "alleged criminality" surrounded Death Row Records and that street gangs were associated with the company and its employees. The suit rumbled on for years. In 2006, a $1.1 million judgment against the city for the cost of legal fees was awarded and then revoked after a district judge discovered the family had information they told the court they did not have access to. A second lawsuit was dismissed in 2010.

There are some who urge caution in accepting Poole's theories at face value, including the lawyer who represented Perez. "I thought that was basically an overzealous investigator [Poole] with an active imagination," said McKesson. "I don't want to mess up your book, but I've never seen any evidence that either my client, Sammy [Martin], or David Mack were in any way involved with Suge Knight.

"I think he [Poole] was an honest man, in that respect. I think he actually believed that. And I really believe that [a senior figure in the LAPD] was trying to suppress that. And so you had those two forces at work. But I saw no evidence to suggest that Poole's theory was anything more than a theory."

McKesson continued, "I'm a big critic of the LAPD, but this is one where I'm not criticizing it. I thought that [the LAPD] took him off the case because [they] thought that Poole really believed these theories that were unsubstantiated by the facts. And he, excuse my language, would somehow fuck up the [Perez] case by talking about that shit. And so, I thought he was removed because they thought that he would make the case more difficult to prove because he would have all these grandiose theories when juries say, 'Well, look, I thought I was gonna hear about Biggie Smalls and Tupac Shakur.'"

The FBI closed its own investigation in 2005 after federal prosecutors decided not to pursue anyone in connection with the murder or any alleged cover-up by Los Angeles Police Department officers. Heavily redacted FBI documents released in 2011 showed the bureau's conclusion that Gaines and other police officers were moonlighting as security for Death Row. They also suggested LAPD involvement in Biggie's murder. One 2002 document supports allegations that police helped carry out and cover up the killing. Despite the edits, the records again raise links between the Rampart scandal, the Mob Piru Bloods, and Death Row.

"Because of the professional manner in which the Wallace murder took place, it is alleged that not only could one gang member [redacted] Mob Piru Blood not pull this off but it would have taken a large contingency of people/officers," the 2002 report said.

"LAPD Officer [redacted] and other alleged LAPD Officers were Mob Piru Blood gang members who worked with and affiliated with Death Row Records. When Tupac was killed, it is alleged by many that Wallace was killed in retaliation and that this was orchestrated by [redacted], his good friend [redacted] and other LAPD Officers that [redacted] associated with."

4.

Almost a quarter century after his death, Tupac's voice rang out on the streets of New Zealand. Kiwis hit the pavement as part of a show of global solidarity with America's Black Lives Matter protests against the killing of George Floyd, a Black man, in Minneapolis by forty-four-year-old white police officer Derek Chauvin, who knelt on Floyd's neck for over nine minutes while he was handcuffed and sprawled across the ground, face down.

Demonstrations sometimes require a unifying anthem, and from speakers powerful enough to ring throughout the streets came the sounds of 2Pac's "Changes." As it blared, the galvanized crowd jumped up and down in bursts of exaltation, their limbs and placards flailing in all directions. A video of the moment was posted online. It was even seen by Bruce Hornsby, writer of the song "The Way It Is," which "Changes" heavily adopts. I've spoken to artists over the years who've hated being sampled, seeing the move as being derivative or lamenting that their message was skewed. Not Hornsby, though. He was moved by what he had helped ignite. "This is so beautiful," the musician posted on social media.

It's strange to consider that 2Pac never heard the version of "Changes" that many have found so poignant, so resonant. His defining statement on police brutality, mass incarceration, the War on Drugs, and economic inequality—and his plea for change—was assembled after his death and added to *Greatest Hits*, a very important, expertly assembled double-disc release that solidified 2Pac's reputation as a legendary rap artist.

"Changes" goes all the way back to Christmas Day 1991. It was at Hyde Street Studios in San Francisco, where Tupac, too restless to stop working even on Yule night, met with "Brenda's Got a Baby" producer Deon "Big D the Impossible" Evans. So surprised was the studio that someone would want to record on the holiday that they'd scheduled maintenance on one of their machines to take place.

Once there, Tupac fondled a cassette tape of Bruce Hornsby and the Range's 1986 hit "The Way It Is" and told Big D he wanted to use it in his own song. As the producer extracted the sample and crafted the beat, 2Pac penned his verses. The version they recorded that night is rougher than the canonical edit released years later, the chief difference being that Big D's original adds the use of a Run-DMC "It's Like That" to the Hornsby sample (when 2Pac declares "That's the way it is," it's punctuated by the Hollis, Queens, legends' utterances of the same words). For the 1998 version, production duo Trackmasters were brought in to smooth the arrangement for mainstream radio.

The rapid spread of rallies under the Black Lives Matter banner was dizzying—I attended them in Dublin in solidarity with activists protesting the murder of George Floyd, and in solidarity with Ireland's Black community. But Black Lives Matter meant a variety of things to those who embraced it. For some, it didn't stretch beyond the statement itself: precious Black life was not being valued by police and needed to be safeguarded. For others, the words primarily referred to an organization of the same name with its own political goals and purpose. To radicals, BLM is in a tradition that counts among its past contributors the Black Panthers—a Marxist movement with various left-wing objectives, including defunding the police, dismantling capitalism, smashing the patriarchy, seeking reparations for slavery, and raising money to bail out Black prisoners awaiting trial.

Released two years after his death, "Changes" encouraged people to remember the best of Tupac. It has been heralded for a message that has felt timeless, prophetic even. When the Black Lives Matter movement took shape in 2013, Tupac's words seemed even more potent. When I heard that a painting of Tupac adorns the home of Colin Kaepernick, it reminded me of a quote credited to him that has proved prophetic: "I'm not saying I'm gonna change the world, but I guarantee that I will spark the brain that will change the world." In tumultuous times, a new generation has hugged him closely.

There's a key section in "Changes," when 2Pac summons activism of the past: "'It's time to fight back,' that's what Huey said / Two shots in the dark, now Huey's dead / I got love for my brother / But we can never go nowhere unless we share with each other." In a small way, any BLM activist moved by "Changes" is infused by the spirit of Huey through Tupac.

One particular lyric took on new meaning in 2009: "And although it seems heaven-sent / We ain't ready to see a Black president." Did 2Pac mean America as a nation simply would not vote in adequate numbers to elect a Black commander in chief, or does the first bar, the idea of false hope, signal a belief that such a president would do little to cure the country's racism? The radical left's disappointment with Obama would suggest the latter. Tupac himself hated American imperialism and war, and likely would have been sickened by the drone bombs unleashed on Obama's watch. Too much civilian death in Afghanistan, Yemen, Pakistan, and Somalia has never been justified.

What's undeniable, though, is how Obama's rise to power electrified the USA and beyond. There on November 4, 2008, was the president-elect with all his charisma, wisdom, and beauty— abolisher of a historically terrible Republican regime; symbol of a blood-soaked nation's racial progress. Just as the famous Che Guevara poster encapsulates rebellion, that stencil portrait of Obama in red, beige, and blue—the word "hope" laid out below—became a symbol of liberal promise and progressive values. (As it happens, designer Shepard Fairey has expressed his dissatisfaction with Obama, singling out the drone strikes for criticism.) As much as there is to lament about Obama's time in office, when I see that poster, I find myself back in 2008. It's like a mental bookmark back to an era when I believed a young, principled politician could operate in the current U.S. system and cure a nation's social ills—an idea that itself feels revolutionary. Jesse Jackson cried tears of joy as he awaited Obama's victory speech. That election night felt like an event worthy of echoing *The Simpsons'* Jasper Beardsley and his astonishment at the sight of a packaged moon pie: What a time to be alive. If only those positive feelings could be bottled and preserved for when we most needed them. Even the Panthers' aging co-founder was moved. "Electoral politics was always an objective of the Black Panther party, so Barack Obama is a part of what we dreamed and struggled and died for," said Bobby Seale, who once ran for mayor of Oakland as a Democrat himself.

In 2012, Jamal Joseph was asked if Obama's presidency had changed anything: "Things changed, in the sense that we have a Black president, and that people were able to rally together to make that happen. But when you have any leader who is presiding over a broken system, there is still a lot of work to be done. Yes, we have a Black president, but the system is still broken. People are struggling; things are hard each and every day.

"I still live in Harlem. It's interesting, because of the contrast of the co-ops and the condo buildings. We have more white neighbors. But when I walk through those streets and those projects—I have kids in my youth program who are homeless, or who are struggling to make ends meet, whose best meal of the day is the one that we given [*sic*] them at Impact [an arts program that he founded]. That reminds me of when I was a Panther, and the best meal of the day was for the kids we fed in the breakfast program. I don't feel this glorious change. The country is more polarized. You have a lot of Americans saying, we don't want him because he's Black. How far have we come really?"

While Obama's record is there to be scrutinized, what you can't deny is the *meaning of Obama*, and the conservative backlash to his symbolism that helped birth Trumpism, and, inversely, intensified the Black Lives Matter movement's pushback. You can spot Tupac's handprints all over the BLM era. *The Hate U Give*, a young-adult book by Angie Thomas, is inspired by the Black Lives Matter movement, but also, as the title suggests, by Tupac and his Thug Life mantra. The plot concerns a sixteen-year-old Black girl who witnesses the fatal shooting of her childhood best friend at the hands of a police officer. The book hit number one on the *New York Times* young adult best-seller list, where it remained for fifty weeks, and it was turned into an equally well-received movie the following year.

Tupac's influence is most palpable through one of his successors: Kendrick Lamar. In 2015, to mark the nineteenth anniversary of Tupac's death, the Compton rapper wrote an ode to his hero: "I was 8 yrs old when I first saw you. I couldn't describe how I felt at that moment. So many different emotions. Full of excitement. Full of joy and eagerness. 20 yrs later I understand exactly what that feeling was. INSPIRED. The people that you touched on that small intersection changed lives forever. I told myself I wanted to be a voice for man one day. Whoever knew I was speaking out loud for u to listen. Thank you."

Kendrick's admiration for Tupac was a core tenet of his 2015 album *To Pimp a Butterfly*, a capsule of American political turmoil during an intensification of activity among organizers of the Black Lives Matter movement, often recognized as one of the greatest rap LPs ever made. The conclusion of *To Pimp a Butterfly* depicts Kendrick speaking to Tupac himself, using the effect of dubbing newly recorded conversation over clips from an old Tupac interview. There's no doubting the voice as soon as you hear it. The accent, the intonation, are instantly recognizable, iconic. He has also said that its original title was *Tu Pimp a Caterpillar*, a backronym to honor his hero.

Kendrick's music had always featured a healthy dollop of references to Tupac. But by calling on Tupac's ghost, Lamar was seeking guidance—not just for himself, but for Black Lives Matter and the nation. *To Pimp a Butterfly* included the song "Alright," undeniably the defining anthem of BLM—a hymn of strength, unity, peace, and defiance—like "Changes," regularly heard chanted at protests. On the back of the album, Kendrick was heralded as a voice of his generation.

It's not surprising that Tupac's life, words, and music should be seen as relevant as blood was being spilled on the streets of Ferguson, Cleveland, New York, Minneapolis, Baton Rouge, and elsewhere. Police brutality had been the center of his music since his debut album—his commentary chillingly came to pass when he was violently arrested for jaywalking in 1991. There are songs such as "Point the Finga," where Tupac describes getting lynched by cops who invariably face no consequences. On "Hellrazor," a song about the degenerative cycle of chaos and violence that can consume a life, he speaks of cops who seek him as part of an investigation, because, he says, "I'm marked for death."

The Black Lives Matter movement echoes much of what Tupac

envisioned Thug Life to be about. It had been the greatest moment of pro-Black activism since the Black Panthers era. "They exist as a continual barometer to measure ourselves against—both in terms of lessons that have been garnered as well as challenges in terms of where we can improve or deepen our analysis," Aislinn Pulley, a co-founder of Black Lives Matter Chicago, said of the Panthers. And there was Tupac, the ideal midpoint between both movements.

In a report that harked right back to the days of COIN-TELPRO, leaked FBI documents indicated that "black identity extremists"—or those who "use force or violence in violation of criminal law in response to perceived racism and injustice in American society"—were among the agency's top counterterrorism priorities under President Donald Trump, even considered a bigger threat than terror groups such as Al Qaeda. Under a cryptic strategy titled "IRON FIST," the leaked documents suggest the bureau plans to use infiltration and other undercover techniques to "mitigate" threats posed by Black extremist groups, including exploiting the felony status of some members.

As U.S. foreign policy has come under scrutiny, Tupac's words again felt relevant. To Scott Pelley's question, "Are the wars in Israel and Ukraine more than the United States can take on at the same time?" President Joe Biden, in a 2023 interview, answered: "No. We're the United States of America for God's sake, the most powerful nation in the history—not in the world, in the history of the world. The history of the world. We can take care of both of these and still maintain our overall international defense."

It was impossible not to remember one of Tupac's most lasting lyrics: "They got money for wars but can't feed the poor."

5.

An obsessive studio loiterer, Tupac recorded more music than he knew what to do with, leaving behind a trove of unheard verses. For a decade after his death, this body of work was transmuted into new albums, some of them double discs, as though *All Eyez on Me* had set a standard length that had to be adhered to. The final 2Pac album, *Pac's Life*, was released in 2006. It sounds nothing like a 2Pac album. The production consists of sounds popular in the era it was released, not the era 2Pac was a part of, padded out with guest artists little more than children when he was alive. For every "Changes," there's a handful of cash-in cuts that are unmitigated disasters. The very fact that most of the verses were initially discarded indicates 2Pac's dissatisfaction with them.

There was, at first, an attempt to handle 2Pac's unreleased work with care. In the wake of his death, Carsten "Soulshock" Schack received a call from Afeni Shakur. With the shaky voice of someone still in deep mourning, she told the producer she was wrenching some of the unheard recordings away from Suge Knight's clutches. This old-hand activist's next fight was for her son's legacy.

The day after Tupac's death, Afeni returned to her home in Stone Mountain, Georgia, and began the painful process of sorting through her son's belongings. Among them, she made a curious discovery: the amateurish three-page handwritten contract presented to Tupac in prison by Suge Knight almost twelve months earlier. The document alarmed the former legal clerk. Worried that Tupac's business arrangement with Death Row had left him undercompensated, Afeni summoned a trusted confidant in New York, attorney Richard Fischbein, who flew out to Los Angeles to help her assert control over the situation. They'd soon realize that Tupac's platinum-selling popularity had yielded only a five-figure life insurance policy (the beneficiary was Sekyiwa), two cars, and a checking account that contained a little over $100,000. The star didn't even own his Woodland Hills home and had not left a will. Maneuvering quickly, Afeni filed court papers to establish herself as the administrator of his estate and the sole living heir.

Death Row maintained that it was Tupac's own spending that left him without assets, claiming it advanced large sums of cash to him to cover recording and video costs, plus more lavish expenses, such as cars and furniture. (Afeni herself was reportedly receiving living expenses of $16,000 a month from her son.) Both sides were now in direct conflict. In an early skirmish, Death Row reached a settlement with the Shakur estate in 1997 in which all 2Pac recordings in the label's possession were to be forfeited. Far from settling the issue of her son's unheard music, Afeni filed an injunction against Death Row a full decade later in an effort to prevent the label from auctioning off more unreleased recordings to pay a $100 million bankruptcy debt.

"Whatever it is I'm doing I do because my son was murdered, and he was not able to complete his work," Afeni said in an interview in support of the release of the 2003 documentary *Tupac: Resurrection*. "So as his mother, my whole job and responsibility is to see to it that that happens for him, and I do that with love."

Speaking to Soulshock over the phone that day, Afeni laid out her vision for the 2Pac verses in her possession: she only wanted collaborators who knew her son to be involved. There was a catch: the precious tapes would not be allowed out of her sight, meaning Soulshock would have to work on the spot and in her presence. Before meeting Afeni the next day, Soulshock tried to get a decent night's sleep.

Afeni showed up to the studio with the precious cargo and a security guard, as tall as six foot eight by Soulshock's estimates, to protect it. A friction developed between producer and giant when Soulshock attempted to explain the need to transfer the tapes to the ADAT format. But the tension evaporated when Soulshock hit play.

"All of a sudden, we hear Tupac. And I'm telling you, this was a really, really, really special emotional moment because I'm sitting and next to me is [Afeni]. We're looking up, literally up, towards heaven. And you got her son talking about, 'I wonder if heaven got a ghetto' . . . I mean, we just started crying."

The song became "I Wonder If Heaven Got a Ghetto." Soulshock and his production partner Karlin ended up creating two versions, both of which appeared on the 1997 album *R U Still Down? (Remember Me)*. The duo also crafted "Do 4 Love," one of the strongest of 2Pac's posthumous singles.

Soulshock & Karlin were called on once again by Afeni to work on *Still I Rise*, a 1999 album credited to 2Pac and the Outlawz.

Their contribution was "Baby Don't Cry (Keep Ya Head Up II)," a song presented as a sequel to one of 2Pac's best-loved songs. This time, Soulshock was dissatisfied with the results. The verse he worked from seemed unfinished, the concept of the song not yet fully realized in 2Pac's mind.

"'Heaven Got a Ghetto' and 'Do for Love,' they were finished vocals, you could hear it, he was present," explained Soulshock. "I mean, really present. It's almost like he was in the studio with us. But on 'Baby Don't Cry' and some of the other stuff they're sending us, there was like a small burst here and there, and we just felt now we were getting into that territory where you are milking it, you know? And I'm not in any way accusing Afeni of doing this, she was proud of her son's work, but we were not happy with 'Baby Don't Cry.'

"I remember after we did that, [Interscope executive] Tom Whalley said, 'There's more.' And I remember, specifically, me and Karlin saying, 'No, no, that's it, boss.' Yeah, I think we got asked to do one more, we actually said no."

6.

"Boots, let me ask you," said soap actor Eric Braeden with arms firmly crossed as he leaned back in his chair. "What have you got against capitalism?"

The scene was Bill Maher's ABC show *Politically Incorrect*, 2002, and opposite Braeden, Boots Riley, leader of rap group the Coup, was attempting to explain the message of his music. Riley was ostensibly there to promote the Coup's fourth album, *Party Music*. With extremely poor timing, the LP was due for release in September 2001 with artwork depicting Riley and his bandmate, Pam the Funkstress, blowing up the World Trade Center. When the towers fell for real, the album was postponed and the cover changed, but Riley was still willing to explain the meaning of the original artwork: it was a depiction of the Coup destroying capitalism.

This certainly jibed with the album's content. Over the slap-you-in-the-face funk of "Ghetto Manifesto," Riley slams landlords, encourages workers to take strike action, and urges listeners to burn an American flag. On "Ride the Fence," he declares himself a "proletarian funkadelic parliamentarian." There's even a song on there called "5 Million Ways to Kill a CEO."

Riley had faced pushback from Maher and the rest of the panel all night. As well as Braeden, there sat conservative activist Erin Shannon and comedian and *Dumb and Dumber* star Harland Williams (he played the cop in the traffic-stop scene). None of the four were on Boots's side when it came to the Enron scandal ("We don't really vote for politicians, we vote for corporate puppets," said Riley) or the Muslim woman who refused to take off her hijab for a driver's license photo ("Now we're getting all of these practices that are being enforced because of September 11 that don't have anything to do with the law"). Williams tried to get a laugh by pointing out that, *shock horror*, Riley had an Afro. But it was Boots's declaration that he was a communist that attracted the most ire.

All four attempted to drown Riley out as he explained his stance ("I think the people should control the profits that they create"), before Maher hastily cut to a commercial. The appearance serves as a microcosm for his music career: marginalized, drowned out, struggling to be heard. He eventually switched mediums and became a movie director. Riley's 2018 satirical dystopian film, *Sorry to Bother You*, is an extension of his music. It captures Riley's fears of free-market capitalism by depicting struggling workers who are forced to sign lifetime contracts with a large company in exchange for basic necessities.

Tupac Shakur is the most famous rapper to take influence from the Black Panthers and other socialist groups, but he's far from being alone. While capitalism's hold on hip-hop remains ironclad, overt socialist ideas are passed around the underground. Among those artists who have been unequivocal in their willingness to operate under a socialist flag since the 1990s are Paris, Immortal Technique, and Dead Prez. Their fan bases are large and loyal, but mainstream success has not been forthcoming.

Paris felt the sting of trying to release music with incendiary political content in 1992, when he recorded "Bush Killa," a protest song against George H. W. Bush's war against Iraq that repeats a decades-old message of righteous Black revolutionary politics: the enemy is not foreign, but domestic; liberation can't always be achieved through nonviolence. The track was due to appear on his second album, *Sleeping with the Enemy*. But the backlash unnerved Tommy Boy Records, then a Warner Bros. Records subsidiary, forcing Paris to eventually put the project out independently.

Married to the cause, Paris never veered from his principles. He declared his 2020 single "Nobody Move" as "The return of authentic hard truth spit / The Trump killa, Pence killa, Bush killa, cop killa," before calling for a new Red revolution: "Convince the proletariat to listen, envision / The uprise and the wise eyes open wide."

While overtly socialist hip-hop has remained rare in the mainstream, you will find plenty of leftist messages. Years before he asked Mark Zuckerberg to invest $1 billion in his ideas, Kanye West loaded his 2004 debut album, *The College Dropout*, with songs that mocked materialism and captured the woes of working in precarious retail employment. He later put out the single "Diamonds from Sierra Leone," which revealed some of the awkward truths about the precious stones rappers rock around their necks, including the deaths of workers in blood diamond mines. Genre stars such as Kendrick Lamar, Talib Kweli, and Earl Sweatshirt have infused their verses with anti-capitalist messages.

The lyric annotation website Genius has dubbed the Wu-Tang Clan's single "C.R.E.A.M." as "arguably one of the most iconic songs in hip-hop," but it's also one of the most misunderstood. In that regard it has much in common with Bruce Springsteen's "Born in the USA," which went from a bitter denunciation of America's treatment of Vietnam veterans to a flag-waving anthem when it was hijacked by prospective presidential candidates. "C.R.E.A.M." is remembered as an ode to moneymaking—a soundtrack for all hustlers, entrepreneurs, and nine-to-five workers to power their pursuit of the almighty "dollar dollar bill ya'll!" But a deeper listen to the lyrics shows the Clan were critiquing the desperate conditions capitalism had imposed on their neighborhoods. Even those famous five words aren't as celebratory when they're released from Method Man's catchy chorus: "Cash rules everything around me."

Isn't that a bad thing? As Mychal Denzel Smith wrote in a 2019 article for *Pitchfork*, "Chasing cash, by whatever means available, is the only option for survival, as it rules everything around us—but should it? Should a lack of money make one's life indistinguishable from prison?"

Rappers born after the Cold War, with no lived experience of the forced Evil Soviet Communism and Good American Capitalism moral binary, have shown an interest in a different type of society. "So when we start over y'all tryna do socialism or communism," posted Chance the Rapper in a tweet in 2020. The earnest, sweet-kid rapper became a genuine genre A-lister despite bucking industry convention by choosing independence over signing to a major label. Beyond the mainstream, Philadelphia rapper Ghais Guevara positioned himself as a clear successor to Paris by presenting as a revolutionary leftist; he even titled one of his albums *Black-Bolshevik*, while also naming both a collective he leads and their inaugural mixtape Free Breakfast for Children, an obvious homage to his Black Panther forebears.

Then there's Noname, the self-declared "socialist sister," who made a significant ideological shift to the left after receiving criticism for a defense she made of Black capitalism on social media in 2019. A fresh outlook saw Noname turn down the chance to record a song for the Fred Hampton biopic *Judas and the Black Messiah* as she felt the film failed to center the Panthers' "radical communist politics," talk openly with Boots Riley about how capitalism can be dismantled, and launch the Noname Book Club, a reading group that has selected openly leftish literature such as *Are Prisons Obsolete?* by Angela Davis, *The Wretched of the Earth* by the anti-colonial theorist Frantz Fanon, and Karl Marx and Friedrich Engels's *The Communist Manifesto*. With her music, Noname has spared nobody from criticism: the poor who defend billionaires, those who stay silent when it comes to violence toward transgender people, superstars Rihanna, Beyoncé, and Kendrick Lamar for performing at the Super Bowl—an event that serves, she says, as "propaganda for the military complex." In isolating herself from such powerhouse names and institutions, Noname's position is set: it's the message over the money.

7.

Black Panthers prefer the term "veterans" to "ex-Panthers" or its derivatives because they survived a war. Few groups are said to be more valued in a society than military vets, so much so that their well-being is a familiar political football that gets kicked around every election cycle. Funny, then, that the word "veterans" also conjures images of the broken, homeless, and drug-addicted— consequences of the ferocity of military service. Panthers felt a sense of duty as strong as any enlistee. For their trouble, many were left with cognitive scars that never healed.

By 2016, one Panther veteran was attempting to create her own floating Shangri-la. It was a world consisting of four house-boats in a pier community in Sausalito, a city in Marin County, an asylum for herself, family members, and friends, with geese, sea lions, and hummingbirds for additional company. Having married Gust Davis, a preacher known to prefix his name with the word "Prophet," twelve years earlier, she'd taken the name Afeni Shakur Davis, but became embroiled in an acrimonious divorce battle, just another skirmish in a life of struggle and fight. Still, a neighbor on the pier knew her as "a gentle soul who genuinely cared about everyone she came in contact with. She was quick to laugh and always had a kind word for everyone."

Living on the same dock as Afeni was one of her son's old col-laborators, Ray Luv, who'd never quite followed 2Pac to rap's high-est peaks, but was still motivated, still making music. Also close by was Sekyiwa and, soon, she and Ray began dating. Both Ray and Sekyiwa were with Afeni on May 2 when, having just returned from a work trip to North Carolina, she began to feel unwell. Con-cerned, Ray left the houseboat to buy some medicine. When he came back, he found that Afeni had collapsed. Ray administered CPR and waited for an ambulance. It was just after 9:30 p.m. when paramedics arrived and tried to resuscitate the patient. Afeni was transported to the Emergency Department at Marin General Hos-pital. She was pronounced dead soon after, aged sixty-nine. The cause of death was a heart attack.

A private memorial was held in Lumberton, her birthplace, a million journeyed miles away. Afeni had never lost sight of these roots. In 2002, she donated $15,000 to her former elementary school and organized a golf tournament to raise additional funds for a new playground and surrounding fence. New York's Panther veterans also held their own event to pay tribute. "She was ready for whatever," said Panther 21 member Dhoruba bin Wahad in requiem. "She had that effervescent spirit. When the guns were drawn, she was there."

Afeni's life had been a masterpiece of pulling back from the brink, from raising her head back above water just as the last of the air was exiting her lungs. As a young woman, activism had been an outlet for her sorrow and rage. The dream that Black liberation could be achieved one served children's breakfast at a time was taken from her by a country lacking the moral consciousness of the Civil Rights and Black Power movements. The setbacks of her youth wired Afeni for years of perpetual struggle—drug addiction, strained relations with her children, a lost sense of purpose. She didn't win every fight along the way, but never did she sink into the canvas.

She was only forty-nine years old when she lost her son, leaving her with grief that was matched solely by her sense of responsibility for his legacy. As well as dealing with the complexities of Tupac's estate, Afeni dedicated herself to guarding his memory. In addition to steering the release of his music, she founded the Tupac Amaru Shakur Foundation in 1997 to bring creative arts training and mental wellness support to young people. Afeni ran the foundation until 2014, before handing stewardship over to Sekyiwa. If Tupac's voice was missed during the Black Lives Matter movement, then let it be said that so was Afeni's.

It shouldn't be ignored that Afeni received some criticism for her handling of the estate. There were the shoddy albums released on her watch. Some felt she controlled Tupac's memory with too tight an iron fist. Wendy Day had hoped to honor her friend's wishes, but the plan was blocked by the woman with ultimate authority. "He told me in writing that if anything happened to him, he wanted a scholarship program in his name to send kids to drama school for acting," Day explained. "And when he passed away, I reached out to some of my friends in Hollywood that were in those circles and asked them if they would want to be on a board of a not for profit that would send kids to school as he had wished. And his mother had the attorney, Richard Fischbein, send me a cease-and-desist letter. I sent back a copy of the letter where Pac was asking me to do this, in his own handwriting, and they never responded. So, at that point, I backed off. Like, who wants to fight a mother over her dead son, you know?"

It's right and proper that we highlight these criticisms of Afeni, that we don't deny she made mistakes and had flaws, because they humanize a woman who has become a paradigm for strong (Black) motherhood, and to construct a paradigm you generally must flatten a life. That Tupac was raised by a warrior is core to every canonical telling of his story, and so Afeni is lionized by those who listen and learn from her son. But when you make a life three-dimensional, the coarse edges can be felt, and without acknowledging those edges, the depths of her strength can't properly be gauged.

I was struck by something the Irish singer Sinéad O'Connor once wrote. In her memoir, penned before the death of her son Shane, O'Connor discussed their relationship in a manner that perhaps encapsulates that of Afeni and Tupac. "I know it is said that children like Shane can be difficult and challenging. But it is actually easy for me, because I am an unusual kind of mother," O'Connor wrote. "Shane is not a square peg to be shoved into a round hole. He is the child who is most like me, I believe, to look at and by his nature."

Unlike O'Connor, Afeni will primarily be remembered through the lens of motherhood. She fought back the tides for the fetus within her to survive, and raised a son as a singular child destined for prominence, instilling in him the strength to endure even his own mother's descent. Everything in its right place for the creation of an icon. Yet remembering her solely through a famous child seems insufficient. Also crucial are Afeni's triumphs against her own enemies and demons, both external and within, that serve as a torchlight in the darkness, when we need to find our better selves.

2Pac performs at New York's Palladium, 1993.

EPILOGUE

WHEN LAS VEGAS POLICE arrested Duane Keith "Keffe D" Davis for the murder of Tupac Shakur in early 2024, it stuck a dagger into the heart of some of the various theories on the crime that had emerged over the years. These theories ranged from the cinematic—the belief that the Notorious B.I.G. met with the killers in Las Vegas on the night of the shooting and provided them with his own .40-caliber Glock pistol—to the collusive, involving shady government forces acting in their own interests to suppress an influential Black leader, using the preferred tactic of assassination. Proving or disproving the various hypotheses falls outside of this book's purview. Still, I do not blame anyone aware of the political history of the Shakur family for considering the possibility that Tupac's murder was provoked by more than a brawl in a hotel lobby.

Once you wade into the murky waters of shadowy government agencies and politically motivated assassinations, you cross the Rubicon into the world of conspiracy theories. False conspiracy theories—from Pizzagate to the racism-fueled allegations regarding President Barack Obama's birthplace—have, in recent years, become a recreation for those on the political right, distracting their believers from the very real societal problems that plague them. And so, the instinct—and duty—of leftists has been to push back, to fact-check, to correct the record. But it's crucial that in defending the status quo from the right, the left doesn't lose sight of the possibility, and probability, of clandestine chicanery from those in positions of authority. From COINTELPRO to Rampart,

I hope this book serves as a reminder to the left of the potential, even likelihood, of absolute power corrupting absolutely.

The ultimate conspiracy theory surrounding Tupac's death is that he is not, in fact, dead. Every now and then a grainy image snapped somewhere in the world appears online showing a figure purported to be him. My favorite hypothesis is that Tupac faked his death to join his fugitive godmother Assata Shakur in Cuba because it places Tupac in the righteous lineage to which he belongs. Picture him in the nation that proved a thorn in the side of many U.S. presidents, living quietly, bettering himself, perhaps waiting to someday return.

Would Tupac have stood with his leftist roots if he'd lived? It's hard to predict what the indignity of aging can do to any person— rappers are no different. There's an internet meme of Ice Cube that mocks his transition from gun-toting renegade to cuddly star of family movies; Snoop Dogg has become a figure embraced, beloved even, by mainstream America. So it's entirely possible that a middle-aged Tupac would have been softened, centrist, less serious. But I think it more probable that like many of his surviving Panther forebears who never lost sight of, or faith in, a better tomorrow, he would have continued to use his voice to stand with the masses, the downtrodden.

When speaking to ex-Panthers and other leftist activists from the same era for this book, I typically finished up by asking a variation of the question "Do you still have faith that the revolution is coming?" It would be understandable if their resolve had been shaken. All of them had experienced crushing repression at the hands of the establishment; as they grew old, they witnessed the rise of dangerous new reactionary politics in America in the form of Trumpism. There was the battering and decimation of Gaza—a heartbreaking topic many of them broached as we spoke—and the sense that humanity's moral philosophy had been desperately corrupted. Yet not a single one of the battle-scarred activists I asked had stopped believing that the revolution would arrive—or, at least, they wouldn't be seen to admit it.

"I have absolute faith because the struggle is a process," insisted Jamal Joseph. "I'm encouraged by the young people that I meet that want to fight that fight, that want to learn. They want to sit with veterans of the movement and ask, 'What was it like? What was it really about? And what can we learn from you in terms of what you did right? And most importantly, what you did wrong?'"

I wonder whether it is this hope in seemingly hopeless times that explains Tupac's enduring appeal. In death, his image has calcified into a symbol for people who tightly hold the spirit of rebellion, a tower of strength when all seems frail.

It might seem strange that many people's takeaway from Tupac's life has been a message of hope. He was born into the wrong side of American capitalism's wealth inequality, watching on as his elders struggled in the aftermath of the failed revolution. Tupac's life became a violent spiral, which eventually led to his demise. Pull back the lens and the Tupac story intersects across many of the ills of the American twentieth century. This is not a happy chronicle. But he was a man who hid very little of himself; he seemed to have little interest in cultivating an image, using interviews to deliver a stream-of-consciousness commentary on the state of the world, or showing his worst side by spitting at reporters. So if contemporary audiences look to the positives, it's perhaps because they have to. This has been necessary because the Panthers' vision has not yet been achieved.

Envisioning alternate history, such as a world where Tupac Shakur had lived, is a trait unique to human beings, an interesting mind game to play. But in the one reality we do find ourselves in, Tupac will never truly be laid to rest.

At the 2012 Coachella festival in California, Tupac appeared onstage next to Dr. Dre and Snoop Dogg as a hologram (technically, it wasn't a hologram, but rather a two-dimensional image projected down onto an angled piece of glass onstage, which in turn reflected onto a special screen). Though Afeni gave the project her blessing, it was poorly received by fans and cultural critics alike amid questions around the morality of puppeting the corpse of a dead artist. Talk of a full tour featuring the hologram did not proceed any further. Yet over a decade later, the development and proliferation of new artificial intelligence technology, a worrying threat to all arts, has led to creation of new music that replicates Tupac. In 2023, the technology was used to generate a 2Pac version of "Too Tight," a song he'd penned for MC Hammer. It's unsettling to hear a voice that sounds much like 2Pac spluttering out verses that are sloppy, confused, and just plain *off*. Even more perplexing was the use of AI to interview Tupac in 2024 about the ongoing war in Gaza. With the advent of such technology, we are increasingly hurtling toward a dystopian future where nobody is allowed to die.

What's clearly less corruptible is Tupac's icon, a natural phenomenon that has blossomed in the years since his death. Icons aren't easily destroyed; in fact, they extrapolate. History fades; symbols remain strong. Yet understanding history proves crucial because history always folds back on itself; it anticipates what is to come. It's a history of resistance in America that charges Tupac's icon, which will endure, even when hope seems depleted, seized by activists old and young who still have faith in upliftment, progress, and even revolution.

For those made of such steel, Tupac left a message tucked in the middle of his song "16 on Death Row," a tidy starting point for anyone who chooses to take up the old cause: "The trick is to never lose hope."

THE BLACK PANTHER PARTY
TEN-POINT PROGRAM

OCTOBER 15, 1966

1. *We Want Freedom. We Want Power to Determine the Destiny of Our Black Community.*

   We believe that Black people will not be free until we are able to determine our destiny.

2. *We Want Full Employment for Our People.*

   We believe that the federal government is responsible and obligated to give every man employment or a guaranteed income. We believe that if the White American businessmen will not give full employment, then the means of production should be taken from the businessmen and placed in the community so that the people of the community can organize and employ all of its people and give a high standard of living.

3. *We Want an End to the Robbery by the Capitalists of Our Black Community.*

   We believe that this racist government has robbed us, and now we are demanding the overdue debt of forty acres and two mules. Forty acres and two mules were promised 100 years ago as restitution for slave labor and mass murder of Black people. We will accept the payment in currency which will be distributed to our many communities. The Germans are now aiding the Jews in Israel for the genocide of the Jewish people. The

Germans murdered six million Jews. The American racist has taken part in the slaughter of over fifty million Black people; therefore, we feel that this is a modest demand that we make.

4. *We Want Decent Housing Fit for the Shelter of Human Beings.*

We believe that if the White Landlords will not give decent housing to our Black community, then the housing and the land should be made into cooperatives so that our community, with government aid, can build and make decent housing for its people.

5. *We Want Education for Our People That Exposes the True Nature of This Decadent American Society. We Want Education That Teaches Us Our True History and Our Role in the Present-Day Society.*

We believe in an educational system that will give to our people a knowledge of self. If a man does not have knowledge of himself and his position in society and the world then he has little chance to relate to anything else.

6. *We Want All Black Men to Be Exempt from Military Service.*

We believe that Black people should not be forced to fight in the military service to defend a racist government that does not protect us. We will not fight and kill other people of color in the world who, like Black people, are being victimized by the White racist government of America. We will protect ourselves from the force and violence of the racist police and the racist military by whatever means necessary.

7. *We Want an Immediate End to Police Brutality and the Murder of Black People.*

We believe we can end police brutality in our Black community by organizing Black self-defense groups that are dedicated to defending our Black community from racist police oppression and brutality. The Second Amendment to the Constitution of the United States gives a right to bear arms. We therefore believe that all Black people should arm themselves for self-defense.

8. *We Want Freedom for All Black Men Held in Federal, State, County and City Prisons and Jails.*

   We believe that all Black People should be released from the many jails and prisons because they have not received a fair and impartial trial.

9. *We Want All Black People When Brought to Trial to Be Tried in Court by a Jury of Their Peer Group or People from Their Black Communities, as Defined by the Constitution of the United States.*

   We believe that the courts should follow the United States Constitution so that Black people will receive fair trials. The Fourteenth Amendment of the U.S. Constitution gives a man a right to be tried by his peer group. A peer is a person from a similar economic, social, religious, geographical, environmental, historical, and racial background. To do this the court will be forced to select a jury from the Black community from which the Black defendant came. We have been, and we are being, tried by all-White juries that have no understanding of the "average reasoning man" of the Black community.

10. *We Want Land, Bread, Housing, Education, Clothing, Justice and Peace.*

   When, in the course of human events, it becomes necessary for one people to dissolve the political bands which have connected them with another, and to assume, among the powers of the earth, the separate and equal station to which the laws of nature and nature's God entitle them, a decent respect of the opinions of mankind requires that they should declare the causes which impel them to the separation.

   We hold these truths to be self-evident, that all men are created equal; that they are endowed by their Creator with certain inalienable rights; that among these are life, liberty, and the pursuit of happiness. That, to secure these rights, governments are instituted among men, deriving their just powers from the consent of the governed; that, whenever any form of government becomes destructive of these ends, it is the right of the people to alter or abolish it, and to institute a new government, laying its foundation on such principles, and organizing its powers in such form, as to them shall seem most likely to effect their safety and happiness. Prudence, indeed, will dictate that governments long established should not be changed for light and transient causes; and, accordingly, all experience hath shown that mankind are more disposed to suffer, while evils are sufferable, than to right themselves by abolishing the forms to which they are accustomed. But, when a long train of abuses and usurpations, pursing invariably the same object, evinces a design to reduce them under absolute despotism, it is their right, it is their duty, to throw off such government, and to provide new guards for their future security.

APPENDIX II

THE CODE OF THUG LIFE

INTRODUCTION

Someone must dare put the street life back on track, because it is clear to anybody that can see—that the hustling game has gone stark raving mad.

The short and long range result, will not only be detrimental to the street game, but more importantly, the combination of the self destruction & turf warfare, coupled with the government's police terrorism, fascist laws designed to capture and keep our Black men and women in prison for the rest of their lives, leaves a defenseless Black community—which will result in our genocide.

For as long as the street game/hustle has existed in our community, which is the result of many factors (and will only be resolved through our liberation), it has been viewed as a necessary tolerance between the legal and illegal economy and culture.

The underground economy has, in many areas, been supportive of the uplifting of the Black community. Although, for a fact, it has been the downfall of individuals, the dynamics of struggle between the do-gooders and the thugs has kept a consistent battle for balance in The Black Community which at least was under our control.

The rules of engagement of the hustle was a code of the thug life. This code was the A, B, C's of how the street game should and would be played. These rules allowed for money to be made by the crews in the different fields of the game, and determined how disputes between and among the players should be handled.

It also allowed the people who were not in the game to pressure the enemy of our people, and allowed the people who would work in the interest of our people (education, health, housing, legal, etc.) to feel that the effort was worth it.

The game today, as it exists, is a complete violation of the code. Historically, the street hustler was hip to the enemy and would never work in the government's interest to destroy their own people.

The thug life is a tool of the enemy as it exists today; it must change. The interests of outside forces are being served by the hustlers, because the crew has no dignity or honor—and this must be corrected. A council must be called to put a code to the thug life.

We accept that the game will go on until our liberation. What we won't accept is that the game will destroy us from within before we get another chance to rumble and rebuild. We will not allow ourselves to be played by the covert operations, COINTELPRO, and low intensity warfare waged by the United States government.

A code must be established. As we look at the West coast, the majority of the life is controlled by gangs (Latin/Chican and of the Black community as well). The gangs are the force behind the underground economy in our hoods.

In the mid-East, the common denominator there is also the gangs, which are responsible for the street life. Politically, culturally, and economically, these forces attempt to put the game back on track and work in the interests of the community and to resist the strategy of the government. They have begun setting down a platform for the street game in full effect—we praise this effort.

The code of the thug life must become a part of East coast street life as well. There must be a common denominator.

The original gangsters behind the walls of the dungeon will take some responsibility to putting force to the council and the code.

We must act now. The Code of the Thug Life will save us to fight another day. If we don't, then we will lose . . .

While other forces attempt to bring peace and unity to the gangs and crews of the street life . . . Although we re [*sic*] down with that, and shout out to those attempts, we have always tried to be real with the people. Some folks may oppose what we say and do.

What we're putting out here is a code to the true dwellers in the thug life. We don't see this as an end of the game, or the street game as a real end. What we need is liberation. But what we do see is the bringing of some honor to being true to the life—and being real to our family which is a giant step to being down with the true thug life.

CODE OF THUG LIFE

1. All new Jacks to the game must know: a) He's going to get rich. b) He's going to jail. c) He's going to die.
2. Crew Leaders: You are responsible for legal/ financial payment commitments to crew members; your word must be your bond.
3. One crew's rat is every crew's rat. Rats are now like a disease; sooner or later we all get it; and they should too.
4. Crew leader and posse should select a diplomat, and should work ways to settle disputes. In unity, there is strength!
5. Car jacking in our Hood is against the Code.
6. Slinging to children is against the Code.
7. Having children slinging is against the Code.
8. No slinging in schools.
9. Since the rat Nicky Barnes opened his mouth, ratting has become accepted by some. We're not having it.
10. Snitches is outta here.
11. The Boys in Blue don't run nothing; we do. Control the Hood, and make it safe for squares.
12. No slinging to pregnant Sisters. That's baby killing; that's genocide!

13. Know your target, who's the real enemy.
14. Civilians are not a target and should be spared.
15. Harm to children will not be forgiven.
16. Attacking someone's home where their family is known to reside must be altered or checked.
17. Senseless brutality and rape must stop.
18. Our old folks must not be abused.
19. Respect our Sisters. Respect our Brothers.
20. Sisters in the Life must be respected if they respect themselves.
21. Military disputes concerning business areas within the community must be handled professionally and not on the block.
22. No shooting at parties.
23. Concerts and parties are neutral territories; no shooting!
24. Know the Code; it's for everyone.
25. Be a real ruff neck. Be down with the code of the Thug Life.
26. Protect yourself at all times.

ACKNOWLEDGMENTS

My foremost thanks go to those who helped convince me that this was a Tupac Shakur story I had to tell. *Words for My Comrades* is, at its core, an attempt to chart Tupac's status as a global icon and, invariably, much gets written and said about global icons. As I worked on the book, different projects across different mediums were released and more are sure to come. And so the question was always pertinent: Why this story? And why me?

Ultimately, I was motivated to discover the cause and meaning of Tupac's iconic status. Too often the analysis of his revolutionary roots has amounted to no more than "Tupac was of Black Panther parentage, ergo, he had the spirit of the Panthers." I had to show the audience what that exactly meant, who the Panthers were, and how that spirit manifested in him. And in telling the story of hip-hop's greatest radical, I found there was also an opportunity to present the story of hip-hop from a radical perspective.

Crucial to keeping me going through the process was my editor Thomas Gebremedhin, who helped me develop the idea and, from that kernel, showed me unwavering support in its realization. Same goes for Johanna Zwirner and everyone else at Doubleday, Lee Brackstone and his team at White Rabbit, my phenomenal agent Chris Clemans, and copy editor Amy Ryan. Writing is said to be a lonely practice. I didn't realize that was true until I discovered what it's like to have a team behind you.

My thanks to Aoife Barry, Amy Bond, Barry Kenna, Carlo Magliocco, Una Mullally, Mark O'Connell, Sinead O'Shea, Daragh

Soden, Mats Utas, and Jeff Weiss for their amazing help. Thanks to my family, Amy's family, and to everyone else who, directly or indirectly, kept me going: the Triumvirate, the Dublin Dinner Club, the Griffith College Cool Kids, the Liverpool Football Club WhatsApp group chat, Alyson Gray, and the rest.

Finally, I have a special gratitude for everyone who agreed to speak to me as part of my research, particularly those who said some variation of "I'm not sure I should be telling you this." It seems to me that many activists of the 1960s and '70s have grown more comfortable with the idea that they're probably not going to get in trouble with the law for revealing certain secrets, and their honesty helped me pursue a more unvarnished version of the truth, but one, I believe, that should only enhance their standing in the eyes of younger activists. My respect and admiration go out to all of America's leftist radicals who never stopped fighting, who never stopped believing.

NOTES

PROLOGUE

3 The text on his original: The most widely accepted story of Tupac's birth certificate is that it originally read "Lesane Parish Crooks" before being amended to Tupac Amuru Shakur—indeed, images of the document bearing the latter are well circulated. However, Afeni Shakur's comrade Jamal Joseph believes she had both documents issued simultaneously upon her son's birth.

3 Amaru II was executed: Miguel La Serna, "'I Will Return and I Will Be Millions!' The Many Lives of Túpac Amaru," *Age of Revolutions*, November 2, 2020.

3 "I wanted him to have": Tashan Reid, "Afeni Shakur Took on the State and Won," *Jacobin*, no. 43, Fall 2021.

4 the rapper's five-foot-nine-inch: Dimensions.com, a website in the business of measuring people and objects, lists Tupac as five feet nine inches tall. However, his California driver's license recorded him as five-foot-ten, while a prison ID claims five-foot-eleven.

4 Throughout this book: This approach was also used in Jeff Weiss and Evan McGarvey, *2Pac vs. Biggie: An Illustrated History of Rap's Greatest Battle*, Voyageur Press, 2013, and has been replicated with Jeff's blessing.

4 "If we had lost Oprah": Tony McKenna, "Tupac Shakur: Radical Poet," *The New Statesman*, September 13, 2012.

4 had to battle authorities: Vanessa Satten, "Afeni Shakur, Survivor," *XXL*, October 2003.

5 Tupac's godparents: Though they're often referred to as Tupac's godfather and godmother, it's unlikely that either Geronimo Pratt or Assata Shakur took part in a ceremony, religious or otherwise, to seal the position. They've also at different times been referred to as his step-uncle and step-aunt.

5 "In my family": Connie Bruck, "The Takedown of Tupac," *The New Yorker*, June 29, 1997.

5 "It was like their words": Ibid.

6 Following the Siege of Sarajevo: Vildana Muratovic, "Tupac in Sarajevo: The Rise of Rebellion Rap in Eastern Europe," *BlackPast*, October 3, 2008. This article was originally written as a paper in 2007.

6 "What makes me saying": Jesse Gissen, "Tupac's Most Memorable Quotes," *XXL*, September 9, 2011.

7 "When I heard Tupac sing": Sunaina Maria, "We Ain't Missing: Palestinian Hip Hop—A Transnational Youth Movement," *CR: The New Centennial Review*, vol. 8, no. 2, 2008, p. 167.

7 "no way Michael Jackson should have": MTV News, "Tupac Talks Donald Trump & Greed in America in 1992 Interview," youtube.com /watch?v=GL-ZoNhUFmc, posted April 19, 2016.

9 "I will live by the gun": Though it's attributed to Tupac on internet quotation websites and graffiti art, it's unclear to me whether Tupac actually said this. For certain, his collaborator Snoop Doggy Dogg, on their joint single "2 of Amerikaz Most Wanted," uttered the words "You see, we live by the gun, so we die by the guns, kid."

9 "The lads would have been": Author interview with Blindboy Boatclub, January 19, 2022.

10 Frederick Douglass fled to Ireland: James Brosnahan and Dan VanDeMortel, "Frederick Douglass Travels 'Home' to Ireland," *Irish Echo*, February 10, 2021.

10 "I have heard many speakers": Frederick Douglass [Letter], Dublin (Great Brunswick Street), September 29, 1845. To William Lloyd Garrison. Foner, Philip (ed), *Life and Writings of Frederick Douglass*, International Publishers, 1950, vol. I, p. 120.

10 "Everyone was very radicalized": Author interview with Tim Brannigan, March 24, 2023.

11 "To all these people": "Irish Give Key to City to Panthers as Symbol," *The New York Times*, March 3, 1970.

11 Devlin befriended Angela Davis: Róisín Spealáin, "When Angela Davis Met Bernadette Devlin: Ireland's fight for Abolition," plutobooks.com.

11 "Róisín must be freed": Ibid.

12 Terence MacSwiney died: For more on MacSwiney, see *74 Days: The Hunger Strike of Terence McSwiney*, director Ciara Hyland, 2020.

12 Garvey even sent telegrams: Brian Dooley, "Black and Green Civil Rights—USA and Ireland," *An Phoblacht*, August 20, 1998.

12 "convey to McSwiney": Dave Hannigan, "Terence MacSwiney and the hunger strike that made world headlines," *The Irish Times*, June 2, 2020.

12 "The time has come": Ray Bassett, "Marcus Garvey and 1916," *An Phoblacht*, December 1, 2016.

14 "I really started to see": Author interview with Jordan Fripp, April 21, 2023.

14 "I don't think you'll see their pictures": *Chris Rock: Bigger and Blacker*, director Keith Truesdall, 1999.

CHAPTER ONE: OF JIM CROW SOIL

18 "the legacy moms": Paul Grein, "Producers Who Arranged the Meeting of 2Pac and B.I.G.'s Mothers at the '99 VMAs Recall the Emotional Moment," *Billboard*, April 9, 2019.

19 Rosa Belle brushed up against death: Dequi Kioni-Sadiki and Matt Meyer, eds., *Look for Me in the Whirlwind: From the Panther 21 to 21st Century Revolutions*, PM Press, 2017, p. 182. The original edition of this book was published in 1971 by Vintage Books with the subtitle *The Collective Autobiography of the Panther 21*.

19 slaves to sharecroppers: Michael Eaton, "A Lovely Day (At Last)," *Risen*, Jan./Feb. 2005; Rob Kenner, "You Are Appreciated: Remembering Afeni Shakur," *Complex*, May 9, 2016.

20 Almost 125,000 North Carolinians: David C. Williard, "North Carolina in the Civil War," NCPedia, 2010; "North Carolina in the Civil War," historic sites.nc.gov.

20 Millie Ann married a white man named Powell: Tayannah Lee McQuillar and Fred L. Johnson III, Ph.D., *Tupac Shakur: The Life and Times of an American Icon*, Da Capo Press, 2010, p. 7. Afeni at times claimed Powell was half white, half Lumbee Indian. In conversation with Jasmine Guy for *Afeni Shakur: Evolution of a Revolutionary* (Atria Books, 2004), Afeni admitted she'd been mistaken, and he was "just a white dude," suggesting that this former Black Panther was at one time moved to dilute her Caucasian blood down as thinly as possible. "It's taken me a long time to deal with the fact that my great-grandmother married a white man," she chuckled.

20 Powell's family disowned him: McQuillar and Johnson, *Tupac Shakur: The Life and Times of an American Icon*, p. 7; Kioni-Sadiki and Meyer, eds., *Look for Me in the Whirlwind*, p. 217.

20 She would walk the dirt roads: Guy, *Afeni Shakur*, p. 40.

20 Millie Ann was one: Ibid., p. 7.

20 She had memories: Kioni-Sadiki and Meyer, eds., *Look for Me in the Whirlwind*, p. 217.

21 "There wasn't anything": Ibid., p. 182.

21 Lumberton became the scene of a conflict: This account of the Lumbee Indians' clashes with the Ku Klux Klan is mostly drawn from Karen I. Blu, *The Lumbee Problem: The Making of an American Indian People*, Cambridge University Press, 1980, pp. 88–89; Adolph L. Dial and David K. Eliades, *The Only Land I Know*, The Indian Historical Press, 1975, pp. 159–162; Malinda Maynor Lowery, "During Civil Rights Era, Native American Communities in the South Armed Themselves Against the Clan," *Scalawag*, January 20, 2020; "Battle of Hayes Pond: The Day Lumbees Ran the Klan out of North Carolina," *Black Then*, August 23, 2022.

21 "There was a lot of camaraderie": Author interview with Chairman John Lowery, September 6, 2022.

22 she would regale: McQuillar and Johnson, *Tupac Shakur: The Life and Times of an American Icon*, pp. 8–9.

22 "There was no real bloodshed": Author interview with Chairman John Lowery, September 6, 2022.

22 the very sad "Kissing Case": For more on the Kissing Case, see Timothy B. Tison, *Radio Free Dixie: Robert F. Williams & the Roots of Black Power,* The University of California Press, 1999.

23 "If the 14th Amendment": Felicia R. Lee, "Outspoken and Feared but Largely Forgotten," *The New York Times,* February 7, 2006.

23 Catholic boys club organized: "The Rolling Snowball," *Time,* February 9, 1959.

23 "We must be willing": Tyson, *Radio Free Dixie.*

23 Her father, a trucker: Peter Castro, "All Eyes on Her," *People,* December 1, 1997.

23 With her husband an unreliable provider: Guy, *Afeni Shakur,* pp. 16–18.

23 a diminutive preacher: Ibid., pp. 22–24.

23 "the tragedy of our family": Taken from the description section of J. Kimo Williams, "Tupac Shakur: My Family Tree Tragedy (A String Quartet)," youtube.com/watch?v=nuWv4uzK9-4, posted July 10, 2023.

24 when Walter Sr. spoke: Ibid.

24 "like fifteen children": Guy, *Afeni Shakur,* p. 22.

24 Walter Sr. had hoped: Ibid., p. 24.

24 "That was my dad's": Ibid.

24 She called her brother: Reid, "Afeni Shakur Took on the State and Won."

24 Alice was eleven years old: Guy, *Afeni Shakur,* pp. 30–32. Speaking to Guy, Afeni said she arrived in New York in 1958, aged eleven. This is reaffirmed by her sister Gloria Jean in the documentary series *Dear Mama: The Saga of Afeni and Tupac Shakur,* director Allen Hughes, 2023, though Staci Robinson's *Tupac Shakur: The Authorized Biography,* Crown, 2023, claims it was 1959.

24 While Gloria Jean found: *Dear Mama,* director Allen Hughes.

24 The smell of the city: Kioni-Sadiki and Meyer, eds., *Look for Me in the Whirlwind,* pp. 230–31.

24 On a salary of about forty dollars: Ibid., p. 231.

25 "Every time somebody": Ibid., p. 230.

25 "Because I was just ferocious": Ibid., p. 271.

25 Alice later attended: Rudy Johnson, "Joan Bird and Afeni Shakur, Self-Styled Soldiers in the Panther 'Class Struggle,'" *The New York Times,* July 19, 1970.

25 she wrote for the school newspaper: Ibid.

25 "seemed to be yearning": Ibid.

25 She was initially drawn: Kioni-Sadiki and Meyer, eds., *Look for Me in the Whirlwind,* p. 294.

26 Alice struck up a young romance: Guy, *Afeni Shakur,* pp. 45–47.

26 Glynn slapped her during an argument: Ibid.

26 "I bet you won't slap me again": Ibid.

26 Alice stormed PA: Ibid.

26 getting drunk: Kioni-Sadiki and Meyer, eds., *Look for Me in the Whirlwind,* p. 294.

26 She failed all but one subject: Johnson, "Joan Bird and Afeni Shakur."

26 "I couldn't relate to that": Ibid.

26 running with the Disciples: Kioni-Sadiki and Meyer, eds., *Look for Me in the Whirlwind*, p. 296.

27 "We were killing": Ibid., p. 308.

27 a boyfriend named Ray: Guy, *Afeni Shakur*, pp. 55–56.

27 His name was Omar: Kioni-Sadiki and Meyer, eds., *Look for Me in the Whirlwind*, p. 405. In Guy, *Afeni Shakur*, Afeni calls him Shaheem. His true name is unclear.

27 "Black is the best": Kioni-Sadiki and Meyer, eds., *Look for Me in the Whirlwind*, p. 406.

28 "This dude was": Ibid.

28 It begins with W. D. Fard: For a crucial early text on the founding of the Nation of Islam, see Erdmann Diane Beynon, "The Voodoo Cult Among Negro Migrants in Detroit," *American Journal of Sociology*, vol. 46, no. 6, May 1938, pp. 894–907. See also C. Eric Lincoln, *The Black Muslims in America*, Beacon Press, 1961; Michael Knight Muhammad, "Remembering Master Fard Muhammad," *Vice*, February 16, 2013.

29 Most tellings of the: The story of Malcolm X is well chronicled in, among other titles, Malcolm X with Alex Haley, *The Autobiography of Malcolm X*, Grove Street, 1965; Manning Marable, *Malcolm X: A Life of Reinvention*, Allen Lane, 2011; Les Payne and Tamara Payne, *The Dead Are Arising: The Life of Malcolm X*, Liveright, 2020.

31 in 2021, Aziz and Islam: John Leland, "Exonerations Only Deepen Mystery Shrouding Malcolm X's Killing," *The New York Times*, November 18, 2021.

31 "I wasn't doing anything": Kioni-Sadiki and Meyer, eds., *Look for Me in the Whirlwind*, pp. 406–7.

31 "They just removed one tube": Kioni-Sadiki and Meyer, eds., *Look for Me in the Whirlwind*, pp. 252–53.

31 "They wouldn't put the baby": Ibid., p. 252.

32 "I was really fucked": Ibid., p. 254.

32 She took a postal job: Johnson, "Joan Bird and Afeni Shakur."

32 "that kind of work": Ibid.

32 walked down 125th Street: Kioni-Sadiki and Meyer, eds., *Look for Me in the Whirlwind*, pp. 455–56; Guy, *Afeni Shakur*, pp. 59–61. A July 1970 *New York Times* report on Afeni and her comrade Joan Bird recounted Afeni seeing Bobby Seale speak "early in 1968." However, in the book *Look for Me in the Whirlwind*, she is quoted as saying it was "early in 1967."

CHAPTER TWO: SELF-DEFENSE

35 Fury filled: This account of Bobby Seale's reaction to the killing of Malcolm X is mostly drawn from Bobby Seale, *Seize the Time*, Random House, 1970, p. 3; Bobby Seale, *A Lonely Rage*, Times Books, 1978, pp. 133–36.

35 "cultural nationalists": Seale, *Seize the Time*, p. 119.

36 The couple would regularly separate: Nadra Kareem Nittle, "Biography of Bobby Seale," ThoughtCo, February 5, 2019.

36 Formal education: Seale, *Seize the Time*, pp. 7–12.

37 at a protest at Merritt: Seale, *Seize the Time*, p. 13; "#blackhistory: On Octo-

ber 15, 1966, Bobby Seale and Huey P. Newton form the Black Panther Party in Oakland, California," California African American Museum, October 15, 2019.

37 Seale decided to test him: Seale, *Seize the Time*, pp. 13–14.

38 a child of Monroe: Dennis Hevesi, "Huey Newton Symbolized the Rising Black Anger of a Generation," *The New York Times*, August 23, 1989.

38 job opportunities were plentiful: Robert McNamara, "Biography of Huey Newton, Co-Founder of the Black Panthers," ThoughtCo, January 28, 2019.

38 "I read it through about five times": Hevesi, "Huey Newton Symbolized the Rising Black Anger of a Generation." Melvin Newton denied his brother Huey graduated high school without knowing how to read. See Hugh Pearson, *The Shadow of the Panther: Huey Newton and the Price of Black Power in America*, Addison-Wesley Publishing Company, 1994, p. 46.

39 North Oakland Neighborhood Anti-Poverty Center: Seale, *Seize the Time*, p. 35; Alondra Nelson, *Body and Soul: The Black Panther Party and the Fight Against Medical Discrimination*, University of Minnesota Press, 2013.

39 When he burst into one: Seale, *Seize the Time*, p. 24.

39 Their revolutionary principles and experience: "On October 15, 1966, Bobby Seale and Huey P. Newton form the Black Panther Party in Oakland, California."

39 The pyre was lit: This account of the killing of Matthew Johnson is drawn from "Hunters Points—Cops Shot Into Community Center Sheltering 200 Children," *The Movement*, vol. 2, no. 9, October 1966; Walter Thompson, "The Fire Last Time," *San Francisco*, August 18, 2016; Gary Kamiya, "Officer's '66 killing of black teen sparked Hunters Point riots," *San Francisco Chronicle*, September 16, 2016.

40 Residents demanded a meeting: Frank Rich, "Why Do America's Race Riots Mirror Each Other," *New York*, May 17, 2015.

40 Police coordinated with local volunteer group: Will Mack, "Hunter's Point, San Francisco Uprising (1966)," *BlackPast*, December 19, 2017.

40 Their roles were set by chance: "The Black Panthers," *Lords of the Revolution*, season 1, episode 3, VH1 Productions, 2009.

40 The Panthers downplayed: Donna Murch, *Living for the City: Migration, Education, and the Rise of the Black Panther Party in Oakland, California*, UNC Press, 2010.

40 The first weaponry: Michael Newton, *Bitter Grain: Huey Newton and the Black Panther Party*, Holloway House Publishing Company, 1980, p. 16.

41 Funds for the nascent Panthers: Newton, *Bitter Grain*, p. 17.

41 "a righteous revolutionary front": Chuck McFadden, "Armed Black Panthers in the Capitol, 50 Years On," *Capitol Weekly*, April 26, 2017.

41 they were in synchronicity: Manning Marable, *Malcolm X: A Life of Reinvention*, Allen Lane, 2011, p. 203.

42 Malcolm had often reflected: Ibid., p. 421.

42 when Newton was asked: Lynn Burnett, "The White Panther Party," Cross Cultural Solidarity, crossculturalsolidarity.com.

42 "We thought the Black Panther Party": Author interview with John Sinclair, July 24, 2023.

42   "I have had enough of religion": Huey Newton, *Revolutionary Suicide*, Harcourt Brace Jovanovich, 1973 (1995 edition, published by Writers and Readers), p. 71.

43   "a human rights document": Author interview with Clayborne Carson, August 2, 2022.

43   marched on the California Capitol: Chuck McFadden, "Armed Black Panthers in the Capitol, 50 Years On," *Capitol Weekly*, April 26, 2017; *The Black Panthers: Vanguard of the Revolution*, director Stanley Nelson, 2015.

44   its selection an intended homage: Author interview with Aaron Dixon, March 10, 2023.

44   "We had our leather jackets on": Ibid.

44   "Somebody told me": *Look for Me in the Whirlwind*, pp. 456–57.

44   In the small hours of October 28, 1967: This account of the killing of John Frey and subsequent trial is mostly drawn from *People v. Newton*, Crim. No. 7753, Court of Appeals of California, First Appellate District, Division Four, May 29, 1970; Newton, *Bitter Grain*; *American Justice on Trial: People v. Newton*, directors Andrew Abrahams and Herb Ferrette; Wallace Turner, "Newton Is Guilty of Manslaughter," *The New York Times*, September 9, 1968; and FBI files.

44   a bully and racist: FBI files, "Trial of Huey Percy Newton, Minister of Defense, Black Panther Party, Oakland, California," August 26, 1968.

46   borrowing a psychedelically painted: David Hilliard and Lewis Cole, *The Side of Glory: The Autobiography of David Hilliard and The Story of the Black Panther Party*, Little, Brown and Company, 1993, p. 3.

46   to save Newton from the death penalty: Paul Alkebulan, *Survival Pending Revolution: The History of the Black Panther Party*, The University of Alabama Press, 2007, p. 6.

47   earned Cleaver reverence: Frank Gunn, "Notes from Underground," *Bookforum*, Summer 2018.

47   Fresh out of jail: Newton, *Bitter Grain*, pp. 23–27.

47   "Nonviolence has died with King": Hilliard and Cole, *This Side of Glory*, p. 182.

48   "went after the cops that night": Lynn Scott and Bill Kauffman, "Reason Interview: Eldridge Cleaver," *Reason*, February 1986.

48   Hilliard, also present: Hilliard, *The Autobiography of David Hilliard and the Story of the Black Panther Party*, pp. 187–92.

48   "I'm not going to let": "Cleaver of Black Panthers is Nominee of Leftists," *The New York Times*, August 19, 1968.

48   "If Eldridge Cleaver is allowed": John Kifner, "Eldridge Cleaver, Black Panther Who Became G.O.P. Conservative, Is Dead at 62," *The New York Times*, May 2, 1998.

49   Eldridge jumped bail: For more on Eldridge Cleaver's time in Cuba and Algeria, see John A. Oliver, *Eldridge Cleaver: Reborn*, Logos International, 1977; Brendan I. Koerner, *The Skies Belong to Us: Love and Terror in the Golden Age of Hijacking*, Broadway Books, 2013.

49   Its home became: Clyde H. Farnsworth, "Black Panthers Open Office in Algeria," *The New York Times*, September 14, 1970.

49 "When I heard him": *Look for Me in the Whirlwind*, pp. 457–58.

50 Cleaver encouraged: Ibid., p. 457.

50 "All of a sudden": Ibid., p. 458.

50 "350,000 considered themselves": Bryan Burrough, *Days of Rage: America's Radical Underground, the FBI, and the Forgotten Age of Revolutionary Violence*, Penguin Press, 2015, p. 61.

51 Cleaver had even hoped: Ibid., p. 184.

51 Sam Melville, connected to eight New York bombings: Burrough, *Days of Rage*, pp. 9–25. Melville was later killed in the Attica prison riots of 1971.

51 "The very first question": Karin Asbley, Bill Ayers, Bernardine Dohrn, John Jacobs, Jeff Jones, Gerry Long, Home Machtinger, Jim Mellen, Terry Robbins, Mark Rudd, and Steve Tappis, "You Don't Need a Weatherman to Know Which Way the Wind Blows," *New Left Notes*, June 18, 1969.

51 "We believe that the Weathermen's action": Vintage & Iconic African American Everything, "Fred Hampton Interviewed by ABC News October 9th 1969," youtube.com/watch?v=Lu2YvfPW91E, posted February 17, 2021.

52 "The Days of Rage symbolized": "Days of Rage Now More Like a Convulsion That Became Blip in History," *Chicago Tribune*, January 8, 1994.

52 "In our hearts": Burrough, *Days of Rage*.

52 "One of the things we felt": Author interview with Bill Ayers, October 25, 2022.

52 dynamite exploded outside: Christopher Zerozek, "The Bombing of the A2 CIA Office," *The Michigan Daily*, October 24, 2006.

53 "Our people did the bombing": Author interview with John Sinclair, July 24, 2023.

53 Panther-operated health-care clinics: "The Black Panther Party Stands for Health," Columbia Mailman School of Public Health, publichealth .columbia.edu, February 23, 2016.

53 The New York Panthers had guns: Jamal Joseph, *Panther Baby: A Life of Rebellion and Reinvention*, Algonquin Books, 2012, p. 62.

54 Core to being a rank-and-file Panther: Alkebulan, *Survival Pending Revolution*, pp. 38–40; Assata Shakur, *Assata: An Autobiography*, Lawrence Hill Books, 1988.

54 Panthers would show up at housing projects: Author interview with Charles Pinderhughes, October 11, 2023.

54 Afeni quickly became: Desire Thompson, "The Black Panther Party Releases Statement on Afeni Shakur's Passing," *Vibe*, May 5, 2016.

54 "strong Black sister": Author interview with Bill Jennings, February 10, 2023.

54 The first breakfast: Alkebulan, *Survival Pending Revolution*, pp. 29–33.

55 Dinner for the whole house: Joseph, *Panther Baby*, pp. 129–30.

55 "We recognized": Huey P. Newton, *To Die for the People: The Writings of Huey P. Newton*, Random House, 1972, p. 104.

55 "Because the people weren't ready": Author interview with Aaron Dixon, March 10, 2023.

56 "Those programs would have helped": Guy, *Afeni Shakur*, pp. 63–64.

56 Afeni first laid eyes: Ibid., pp. 76–78.

56 Odinga and Lumumba went way back: Burrough, *Days of Rage*, p. 179.

57 In the late 1950s: Guy, *Afeni Shakur*, pp. 73–74.

57 "The penitentiary": Joseph, *Panther Baby*, p. 110.

57 Little did Anthony know: Burrough, *Days of Rage*, p. 180.

57 "Malcolm X is a very beautiful brother": Ibid.

57 "I went in search of Malcolm": Ibid.

57 After a brief drift: Ibid., pp. 180–81.

58 Odinga taking on the same role: *Can't Jail the Spirit: Political Prisoners in the U.S.: A Collection of Biographies*, produced by the National Committee to Free Puerto Rican Prisoners of War and the Committee to End the Marion Lockdown, 1992.

58 banned the wearing of dashikis: Burrough, *Days of Rage*, p. 181.

58 Suddenly, Afeni was: Guy, *Afeni Shakur*, p. 70.

58 The couple married in the bedroom: Author interview with James Small, March 30, 2023.

58 "Once I read the Koran": Guy, *Afeni Shakur*, p. 72.

59 "No, she didn't like it": Ibid., p. 81.

59 "I didn't care": Kioni-Sadiki and Meyer, eds., *Look for Me in the Whirlwind*, p. 461.

59 It was Panther philosophy: Safiya Bukhari, "On the Question of Sexism in the Black Panthers," March 9, 1995.

59 Within the Panther pads: Alkebulan, *Survival Pending Revolution*, pp. 29–33.

59 "You had a revolutionary duty": Author interview with Kit Kim Holder, May 25, 2024.

59 "It is extremely important": Bukhari, "On the Question of Sexism in the Black Panthers."

60 Afeni inspired many: Thompson, "The Black Panther Party Releases Statement on Afeni Shakur's Passing."

60 When fifteen-year-old Jamal Joseph: Joseph, *Panther Baby*, p. 44.

60 the robbery of a tollbooth: Guy, *Afeni Shakur*, pp. 78–79.

60 the sanctioning of armed robbery: Pearson, "Shadow of the Panther," pp. 183–85.

61 "That's why I know God": Guy, *Afeni Shakur*, p. 79.

CHAPTER THREE: THE SWEEPING OF THE BARS

63 What they knew for sure: This account of the media burglary draws from Betty Medsger, *The Burglary: The Discovery of J. Edgar Hoover's Secret FBI*, Knopf, 2014; *1971*, director Johanna Hamilton, 2014.

66 "enhance the paranoia": Fred P. Graham, "F.B.I. Files Tell of Surveillance of Students, Blacks, War Foes," *The New York Times*, March 25, 1971.

67 "If Hoover had been asked": Beverly Gage, *G-Man: J. Edgar Hoover and the Making of an American Century*, Viking, 2022, p. 681.

67 In April 1968, it anonymously mailed: Arthur J. Magida, *Prophet of Rage: A Life of Louis Farrakhan*, Basic Books, 1996, p. 105.

67 he approved a plan to target the actress Jean Seberg: Medsger, *The Burglary*, pp. 348–49.

68 William O'Neal was in charge: Michael Ervin, "The Last Hours of William O'Neal," *The Chicago Reader*, January 25, 1990.

68 In mid-November 1969, O'Neal sat down: Ward Churchill and Jim Van Der Wall, *The COINTELPRO Papers: Documents from the Federal Bureau of Investigation's Secret Wars Against Dissent in the United States*, South End Press, 1990, p. 139; Jeffrey Haas, *The Assassination of Fred Hampton: How the FBI and the Chicago Police Murdered a Black Panther*, Lawrence Hill Books, 2010 (2019 edition), p. 195.

68 the early hours of December 4, 1969: This account of the killing of Fred Hampton draws from Churchill and Van Der Wall, *The COINTELPRO Papers*; Haas, *The Assassination of Fred Hampton*; Jeffrey Haas interview with author, March 20, 2023. Also on December 4, 1969, in Brooklyn, Jay-Z was born. He referenced this fact on the 2011 song "Murder to Excellence" by rapping, "I arrived on the day Fred Hampton died." This irritated Hampton's son, Fred Hampton Jr., who asserted, "Fred Hampton didn't die. He was assassinated. Saying Fred Hampton died is like the schoolteacher telling students that Christopher Columbus discovered America." Years earlier, as part of rap's East Coast–West Coast war, 2Pac took aim at Jay-Z, rapping, "I'm a Bad Boy killer, Jay-Z die too."

69 FBI agent Robert Piper sent a memo: Churchill and Van Der Wall, *The COINTELPRO Papers*, p. 140.

69 "deliberately set up": John M. Crewdson, "Former F.B.I. Agent Tells Investigators of Widespread Abuse and Corruption," *The New York Times*, January 20, 1979.

69 O'Neal entered the federal Witness Protection Program: Michael Ervin, "The Last Hours of William O'Neal," *The Chicago Reader*, January 25, 1990.

69 "Do I feel like I betrayed someone?": Nick Pope, "The Strange, True Story of William O'Neal in Judas and the Black Messiah," *Esquire*, February 12, 2021. This portion of the interview did not originally air.

69 "no legal authority or justification": *Socialist Workers Party v. Attorney General of U.S.*, 642 F. Supp. 1357, Southern District Court of New York, August 25, 1986.

70 five NYPD officers stormed: Murray Kempton, *The Briar Patch: The People of the State of New York v. Lumumba Shakur et al.*, E. P. Dutton Co., 1973, p. 1.

70 "Police! If you move": Robinson, *Tupac Shakur: The Authorized Biography*, p. 4.

70 That morning, more than 150 NYPD officers: Orisanmi Burton, "Revolution Is Illegal: Revisiting the Panther 21 at 50," *Spectre*, April 21, 2021.

70 "If you move, I'll blow your brains out": Kempton, *The Briar Patch*, p. 3.

71 a conviction for conspiring: "New York: The Monumental Plot," *Time*, February 26, 1965; Murray Kempton, "Free at Last?," *The New York Review of Books*, June 17, 1971.

71 By eleven a.m.: Burton, "Revolution Is Illegal."

71 twenty-one Black Panthers were being charged: Kioni-Sadiki and Meyer, eds., *Look for Me in the Whirlwind*, pp. 22–23.

71 police made ten arrests: Many members of the Panther 21 changed their

name to reflect their African heritage. News reports at the time, however, were inconsistent—some refer to them by their original names and some to their chosen names. Lumumba and Afeni Shakur were rarely referred to by their birth names; Cetewayo, however, was often called Michael Tabor. It's difficult to discern when some of the changes occurred and to what degree those who did change their names still used their government name. Therefore, I've made the decision to refer to members by their chosen names, though it's possible some may not have made the alteration until after the events depicted here. Sundiata Acoli, for example, doesn't appear in news clippings I've seen under that name until 1973. Though I refer to him here as Dharuba, he has at different times gone by Analyle Dhoruba/ Dhoruba and Dhoruba bin Wahad. I have at various opportunities included each Panther's original name, for anybody who wishes to research them further.

71   No roughhouse tactics: Trip Gabriel, "Lee Berry, Black Panther in a 'Radical Chic' Time, Dies at 78," *The New York Times*, March 26, 2024.

72   Determined to avoid the NYPD's dragnet: This account of Sekou Odinga's escape is mostly drawn from Burrough, *Days of Rage*, pp. 182–83.

73   A twenty-second soul: Peter L. Zimroth, *Perversions of Justice: The Prosecution and Acquittal of the Panther 21*, Viking Press, 1974, p. 13.

73   Writing in 1974: Zimroth, *Perversions of Justice*, p. 49.

73   "has been working closely": Kioni-Sadiki and Meyer, eds., *Look for Me in the Whirlwind*, p. 97.

73   Jamal Joseph had once observed: Joseph, *Panther Baby*, pp. 5–6.

73   "an emotional sister": Kempton, *The Briar Patch*, p. 222.

74   "It wasn't something that we thought about": Author interview with Aaron Dixon, March 10, 2023.

75   deployed to help fill the leadership void: Author interview with Kit Kim Holder, May 25, 2024.

75   Photographed at one rally: Stephen Shames and Ericka Huggins, *Comrade Sisters: Women of the Black Panther Party*, ACC Art Books, 2022, p. 81.

75   Long went to greet the caller: Author interview with Steve Long, May 1, 2023.

75   Leonard Bernstein hosted: Tom Wolfe, "Radical Chic: That Party at Lenny's," *New York* magazine, June 8, 1970.

75   "Tom Wolfe's article really": Author interview with Jamal Joseph, February 28, 2024.

75   On the night of February 21, 1970: Burrough, *Days of Rage;* Emanuel Perlmutter, "Justice Murtagh's Home Target of 3 Fire Bombs," *The New York Times*, February 22, 1970.

76   "tendency to consider only bombings": Carl Davidson, "Whither the Weatherman," *The Guardian*, December 26, 1970 (accessed via marxists.org).

76   "La Pasionaria of the lunatic left": Burrough, *Days of Rage*, p. 65.

76   "We couldn't resolve the question": Author interview with Bill Ayers, October 25, 2022.

77   Phillips had spent a year: Nick Ravo, "Joseph Phillips, 65, Prosecutor in Criminal Justice Investigation," *The New York Times*, August 27, 1997.

77 a *New York Times* profile: Victor S. Navasky, "Right On! With Lawyer William Kunstler," *The New York Times*, April 19, 1970.

77 to focus on the Chicago Eight: Author interview with Gerald Lefcourt, November 8, 2023.

78 Attorneys involved suspected: Ibid.

78 leading a ticket that consisted of: Kempton, *The Briar Patch*, p. 34.

78 "It was obvious": Gerald Lefcourt interview with author, November 8, 2023.

78 a small explosion shattered: This account of the January 17, 1969, explosions and shoot-out is drawn from Kempton, *The Briar Patch*; Zimroth, *Perversions of Justice*; Johnson, "Joan Bird and Afeni Shakur."

79 "Joan is a very sensitive girl": Johnson, "Joan Bird and Afeni Shakur."

79 "I read their Ten-Point Program": Lesley Oelsner, "Joan Bird Freed in $100,000 Bail," *The New York Times*, July 7, 1970.

80 That same evening: *Perversions of Justice*, pp. 147, 177.

80 The Panthers even claimed the torture: Ibid., pp. 104–5.

80 this meant being held: Kempton, *The Briar Patch*, pp. 31–32.

81 "You haven't got a chance": Ibid., p. 33.

81 "Carol Lefcourt had a tiny": Guy, *Afeni Shakur*, p. 97.

81 "Because they were so scary": Author interview with Gerald Lefcourt, November 8, 2023.

82 "It wasn't so much": Author interview with Jamal Joseph, February 28, 2024.

82 "fuck it up": Guy, *Afeni Shakur*, p. 98.

83 On January 30, Afeni left: "Churches Provide $100,000 Bail Here for Black Panther," *The New York Times*, January 31, 1970.

83 By the time it reached court: Kioni-Sadiki and Meyer, eds., *Look for Me in the Whirlwind*, pp. 22–23.

83 Joan Bird was finally uncaged: Oelsner, "Joan Bird Freed in $100,000 Bail."

84 On September 24, 1969: Jason Epstein, "The Trial of Bobby Seale," *The New York Review of Books*, December 4, 1969; Professor Douglas O. Linder, "The Chicago Eight Conspiracy Trial: An Account," famoustrials.com; *The Black Panthers: Vanguard of the Revolution*, director Stanley Nelson Jr., 2015.

84 In total, authorities indicted nine people: Among those indicted was Ericka Huggins, founder of the New Haven chapter of the Black Panther Party, after it was claimed that her voice appeared on a taped recording of the interrogation of Rackley before his murder. She was eventually acquitted.

85 his reprieve came in May 1970: Pendarvis Harshaw, "Huey Newton Was Freed 50 Years Ago. What's Really Changed?" KQED, August 5, 2020.

85 Crowds swelled as he emerged: Tim Findley, "Huey Newton: Twenty-Five Floors from the Street," *Rolling Stone*, August 3, 1972.

86 "I was out in California": Reggie Schell, "A Way to Fight Back," *They Should Have Served That Cup of Coffee*, ed. Dick Cluster, South End Press, 1999, pp. 61–62.

86 "I have never seen anybody": Author interview with Denise Oliver-Velez, November 27, 2023.

86 "Huey had a fucking fit": Ibid.

87　Newton expelled the highly respected Geronimo Pratt: Kate Coleman, "Elmer 'Geronimo' Pratt: The Untold Story of the Black Panther Leader, Dead at 63," *The New Republic*, June 27, 2011.

87　Newton ordered members: Ibid.

87　a key witness was an informant: In re Elmer Gerard Pratt on Habeas Corpus, no. A267020, Superior Court of Los Angeles County, February 16, 1999.

87　Cleaver received a curious letter: John Kifner, "F.B.I. Sought Doom of Panther Party," *The New York Times*, May 9, 1976.

87　A directive produced on counterfeit: Ibid.; Lowell Bergman and David Weir, "Revolution on Ice," *Rolling Stone*, September 9, 1976.

87　Newton too received letters: Smith, "History of the Black Panther Party," *Red Star*, Fall–Winter 2019.

88　"counter-revolutionary actions": "Enemies of the People," *The Black Panther*, vol. 6, no. 3, February 13, 1971.

88　Enlisted to assist Cetewayo: This account of Cetewayo and the group's escape to Canada draws from author interview with Denise Oliver-Velez, November 27, 2023; author interview with Jamal Joseph, February 24, 2024.

89　Cleaver agreed to appear: Burrough, *Days of Rage*, pp. 186–87; *The Black Panthers: Vanguard of the Revolution*, director Stanley Nelson.

89　He denounced Newton loyalist: Julia T. Reed, "Newton-Cleaver Rift Threatens Panthers," *The Harvard Crimson*, March 23, 1971.

89　there may have been groups: Jalil Muntaqim, *On the Black Liberation Army*, Abraham Gillen Press/Arm the Spirit, 1997 (2002 edition), p. 3.

90　"The Black Liberation Army was not a centralized": Assata Shakur, *Assata: An Autobiography*, p. 241.

91　"premature": Ibid., p. 11.

91　The most notorious attack: This account of the killing of Waverly Jones and Joseph Piagentini draws from Burrough, *Days of Rage*, pp. 175–76; Joseph P. Fried, "2 Policemen Slain by Shots in Back; 2 Men Are Sought," *The New York Times*, May 22, 1971; Daniel A. Gross, "The Eleventh Parole Hearing of Jalil Abdul Muntaqim," *The New Yorker*, January 25, 2019; Mike Wood, "Why the Murders of NYPD Officers Jones and Piagentini Still Resonate," *Police1*, March 23, 2018.

92　two packages were delivered: Burrough, *Days of Rage*, p. 176.

92　"Armed goons of this racist government": Ibid.

92　President Richard Nixon met with: Ibid., pp. 196–97.

93　"I wanted to have sex": Castro, "All Eyes on Her."

93　Legs was returned to prison: Robinson, *Tupac Shakur: The Authorized Biography*, p. 14.

93　she made a visit to Harlem Hospital: Kempton, *The Briar Patch*, pp. 123–25.

93　"At a time when the court's calendar": Edith Evans Asbury, "Panther Jury in Case Here Is Complete," *The New York Times*, October 16, 1970.

93　During one session: Edith Evans Asbury, "Murtagh Scores Panther Lawyer," *The New York Times*, September 29, 1970.

94　"We actually impaneled": Author interview with Jamal Joseph, February 29, 2024.

94　"The district attorney and his agents": Lesley Oelsner, "Accused Black Panthers Tell Jury Here That Their Party Is on Trial," *The New York Times*, October 21, 1970.

94 wearing a fashionable: Ibid.

94 "I was young": Guy, *Afeni Shakur*, p. 98.

94 Dharuba and Cetewayo's decision: Zimroth, *Perversions of Justice*, pp. 205–6.

94 Afeni and Joan Bird had their bail revoked: Kempton, *The Briar Patch*, p. 184.

95 "The conditions are not just abominable": Ibid., p. 186.

95 "There she stood between": Ibid., p. 188.

95 "the unborn baby": *Look for Me in the Whirlwind*, pp. 528–29.

95 hinged on its inclusion: Guy, *Afeni Shakur*, pp. 89–90.

96 the other four pleaded guilty: Robert D. McFadden, "Four Panthers Admit Guilt in Slaying," May 22, 1973.

96 Older inmates showed: Guy, *Afeni Shakur*, pp. 111–12.

96 "I had support": Ibid.

96 "This is my prince": Robert Sam Anson, "To Die like a Gangsta," *Vanity Fair*, March 1997.

96 "I had come from court": Hugh Ryan, *The Women's House of Detention: A Queer History of a Forgotten Prison*, Bold Type Books, 2023.

96 "Crooksie had a rep in the joint": Author interview with Denise Oliver-Velez, November 27, 2023.

97 Afeni, it was claimed, had cooked up a plan: Kempton, *The Briar Patch*, p. 163.

97 "You misunderstand me": Ibid.

97 "The Bureau of Special Services was an outfit": Author interview with Gerald Lefcourt, November 8, 2023.

97 "We doubled down": Ibid.

97 The state summoned: Edith Evans Asbury, "Black Panther Party Members Freed After Being Cleared of Charges," *The New York Times*, May 14, 1971.

98 infiltrated the security detail of Malcolm X: Marable, *Malcolm X: A Life of Reinvention*, pp. 436–39.

98 he recalled many meetings: Zimroth, *Perversions of Justice*, p. 161.

98 "Isn't it a fact": Ibid., p. 170.

98 he revealed that no exact date: Ibid.

98 "You really didn't think anything": Kempton, *The Briar Patch*, p. 220.

98 White described an August 1968 trip: Edith Evans Asbury, "Agent Got 'High' with Panthers," *The New York Times*, February 2, 1971.

99 on the eve of the roundup: Zimroth, *Perversions of Justice*, p. 171.

99 White described witnessing: Ibid., pp. 147, 177.

99 "His testimony put dynamite": Author interview with Gerald Lefcourt, November 8, 2023.

99 He drank, he smoked weed: Zimroth, *Perversions of Justice*, pp. 198–99.

99 He slept with Panther women: Ibid.

99 falsifying expense reports to his own financial benefit: Ibid.

99 "You want to know the truth?": Ibid., p. 205.

100 "Why, Yedwa, have you": Kempton, *The Briar Patch*, p. 232.

100 "As far as your involvement": All transcripts of the testimony of Ralph White are taken from Kempton, *The Briar Patch*, pp. 239–40.

101 "I don't know what I'm supposed to say": Ibid., pp. 268–69.

101 "Standing there in front of the jury": Author interview with Gerald Lefcourt, November 8, 2023.

102 Phillips used his closing statement: Zimroth, *Perversions of Justice*, pp. 261–62.

103 "mop up operation": Ibid., pp. 389–90.

103 Many also saw the judge: Ibid., p. 374.

103 "request denied": Ibid., p. 316.

103 "Where'd you find out": Kempton, *The Briar Patch*, p. 280.

104 Afeni found sanctuary: Ryan, *The Women's House of Detention*, p. 281; author interview with Giles Kotcher, February 3, 2024.

104 the women would send Kotcher: Author interview with Giles Kotcher, February 3, 2024.

104 Parish, it was claimed: Ryan, *The Women's House of Detention*, p. 282.

104 "That's what was on the paper": Robinson, *Tupac Shakur: The Authorized Biography*, p. 23.

105 "romanticizing it": Author interview with Giles Kotcher, February 3, 2024.

105 "We should be willing to discuss": *The New Huey P. Newton Reader*, Seven Stories Press, 2002 (2019 edition), p. 172.

105 traveled to the United States: Noel Halifax, "When Gays and Panthers Were United," *Socialist Worker*, no. 404, June 30, 2015.

106 Zayd Shakur helped: Lynn Burnett, "Jean Genet," Cross Cultural Solidarity, crossculturalsolidarity.com.

106 She observed that not only did Genet: Halifax, "When Gays and Panthers Were United."

106 "Afeni did not get support": Author interview with Denise Oliver-Velez, November 27, 2023.

107 On May 2, 1973: This account of the New Jersey Turnpike shoot-out mostly draws from Burrough, *Days of Rage*; Joseph F. Sullivan, "Panther, Trooper Slain in Shoot-Out," *The New York Times*, May 3, 1973.

108 "I am ashamed": Walter H. Waggoner, "Joanne Chesimard Convicted in Killing of Jersey Trooper," *The New York Times*, March 26, 1988.

108 Zayd Shakur was laid to rest: C. Gerald Fraser, "Panther Buried in U.S. Cemetery," *The New York Times*, May 8, 1973.

109 At a small social gathering: Mark Stillman, "Eldridge Cleaver's New Pants," *The Harvard Crimson*, September 26, 1975.

109 his children's adoption of the French language: Eldridge Cleaver, *Soul on Fire*, Word Books, 1978, pp. 208–9.

109 He retreated to an apartment: Ibid., pp. 211–12.

109 The airplane touched down: John A. Oliver, *Eldridge Cleaver: Reborn*, Logos International, 1977, p. viii.

110 "It's ridiculous to ask me": Ibid.

110 "Lots of people believe I left": Eldridge Cleaver, "Why I Left the U.S. and Why I Am Returning," *The New York Times*, November 18, 1975.

110 Cleaver served eight months: Rupert Cornwell, "Obituary: Eldridge Cleaver," *The Independent*, May 3, 1998.

111 Cleaver agreed to an interview: "Interview Eldridge Cleaver," *Frontline*, pbs .org.

CHAPTER FOUR: THIS SHOULD MOVE YA

115 a pitiful, bloodstained: *Takeover: How We Occupied a Hospital and Changed Public Health Care*, director Emma Francis-Snyder, 2021.

116 When the Bolsheviks: Maurice Isserman, "When New York City Was the Capital of American Communism," *The New York Times*, October 20, 2017.

117 In the mid-1920s: *At Home in Utopia*, director Michal Goldman, 2009.

117 five-story complexes: Murray Schumach, "Reunion Hails Bronx Housing Experiment of 20's," *The New York Times*, May 2, 1977.

117 Righteous slogans: Ibid.

117 a reference to the wrongful conviction: West Side Workers Forum, "Save the Scottsboro Boys: Smash All Racism" flier, 1933.

117 "There are a few thousand people": Vivian Gornick, *The Romance of American Communism*, Basic Books, 1977 (2020 edition, published by Verso), p. 53.

117 With the cold wind: Isserman, "When New York City Was the Capital of American Communism."

117 Before McCarthyism: Marable, *Malcolm X: A Life of Reinvention*, p. 158; "Davis, Benjamin Jefferson, Jr.," Stanford: The Martin Luther King, Jr. Research and Education Institute, kinginstitute.stanford.edu/davis-benjamin -jefferson-jr.

118 "You can't operate a capitalistic system": Ray Smith, "Malcolm X: 'You Show Me a Capitalist, I'll Show You a Bloodsucker,'" *The Communist*, February 23, 2015.

118 The Bronx went from: Evelyn Gonzalez, *The Bronx*, Columbia University Press, 2004.

118 "Black kids didn't play on white blocks": Joseph, *Panther Baby*, p. 12.

118 In the early morning of July 14, 1970: This account of the Lincoln Hospital Takeover draws from author interview with Cleo Silvers, February 13, 2023, and December 6, 2023; *Takeover*, director Francis-Snyder; Alfonso A. Narvaez, "Young Lords Seize Lincoln Hospital," *The New York Times*, July 15, 1970.

119 the tuberculosis mortality rate: "Tuberculosis Death Rate Here Declines 12 Per Cent from the Level of a Year Ago," *The New York Times*, June 10, 1954.

119 The group allied with: Stephen Torgoff, "HRUM Sums Up Hospital Organizing," *The Guardian*, December 27, 1972 (accessed via Marxists.org).

119 A precursor to the hospital: Alfonso A. Narvaez, "The Young Lords Seize X-Ray Unit," *The New York Times*, June 18, 1970.

119 "It took us a couple of months": Author interview with Cleo Silvers, December 6, 2023.

120 "To watch people": Author interview with Jennifer Dohrn, March 24, 2023.

121 "It happened because of the struggle": Author interview with Cleo Silvers, February 13, 2023.

121 "Those poets were revolutionaries": Author interview with Jamal Joseph, February 28, 2024.

122 Apartment buildings would be emptied out: David Gonzalez, "How Fire Defined the Bronx, and Us," *The New York Times*, January 20, 2022.

122 By the end of the arson wave: Zhandarka Kurti, "Why the Bronx Burned," *Jacobin*, August 10, 2019.

123 As a DJ, Bambaataa: Steve Knopper, "Afrika Bambaataa: Crate-digger, collector, creator," *Chicago Tribune*, May 5, 2011.

124 has been referred to as the first political hip-hop tune: Adam Bradley and Andrew DuBois, eds., *The Anthology of Rap*, Yale University Press, 2010, p. 33.

124 "I got revved up": Ibid.

124 Plotting a revolutionary hip-hop record: Ibid.

125 "We were in a place": "How the Burning Bronx Led to the Birth of Hip-Hop," November 4, 2019, pbs.org/independentlens.

125 gold within eleven days: Caroline Sullivan, "How We Made: Jiggs Chase and Ed Fletcher on The Message," *The Guardian*, May 27, 2013.

125 "the most powerful pop record": Robert Palmer, "In Hard Times, Pop Music Surges with Fresh Energy," *The New York Times*, December 26, 1982.

126 "Public Enemy has been dubbed": Richard Harrington, "Public Enemy's Assault on the Airwaves," *The Washington Post*, July 30, 1988.

CHAPTER FIVE: REMEMBER THIS HOUSE

129 he had moved home twenty times: Bruck, "The Takedown of Tupac."

130 In another social meetup: Fox was later called "probably Guyana's most prolific composer of classical music," though he was not a natural ally of Afeni. "The Panthers didn't want me no way," he'd say. "They saw me as the Black bourgeoisie."

130 "Love, Parish": A 1972 *New York* magazine article written by Catherine Breslin refers to Afeni's baby as Parish Shakur, suggesting there was a period when the new mother used a halfway name between her son's birth name, Lesane Parish Crooks, and the name he would become eternally known by, Tupac Amaru Shakur.

131 Afeni took him to see: Robinson, *Tupac Shakur: The Authorized Biography*, p. 27.

131 Afeni stayed in the role for a decade: Peter Carlson, "The Gangsta Rapper's Radical Mama," *The Washington Post*, September 22, 2003.

131 Crooks was running: J. B. Nicholas, "August Rebellion: New York's Forgotten Female Prison Riot," *The Village Voice*, August 30, 2016.

131 The worst of her troubles: This account of the beating of Carol Crooks mostly draws from Women Against Prison, "Dykes Behind Bars," *DYKE, A Quarterly*, no. 1, 1975; Amber Baylor, "Centering Women in Prisoners' Rights Litigation," *Michigan Journal of Gender and Law*, vol. 25, 2018, Texas A&M University School of Law Legal Studies Research Paper No. 19-29125.

A 2016 article in *The Village Voice* gives a different version of the incident. In this account, there's no mention of a migraine. Instead, Crooks walked past the guard and down a flight of stairs to the mess hall for a glass of milk, ignoring requests to stop. Crooks then returned to her cell, took off her glasses, and "attacked four guards, knocking two of them out with her fists." The article also adds the extra detail of Crooks striking the other two guards with a flowerpot and two table legs.

132 Crooks managed to get word: Baylor, "Centering Women in Prisoners' Rights Litigation."

132 a successful lawsuit: *Wallace v. Kern*, 371 F. Supp. 1384 (E.D.N.Y. 1974).

132 Latimer arrived: Baylor, "Centering Women in Prisoners' Rights Litigation," p. 125.

132 The lawsuit set a precedent: Nicholas, "August Rebellion."

133 After five months: Ibid.

133 On August 29: This account of the August Rebellion mostly draws from Women Against Prison, "Dykes Behind Bars"; J. B. Nicholas, "August Rebellion"; Baylor, "Centering Women in Prisoners' Rights Litigation."

134 Abdul Majid, an ex-Panther: Saeed Shabazz, "Political prisoner Abdullah Majid dies after 33 years in jail," *New York Amsterdam News*, April 7, 2016.

134 Twymon Myers, the Black Liberation Army soldier: "Commissioner Says Myers' Shooting Means Last of Black Liberation Army," *The Argus Leader*, November 15, 1973.

135 Afeni punished mischief: Anson, "To Die like a Gangsta."

135 One of his first chores: djvlad, "Mopreme Shakur Details Early Life of Growing Up with 2Pac," youtube.com/watch?v=ctRGIFHqsEQ, posted June 4, 2015.

136 An apartment in historic Harlem: This account of Akinyele Umoja's visit to the Shakur home draws from author interview with Akinyele Umoja, December 16, 2022; "Akinyele Umoja, ''You Are Appreciated': My Memories of Afeni Shakur," *The Black Scholar*, May 18, 2016.

137 Pan-Africanism emerged: British historian Hakim Adi's book *Pan-Africanism: A History* (Bloomsbury, 2018) goes back further, beginning with the abolition movement and figures like Olaudah Equiano and Ottobah Cugoano, two former slaves turned British abolitionists who founded an organization called the Sons of Africa. For Adi, this attempt to use "Africa" and "African" as a designation for a political membership that at the time was anti-slavery, but would later become anti-racist and anti-imperialist, suggests a much longer history of thinking about Pan-Africanism.

138 The RNA saw itself: William Rosenau, *Tonight We Bombed the U.S. Capitol*, Atria, 2020, p. 32.

138 the Black Belt thesis: James R. Forman, *Self-Determination and the African-American People*, Open Hand Publishing, 1981; Denise Lynn, "The Marxist Proposition, Claudia Jones, and Black Nationalism," *Black Perspectives*, aaihs.org, November 1, 2017.

139 "a worldwide monster": Karin Ashley, Bill Ayers, Bernardine Dohrn, John Jacobs, Jeff Jones, Gerry Long, Home Machtinger, Jim Mellen, Terry Rob-

bins, Mark Rudd, and Steve Tappis, "You Don't Need a Weatherman to Know Which Way the Wind Blows," *New Left Notes,* June 18, 1969.

139 "White stood for": Author interview with Akinyele Umoja, December 16, 2022.

139 "I am not going to stand up": Steve Wyche, "Colin Kaepernick Explains Why He Sat During National Anthem," NFL.com, August 27, 2016.

140 being asked by a minister: Anson, "To Die like a Gangsta."

140 "We wanted, on the one hand": Author interview with Jeffrey Haas, March 20, 2023.

140 she journeyed to California: Robinson, *Tupac Shakur: The Authorized Biography,* p. 30.

140 "They were pretty charged": Author interview with Jeffrey Haas, March 20, 2023.

141 Mutulu Shakur was born: This account of Mutulu Shakur's formative years mostly draws from John Castellucci, *The Big Dance: The Untold Story of Weather-Man Kathy Boudin and the Terrorist Family That Committed the Brink's Robbery Murders,* Dodd, Mead & Co., 1986; Burrough, *Days of Rage;* Rosenau, *Tonight We Bombed the U.S. Capitol;* Akinyele Umoja, "Straight Ahead: The Life of Resistance of Dr. Mutulu Shakur," *Souls,* vol. 23, nos. 1–2, January–June 2022; mutulushakur.com.

142 He wrote a popular autobiography: Carson's son, Lumumba Carson, became better known as Professor X, a member of rap group X Clan.

142 introduced to acupuncture: Eana Meng, "Reflections on (Re)making History," *Asian Medicine* 16, 2021, p. 298.

143 he began prefixing his name: On his website, Mutulu also claimed that 1976 was the year he became certified and licensed to practice acupuncture in the state of California. It should be noted that half a century on, mainstream medicine still considers acupuncture quackery.

143 "The view at Lincoln Detox": Author interview with Jennifer Dohrn, March 24, 2023.

143 A report to Mayor Ed Koch: Ronald Sullivan, "Bronx Drug Program Called a 'Ripoff,'" *The New York Times,* November 28, 1978.

144 "Despite public knowledge": Ibid.

144 The clinic was finally shut down: Burrough, *Days of Rage,* pp. 466–67.

144 It was in 1976 when: Ibid., p. 453.

144 Sekou Odinga had slipped back into the country: Ibid., 455.

144 "I couldn't even tell you": Ibid.

145 the trio targeted an armored car: Castellucci, *The Big Dance,* p. 62; Burrough, *Days of Rage,* pp. 455–56.

145 During an eighteen-month period: Rosenau, *Tonight We Bombed the U.S. Capitol,* p. 54.

146 may have been funneling money: Ibid.

146 "We felt that just robbing": Arnold H. Lubasch, "Killer Says He Helped in Chesimard's Escape," *The New York Times,* December 2, 1987.

146 busting Assata Shakur out of prison: This account of the liberation of Assata Shakur mostly draws from Castellucci, *The Big Dance;* Burrough, *Days of*

Rage, pp. 474–79. Robert Hanley, "Miss Chesimard Flees Jersey Prison, Helped by 3 Armed 'Visitors,'" *The New York Times*, November 3, 1979; Arnold H. Lubasch, "Brink's Testimony Examining Escape," *The New York Times*, May 15, 1983.

147 a former youth worker: Safiya Bukhari, "Lest We Forget," *Liberation*, February 25, 2020.

148 "I have no contentions": "Freed Panther Sekou Odinga on Joining the Panthers, COINTELPRO & Assata Shakur's Escape," *Democracy Now!*, October 26, 2016.

148 On one expedition in February 1980: Burrough, *Days of Rage*, pp. 493–94.

148 The group trailed a Brink's armored truck: Castellucci, *The Big Dance*, p. 62; Burrough, *Days of Rage*, pp. 455–56; Peter Kihiss, "A Brink's Guard Is Shot to Death in Bronx Attack," *The New York Times*, June 3, 1981; "Thieves Cooly Ambush Armored Car in the Bronx," UPI, June 3, 1981.

150 The location of the job: This account of the Big Dance mostly draws from Castellucci, *The Big Dance*; Burrough, *Days of Rage*; Susan Braudy, *Family Circle: The Boudins and the Aristocracy of the Left*, Alfred A. Knopf, 2003; Rosenau, *Tonight We Bombed the U.S. Capitol*; Mark Gado, "Ambush: The Brinks Robbery of 1981," crimelibrary.org; *United States v. Shakur*, 565 F. Supp. 123, Southern District Court of New York, June 21, 1983.

152 Trombino would survive: Lee Trombino returned to work and served as a Brink's guard for another twenty years. He did die an untimely death, however. On the job, he was making a pickup in the basement of the World Trade Center on September 11, 2001, and died in the terrorist attack.

156 "I'm all right": Castellucci, *The Big Dance*, p. 35. Joseph was never charged with an offense connected with being at the scene of the robbery or shootout with police, but was convicted of harboring a fugitive.

156 Odinga later claimed that his comrade: "Freed Panther Sekou Odinga on Joining the Panthers, COINTELPRO & Assata Shakur's Escape"; sekouodinga.com/about.html.

157 "The story of the combatants": "Interview with David Gilbert," Kersplebedeb, kersplebedeb.com, April 2, 1985 (posted online January 8, 2011).

157 "When I would feel he needed me": Bruck, "The Takedown of Tupac."

157 "He had to keep secrets": Ibid.

CHAPTER SIX: I AM SOCIETY'S CHILD

159 likely because of her connection: McQuillar and Johnson, *Tupac Shakur: The Life and Times of an American Icon*, p. 41.

159 "our way of socializing": Ronin Ro, *Have Gun Will Travel: The Spectacular Rise and Violent Fall of Death Row Records*, Quartet Books, 1998, p. 139.

160 "the pit of the garbage can": Carlson, "The Gangsta Rapper's Radical Mama."

160 These years were dubbed the "Crack Era": For more on the Crack Era, see Gary Webb, *Dark Alliance: The CIA, the Contras, and the Crack Cocaine Explosion*, Seven Stories Press, 1998; Donovan X. Ramsey, *When Crack Was King*,

One World, 2023; *Crack: Cocaine, Corruption & Conspiracy*, director Stanley Nelson Jr., 2021.

160 Afeni sought to move the family: Robinson, *Tupac Shakur: The Authorized Biography*, pp. 59–61.

161 he penned a collection: Carlie Portefield, "Tupac Shakur's Unseen Childhood Poetry Written for an Incarcerated Black Panther Is up for Sale," *Forbes*, April 14, 2022.

161 "This is dedicated": Sotheby's New York, *The Art and Influence of Hip-Hop*, lot 100, March 30, 2022.

161 When Tupac was twelve: Robinson, *Tupac Shakur: The Authorized Biography*, pp. 62–66; "Tupac Amaru Shakur: Native Harlemite," *The Amsterdam News*, September 13, 2016.

162 "The night of that show": Author interview with Levy Lee Simon, July 6, 2023.

162 Sekyiwa would accompany her brother: McQuillar and Johnson, *Tupac Shakur: The Life and Times of an American Icon*, p. 44.

162 When members of the company: Sheldon Pearce, *Changes: An Oral History of Tupac Shakur*, Simon & Schuster, 2021, pp. 11–12.

162 on her father's side: Guy, *Afeni Shakur*, p. 36.

162 agreed to take the family: Robinson, *Tupac Shakur: The Authorized Biography*, p. 66.

162 Legs was in prison: Cathy Scott, *The Killing of Tupac Shakur*, Huntington Press, third edition, p. 108; Anson, "To Die like a Gangsta."

162 "I miss my daddy": Kevin Powell, "This Thug's Life," *Vibe*, February 1994.

163 "handwritten verses now reside": John Lewis, "Tupac Was Here," *Baltimore* magazine, September 2016.

164 The library has been in possession: Ibid.

164 "That was the start, right there": The flier advertises the final as taking place at a different branch, though Parker's account is supported by *Back in the Day: My Life and Times with Tupac Shakur* (Da Capo Press, 2002), a memoir by Tupac's childhood friend Darrin Keith Bastfield, who wrote that "Library Rap" was performed at Cathedral Hill.

165 Once the apartment was the Shakurs': Robinson, *Tupac Shakur: The Authorized Biography*, p. 72.

165 Tupac was enrolled: Lewis, "Tupac Was Here."

166 "It was a masterful consideration": Bastfield, *Back in the Day*, p. 18.

166 destiny dictated that he take a seat: Lewis, "Tupac Was Here"; "Tupac Shakur's Close Friends Dana Smith and Darrin Bastfield Reminisce on the Rapper's Formative Years in Baltimore," *Baltimore* magazine Facebook page (Facebook Live), facebook.com/Baltimoremagazine, August 31, 2016.

166 Tupac wasn't super-popular: Ibid.

166 Mouse was often questioned: Bastfield, *Back in the Day*, pp. 21–23.

167 A reward for Tupac and Mouse's endeavor: This account of Tupac and Mouse's Cherry Hill rec center performance mostly draws from Bastfield, *Back in the Day*; Robinson, *Tupac Shakur: The Authorized Biography*; author interview with Virgil Simms, March 11, 2023.

167 into the respected British rock publications: Paul Mathur, "Mantronix: The Album (10)," *Melody Maker*, March 22, 1986; "NME's Best Albums and Tracks of 1986," accessed via NME.com.

168 drafting love letters to a girl named Averil: In 2018, the letters were made available to view online when put up for sale by autograph dealers Moments in Time.

169 For the audition: Lewis, "Tupac Was Here."

169 The audition lasted: M. Dion Thompson, "20 Years After Tupac Shakur's Death, Remembering His Baltimore Beginnings," *The Baltimore Sun*, September 21, 1996 (republished September 13, 2016).

169 "The empathy": Wesley Case, "Tupac Shakur in Baltimore: Friends, Teachers Remember the Birth of an Artist," *The Baltimore Sun*, March 31, 2017.

169 a carload of white strangers: Robinson, *Tupac Shakur: The Authorized Biography*, pp. 91–92.

171 "I love Shakespeare": Chuck Philips, "Q&A with Tupac Shakur: 'I Am Not a Gangster,'" *Los Angeles Times*, October 25, 1995.

171 One he named Redbone: The word "redbone," historically popular in the southern United States to denote a multiracial person or culture, reentered the popular music lexicon when Childish Gambino released a song of the same name. An unauthorized version featuring verses from 2Pac and the Notorious B.I.G. became popular online. "I would consider this one of the best mashups I have heard," wrote one YouTube commenter.

172 During one prom: Thompson, "20 Years After Tupac Shakur's Death, Remembering His Baltimore Beginnings."

172 her school organized a field trip: Robinson, *Tupac Shakur: The Authorized Biography*, p. 76.

172 "You look just like him": Ibid.

172 On what appeared like it: The Boss Playa, "2Pac—Christmas Interview (1992) (MTV)," youtube.com/watch?v=oaAwFbFwuVU, posted December 25, 2020.

173 once a navy man: "Progressive Baltimore Icon Margaret Baldridge Honored on Her 80th," *People's World*, December 13, 2022.

173 "Happy birthday to our brother and comrade": @communistsusa, X (previously Twitter), June 17, 2019, retrieved from x.com/communistsusa/status/1140414143943589888.

173 named the Tupac Shakur Club in his memory: Jordan Farrar, "Baltimore Students Protest Cuts," *People's World*, May 13, 2011.

173 They also joined the Yo-No: Bastfield, *Back in the Day*, pp. 64–67.

174 staunch criticism of Reagan's War on Drugs: For more on Schmoke's opposition to Reagan's War on Drugs, see Ron Cassie, "Back to the Future," *Baltimore* magazine, April 2018.

174 "If you're a kid growing up": Wesley Case, "More Stories of Tupac Shakur's Time in Baltimore, from Town Hall Meetings to School Sleepovers," *The Baltimore Sun*, July 1, 2019.

175 a mother who struggled: McQuillar and Johnson, *Tupac Shakur: The Life and Times of an American Icon*; Zach Seemayer, "Jada Pinkett Smith's Mom

Adrienne Banfield-Norris Celebrates 31 Years of Living Clean After Drug Addiction," *ET,* December 22, 2021.

175   Panther cub schooled Jada: Molly Monjauze, *Tupac Remembered: Bearing Witness to a Life and Legacy,* Chronicle Books, 2008, p. 32.

175   Tupac assuring Jada: Ibid., p. 30.

175   without his biological father: Ibid., p. 36.

176   Tupac began spending: McQuillar and Johnson, *Tupac Shakur: The Life and Times of an American Icon,* p. 67.

176   he worked busing tables: Case, "Tupac Shakur in Baltimore."

176   took part in recitals: Robinson, *Tupac Shakur: The Authorized Biography,* p. 100.

176   sought to recruit: Bastfield, *Back in the Day,* pp. 45–46.

177   "He lived in a very rough": Case, "Tupac Shakur in Baltimore."

177   culminated in the formation: Bastfield, *Back in the Day,* p. 89.

177   "We rapped, wrote our stuff": Lewis, "Tupac Was Here."

177   Tupac had been raised to believe: Pearce, *Changes,* p. 21.

178   was finally arrested in Los Angeles: Arnold H. Lubasch, "2 Ex-Fugitives Convicted of Roles in Fatal Armored-Truck Robbery," *The New York Times,* May 12, 1988.

178   capture in a diner in Dobbs Ferry: Robert D. McFadden, "Fugitive in $1.6 Million Brink's Holdup Captured," *The New York Times,* May 12, 1985.

178   Mutulu was sentenced: John M. Doyle, "Lengthy Terms for Two Convicted in Bloody Brink's Robbery," Associated Press, August 3, 1988.

178   "gifted and capable": Ibid.

178   "the malignant cancer": Ibid.

179   "I am not guilty": Ibid.

179   "It took the ambulance": Author interview with Jennifer Dohrn, March 24, 2023.

179   the boy cried: Case, "Tupac Shakur in Baltimore: Friends, Teachers Remember the Birth of an Artist."

179   "On the other side of the Golden Gate Bridge": *I Want It All Now!,* director Joseph DeCola, 1978.

180   Marin City rose: Jennifer Warren, "California Album: The Other Marin," *Los Angeles Times,* December 20, 1992.

181   When Afeni finally did show up: Robinson, *Tupac Shakur: The Authorized Biography,* pp. 132–33.

181   Tupac performed in Chekhov's *The Bear:* Monjauze, *Tupac Remembered,* p. 41.

181   "I want you all to remember": Zach Ruskin, "Tupac Shakur's Life in Marin," *Marin* magazine, August 23, 2019.

181   Tupac volunteered to appear: Robinson, *Tupac Shakur: The Authorized Biography,* pp. 135–37.

182   "There should be a class on drugs": Historic Films Stock Footage Archive, "Tupac Shakur 1988 High School Interview," youtube.com/watch?v=v_XT9-C5Qu8, posted June 12, 2017.

182   "That's my favorite song": Monjauze, *Tupac Remembered,* p. 41.

182 Tupac dropped out: Anson, "To Die like a Gangsta," *Vanity Fair,* March 1997.

182 a military brat: Pearce, *Changes,* p. 34.

182 It was Rollins: Ibid., p. 37.

183 "I was broke": *Tupac: Resurrection 1971–1996,* editors Jacob Hoye and Karolyn Ali, Atria Books, 2003, p. 69.

183 an excursion to Los Angeles: Anson, "To Die like a Gangsta"; Tupac Facts, "Watani Tyehimba on Tupac: First Impressions, Tupac's Duality, What He Misses About Tupac + More," youtube.com/watch?v=3aFubvxGMuI, posted May 3, 2021.

183 in a park: Anson, "To Die like a Gangsta."

183 the grass outside Bayside Elementary School: Bronwyn Garrity, "The Music Is the Message," *Los Angeles Times,* April 2, 2002.

183 "That's a good one": Anson, "To Die like a Gangsta."

184 "Give me a break": Garrity, "The Music Is the Message."

184 Ray came from a home: Mike Su, "Maya Angelou Tells Dave Chappelle About That Time She Met Tupac," *Upworthy,* April 16, 2015.

184 "We knew very quickly": *Dear Mama,* director Allen Hughes.

184 "The number one thing": Author interview with Raymond "Ray Luv" Tyson, May 15, 2024.

184 she became pregnant: Guy, *Afeni Shakur,* pp. 137–43.

185 she would fill the role of chauffeur: Author interview with Raymond "Ray Luv" Tyson, May 15, 2024.

185 "Sure, send me a videotape": Christopher R. Weingarten, "I Get Around: The Oral History of 2Pac's Digital Underground Years," *Rolling Stone,* April 6, 2017.

185 Their first meeting: This account of Tupac's first meeting with Shock G mostly draws from Weingarten, "I Get Around."

186 "Yeah, I'll do it": Monjauze, *Tupac Remembered,* p. 57.

186 "He took a trip to Los Angeles": Author interview with Kendrick Wells, April 25, 2023.

187 the boy pitched a big idea: Author interview with Akinyele Umoja, December 16, 2022.

187 He was finally freed in 1997: Robert J. Lopez, "Elmer 'Geronimo' Pratt Dies at 63; Former Black Panther Whose Murder Conviction Was Overturned," *Los Angeles Times,* March 16, 2014.

187 "It took everybody by surprise": Author interview with Akinyele Umoja, December 16, 2022.

188 a story was breaking: B. Drummond Ayres Jr., "Virginia Beach Is Quiet After Violence," *The New York Times,* September 5, 1989; D. L. Chandler, "Little Known Black History Fact: 1989 Greekfest Riots," BlackAmerica Web.com, September 4, 2014.

188 This followed the killing: Arnold H. Lubasch, "Juries Acquit 2 in Murder Case in Bensonhurst," *The New York Times,* February 8, 1991.

189 "When my mother gave me Tupac": RBGStreetScholar, "RBG Tupac Shakur Speaks—National Chairman for the New Afrikan Panther Party

(1989) pt 1 of 2," youtube.com/watch?v=MW8JeFKEAxM, posted April 13, 2010.

189   he discussed with other New Afrikan Panthers: *Dear Mama*, director Allen Hughes.

190   "I think it was something": Author interview with Kendrick Wells, April 25, 2023.

190   her phone rang shrilly: Author interview with Becky Mossing, February 24, 2023.

192   "Pac would invite": Weingarten, "I Get Around."

193   Huey P. Newton was shot three times: Mark A. Stein and Valarie Basheda, "Huey Newton Found Shot to Death on Oakland Street," *Los Angeles Times*, August 22, 1989; "Arrest in Murder of Huey Newton," *The New York Times*, August 26, 1989.

193   Tupac attended a memorial for Newton: Robinson, *Tupac Shakur: The Authorized Biography*, p. 157.

194   drinking two quarts of cognac a day: Dennis Hevesi, "Huey Newton Symbolized the Rising Black Anger of a Generation," August 23, 1989.

194   "It means just the opposite": Newton, *Revolutionary Suicide*, p. 5.

197   she asked Afeni to attend: Guy, *Afeni Shakur*, pp. 170–78.

CHAPTER SEVEN: SOMETHING WICKED

200   Evans had previously: "Deon 'Big D the Impossible' Evans Tears Open His Vault of Unreleased Tupac Songs (Interview)," 2PacLegacy.net, April 15, 2022.

200   Even Digital Underground's label: Robinson, *Tupac Shakur: The Authorized Biography*, pp. 180–81.

200   Gregory heard about a new label: Ibid., pp. 190–93.

201   "He's so handsome": Ibid., p. 192.

201   Tupac inked the contract: Ibid.

201   Ray Luv's discarded lyrics: Robinson, *Tupac Shakur: The Authorized Biography*, p. 160.

202   The night of March 2, 1991: The Rodney King beating has been pored over in many different places. This account mostly draws from the Report of the Independent Commission on the Los Angeles Police Department, 1991; Stacey C. Koon with Robert Deit, *Presumed Guilty: The Tragedy of the Rodney King Affair*, Gateway Books, 1992; Rodney King, *The Riot Within: My Journey from Rebellion to Redemption*, HarperCollins, 2012; Lou Cannon, "The King Incident: More Than Met the Eye on Videotape," *The Washington Post*, January 24, 1998; Douglas Linder, "The Rodney King Beating Trials," *Jurist*, December 1, 2001; publicly available FBI files. The tape itself is easy to find online.

205   Photos taken of King: Anjuli Sastry Krbechek and Karen Grigsby Bates, "When LA Erupted in Anger: A Look Back at the Rodney King Riots," NPR, April 26, 2017.

206   "a crushed can": Cannon, "The King Incident."

206 "Television used the tape": Ibid.

206 "The beating was not the aberration": Henry Weinstein and Ronald L. Soble, "Crisis in the LAPD: The Rodney King Beating," *Los Angeles Times*, April 15, 1991.

208 Tupac came across a newspaper story: Robinson, *Tupac Shakur: The Authorized Biography*, pp. 186–87.

208 Two maintenance men: James C. McKinley Jr., "Baby Saved from Compactor, Where Mother, 12, Says She Put Him," *The New York Times*, March 28, 1991.

208 "When this song came out": Bruck, "The Takedown of Tupac."

209 Bishop had never truly left him: Pearce, *Changes*, p. 72.

209 suggested Tupac go along: Davey D, "On the Line with . . . 2Pac Shakur," www.daveyd.com.

209 "The thing that he came with": Ronda Racha Penrice, "*Juice* at 25: Director Ernest Dickerson Talks Tupac, Hip-Hop and the Film's Enduring Legacy," *The Root*, June 13, 2017.

209 "not a hip-hop movie": Ibid.

210 he came across a newsstand: *Thug Immortal*, director George Tan, 1997.

211 he was stopped by two cops: Robinson, *Tupac Shakur: The Authorized Biography*, pp. 197–200; *Dear Mama*, director Allen Hughes.

211 being in captivity meant: *Dear Mama*, director Allen Hughes.

211 doggedly been pursuing Boyovich and Rodgers: Author interview with John Burris, February 28, 2024.

211 "The main dollar sum": Ibid.

CHAPTER EIGHT: A THUG LIFE LESS ORDINARY

215 Tupac Shakur was on the set: This account of Tupac leaving the set of *Poetic Justice* draws from Yvonne Villarreal, "John Singleton Looks Back on the 1992 L.A. Riots in New Documentary," *Los Angeles Times*, April 18, 2017; *L.A. Burning: The Riots 25 Years Later*, directors One9 and Erik Parker, 2017.

215 twice the budget: Rich Juzwiak, "*Poetic Justice* Is a Movie-Long Exploration of Why Janet Jackson Isn't Smiling," *Jezebel*, July 13, 2020.

216 "I lost thirteen good friends": Author interview with Aqeela Sherrills, December 7, 2002.

216 the reported number of gang-related homicides: Elizabeth Hinton, "Los Angeles Had a Chance to Build a Better City After the Rodney King Violence in 1992. Here's Why It Failed," *Time*, May 18, 2021.

217 total of 383 fatalities: "American War and Military Operations Casualties: Lists and Statistics," Congressional Research Service, crsreports.congress .gov.

217 its citizens were mostly: William J. Aceves, "The Watts Gang Treaty: Hidden History and the Power of Social Movements," *Harvard Civil Rights–Civil Liberties Law Review*, 2022, vol. 57, no. 1, p. 121.

217 the highest concentration: Ibid., p. 122; John Buntin, "What Does It Take to Stop Crips and Bloods from Killing Each Other?," *The New York Times*, July 10, 2013.

217 these projects were almost entirely Black: Jennifer Bowles, "'60s Watts Riots Still Afire in Memories," Associated Press, August 13, 1995; "History of Watts," wattsnc.org.

218 On August 11, 1965: "Mrs. Frye's Fuse," *Time*, November 12, 1965.

218 Thirty-four people died: "Granddaddy of Civil Disturbance: The Watts Riots, 50 Years Later," cbsnews.com, August 11, 2015.

218 "After visiting Watts": Clayborne Carson, ed., *The Autobiography of Martin Luther King, Jr.*, Abacus, 1998, p. 291.

218 "kid gloves": James Queally, "Traffic Stop Was the Spark That Ignited Days of Destruction in L.A.," *Los Angeles Times*, July 29, 2015.

219 "We traded a lot of bodies": Author interview with Aqeela Sherrills, December 7, 2002.

219 Louis Farrakhan invited gang members: Charisse Jones, "Farrakhan to Speak to 900 Gang Leaders to 'Stop the Killing,'" *Los Angeles Times*, October 6, 1989.

220 "The idea of retaliation": Author interview with William J. Aceves, November 25, 2022.

220 Daude asked fellow activist: Aceves, "The Watts Gang Treaty," pp. 132–34.

221 "the Multi-Peace Treaty–General Armistice Agreement": For a copy of the agreement, also known as the Watts Gang Treaty or Watts Truce, see Rasheed L. Muhammad, *Original Gang Truce of 1992*, 1995 (first edition).

221 "I accept the duty to honor": Jesse Katz and Andrea Ford, Ex–Gang Members Look to Mideast for a Peace Plan," *Los Angeles Times*, June 17, 1992.

221 a delegation of a dozen Grape Street Crips: This account of the Imperial Courts meeting mostly draws from Aceves, "The Watts Gang Treaty"; author interview with William J. Aceves, November 25, 2022; author interview with Aqeela Sherrills, December 7, 2022.

221 while standing in the doorway: Jesse Katz, "Corrupting Power of Life on the Streets," *Los Angeles Times*, May 15, 1992.

222 "It didn't happen that way": Author interview with Aqeela Sherrills, December 7, 2002.

222 "There really wasn't an official signing": Author interview with William J. Aceves, November 25, 2022.

223 Property damage in Watts: Elizabeth Hinton, "Los Angeles Had a Chance to Build a Better City After the Rodney King Violence in 1992. Here's Why It Failed," *Time*, May 18, 2021.

223 Developed with Jamal Joseph: Robinson, *Tupac Shakur: The Authorized Biography*, pp. 224–25.

223 "something that I'd heard about vaguely": Author interview with Aqeela Sherrills, December 7, 2002.

223 "These were summits": Westhoff, *Original Gangstas*, Hachette, 2016.

225 "wasn't the mother of all bad ideas": McQuillar and Johnson, *Tupac Shakur: The Life and Times of an American Icon*, p. 100.

226 "I don't consider myself": Blank on Blank, "Tupac Shakur on Life and Death," youtube.com/watch?v=6x2FqX2YZws, posted December 3, 2013.

226 gang homicides in L.A. County fell: Aceves, "The Watts Gang Treaty," pp. 142–43.

226 Tony Bogard was tragically killed: Katz, "Corrupting Power of Life on the Streets."

227 "burying our own kids": Andrea Ford, "Gang Truce Lets Residents Rediscover Their Freedoms," *Los Angeles Times*, August 14, 1992.

227 "When Watts reached": Author interview with Aqeela Sherrills, December 7, 2002.

227 "I think it was a real": Author interview with Tracy "Big Tray Deee" Davis, April 26, 2024.

227 "If the truce ends tomorrow": Ford, "Gang Truce Lets Residents Rediscover Their Freedoms."

228 Latasha Harlins, a fifteen-year-old: Erika D. Smith, "The Killing of Latasha Harlins Was 30 Years Ago. Not Enough Has Changed," *Los Angeles Times*, March 17, 2021; "Latasha Harlins' Death and Why Korean-Americans Were Targets in the '92 Riots," *LAist*, April 28, 2017.

229 convince malt liquor company: Gerrick D. Kennedy, "Ice Cube Reflects on the 25 Years Since the Release of 'Death Certificate,'" *Los Angeles Times*, June 30, 2017.

229 take the case away from Judge Kamins: Sheryl Stolberg and Tracy Wilkinson, "Appeals Court Bars Kamins from King Case," *Los Angeles Times*, August 22, 1991.

230 L.A. began to burn: For more on the Los Angeles Riots, see Anjuli Sastry Krbechek and Karen Grigsby Bates, "When LA Erupted in Anger: A Look Back at the Rodney King Riots," NPR, April 26, 2017; *Birth of a Nation*, director Matthew McDaniel, 1993; *Race + Rage: The Beating of Rodney King*, aired on CNN, 2011.

230 "By having this verdict": *Race + Rage: The Beating of Rodney King*, aired on CNN, 2011.

230 "ground zero": Esmeralda Bermudez, "Fading Memories at Florence and Normandie," *Los Angeles Times*, April 29, 2012.

231 "We were all taking stuff": Josh Eells, "The Trials of Kendrick Lamar," *Rolling Stone*, June 22, 2015.

231 Sylvester Monroe witnessed: Sylvester Monroe, "'Burn, Baby, Burn': What I Saw as a Black Journalist Covering the L.A. Riots 25 Years Ago," *The Washington Post*, April 28, 2017.

232 "Everybody was just so bugging out": djvlad, "Kool G. Rap Was Part of the L.A. Riot with 2Pac (Flashback)," youtube.com/watch?v=5W2sptoaRLY, posted June 15, 2020.

233 "whatever force is necessary": "Address to the Nation on the Civil Disturbances in Los Angeles, California," The American Presidency Project, presidency.ucsb.edu.

233 Two thousand riot-trained federal officers: Hinton, "Los Angeles Had a Chance to Build a Better City After the Rodney King Violence in 1992. Here's Why It Failed."

233 Among them were Border Patrol agents: Shereen Marisol Meraji, "As Los Angeles Burned, the Border Patrol Swooped In," NPR, April 27, 2017.

233 more than 20,000 law enforcement officers: Hinton, "Los Angeles Had a

Chance to Build a Better City After the Rodney King Violence in 1992. Here's Why It Failed."

233 "I hate to say I told you so": "2Pac's Interview with Swedish Reporter About L.A. Riots," 2paclegacy.net, July 20, 2018.

233 On a location scout: Veronica Chambers, "Conversations with Tupac," *Esquire*, August 25, 2022.

234 "We would go to dailies": Author interview with Dawn Gillem, February 3, 2023.

234 He often acted jittery: Author interview with Joe Torry, July 18, 2023.

235 "That's everybody's grandmother": Author interview with Joe Torry, July 18, 2023.

235 "Do you know how much": Peetvader, "Maya Angelou Talks About Tupac (Very Rare)," youtube.com/watch?v=Os6Sl6SORqk, posted February 23, 2009.

235 "I don't believe you actually spoke": Strombo, "Maya Angelou's Conversation with Tupac Shakur," youtube.com/watch?v=vVVA_siR-xg, posted December 23, 2013.

235 Gillem had recently trimmed: Author interview with Dawn Gillem, February 3, 2023.

236 "I can't take this shit": Veronica Chambers, "Conversations with Tupac."

237 "Bad on him for allowing": Torri Minton, "Marin City Haunted by Boy's Shooting," *San Francisco Chronicle* (article accessible via SFGate), November 3, 1995.

237 Teal stared into the distance: Michel Marriott, "Shots Silence Angry Voice Sharpened by the Streets," *The New York Times*, September 16, 1996.

CHAPTER NINE: NIGHTMARES

240 "The funnest day of my life": *Dear Mama*, director Allen Hughes.

240 Tupac visited Digital Underground's tour bus: Robinson, *Tupac Shakur: The Authorized Biography*, pp. 211–12.

241 "I have headaches": Kevin Powell, "Ready to Live," *Vibe*, April 1995.

242 *Troublesome '21* was eventually scrapped: Only fragments of the album surfaced until December 10, 2021, when a cassette tape containing the project in its entirety sold to an unknown buyer for $3,000. And at the start of 2022, thirty years after its initial conception, *Troublesome '21* was leaked online.

243 "What do you think about all the efforts": Chang, *Can't Stop Won't Stop*.

244 "the oppressive ruling class": Brenda Hyson, "New York City Passed New Abortion Law Effective July 1, 1970," *The Black Panther*, July 4, 1970.

244 "turn into involuntary abortion": Ibid.

244 as many as seventy thousand women: Jorge Juan Rodríguez V, "The Last Time the US Wanted a Wall, 70,000 People Were Sterilized," *Truthout*, February 12, 2019.

245 Panther Cleo Silvers remembered: Author interview with Cleo Silvers, February 13, 2023.

245 "The white movement tends": Author interview with Denise Oliver-Velez, November 27, 2023.

246 Interscope asked that an alteration: Mitchell Steinfeld, "Interscope Records Censored Tupac's 'Holler if Ya Hear Me' Message, Video Director Alleges," hiphopdx.com, December 16, 2014; author interview with Stephen Ashley Blake, February 23, 2023.

246 a member of the production staff: Author interview with Stephen Ashley Blake, February 23, 2023.

247 "Well, he got furious": Ibid.

248 "What do you mean?": Ibid.

249 "When did I ever say": Jacob Hoye and Karolyn Ali, eds., *Tupac: Resurrection 1971–1996*, Atria Books, 2003, p. 132.

249 Two of his objectives: "How Ya Livin Biggie Smalls?": *Fader*, May 25, 2011.

250 "Yo, what else": Ibid.

250 "While we were running around": Ibid.

250 Lil' Cease has spoken of his mentor: Cheo Hodari Coker, *Unbelievable: The Life, Death, and Afterlife of the Notorious B.I.G.*, p. 120.

251 young Christopher enjoyed: The story of the Notorious B.I.G. is well chronicled in Coker, *Unbelievable*; Justin Tinsley, *It Was All a Dream: Biggie and the World That Made Him*, Abrams Press, 2022.

252 "I went to the Soul Train": Madeline Hirsh, "TBT: Madonna and Tupac Secretly Dated in the Early '90s," Yahoo! Money, April 7, 2022.

252 Tupac showed up to Snoop: Author interview with Nanci Fletcher, November 24, 2023.

253 Tupac went on *The Arsenio Hall Show*: Interview available via Tupac Facts, "RARE: Tupac on the Arsenio Hall Show 1993 [FULL EPISODE]," youtube.com/watch?v=_iaH0rizTcw, posted November 27, 2022.

253 scuffled with a limo driver: Ro, *Have Gun Will Travel*, p. 144.

253 Tupac was accused of swinging: Ibid.; Chuck Philips, "Who Killed Tupac Shakur?," *Los Angeles Times*, September 6, 2022; "Tupac Was Arrested to Hit Chauncey Wynn (M.A.D.) with a Baseball Bat," 2PacLegacy.net, February 13, 2016.

253 Tupac was involved in a brawl: Robinson, *Tupac Shakur: The Authorized Biography*, pp. 230–33.

254 "Tupac, why are you acting": Ibid.

254 "They fired me": She Be Allah, "Today in Hip-Hop History: Tupac Admits to Hughes Brothers Assault on 'Yo! MTV Raps' 27 Years Ago," *The Source*, July 16, 2020.

254 Tupac even pulled through Fulton and Washington: Coker, *Unbelievable*, p. 121.

255 Tupac purchased a house: Robinson, *Tupac Shakur: The Authorized Biography*, pp. 247–48.

255 a local drug dealer: Ibid., p. 149.

255 spotted him at a Manhattan club: Ben Westhoff, *Original Gangstas*.

255 "I'm glad I met you": *Hip-Hop Uncovered*, director Rashidi Natara Harper.

255 One curious kid: J. B. Powell, "The Rumpus Interview with Ayize Jama-Everett," *The Rumpus*, February 19, 2013.

256 Halloween 1993: This account of the shooting of Mark and Scott Whitwell mostly draws from Ronald Smothers, "Rapper Charged in Shootings
of Off-Duty Officers," *The New York Times*, November 2, 1992; Marco Mar-
garitoff, "Inside the Story of Tupac's 1993 Shootout With Off-Duty Police
Officers—and How He Got Away with It," All That's Interesting, February 7, 2022; *Dear Mama*, director Allen Hughes. The Whitwells later sued
in civil court. Mark Whitwell's suit was settled out of court. In 1998, Scott
Whitwell's suit resulted in a default judgment against Tupac's estate. He was
awarded $210,000.

259 "When Tupac got to L.A.": The 85 South Comedy Show, "Too Short in
the Trap! With Karlous Dc Chico and Clayton," youtube.com/watch?v
=txAV1HeqPD8, posted September 24, 2022.

260 Jackson and Tupac's depictions: Ayanna Jackson's account of these days is
mostly drawn from djvlad, "Ayanna Jackson on Meeting 2Pac, Sexual Assault,
Trial, Aftermath (Full Interview)," youtube.com/watch?v=0CVBOv9O1GA,
posted February 13, 2018, and a statement she released anonymously in
1994, accessed via "The Rape Case: Ayanna Jackson's Story," 2PacLegacy
.net, November 28, 2015. Tupac's version of events is mostly drawn from
Powell, "Ready to Live." Supporting these sources throughout are publicly
available court documents.

260 "When I first met Tupac": "The Rape Case: Ayanna Jackson's Story,"
2PacLegacy.net.

260 "It was all in good fun": djvlad, "Ayanna Jackson on Meeting 2Pac, Sexual
Assault, Trial, Aftermath (Full Interview)."

260 Jackson bought a new dress: *People v. Shakur*, 169 Misc. 2d 961, Supreme
Court, New York County, April 12, 1996.

261 "So we get in the room": Powell, "Ready to Live."

262 "You know what happened": djvlad, "Ayanna Jackson on Meeting 2Pac,
Sexual Assault, Trial, Aftermath (Full Interview)."

262 John Singleton was forced: Alston, "To Die like a Gangsta."

262 "It bothers me so much": Tupac Facts, "Tupac's Second Appearance on
the Arsenio Hall Show. March 8, 1994," youtube.com/watch?v=TEmCW
mVANh0, posted March 8, 2022.

262 the sentence came down: Chuck Philips, "Rapper Gets 15 Days in Jail for
Attack on Film Director," *Los Angeles Times*, March 11, 1994.

264 Indictments were entered on: "Rapper Shakur Indicted on Sodomy, Sex
Abuse, Weapons Charges," UPI, November 24, 1993; Bruck, "The Takedown of Tupac."

264 It stirred a suspicion in his mind: Bruck, "The Takedown of Tupac." Agnant
pleaded guilty on three misdemeanor charges relating to the incident. In
1998, he filed a libel suit against Tupac's estate, among others, for claims
made in the song "Against All Odds" that he was an informant. See *Agnant v.
Shakur*, 30 F. Supp. 2d 420, Southern District Court of New York, December 16, 1998. Agnant's defamation suit was ultimately dismissed.

265 "They set her up": "Opening Arguments in Shakur Rape Case," UPI,
November 9, 1994.

265 "Anytime you're in the public eye": Ibid.

265 "No matter what happens": 2PacLegacy.net, "Full Interview: Tupac Outside Courthouse, N.Y.—November 29, 1994 (#2PacLegacy.net)," youtube .com/watch?v=o9j8fs6SSfc, posted December 17, 2016.

266 he reached Quad Recording Studios: The November 1994 shooting of Tupac has been depicted many times in many places. This account mostly relies on Eric Berman, Rob Kenner, Ian Landau, Danyel Smith, Joe Tirella, Josh Tyrangiel, Mimi Valdes, and Elizabeth Yo, "Sweatin' Bullets—Tupac Shakur Dodges Death but Can't Beat the Rap," *Vibe*, February 1995; Robinson, *Tupac Shakur: The Authorized Biography*, pp. 272–75; djvlad, "Lil Cease on Seeing 2Pac Shot, Shooters Pointed Guns at Him, Telling Biggie What Happened (Part 12)," youtube.com/watch?v=Z3lot1zKxRc, posted December 23, 2021.

268 she called her old Panther comrade: Author interview with Denise Oliver-Velez, November 27, 2023.

268 Jurors had even felt: Pearce, *Changes*, p. 143.

269 Devitt also alleged: Ibid., p. 146. No other juror has made a statement in relation to Devitt's account of deliberations.

269 startled jurors nudged one another: Richard Perez-Pena, "Wounded Rapper Gets Mixed Verdict in Sex-Abuse Case," *The New York Times*, December 2, 1994.

269 checked into Metropolitan Hospital Center: Berman, Kenner, Landau, Smith, Tirella, Tyrangiel, Valdes, and Yo, "Sweatin' Bullets."

270 "The mixed verdict": Perez-Pena, "Wounded Rapper Gets Mixed Verdict in Sex-Abuse Case."

270 found an awful sight: Robinson, *Tupac Shakur: The Authorized Biography*, pp. 280–81; *Dear Mama*, director Allen Hughes.

272 "We of the South have never": Speech of Senator Benjamin R. Tillman, March 23, 1900, Congressional Record, 56th Congress, 1st Session, 3223–4, reprinted in Richard Purday, ed., *Document Sets for the South in U. S. History*, D. C. Heath and Company, 1991, p. 147.

272 Jackson herself believed that authorities: djvlad, "Ayanna Jackson on Meeting 2Pac, Sexual Assault, Trial, Aftermath (Full Interview)."

273 Jackson filed a civil suit: *Doe v. Shakur*, 164 F.R.D. 359, United States District Court, S.D. New York, January 22, 1996.

274 "This album was made before": Ralph Bristout, "Poetry, Power, Pistols: An Oral History of 2Pac's 'Me Against the World,'" *Revolt*, March 14, 2016.

274 Tupac had one rule: Author interview with Carsten "Soulshock" Schack, August 23, 2023.

274 the same sessions yielded: Jake Brown, *Tupac Shakur (2Pac) in the Studio: The Studio Years (1989–1996)*, Colossus Books, 2005, p. 29.

274 "Pac was definitely like": Ibid., p. 17.

275 was asked to come to Rucker Park: Bristout, "Poetry, Power, Pistols."

275 Soulshock noted 2Pac as a dream rapper: Author interview with Carsten "Soulshock" Schack, August 23, 2023.

275 "I know who the fuck you are": Ibid.

276 Karlin decided to bail: Author interview with Carsten "Soulshock" Schack, August 23, 2023.

277   the stuff of tabloid intrigue: In 1992, Rison was charged with aggravated assault following an alleged altercation with Lopes. The charges were dropped the following year. In 1994, Lopes pleaded guilty to arson after setting fire to Rison's home.

277   After hearing a demo tape: Bristout, "Poetry, Power, Pistols."

277   "I like most of": Ibid.

278   "Inmate Shakur is": Paul Grondahl, "When Inmate Tupac Shakur Caused a Stir at Dannemora," *Times Union*, January 15, 2019.

278   He consumed *The Art of War*: Robinson, *Tupac Shakur: The Authorized Biography*, p. 290.

279   Tupac was approached: Michael Daly, "Tupac Shakur's Race-Killer Prison Pal Talks," *The Daily Beast*, July 29, 2014.

279   who told Tupac who Fama was: *SOCIAL the Lifestyle Magazine*, "Best interview ever about Donald Trump, Tupac Shakur & Mike Tyson by: Rev Al Sharpton," youtube.com/watch?v=LqKzpdP6xz, posted December 18, 2017.

279   Serving as witnesses: Grondahl, "When Inmate Tupac Shakur Caused a Stir at Dannemora."

280   he penned seductive letters: These letters were later compiled in Angela Ardis's book *Inside a Thug's Heart: With Original Poems and Letters by Tupac Shakur*, Kensington Publishing Corp., 2004.

280   "I'm not good": Author interview with Carsten "Soulshock" Schack, August 23, 2023.

281   "I imagine Tupac": Jake Paine, "Jimmy Iovine Reveals He Was Behind Suge Knight Bailing Tupac Out of Jail," *Ambrosia for Heads*, July 2017.

281   O. J. Simpson discovered: For more on the story of O. J. Simpson, see *O.J.: Made in America*, director Ezra Edelman, 2016.

282   "lying, perjuring, genocidal racist": Edward Helmore, "OJ Defence Rails at Racist Police 'Devils,'" *The Independent*, September 28, 1995.

282   "worst LAPD has to offer": "Excerpts of Marcia Clark's Closing Arguments," *The New York Times*, September 27, 1995.

CHAPTER TEN: WINTER IN AMERICA

285   the white rap music executive: "Police Investigate 48-Hour Disappearance of Rap Figure," *Los Angeles Times*, August 30, 1995.

285   they backed out of recording: Ro, *Have Gun Will Travel*, p. 25; Tasha Stanley, "The Untold Story of Home Boys Only," *In Touch with Tasha*, July 3, 2020.

286   Lynwood had the temerity: Ro, *Have Gun Will Travel*, pp. 85–87.

286   Nobody would give a statement: Stanley, "The Untold Story of Home Boys Only"; Bruck, "The Takedown of Tupac."

287   Knight's parents: Ro, *Have Gun Will Travel*, p. 10.

287   taking with them: Laura Martin, "*THEM* Tells a True Story of the Racist Horror That Followed the Great Migration," *Esquire*, April 9, 2021.

288   The rise of the Crips: Carman Tse, "How Compton Became the Violent City of 'Straight Outta Compton,'" *LAist*, August 13, 2015.

288 Marion Sr. had been a high-school football star: Ro, *Have Gun Will Travel*, p. 14.

288 offensive tackle Robert Cox: Chris Dufresne, "NFL Players Strike Day 3: Rams," *Los Angeles Times*, September 25, 1987; Justin Tinsley, "Life Before Death Row: The Brief Football Career of Suge Knight," *Andscape*, September 12, 2017.

288 Suge and his goons: For more about this story, see Sullivan, *LAbyrinth*, p. 56; Best Westhoff, "Did Suge Knight Really Dangle Vanilla Ice Off of a Balcony?," *LA Weekly*, November 20, 2012.

289 pulled out a gun: Lindsey India, "Vanilla Ice Gives His Side of the Suge Knight Balcony Story," *XXL*, July 18, 1997; Blair R. Fischer, "To the Extreme and Back," *Rolling Stone*, March 12, 1998.

289 A crucial relationship: Ro, *Have Gun Will Travel*.

289 He wouldn't, in fact, be released: "Revisiting Michael 'Harry-O' Harris' Incredible Story of Redemption," Spectrum News 1, June 26, 2023.

290 Knight ushered a couple of mean henchman: Ro, *Have Gun Will Travel*, pp. 53–54; Allison Samuels, "Suge Knight Is Back in Business," *Newsweek*, April 22, 2001.

291 "I hadn't seen that in any Black artist": Author interview with Jerry "Swamp Dogg" Williams, February 3, 2023.

291 In August 1991: "Dr. Dre Sentenced to Eight Months," UPI, August 30, 1994.

291 he pled guilty to battery: Chuck Philips, "The Violent Art, Violent Reality of Dr. Dre," *Los Angeles Times*, December 15, 1992.

291 Dre's Calabasas home caught fire: "Fire Damages Rap Singer's House, Injures 2 Firefighters," *Los Angeles Times*, June 29, 1992.

292 "1992 was not my year": Philips, "The Violent Art, Violent Reality of Dr. Dre."

292 Above the Law's Cold187um: Shawn Setaro, "Dr. Dre Perfected G-Funk, but He Didn't Invent It—Gregory Hutchinson Did," *Complex*, July 11, 2017.

292 "We would stay up": *Welcome to Death Row*, directors S. Leigh Savidges and Jeff Scheftel, 2001.

292 As Snoop found: Ro, *Have Gun Will Travel*, p. 112.

292 Dre was conducting: Del F. Cowie, "Dr Dre: The Pioneer," exclaim!, May 29, 2011.

292 "The very last night": Author interview with Nanci Fletcher, November 24, 2023.

293 "They told me that it would cost them": Tim Sanchez, "Exclusive: Chris 'The Glove' Taylor Talks Death Row, Aftermath, and Dr. Dre (Part 1)," AllHipHop.com, January 28, 2012.

293 Anyone Knight thought: Ro, *Have Gun Will Travel*, p. 103; Burhan Wazir, "Mutha Knows Best," *The Guardian*, August 5, 2001.

293 A party was planned: Ro, *Have Gun Will Travel*, pp. 134–35; Westhoff, *Original Gangstas*.

294 In the crowd: Author interview with Michael A. Gonzalez, October 27, 2023.

295 It all prompted the Roots' sage-like drummer Questlove: Ahmir "Quest-

love" Thompson, "The Day Hip-Hop Changed Forever," *Time*, August 10, 2023.

295   "Suge was jealous": Author interview with Nanci Fletcher, November 24, 2023.

295   Knight wasn't always a fan: Ro, *Have Gun Will Travel*, p. 136.

296   it was rejected: Chuck Philips, "Q&A with Tupac Shakur: 'I Am Not a Gangster,'" *Los Angeles Times*, October 25, 1995.

296   the rapper left LAX: Robinson, *Tupac Shakur: The Authorized Biography*.

297   After arriving at the studio: Author interview with Kendrick Wells, April 25, 2023.

298   "Me and my producer": Ibid.

298   Johnny J eventually: Pearce, *Changes*, p. 187.

298   "Fuck it, I can say it": "The Making of Tupac's All Eyez on Me (XXL)," 2PacLegacy.net, December 15, 2015.

299   It's typically credited: Paul Arnold, "Laylaw Discusses His History with Dr. Dre, 2Pac, Ghost-Producing 'California Love (Remix),'" *HipHopDX*, June 7, 2011.

299   Laylaw called up everyone: Ibid.

299   "A lot of the credits got fucked up": "The Making of Tupac's All Eyez on Me (XXL)."

299   "Nobody came to me": Author interview with Nanci Fletcher, November 24, 2023.

301   "When he named me Mussolini": Robinson, *Tupac Shakur: The Authorized Biography*, p. 313.

301   Soulshock was delighted: Author interview with Carsten "Soulshock" Schack, August 23, 2023.

302   spotted his old Oakland: Author interview with Garrick "Numskull" Husbands, March 5, 2025.

302   "I hated to see it": Ibid.

303   "This is our city": Randall Sullivan, *LAbyrinth: Corruption and Vice in the L.A.P.D.: The Truth Behind the Murders of Tupac Shakur and Biggie Smalls*, Canongate, 2002, p. 132.

303   Sitting in a production trailer: Author interview with Tracy "Big Tray Deee" Davis, April 26, 2024.

303   "He told me everything about the Biggie incident": Author interview with Nanci Fletcher, November 24, 2023.

304   Afeni Shakur advised her son: Paul Meara, "Tupac Shakur's 'One Nation': Associates Share Story Behind Late Rapper's Unreleased Album," *Billboard*, September 13, 2016.

304   Biggie allegedly cried: Gwinin Entertainment, "DJ Self Interviews Lance 'Un' Rivera," youtube.com/watch?v=8FTeZgoadww, posted Jun 29, 2017.

305   did pass away: Jon Caramanica, "Prodigy of Mobb Deep Dies at 42," *The New York Times*, June 20, 2017.

305   "I was disappointed": Author interview with Jamal Joseph, February 29, 2024.

305   he plotted a coast-fusing collaboration: Paul Meara, "Tupac Shakur's 'One Nation.'"

306 "Some of the rooms": Author interview with Darrell "Steele" Yates, April 2, 2024.

307 "His take on leaving Death Row": Author interview with Wendy Day, January 18, 2024.

307 "Selfishly, I wanted to be": Author interview with Gobi Rahimi, October 17, 2023.

308 "Once I experienced his sincerity": Tupac Shakur, "Rashida Jones Remembering a Conversation with Tupac," youtube.com/watch?v=k1uzrsuAp30, posted May 8, 2011.

308 "This movie is really about friendship": Emsnightmare, "Tupac Unseen Gridlock'd Interview (1996)," youtube.com/watch?v=TB9wFFXgzeQm, posted April 23, 2023.

308 The suits above writer and director Jim Kouf: Author interview with Jim Kouf and Lynn Kouf, November 23, 2023.

309 Tupac Shakur was suggested: Ibid.

309 "We would rap together": Drew Weisholtz, "Jim Belushi Reflects on 'Very Special Connection' He Had with Tupac Shakur," *USA Today*, January 21, 2022.

309 Tupac insisted on the authenticity: Author interview with Jim Kouf and Lynn Kouf, November 23, 2023.

309 "You're not watching my back": Ibid.

309 "It was at that point we all thought": Ibid.

310 One night, Tupac and Belushi: Rosy Cordero, "Jim Belushi Reveals Why He Thinks of Tupac Every Time He Watches a Sunrise," *Entertainment Weekly*, June 9, 2021.

311 he cocked his fist: Sharon Waxman, "Rap Giant Gets Nine Years After Assault," *The Washington Post*, February 28, 1997.

312 "Tupac only wore it": Cathy Scott, *The Killing of Tupac Shakur*.

312 Tupac spotted two familiar faces: McQuillar and Johnson, *Tupac Shakur: The Life and Times of an American Icon*; *The Late Late Show with James Corden*, "Marlon Wayans Shares Biggie and Tupac Memories," youtube.com/watch?v=OifbgY8bguw, October 11, 2022.

316 Keffe D was described by authorities: Rio Yamat and Ken Ritter, "Last Living Suspect in 1996 Drive-By Shooting of Tupac Shakur Indicted in Las Vegas on Murder Charge," Associated Press, September 30, 2023.

316 Keffe D's lawyers called his tales: Favour Adegoke, "Tupac's Murder Suspect Claims Comments on Rapper's Death Were for 'Entertainment,'" Yahoo! Entertainment, December 19, 2023.

316 a reference to the year: Travis Kitchens, "Unfortunate Son: The Roots of Tupac Shakur's Rebellion," *The Baltimore Sun*, June 28, 2019.

317 "At this point in my life": Keefe D with Yusuf Jay, *Compton Street Legend*, pp. 107–8.

317 Three bullets had punctured: Robert Macy, "Tupac Shakur's lung removed after shooting," *South Coast Today*, September 10, 1996.

317 handed a bag of bloodstained clothes and jewelry: McQuillar and Johnson, *Tupac Shakur: The Life and Times of an American Icon*, p. 241.

317 "Tupac's been shot": Anson, "To Die like a Gangsta."

318 "I didn't think he would die": Author interview with Wendy Day, January 18, 2024.

318 Jones spoke to her fiancé: Elahe Izadi, "'Tupac Was the Love of My Life': Kidada Jones on Her Relationship with the Slain Rapper," *The Washington Post*, September 13, 2016.

CHAPTER ELEVEN: HOW MUCH A DOLLAR COST?

322 Kurtis Blow inked a deal: Ogden Payne, "Hip-Hop Pioneer Kurtis Blow on Life, Legacy and the Universal Hip-Hop Museum," *Forbes*, January 28, 2019.

322 the first rap single to sell over a million copies: Dan Charnas, "The Rise and Fall of Hip-Hop's First Godmother: Sugar Hill Records' Sylvia Robinson," *Billboard*, October 17, 2019.

322 first-ever endorsement deal: Jael Rucker, "The History and Legacy of the Run-DMC Adidas Partnership," Yahoo.com, January 20, 2023.

323 "The tension between culture and commerce": Jeff Chang, *Can't Stop Won't Stop: A History of the Hip-Hop Generation*, Picador, 2005.

324 "The head's always strong": Shirley Ju, "Dame Dash's Message to Aspiring Entrepreneurs: 'It Costs Nothing to Dream, So Why Dream Small?,'" *Revolt*, April 14, 2021.

325 50 accepting a 10 percent stake in Glacéau: Le Goldman, "Forbes and 50 Cent 'Get Money,'" *Forbes*, September 18, 2007; Zach O'Malley Greenburg, "50 Cent's Next Beverage Bonanza," *Forbes*, March 27, 2013.

326 a number of sexual misconduct allegations: Claudia Rosenbaum, "A Guide to the Many Lawsuits Against Diddy," *Vulture*, first published March 28, 2024, and regularly updated thereafter. Most recently accessed for this book on December 3, 2024.

326 The vetting of his business: Erin Carlyle, "Trump Exaggerating His Net Worth (by 100%) in Presidential Bid," *Forbes*, June 16, 2015; Corky Siemaszko, "Donald Trump's Failed Business Ventures Are Back in the Spotlight," nbcnews.com, March 8, 2016.

327 "This world is such a": MTV News, "Tupac Talks Donald Trump & Greed in America in 1992 Interview," youtube.com/watch?v=GL-ZoNhUFmc, posted April 19, 2016.

327 Obama preluded his speech: C-SPAN, "President Obama at the 2011 White House Correspondents' Dinner," youtube.com/watch?v=n9mzJhvC-8E, posted May 1, 2011.

328 "If an eleven-year-old were to imitate Cam'ron": BigPurp1, "Camron and Billy Orielly," youtube.com/watch?v=HBYQzS36LFQ, posted January 13, 2006.

328 the median household wealth: "Study: Median Wealth for Single Black Women: $100, Single Hispanic Women: $120, Single White Women: $41,000," *Democracy Now!*, March 12, 2010.

329 "hip-hop's first billionaire": Todd Martens, "Dr. Dre Declares Himself 'the First Billionaire in Hip-Hop'"; *Los Angeles Times*, May 9, 2014. Whether

the sale of Beats did make Dre a billionaire was disputed by, among others, *Forbes* reporter Zack O'Malley Greenburg.

329 Knight decided to pay an unannounced visit: Matt Diehl, "The Endless Fall of Suge Knight," *Rolling Stone*, July 6, 2015.

330 Knight pleaded no contest: "Suge Knight Trial: Rap Mogul Pleads No Contest over Hit-and-Run Death," BBC.com, September 21, 2018.

332 The Master P story: This biography of Master P mostly draws from *No Limit Chronicles*, director Mario Diaz, 2020, as well as Neil Strauss, "How a Gangsta Rapper Turns Entrepreneur," *The New York Times*, May 13, 1998; Mark Montieth, "Pushing His Limits," *The Indianapolis Star*, November 12, 1998; Paul Thompson, "The Ice Cream Man Cometh," *The Ringer*, April 19, 2021.

333 that entitled No Limit to between 80 and 85 percent: Dan Runcie, "What Hip-Hop Gets Wrong About Master P and No Limit," *Trapital*, March 26, 2019; Betsy Wagner, "How Master P Turned $10,000 Into a $250 million Fortune," Yahoo! Finance, July 19, 2019.

334 "Do you know J.J.": Author interview with Charlie Braxton, July 19, 2021.

334 "He understood the mom-and-pop retail": Ibid.

334 "I tell people": Jen Rogers, "From Rapper to Restauranteur: How Master P Built a Diverse $250 Million Empire," Yahoo! Finance, August 30, 2019.

335 "There ain't no goal to stop at": Strauss, "How a Gangsta Rapper Turns Entrepreneur."

336 "Because P was a capitalist": Author interview with Charlie Braxton, July 19, 2021.

336 Universal Studios had the terrible idea: "Brian De Palma: You Have to Battle," *The Talks*.

337 "a joke about consumerism (and capitalism)": Pauline Kale, "The Fake Force of Tony Montana," *The New Yorker*, December 19, 1983.

338 "Especially in that neighborhood": David Kohn, "The King of Rap," CBS News, November 18, 2002.

339 Shawn was introduced: Zack O'Malley Greenburg, *Empire State of Mind*, Portfolio, 2011, pp. 20–21.

339 "nickeled and dimed": Ben Westhoff, "Former Jay-Z Associate De-Haven Tells His Side," *Vulture*, November 29, 2007.

340 "His story is the American Dream": O'Malley Greenburg, *Empire State of Mind*, p. 2.

342 "the studio is now a shell": "Settlement Reached for Master P Studio," *Billboard*, February 21, 2002.

342 he pled guilty: Elva Aguilar, "This Day in Rap History: Master P Pled Guilty for Tax Violation," *Complex*, February 5, 2014.

342 successfully sued for compensation: "Master P Sued: No Money, Mo' Problems," TMZ, September 4, 2011.

CHAPTER TWELVE: SPARK THE BRAIN THAT WILL CHANGE THE WORLD

346 ethnic tensions reached an apex: This account of the Guadalcanal Revolutionary Army uprising and the West Side Outlaws mostly draws from

George Wehrfritz, "Rebels of the Pacific," *Newsweek*, August 15, 1999; George Wehrfritz, "The Tupac Uprising: Outlaws with a Cause," *Newsweek*, August 15, 1999.

347 two hundred people were killed: Nat Hill, "Genocide Warning: The Solomon Islands," Genocidewatch.com, December 15, 2021.

347 Bob Marley, Rambo, and Tupac: For Marc Sommers's complete analysis on these three cultural icons and their influence on the child soldiers of Sierra Leone, see *We the Young Fighters: Pop Culture, Terror, and War in Sierra Leone*, University of Georgia Press, 2023.

348 For the West Side Boys: "Who are the West Side Boys?," BBC News World Edition, August 31, 2000.

349 "youth revolution": Mats Utas and Magnus Jörgel: "The West Side Boys: Military Navigation in the Sierra Leone Civil War," *The Journal of Modern African Studies*, vol. 46, no. 3 (Sept. 2008), pp. 498–99.

349 "It wasn't just the humiliation of poverty": Author interview with Kieran Mitton, August 3, 2023.

349 The near decade-long conflict: Samuel Momodu, "The Sierra Leone Civil War (1991–2002)," *BlackPast*, January 16, 2017.

350 2Pac's music was a potent propellant: "Rap Music Inspires Libyan Rebels to Defeat Gadhafi," *San Diego Union Tribune*, September 2, 2016.

350 "When the besieged Colonel Gaddafi": Paul Rogers, "African Rebel Soldiers and Their Eerie Obsession with Tupac Shakur," *LA Weekly*, September 12, 2011.

350 "I only listen": Ibid.

351 "We used to be into Bob Marley": Wehrfritz, "The Tupac Uprising."

351 Tupac created the alias: Ural Garrett, "The Oral History of 2Pac's 'Makaveli' Album: How a Michael Jackson Feature Almost Happened," BET, June 16, 2022.

351 "The Italians I speak about": "Reason Why Tupac Changed His Name to Makaveli," *Tupac Uncensored*, tupacuncensored.com, November 4, 2022.

353 "some slow, thuggish shit": Adam Matthews, "Straight Spittin'," *XXL*, October 2003.

353 "He threw his hands up": Ibid.

353 "He got real deep on there": Ibid.

354 outside a music industry party: Matt Lait, "Police Suspect Conspiracy in Slaying," *The Washington Post*, March 27, 1997.

354 There is an eeriness: Jeff Leeds and Jim Newton, "Death Row Records Under Investigation," *The Washington Post*, September 26, 1996.

355 Police impropriety was evident: Chuck Philips, "Officers May Have Seen Rap Killing," *Los Angeles Times*, April 23, 1997.

355 He died of a heart attack: Daniel Kreps, "Russell Poole, Notorious B.I.G. Murder Investigator, Dead," *Rolling Stone*, August 20, 2015.

356 But eyewitnesses and CCTV footage: Randall Sullivan, *LAbyrinth: Corruption and Vice in the L.A.P.D.: The Truth Behind the Murders of Tupac Shakur and Biggie Smalls*, Canongate, 2002, pp. 20–21.

356 The city later settled: "Rampart Scandal Timeline," *Frontline*, pbs.org.

356 Found taped to the back: Sullivan, *LAbyrinth*, p. 33.

356   Poole heard whispers: Peter J. Boyer, "Bad Cops," *The New Yorker*, May 13, 2001.

357   armed men pulled off a daring heist: "Rampart Scandal Timeline," *Frontline*, pbs.org.

357   she secretly ushered the robbers: Eric Lichtblau and Matt Last, "Officer Charged in Bank Heist That Netted $722,000," *Los Angeles Times*, December 18, 1997.

357   What piqued Russell: Sullivan, *LAbyrinth*, p. 180.

357   "For the first time in my career": Ibid., p. 234.

359   "When Perez decided": Author interview with Winston Kevin McKesson, May 1, 2024.

359   Biggie's family brought: Dan Martin, "Notorious BIG Death Lawsuit Dismissed," *The Guardian*, April 19, 2010.

359   The suit alleged: "Notorious B.I.G. Heirs Sue LAPD, Officials," CNN, April 11, 2002.

359   a $1.1 million judgment: Dan Martin, "Notorious BIG Death Lawsuit Dismissed," *The Guardian*, April 19, 2010.

359   A second lawsuit: Ben Sisario, "Wrongful-Death Lawsuit over Rapper Is Dismissed," *The New York Times*, April 19, 2010; Gary Susman, "FBI Ends Investigation into Biggie's Murder," *Entertainment Weekly*, March 11, 2005.

359   "I thought that was basically an overzealous investigator": Author interview with Winston Kevin McKesson, May 1, 2024.

360   The FBI closed: Tim Molloy, "Notorious B.I.G. FBI Documents Link LAPD to His Murder—But Still No Charges," TheWrap, April 6, 2011.

360   "Because of the professional manner": FBI files, accessed via vault.fbi.gov.

361   "This is so beautiful": @BruceHornsby, X (previously Twitter), June 5, 2020, retrieved from x.com/brucehornsby/status/1268696943053680640.

361   Christmas Day 1991: 2PacForumChannel, "Deon 'Big D' Evans Breaking Down the Song Changes (Rest in Peace)," youtube.com/watch?v=OlIQci 2pNcE, posted October 25, 2015.

363   "Electoral politics was always an objective": Dave Davies, "Bobby Seale's Still Cookin'," *The Philadelphia Inquirer*, November 12, 2008.

364   "Things changed, in the sense that": Andrew Sachs, "From Gun-Toting Black Panther to Ivy League Professor," *Time*, February 9, 2012.

364   "I was 8 yrs old when I first saw you": Even Minsker, "Kendrick Lamar Writes Tribute to 2Pac," *Pitchfork*, September 13, 2015.

366   "They exist as a continual barometer": Andrew R. Chow, "How the Black Panther Party Inspired a New Generation of Activists," *Time*, February 12, 2021.

366   In a report that harked right back: Benjamin Fernow, "FBI Ranks 'Black Identity Extremists' Bigger Threat Than Al Qaeda, White Supremacists: Leaked Documents," *Newsweek*, August 12, 2019.

366   To Scott Pelley's question: Scott Pelley, "President Joe Biden: The 2023 60 Minutes Interview Transcript," CBS News, October 15, 2023.

367   she made a curious discovery: Mark Stuart Gill, "Tupac's Missing Millions," *Entertainment Weekly*, July 25, 1997.

367 Death Row reached a settlement: "Tupac's Mom Files Injunction Against Death Row," *Spin*, July 24, 2007.

368 "Whatever it is I'm doing": "Afeni Shakur, Mother of Tupac and Former Black Panther, Dies Aged 69," *The Guardian*, May 3, 2016; "Tupac's Mom Brings Rapper's Dream to Life," *Today*, November 12, 2003.

368 "All of a sudden": Author interview with Carsten "Soulshock" Schack, August 23, 2023.

369 "they were finished vocals": Ibid.

369 the album was postponed: Joanna Glasner, "Eerie Image Pulled from CD," *Wired*, September 13, 2001.

372 "Chasing cash, by whatever means available": Mychal Denzel Smith, "Wu-Tang Clan's 'C.R.E.A.M.' Is Not the Capitalist Anthem You Think It Is," *Pitchfork*, September 10, 2019.

373 Having married Gust Davis: Lindsay Kimble, "Tupac Shakur's Mother Afeni Shakur Davis Dies at 69: Police," *People*, May 3, 2016.

373 embroiled in an acrimonious divorce battle: "Tupac's Mom: Husband Wants a Piece of Tupac's Pie in Divorce," TMZ, March 18, 2015; "Afeni Shakur's Divorce Case Shows Importance of Prenups," hardinlawform.com, April 8, 2016.

373 "a gentle soul": "Afeni Shakur—Tupac's Mother—Dies on West Pier," *Floating Times*, May 4, 2016.

373 when paramedics arrived: "Death Investigation of Afeni Shakur-Davis," Marin County Sheriff's Office, May 3, 2016.

374 In 2002, she donated $15,000: "Shakur's Mom Aids N.C. School," *Star News*, November 29, 2002.

374 "She was ready for whatever": Chauncey Alcorn and Rich Schapiro, "Afeni Shakur, Mother of Tupac Shakur, Remembered as Fearless Former Black Panther Who Inspired Slain Rapper," New York *Daily News*, June 26, 2016.

374 "He told me in writing": Author interview with Wendy Day, January 18, 2024.

375 "I know it is said that children like Shane": Sinéad O'Connor, *Rememberings*, Sandycove, 2021.

EPILOGUE

377 When Las Vegas police arrested Duane Keith: Yamat and Ritter, "Last Living Suspect in 1996 Drive-By Shooting of Tupac Shakur Indicted in Las Vegas on Murder Charge."

378 "I have absolute faith": Author interview with Jamal Joseph, February 29, 2024.

379 Afeni gave the project her blessing: "Tupac's Mom: Coachella Hologram Was Frickin' AMAZING," TMZ, April 16, 2012.

379 the technology was used: This AI version of "Too Tight" was accessed via youtube.com/watch?v=pwqqAlB4Ib8. The existence of 2Pac's reference track—a recording provided by the songwriter to act as a guide for the artist—had previously surfaced only as snippets caught by a videographer

present in the studio as Tupac and singer Nanci Fletcher worked on the song. For the unreleased MC Hammer version of "Too Tight" and other details of the song's history, see Parfit, "A Track Tupac Produced & Wrote for MC Hammer Surfaces & It's Too Tight," *Ambrosia for Heads*, February 23, 2016.

INDEX

Page numbers in *italics* refer to illustrations.

ILLUSTRATION CREDITS

ABOUT THE AUTHOR

DEAN VAN NGUYEN is a music journalist and cultural critic for *Pitchfork*, the *Guardian*, Bandcamp Daily and *Jacobin*, among other publications. He is based in Dublin, Ireland.